UNCERTAIN GUARDIANS

INTERPRETING AMERICAN POLITICS

MICHAEL NELSON, SERIES EDITOR

THE NEWS MEDIA AS A POLITICAL INSTITUTION

UNCERTAIN
GUARDIANS

BARTHOLOMEW H. SPARROW

THE JOHNS HOPKINS UNIVERSITY PRESS   BALTIMORE AND LONDON

© 1999 The Johns Hopkins University Press
All rights reserved. Published 1999
Printed in the United States of America on acid-free paper
9 8 7 6 5 4 3 2 1

The Johns Hopkins University Press
2715 North Charles Street
Baltimore, Maryland 21218-4363
www.press.jhu.edu

Library of Congress Cataloging-in-Publication Data will be found
at the end of this book.
A catalog record for this book is available from the British Library.

ISBN 0-8018-6035-0
ISBN 0-8018-6036-9 (pbk.)

To my parents, Lydia Huntington Sparrow and Edward G. Sparrow

CONTENTS

SERIES EDITOR'S FOREWORD

ONE OF THE MOST WIDESPREAD ASSUMPTIONS ABOUT AMERICAN politics among the general public (and, especially, among college students) is that the news media are tainted by a liberal bias. It would be remarkable if they thought otherwise, considering that conservative politicians and pundits have protested alleged media bias much longer and louder than have liberal politicians and pundits. What is more, conservatives have been better able to bring circumstantial evidence to bear to support their indictment of the media. For example, one study of the political views of 2,700 journalists and 3,000 "average" Americans found that the journalists' personal opinions on issues such as abortion, school prayer, gun control, and government regulation of business were far more liberal than the general public's. In 1992, to cite another study, 80 percent of media leaders in Washington, D.C., voted for Bill Clinton for president, compared with 43 percent of the national electorate. In a 1996 survey, members of the television industry were more likely to describe themselves as liberals than were union leaders or government bureaucrats, much less lawyers and business leaders.

Bartholomew Sparrow's study is about much more than alleged liberal bias in the news media. But his book certainly helps to shed light on that charge. As Sparrow reminds us, whatever their personal views, political journalists are employees of large, profit-making corporations with a steady eye on the bottom line. (Of the *Fortune* 100 corporations, as measured by market value, for example, four are media conglomerates.) Under the steady and scrutinizing gaze of their shareholders, these companies have every incentive not to alienate any substantial part of their audience. As Craig Whitney of the *New York Times,* who is quoted by Sparrow, explains, if a news organization imposes an opinion on the public, it "risk[s] losing the trust of people who hold different views. We sell a million copies of this paper every day. You want both sides of the question to keep reading you and not feel you're shading information one way or another."

In addition to liberal bias being bad business, two other reasons help to explain why journalists' liberal views seldom determine the coverage of political events that actually appears in the news media. One reason is that journalists regard themselves as members of a profession, bound by an ethical duty to report the news fairly and without favor. No one thinks that Democratic surgeons work less carefully on Republican patients than on their fellow Democrats. Why, then, should one assume that liberal journalists would be especially hard on conservative politicians and causes? The second reason is that journalists are not free agents. Even if bias crept into their reporting, a hierarchy of editors, publishers, and other executives—many of them far more conservative than the reporters are—stands ready to scrutinize their work.

Having deflated the liberal bias stereotype of the news media, Sparrow goes on to deflate many more casually held assumptions. In the course of doing so, he offers a provocative interpretation of the place of the media in our political system.

MICHAEL NELSON

PREFACE

THE NEWS MEDIA ARE AN INTEGRAL PART OF THE AMERICAN POLITICAL system. An assessment of a political issue, an evaluation of a candidate's qualifications for electoral office, or an appraisal of the performance of a government agency can hardly be undertaken without examining the communication of that issue (e.g., campaign finance reform), the representation of that person in the news (e.g., a presidential candidate), or the media coverage of that department, bureau, or agency (e.g., the Food and Drug Administration). The news media affect most aspects of the American political system, even the most salient of political issues and processes. Public perceptions of national politics greatly depend on the mediation of journalists and news organizations.

Most Americans and most students of U.S. national politics sense the importance of the news media, but what is less appreciated is how the routines and conventions that journalists and news organizations use to produce the news systematically affect national politics. The practices and procedures of news organizations take on a life of their own, influencing the conduct and character of national politics. These media practices ultimately have adverse effects on national politics and democratic government.

All the while, the news media lead the public to believe that they are a positive political influence, reporting the news that people need to know and keeping the government in check, as epitomized by the role of the press in the Watergate affair. The reality is that news organizations are greatly constrained, and shaped, by the political and economic environment in which they operate. In short, they are unable to serve as guardians of the public interest.

THE ALLEGATIONS THAT PRESIDENT CLINTON HAD SEXUAL RELATIONS with Monica Lewinsky and then lied about it under oath, first published in the nation's newspapers on the morning of Wednesday, January 21, 1998, indicate the intimate role of the news media in public affairs. The circumstances of this piece of recent—and still incomplete—history illustrate a number of themes contained in the book.

■ A series of key decisions by editors, publishers, and news executives was necessary for the story to break. Indeed, the story almost never came into public view. *Newsweek* killed reporter Michael Isikoff's story about the president and the twenty-one-year-old female intern (Isikoff had been working on a story about the president's troubles with women for three years and on the Lewinsky case for one year), but Matt Drudge, the Internet gossip columnist, put the story—including the story of *Newsweek*'s spiking the story—on his Web page. Only then did *Newsweek* put the story out on America Online, and the *Washington Post* and the *Los Angeles Times* printed stories in their Wednesday papers. The rest of the media quickly followed suit.

Yet the *Washington Post, Newsweek,* and other major news organizations have routinely ignored other Drudge "exclusives." Drudge himself admits that he is only "about 80 percent accurate" (although it is unclear how he is able to get such a figure).[1] Furthermore, if the story had been around for weeks (although Linda Tripp did not contact Kenneth Starr's office until the evening of January 12, 1998), why was *Newsweek*'s Isikoff the only one on the story? Where were the reporters (and editors' assignments) from the other magazines and newspapers?[2]

■ The scandal has affected national as well as international politics. President Clinton, his staff, and Hillary Rodham Clinton have had to devote precious time and valuable resources (and at least one new aide) to responding to charges that Clinton had sex—however defined—with Lewinsky. Meanwhile, the prevalence of the story in the news either drowned out or pushed aside other important news of early 1998: the policy initiatives contained in the State of the Union speech and budget initiatives for fiscal 1999, discussion of the specific objectives that would be achieved by threatened U.S. military strikes against Iraq, the content and conditions of hundreds of billions of International Monetary Fund dollars being channeled to the Indonesian, Korean, and Thai economies, talks with Yassir Arafat and Benjamin Netanyahu on the peaceful resolution of the controversial Israeli settlements on the West Bank, and Pope John Paul II's visit to Cuba, among other stories.

▪ The Lewinsky story has been played out through the deliberate use of the news media by the staff and lawyers from Kenneth Starr's investigatory team, the Clinton White House, and others. The story results from the actions of the independent prosecutor and the moves by opposing teams of lawyers, but it also necessarily involves the news media, which have printed or publicized leaks by Starr and his staff, the president and his advisors, Lewinsky's lawyer, William Ginsburg, Lewinsky's friend and confidante Linda Tripp, and the New York literary agent Lucianne Goldberg, among others.

▪ The story is a study of the media sinking to a new (low) standard of sensationalist news coverage. Stories of the president's relationship with Lewinsky dominated front pages and front sections of newspapers, newsmagazines, and television news programs. Yet many of the stories were reported secondhand, and articles had to be retracted from the *Wall Street Journal* and the *Dallas Morning News.* Moreover, the *New York Times,* ABC News, *Newsweek, Time,* and other news organizations ran the story that Monica Lewinsky had a dress given to her by the president which was stained with semen. None of these news organizations independently verified the report prior to publication or broadcast. Lucianne Goldberg admits to having leaked the story to shake things up.

This news sells, however.[3] *Time,* for instance, devoted 43 of 80 total pages to the scandal in its February 2 issue and 37 of 112 total pages in its February 9 issue; the *New Yorker* devoted an entire "Talk of the Town" section and its lead article, eight pages long, to the sex story. The *New York Times* defended its front-page coverage of the story by arguing that President Clinton's involvement and unconvincing response to the situation merited it. The *Times's* defense ignores the extraordinary resources the newspaper devoted to the story—beyond simply front-page coverage—and the anecdotal accounts that were repeated in the *Times's* reportage.[4] The tabloid niche is becoming less and less a niche.

The history of the scandal suggests that news organizations are unaccountable and irresponsible. Consider that it is illegal to leak grand jury testimony and that the president's lawyers and advisors have sharply criticized

Starr's office for doing so (criticism widely circulated in the media). Others claim that the damaging leaks have come from the White House so that the special prosecutor can be blamed for undermining the judicial system. But what about the responsibility of journalists to uphold the legal system? They are partners (co-conspirators?) in this battle of a thousand leaks.

The Clinton-Lewinsky story illustrates the new media at work in the late 1990s: the hourly, almost instantaneous news cycle, thanks to cable television, CNN, and the Internet. With the news organizations posting their stories on the Internet as they are being composed, news is being released at an ever-faster pace. This means less and less time for scrutiny, deliberation, and the exercise of judgment. Instead, the pressure is on news organizations to get the story out once it has broken.

In short, we see the reciprocal effect that the individual decisions of a few editors, producers, publishers, and news executives have on national politics. We see, too, how the news affects the operations of the government (in this case the White House, the independent prosecutor, the Secret Service, and the Department of Justice). The attention shown by the leading U.S. news organizations to the scandalous rather than the sober, to the sordid rather than the serious, further suggests the importance of the bottom line to contemporary journalism. We also see how news media report leaks with little discrimination, perhaps because sources would feel burned were reporters to contextualize or criticize the leaks and the practice of leaking. In doing so, journalists are implicitly cooperating with government officials and misleading their audiences as to the truth of the matter—as far as it can be known.

IN THIS BOOK, I EXPLAIN WHY THE NEWS MEDIA MAY BE CONSIDERED a political institution and why this matters to students of American politics. In making the case that the news media are a single political institution, I draw on the empirical evidence provided by scholars and journalists and also make normative claims. As we know from the debates at the constitutional convention in Philadelphia and from the arguments of Alexander Hamilton, James Madison, and John Jay in the *Federalist Papers,* the study of institutions and institutional design is necessarily in part a normative exercise.

This book was motivated by two personal concerns. One is grounded in my own youth as an American growing up in the 1960s and 1970s, during the Vietnam War and the Watergate era. This early political exposure led me to believe that the most prominent news organizations in this country were essentially progressive. They seemed concerned with the larger public interest of voters and nonvoters alike, rather than with individual reporters' objectives, the profit-making or market-share goals of separate news organizations, or the aims of other particular political or economic actors. Also, they appeared to be staffed by smart, sophisticated, and broad-minded people. Journalists (and the news media) were a positive influence on the American polity, I believed, capable of standing for a public good beyond the often parochial concerns of Congress, the narrow objectives of the departments, agencies, or bureaus of the federal government, the particular visions of individual U.S. presidents, and the limited interests of the separate states. Indeed, the news media proclaim as much in their own professional codes of ethics (see Chapter 1).

Yet it has become increasingly clear that the news media are considerably less progressive than they appear. Their embeddedness in present-day politics and economics makes them unable to be the progressive actors I once thought they were. Instead of acting as a check on the excesses of the other branches or holding the government accountable, the news media, because of their large stakes in the politics and policies of the status quo, severely compromise their coverage of the major issues of the day—for example, issues of national security (e.g., the Persian Gulf War and the cold war), the political economy (the savings and loan crisis) and public health (AIDS and cancer research), as I show in Chapter 6.

The other origin of this book came out of research I did for an earlier work on the American state in the 1940s. In that volume, I used a resource-based approach to explain the form and persistence of changes in the organization of American government and society before, during, and after World War II.[5] Although the resource-dependence perspective allowed me to explain much governmental and societal change in the 1940s, it became apparent to me that resources were only part of the explanation of the incredible mobilization by various individual citizens, businesses, labor unions, and associations during World War II and, later, during the cold war. This extraordinary mobilization also arose because Americans of the 1940s were acquiring new ideas about their national government and their own identities as Americans.

An interest in what the great journalist Walter Lippmann identified as the pictures of the world people have in their heads led me to the study of the news media and their coverage of national politics: if Americans' new pictures of the world were a source of national unity and political order in the early 1940s, I wanted to know how they were being communicated.[6] Instead of writing on World War II and the early years of the cold war, however, I chose to examine the contemporary United States, given the dominant role that the news media and political communication now play in the American political system. Questions of national identity and political order are every bit as relevant today as they were in the 1940s.

For both reasons—my early political socialization and my evolution as a student of American politics—I decided to revisit and reinterpret the news media's role as a "fourth branch" of the American political system. Despite the contrast in subject matter and time frame between this project and my previous research, several interests carry over from the earlier work. One is a concern with the organizational and institutional foundations of individual behavior, or how large-scale outcomes can be accounted for at the individual level. There is also an abiding emphasis on empirical accuracy as the basis for political and social science. Finally, there is a long-standing concern with the establishment and maintenance of political order in a large and heterogeneous United States.

ALTHOUGH I REACH DISTURBING CONCLUSIONS ABOUT THE ROLE OF the news media in American politics, this is hardly new. There is a tradition of political science scholarship critical of the American political system.[7] The works of Grant McConnell (*Private Power and American Democracy*) and Theodore Lowi (*The End of Liberalism*) are especially prominent.[8] Both McConnell and Lowi write of the deleterious effects of the pressure-group system on the American polity. McConnell exposes the unrepresentative and antidemocratic politics of private interests; Lowi exposes the moral hollowness of "interest-group liberalism." What matters for my purpose, however, is that neither scholar includes the press or news media in his exposition of the pressure-group system. Yet much of what they write applies to a study of the power of the news media, particularly that of the largest and most prestigious news organizations, in the United States today. Consider McConnell's formulation:

> Deference of government to private groups does not eliminate the phenomenon of power. Power exists in the hands of these groups. It is both inward looking and outward looking: it is power over members of the groups and it is also power over matters affecting the larger community . . . Unfortunately, the governing systems of most private associations do not have the checks upon power or the protections for individuals that have developed out of long experience in the constitutional order of the United States. . . [and] the fewer these parties and interests and the smaller the compass in which they act, the more easily do they concert and execute their plans of oppression. Far from providing guarantees of liberty, equality, and concern for the public interest, organization of political life

by small constituencies tends to enforce conformity, to discriminate in favor of elites, and to eliminate public values from effective political consideration.[9]

The news media *are* private actors that represent a narrow slice of the American public—a narrower slice than they care to admit and one that has power over matters that affect the larger community. Like other pressure groups, the news media operate free from the constitutional checks imposed on the formal institutions of government and are highly concerned with the stability of the American political (and economic) system.

Although McConnell's point about pressure groups' limited representativeness might seem not to apply to the news media, which appeal to broad audiences, it is consistent with an analysis of the news media because there is little direct feedback from viewers and readers to journalists. The popular representation of news organizations emerges more through data on audience share and circulation than through qualitative communication. In fact, the mass audience may not be the only or even the most important audience: politicians and advertisers are every bit as crucial to the success of a leading news organization (see Chapters 3 and 4).

Lowi elaborates on the problems of pluralist government in his exposition on "interest-group liberalism." One reason he condemns pluralist politics is that it advocates the (false) notion that a system built primarily on groups and bargaining is inherently self-correcting. A second is that interest-group liberalism neglects the fact that when policies are assigned to a particular agency (and therefore to the small number of organized interests surrounding it), the situation changes "from one of potential competition to one of potential oligopoly"; there is less likely to be countervailing power and "more likely to be accommodating power." Lowi's third objection is that interest-group liberalism idealizes the group; pluralism makes private associations into a good, whereas for James Madison they were factions—"adverse to the aggregate interests of the community." As Lowi summarizes, "Interest-group liberalism seeks pluralist government, in which there is no formal specification of means or of ends. In a pluralist government, there is, therefore, no substance. Neither is there procedure. There is only process."

Lowi's concerns are worth minding. The news media are critical in interpreting national politics in terms of interest-group liberalism and posing themselves as safeguards of a pluralist system and correctives to its potential defects. The actions of the news media are also complicit in the defects of pluralist politics, given that the media rarely explore or examine the "accommodating power" of policy and economic interests. They typically endorse the beneficial effects of private power in their interpretations of national politics and their definition of what constitutes the public or national interest.

Consistent with McConnell's and Lowi's work, I find that the coverage of political news by the media is frequently devoid of "formal specification of means or of ends," as Lowi asserts, and that the media are concerned more with process than with substance.[10] Like most interest groups, the news media have particular political and economic interests to which they have to attend; unlike other interest groups, however, they play a crucial role in articulating the politics of American society.

Studying the news media as an institutional actor within the American political system addresses the same questions that Lowi raises in *The End of Liberalism*—those of the "older and almost forgotten [issues] of what kind of government, what ends of government, what forms of government, and what consequences of government—for our time and for the future."[11] My intention in this book is to explain the institutional nature of a key component of the American political system—the news media—and to show why they, like other interest groups, do not serve democratic values and a broader public interest. My hope is that this book will be read with the works of McConnell and Lowi in mind.

I would like to note that an exploration into the news media as a political actor—even if an uncomfortable exploration—is fundamentally an act of optimism. It reflects confidence in the ability of voters and policy makers to face politics as they are—no matter how bleak—and in the capacity of the political system to reform. Nothing can happen without an understanding of the political system as it currently exists. Only then is it possible for policy makers, journalists, organized political actors, and the public to know what might be done.

ACKNOWLEDGMENTS

THERE ARE MANY TO WHOM I AM GRATEFUL. THE UNIVERSITY OF TEXas's University Research Institute supported my interviews and participant observation in Washington, D.C., in the Summer of 1995, and I am very appreciative of all those who cooperated with me. These persons, most of whom I cite in the text and acknowledge in the notes, took valuable time out of their days to talk with me, answer my questions, and take me around their facilities and on their news beats. One person whom I did not interview but who was extremely helpful was Jack Nelson, the long-time chief of the *Los Angeles Times*'s Washington bureau. Others who were of help but whom I did not interview include editors and staff at the *New York Times*'s Washington bureau, *U.S. News and World Report,* the *Washington Post,* and the *Wall Street Journal*'s Washington bureau. I owe a special debt to Sarah Crass and Mary Batts Estrada for helping me contact many of those I interviewed. I thank them all.

A research fellowship in the fall of 1996 at the Joan Shorenstein Center on the Press, Politics and Public Policy at Harvard University's John F. Kennedy School of Government gave me the chance to draft much of the manuscript. Marvin Kalb, director, Pippa Norris, director of research, and Edie Holway, fellows and program director, made my stay at the center at once productive and enjoyable. I thank them, my fellow Fellows—John Dancy, Nachman Shai, Richard Sobel, and Fred Wertheimer—and the other faculty and staff at the center for their generous assistance and support.

Early encouragement of my project came from two sources in particular. Elisabeth Noelle-Neumann, the founder and former director of the Institut für Demoskopie Allensbach, was a teacher of mine at the University of Chicago and generously provided me with an internship to spend a semester at Allensbach, Germany, in the fall of 1990—an opportunity that gave me time to read about and reflect on the study of political communication. Henry Y. K. Tom, executive editor at the Johns Hopkins University Press, also merits special mention. Henry agreed to work with me on this project from very early on, suggested that I interview political reporters, columnists, and political and media consultants to get a better feel for the news-making process, recommended that I include a section on the reform of the news media, and saw my project through the various stages of the publication process. Henry has shown exemplary patience by repeatedly extending deadlines on my behalf. He was a pleasure to work with.

Michael Nelson, editor of the Interpreting American Politics series at Hopkins, was most helpful, for both his commentary and his encouragement. The book is clearer and more accurate thanks to his careful reading.

Deborah Klenotic, my copyeditor, was thorough, resourceful, diligent, and a pleasure to work with. She improved much of my writing, insisted on proper documentation, and saved me from numerous errors. Julie McCarthy, MaryKatherine Callaway, and others at the Johns Hopkins University Press were also most helpful.

Friends and colleagues who have responded to my arguments, and thereby made this a better book, include Roderick Hart, Timothy Cook, William Gamson, Martha Kumar, Richard Parker, Richard Sobel, Russell Neuman, Thomas Patterson, and an anonymous reviewer for the Johns Hopkins University Press. I am very grateful for their important contributions; the manuscript is much improved because of them. Tom Wicker and the late Edwin Diamond were also generous with their help beyond the call of duty. My friends Chris Brown and Mike Dennis helped me decide who and how to interview. I am further grateful for the extraordinary assistance and generosity of John Keppel and the late Christopher Bird. I am also appreciative of the help of David and Jeanne Bird in the fall of 1996.

My colleagues in the Department of Government at the University of Texas were also of great help. David Braybrooke, Rudy de la Garza, Phil Paolino, H. W. Perry, David Prindle, and Daron Shaw all read and commented on parts of this book. Joy Howell, Byung-Guk Min, Hannah Kim, Sarah Cunningham, Andra Blum, Rich MacKinnon, Paul Ciavarri, and Quinn Stewart also helped make this a clearer and better-researched book. And Chris Thim solved the computer problems. I owe an additional debt of thanks to several classes of University of Texas undergraduates. Their questions and comments helped me sort through the issues I address herein. The book is very much for them: they are the future. None of the above is to be blamed for the book's errors or omissions—alas, I get stuck with that responsibility.

I owe particular thanks to Edward G. and Margaret K. Sparrow for their careful reading of, responses to, and interest in my work.

UNCERTAIN GUARDIANS

INTRODUCTION

The reporter is the recorder of government but he is also a participant [helping] to shape the course of government. He is the indispensable broker and middleman among the subgovernments of Washington. He can choose from among the myriad events that seethe beneath the surface of government which to describe, which to ignore. He can illumine policy . . . giving it sharpness and clarity; just as easily, he can prematurely expose policy and, as with an undeveloped film, cause its destruction. At his worst, operating with arbitrary and faulty standards, he can be an agent of disorder and confusion. At his best, he can exert a creative influence on Washington politics.—Douglass Cater, The Fourth Branch of Government, 1959

When you come to a crossroads, take it.—Yogi Berra

POLITICAL EVENTS OF THE LAST FEW DECADES HAVE CAUSED AMERIcans to expect much of the news media. Print and television publicity of the Viet Cong's Tet offensive in early 1968 turned a U.S. military victory on the battlefield into a political defeat at home. The Viet Cong's demonstrated ability to mount a formidable assault against American and South Vietnamese forces dramatically contradicted the Johnson administration's upbeat image of the war.[1] There was no light at the end of the tunnel; the United States had not suppressed its adversary. The subsequent publication of the Pentagon Papers in 1971 by the *New York Times* and the *Washington Post* despite a court injunction against publication requested by the Nixon administration—an injunction soon overturned by the U.S. Supreme Court—further showed the significance of an independent press in the American political system.[2]

The investigation of the Watergate break-in and cover-up in 1972 and

1973 firmly established in Americans' minds the perception that the news media are public guardians, able to protect the national interest against government corruption. The Watergate scandal, dramatized in the movie *All the President's Men,* demonstrated emphatically the power of the news media, and of the *Washington Post* in particular. The *Post* and the other news organizations on the story—CBS News, *Time,* the *New York Times,* and a handful of others—published or broadcast stories that prompted official proceedings that ultimately led to the resignation of President Richard Nixon, the first ever by an American president. The Watergate break-in was at least the "story of the decade,"[3] and quite possibly one of the stories of the century.

Earlier reportage laid the groundwork for the coverage of Vietnam and Watergate. In 1954 CBS News correspondent Edward R. Murrow famously spoke out against Senator Joseph McCarthy on the television program *See It Now,* and ABC News's live coverage of the Army-McCarthy hearings, also in 1954, revealed McCarthy to be a bully. The coverage marked the beginning of the senator's downfall.[4] In 1961, soon after taking office, President John F. Kennedy stated publicly that he wished that the *New York Times* had run a story on the ill-fated Bay of Pigs invasion of Cuba. Five years later, *Times* editor Clifton Daniel pronounced that the newspaper's position on the Bay of Pigs story had been wrong, and he encouraged his staff to expose "lies, failures, and abuses in high places"; in doing so, he may have helped to inaugurate an era of adversarial journalism.[5] In addition, televised coverage of "Bull" Connor's use of cattle prods, dogs, and water cannons against blacks—even black children—together with the newspaper coverage of the three murders in Mississippi in the summer of 1964, propelled the civil rights movement and the cause of African Americans in the South and across the entire United States.[6]

Subsequent reporting has been of a piece. Watergate was followed by the revelations of the Iran-Contra affair in the late 1980s; the *Miami Herald* revealed in 1988 that former U.S. Senator and presidential candidate Gary Hart was committing adultery, thereby effectively ending Hart's bid for the presidency; and the *New York Times,* the *Wall Street Journal,* and the *Washington Times,* among other publications, prominently pursued the Whitewater story throughout the first term of the Clinton presidency. There were also the news media's investigations of the Clinton administration's firing of White House Travel Office employees, its treatment of approximately nine hundred confidential personnel files remaining from the Bush administration, and its use of the White House in the solicitation of political contributions. The list goes on.[7]

Not surprisingly, then, the watchdog image of the press and news media persists. Former Secretary of State James A. Baker remarks that the press "is indispensable to a free society . . . Many things that would otherwise never be known or exposed become known and exposed because we have a very free press and because we do have a First Amendment. I think it is one of the strengths of American democracy." The political scientist Thomas Patterson simply comments that "watchdog journalism" is the "traditional role" of the news media. The political scientist Doris Graber observes that the news media "serve as powerful guardians of political norms because the American people believe that a free press should keep them informed about the wrong-doings of government."[8]

The news media hold themselves up to this same standard: the purpose of journalism "is public enlightenment," according to the Radio-Television News Directors Association's Code of Broadcast News Ethics. "The responsibility of radio and television journalists is to gather and report information of importance and interest to the public accurately, honestly and impartially." Broadcast journalists are to "evaluate information solely on its merits as news, rejecting sensationalism or misleading emphasis in any form." Similarly, the ethical code of the Society of Professional Journalists states, "The public's right to know of events of public importance and interest is the overriding mission of the mass media. The purpose of distributing news and enlightened opinion is to serve the general welfare." Nor is this obligation to be taken lightly: "Freedom of the press is to be guarded as an inalienable right of people in a free society. It carries with it the freedom and responsibility to discuss, question, and challenge actions and utterances of our government and of our public and private institutions. Journalists uphold the right to speak unpopular opinions and the privilege to agree with the majority."[9] Journalists have awesome responsibilities, it would seem.

Most journalists and many social scientists see the news media as a "Fourth Estate," as the former Supreme Court justice Potter Stewart put it, a political institution able to act independently from the other branches of government and capable of safeguarding democracy in the United States.[10] So does most of the public. A national survey by the Roper Center shows that in 1992, a full 80 percent of Americans believed that the press—newspapers, magazines, television, and radio—is crucial to the functioning of a free society, and 88 percent said they want to know what their government is doing. Fifty-seven percent of Americans agreed that the "media hold candidates accountable" (37% disagreed), and 59 percent agreed that "media cover issues important to people my age" (38% disagreed).[11]

This picture of an active press, protective of the public welfare, dates back to the Progressive Era of the early twentieth century: by being able to publicize political information, the press is able to prevent tyranny on the part of either elected or nonelected leaders.[12] As the former CBS News anchorman

Walter Cronkite asks, "Why can't the American people see that freedom of the press is not some privilege extended to a favored segment of the population but is purely and simply their own right to be told what their government and its servants are doing in their name?" In the words of Dan Rather, Cronkite's successor at CBS News, the freedom of the press is guaranteed "for the benefit of listeners and viewers and readers. The cause is America." According to Fox News correspondent Brit Hume (formerly with ABC News), "we don't see ourselves . . . as a bunch of journalists out there faithfully reporting what's happening day by day . . . We have a much grander view of ourselves: we are the Horatio at the national bridge. We are the people who want to prevent the bad characters from crossing over into public affairs."[13]

The watchdog function is, in fact, the news media's main role in the political system; as I see it, other views of the media's role relate back to the watchdog image. Some argue that the news media should be a neutral observer and transmit information—but this is so that voters may be informed and the government may be held accountable (as Thomas Jefferson pointed out). Others say the news media should be a participant or an advocate in politics, especially for minority or marginal populations—yet this is to counterbalance a presumed deficit of such advocacy on the part of politicians and civic leaders. The news media are also described as a forum for expression of diverse views—this is because the "marketplace of ideas" available to citizens needs to be enriched. Finally, it is seen as important that the news media be a guardian of public and personal morals—precisely to the extent that such guardianship is lacking from other political actors.[14] I therefore take as essential the watchdog, or guardian (in more than the moral sense), role of the news media in the American political system.

For all of the preeminence of the watchdog or guardian role of the news media, I argue that the "fourth estate" model of the news media is fundamentally wrong. Only rarely and to a limited extent are the news media able to act as significant checks on national government or as advocates of a broader public interest. Instead, the individual news organizations and news departments that make up the news media are, for several reasons, highly constrained in their coverage of politics and economics in the United States. Furthermore, almost all news organizations are similarly constrained, given the larger political and economic environment in which they operate. Consequently, they are unable to fulfill their Progressive Era role as independent guardians of the national interest. The news media's cause is not America; they do not stand as a collective "Horatio at the national bridge."[15]

My argument is based on an open-systems approach: news organizations exist in an uncertain political and economic environment, one in which they have to stabilize their position in order to flourish. That is to say, the news media exist in an interorganizational field of other political communicators (both media and nonmedia) and other market actors (both media and nonmedia). To succeed in this interorganizational field (by which I mean "a community of organizations that partakes of a common meaning system and whose participants interact more frequently and fatefully with one another than with actors outside of the field"),[16] news organizations establish ties with and develop set practices for handling the political and economic actors on whom they depend.

That the news media are to a significant degree subject to external control has three implications. First, the relationships that journalists and news executives establish with politicians and government officials, on the one hand, and with advertisers and audiences, on the other hand, exert their own effects on U.S. national politics. Second, given their similar environment, the largest news organizations develop and use the same practices by which to cover national political news.[17] Finally, the systematic effects of the news media on the American political system, on which I elaborate throughout this book, and the shared practices used by journalists in covering politics cause the news media often to violate their own ethical standards and, indeed, the norms of democratic government.

History of the Concept of the News Media as a Political Institution

The concept of the news media as constituting a separate political actor is not new, of course. As the essayist Thomas Carlyle tells it in 1841, the British statesman "[Edmund] Burke said there were Three Estates in Parliament; but in the Reporters' Gallery yonder, there sat a Fourth Estate more important far than they all." The founders of America likewise spoke of the importance of a free press as an independent political actor. In Thomas Jefferson's words, "when man is free and every man able to read, all is safe . . . The people are the only censors of their governors . . . [and were] it left to me to decide whether we should have a government without newspapers or newspapers without a government, I should not hesitate a moment to prefer the latter." James Madison notes that the right to "freely examine public characters and measures and offer communication thereon [is] the only effective guardian of every other right."[18] The implication of Jefferson's and Madison's statements is that the press may be considered as an independent actor in the American political system.

In 1922 the journalist Walter Lippmann writes that the press had essentially changed the nature of democratic government. Democracy needs to be assisted by policy and communications experts, Lippmann asserts, since public opinion cannot be left to chance, and the press are these experts. But it fell to Douglass Cater, a journalist, author, and aide to President Lyndon B. Johnson to elaborate on the notion of the American news media as a "fourth branch of government."

Cater's 1959 study of the systematic features of political reporting and of journalists' interactions with White House officials and members of Congress is the first attempt at a comprehensive analysis of the role of the news media in the American political system. Cater points out that it is the looseness of the framework of the American political system that allows the news media to insert themselves as another branch of the government. In no other political system (he compares the American political system with those of Great Britain and the then Soviet Union) do journalists have such a continual and prominent place in national government or such access to public officials. Cater argues that the Marshall Plan (which provided for American aid for the reconstruction of Europe after World War II) would not have passed the U.S. Senate had it not been for the cooperation of the major news media. He likewise observes that the news media were of critical importance to the impact that Senator McCarthy had on national politics.

Cater also notes that the presence of television cameras allows reporters to be more interpretive than they could be before television. Observing that the U.S. government is being increasingly driven by publicity, he maintains that this fact effectively alters the qualifications for who runs for office and who gets elected. Indeed, Cater's discussion of the strategic use of news coverage by the Eisenhower-Nixon "Research Associates" foreshadows the routineness with which such research is conducted by today's presidential candidates as well as incumbent presidents, and his comment on the management and manipulation of the press by President Eisenhower's acclaimed press secretary, James Hagerty, anticipates the roles played by subsequent press secretaries and White House communications directors.[19] Cater addresses many of the ingredients of the press as a participant in the American political system (as the epigraph to this chapter suggests).

Since Cater wrote *The Fourth Branch of Government*, other students of the news media and American politics have written about the news media as an institution or fourth branch,[20] yet most of these scholars, for all their contributions, merely mention that the news media constitute an institution and do not explain why or carefully define "institution." Neither do they typically examine how and why the news media are *independent* actors in the American political system for analytic and practical purposes. The upshot is that there is no general recognition or acceptance among students of American politics or mass communications that the news media constitute a political institution, much less any agreement on how they are to be so conceived.

Most political scientists and scholars of mass communications after World War II followed the stimulus-response model, borrowed from psychology, rather than the institutional approach of Cater and a handful of other scholars. They looked at "media effects": a unidirectional model of political communication whereby a message originates from elites and is then disseminated to and received by a mass audience. The media-effects research focused on political campaigns especially, but it bore meager fruit.[21]

The political scientist Bernard Cohen helped shift the focus of media research. As Cohen rephrased it, the press "may not be successful much of the time in telling readers what to think, but it is stunningly successful in telling readers what to think *about*." Communications scholars Maxwell McCombs and Donald Shaw subsequently explored and established "agenda setting" as a major field of media research. They and others found that the news media shape not only what people think about, but also how they think about it and, therefore, in the end, what they think.[22]

Yet researchers studying the media's agenda setting have also had inconsistent success in finding strong or decisive results with respect to Harold Lasswell's famous formulation of 1948: "*Who* says *what* in which *channel* to *whom* with *what effect*."[23] As the sociologist Denis McQuail observes, "the problem is to prove the connections and quantify the links. The 'facts' are so scarce, open to dispute and often puny in stature that the question is often answered by reference to alternative theories." Doris Graber points out that the media-effects research is poor at measuring the news media's "highly complex and elusive" effects on individuals.[24]

In fact, Cater's assertion in 1959 that "the political scientist has so long neglected the study of the interaction between government and the press" was not only accurate then, but also prescient of the next three decades.[25] Not much political science has focused on political communication before it's disseminated—that is, the study of how the "what" in Lasswell's phrase is determined—or to the political case histories that record "what effect" the news media have had. "Little scholarly attention" has been paid to the quality of information reaching the public and to the manufacture of public information, observes the political scientist John Zaller. Such an inquiry requires an understanding of "the politics of expert communities as they relate to the generation and diffusion of knowledge claims, policy recommendations, and general frames of reference." To the extent that the news-making process has been studied, it has mostly been the domain of sociologists, scholars of mass communications, and journalists, rather than political scientists.[26]

In this book I build on the work of Cater and his successors, Leon Sigal and Herbert Gans in particular, to explain why the news media effectively constitute a political institution and why this fact matters to students of American politics. Both Cater and Sigal merit updating and amendment in a world of CNN, C-SPAN, and cyberspace. Cater writes mostly about Congress and the printed press, not surprisingly since he wrote in the 1950s, whereas television dominates the present-day communication of news on politics and government. More seriously, Cater does not explain exactly how the news media can be considered a "fourth branch" of government, analogous to the other three, or present a clear framework by which the descriptions and analyses of the press come together into a whole (as we would expect for an argument that the media are a fourth branch).

Sigal concentrates on foreign policy and defense issues to the exclusion of domestic policies, federal elections, and the courts. Like Cater, he provides more a description of the interplay that exists between journalists and government officials than a thorough analysis of the role of the news media in the American political system and a coherent perspective by which to grasp it. Key questions remain: If the press discusses only the "surface" of political issues and only "samples" reality, what effect does their superficiality and sampling have on democratic government? What impact does the interaction between newspaper publishing (Sigal uses the *New York Times* and the *Washington Post* as examples) and government public relations have on policy outcomes? Are all of the uncertainties that reporters face of equal significance, or is there an order or priority among the routines and conventions of news production?[27]

The purpose here is to attend to how individual journalists and news executives handle the fundamental uncertainties of news production and how their actions may thereby be aggregated into a single institution. By emphasizing the external context of news organizations—on the assumption that the practices of individual media personnel and news organizations derive from their external environment and its resultant pressures—my argument is structural. As McQuail points out, "editorial decision-makers are most directly constrained by the *structure* of constitutional conditions, media laws, the market, and social norms."[28]

By presenting a general interpretation of the institutional status of the news media, I address an unstated assumption of recent scholarship on "the news media," "media politics," "political communication," and "the press": that the news media (or press) *can* be considered a single, separate actor. Almost all writing on political communication implies the more-or-less independent status of the news media, without explicitly explaining why the news media may be viewed as independent or what consequences follow from the existence of the news media as a distinct political actor.[29]

In contrast to the "minimal effects" findings of the earlier media research, however, I argue that the news media exert large and important effects on the American political system. "The mass media do have important consequences for individuals, for institutions, and for society and culture," Mc-Quail notes, although he believes "we cannot trace the very precise causal connections or make reliable predictions about the future." He adds,

> Control over the mass media offers several important possibilities. First, the media can attract and direct attention to problems, solutions or people in ways that can favour those with power and correlatively divert attention from rival individuals and groups. Second, the mass media can confer status and confirm legitimacy. Third . . . the media can be a channel for persuasion and mobilization. Fourth, the mass media can help to bring certain kinds of publics into being and maintain them.[30]

After all, most of what citizens know about government and politics is mediated through the news that is printed in newspapers and newsmagazines, broadcast electronically, or transmitted through cable. How people conceptualize "American democracy" or the "United States" depends in large part on the words, categories, associations, and expectations contained in the media's stories about politics and government.[31]

An Institutional News Media

"Institution" Defined

Institutions, as the economist and Nobel laureate Douglass North writes, "provide the framework through which human beings interact. They establish the cooperative and competitive relationships which constitute a society and more specifically an economic order . . . it is the institutional framework which constrains people's choice sets."[32] Institutions guide and channel choice sets; they are at once delimiting (since some actions may be foreclosed) and empowering (since some decisions may be easier and some choices more certain).

The political scientists Kathleen Thelen and Sven Steinmo use similar words in their definition of institutions, which they maintain include "both formal structures and informal rules and procedures that structure conduct." Thelen and Steinmo thus seem to be in fundamental agreement with North that institutions channel decision making, shaping subsequent individual, societal, and governmental actions.[33]

Following the work of North and of Thelen and Steinmo, I define the news media as an institution in the sense that the production of news by the media—indeed, often their simple presence—provides a regular and persisting framework by which and within which other political actors operate. As an institution, the news media constrain the choice sets of these other political actors; that is, they structure—that is, guide and limit—the actions of those working in the three formal branches of government, in public administration, and at various stages or parts of the political process.[34] The news media thereby exert important effects on other political actors in the American political system.

Yet individual news organizations do not explicitly coordinate their actions. Rather, an understanding of the news media as a political institution has to be grounded in specific, independent individual and organizational behaviors. The relationship of the news media to other institutions of American government, such as the legislative, executive, and judicial branches, federalism, and the electoral system, has to be anchored in the discrete actions of the journalists and organizational executives who gather, select, edit, publicize, and sell political information. I therefore base my macropolitical understanding of the news media as an institution on the microfoundations of another set of institutions, since institutions exist on more than one level. These microfoundations are the smaller-scale, everyday practices used by media personnel and news organizations to produce news about politics and the political system.[35]

Institutions may also consist of the formal or informal rules and norms that persons use in their daily existence, as the organizational and institutional theorists James March and Johan Olsen observe. Individuals do what they consider appropriate and expected of them. What is "appropriate" depends on the roles and behaviors within which persons are embedded. Individual preferences are matched to specific organizational and social conditions, then, rather than resulting from prior disposition or heredity.[36] In other words, individuals depend on shortcuts to navigate through life, using learned behavioral cues to survive, and possibly succeed, in a disorderly universe. Institutions are these shortcuts.

I therefore combine an attention to the news media as a societywide actor with a focus on the actual practices of news production used by journalists and news organizations. Attending to these specific "media practices" (I refer to these lower-level institutions as "media practices" to avoid using "institution" in a second sense) of shared journalistic techniques and organizational behaviors provides a foundation for understanding the news media as a macropolitical institution. Let me therefore discuss more fully the news media's existence as an institution, first, in the sense that they channel or structure national politics and, second, in the sense that they rely on set standard practices to produce political news.

The Media's Structuring of Politics

The news media are an inextricable and ineluctable part of the American political system: their actions direct, channel, and constrain the behavior of other political actors, effects that persist over time. It is a role they—the printed press for most of American history, of course—have played since the founding of this country. Thomas Paine's pamphlet *Common Sense* served to unify American colonists against the English. Shortly thereafter, the political writings of James Madison, Alexander Hamilton and John Jay were published in the New York press (and then compiled as the *Federalist Papers*); they helped secure the ratification of the Constitution. George Washington's farewell address as he ended his term as president was printed in the *Pennsylvania Packet and Daily Advertiser* on September 19, 1796, rather than delivered to Congress.

From the late eighteenth century through the early twentieth century, the press was vital to the creation and maintenance of the political parties. Printers and publishers cooperated with, were subsidized by, and were sometimes coerced by the political parties to publish partisan materials. As the political scientist Richard Rubin observes, "both of the chief instruments of mass mobilization and communications, the party and the press, served to increase partisan organizational activity and reinforce lines of electoral cleavage." The press entrenched the two-party system.[37]

At the end of the nineteenth century, the "yellow press" of inexpensive, non-party newspapers, led by Joseph Pulitzer's *New York World* and William Randolph Hearst's *New York Journal*, succeeded in getting the U.S. Congress and, ultimately, the McKinley administration to go to war against Spain. During the two world wars, journalists and news organizations cooperated with the Wilson, Roosevelt, and Truman administrations in support of the war efforts. They helped to mobilize a nation and unite it against a common enemy.[38]

The news media played a part in the election of President John F. Kennedy in 1960 (through communication of the president's personality and his stage presence), in the decision of President Lyndon B. Johnson not to seek reelection in 1968 (through adverse publicity on Vietnam), and in the resignation of President Richard Nixon in 1974 (through coverage of the Watergate affair). Today the news media occupy a prominent, even dominant, role in electoral campaigns, especially in the primaries (see Chapter 2). They often determine frontrunner status, build up or attack particular candidates or campaigns, probe into candidates' backgrounds, and discover errors and inconsistencies in candidates' statements.[39]

Nor can the functioning of many federal departments and agencies be understood without attending to the news media. United States diplomacy depends on the cooperation of the major news media to relay political messages. The Department of Defense has its own large public affairs system, complete with a separate program of study for its public affairs officers and large public relations and advertising budgets. The behavior of the Department of Justice and, within it, the Federal Bureau of Investigation, is likewise significantly affected by the actual or potential presence of the news media, as the Ruby Ridge, Waco, and Richard Jewell incidents of the early and mid-1990s make clear. The same is true of the Drug Enforcement Agency (also in the Department of Justice) and the Bureau of Alcohol, Tobacco and Firearms (in the Department of the Treasury). The tasks and budgets of the Department of Health and Human Services, the Federal Aviation Authority, the Department of Agriculture, and other departments and agencies are likewise routinely and significantly affected by the news media.[40]

In short, little of the contemporary American political system is not communicated by, and therefore affected by, journalists and their news organizations. It is impossible to study the presidency, the Congress, the Supreme Court, federal departments, bureaus, and agencies, and national elections with any claim to a comprehensive understanding without heeding the news media. For example, studies of the election of President Clinton in 1992 and his reelection in 1996 would be seriously incomplete without an examination of the president's relationship to the news media. The presence and influence of the national news media were crucial to the promulgation and then demise of the Clintons' health plan in 1993, to name just one instance. Likewise, it is not possible to make sense of the legislative successes and failures of the Republican 104th Congress in 1995 without attending to the news media.[41] The same holds for an analysis of the Social Security system.[42] Decidedly, the news media amount to a political institution in their effects on politicians, politics, and policies.

Media Practices

The fact that the various news media follow similar practices in their production of political news also allows them to be thought of as a political institution. It is not that journalists are identically trained or predisposed (although there are similarities among journalists as a population, to be sure) or that journalists and corporate executives coordinate their news decisions with each other (although they closely observe what rival news organizations are doing).[43] Rather, the national and larger regional news organizations inhabit an interorganizational field that they share with other communicators of political information, other news organizations, and other commercial enterprises. From journalists' and news organizations' similar positions (from which reporters and their editors and producers cover national politics), I argue, come similar behaviors.

News organizations have to secure their places in the interorganizational field, given their informal status: the existence of any single news organization among the authoritative voices on politics and government is not legally or constitutionally guaranteed. News organizations therefore have to develop means by which to stabilize their existence and to secure their status in their environment.[44]

Reporters, editors and producers, and news executives establish reliable connections with politicians and public officials, and they distinguish themselves from other (less prestigious) news organizations and from other political communicators (e.g., political parties, interest groups, government bureaus, or election campaign teams). Similarly, journalists and news organizations work to reach their commercial goals so as to remain economically viable.[45] The standing of any one news organization or news department as an authoritative political voice is by no means a given.

Consider that as recently as the 1970s, the *Washington Star* stood as a formidable cross-town rival of the *Washington Post*. In the 1980s, Gannett grew from a small newspaper chain into the largest newspaper group in the United States. From that decade into the 1990s, the Cable News Network (CNN) rose from a lowly position that invited the label "Chicken Noodle Network" to one so solidified that the network is held responsible for the "CNN Effect"—the notion that televised news may exert an instantaneous and international impact on foreign policy making.[46] Over the same decades, CBS fell from being the most profitable and most prestigious of the television networks—the "Tiffany network"—to becoming the fourth-ranked network behind NBC, ABC, and Fox in 1995 (CBS has since rebounded to second place).[47]

The leading news organizations in the United States are at pains, then, to support and reinforce their relative positions of authority as communicators of political news amid the competing sources of political information and entertainment. Leon Sigal's work is seminal here. Sigal was the first to place emphasis on the uncertainty of news production, given the crucial importance of the relationships between journalists and political officials, on the one hand, and between journalists and those who make the financial decisions about attracting audiences and targeting advertisers, on the other hand.

Although any individual person, organization, or industrial sector may be viewed through the perspective of uncertainty, the uncertainty of reporting on national politics and government is especially significant. No other single industry similarly provides the texts and visual images from which other political actors and the public at large routinely learn about their elected representatives, public policy, government agencies, the national economy, and their fellow citizens. The ways in which the news media handle the several uncertainties of news production thus have particular importance for the political community. Ideas are not widgets.

Whereas other writers note the uncertainty inherent in news production, Sigal makes uncertainty the cornerstone of his work. Sigal refers to the different uncertainties that journalists face in the production of political news: the uncertainty of reporters' access to political information, the uncertainty of the political reality that news organizations have to communicate, and the uncertainty of the economic foundations of news organizations. He points out that journalists mitigate their uncertainties through the use of norms and common practices. "The routines of newsgathering yield certified news—stories that other news organizations probably run concurrently or stories that replicate others run in the past whose validity went unquestioned." Furthermore, "The conventions of newsmaking authenticate the news that they [news organizations] publish, as well as legitimating their procedures for obtaining it." These conventions provide journalists "with a modicum of certitude that enables them to act in an otherwise uncertain environment." Once established, the routines "take on a life of their own. Learned during apprenticeship, reinforced in daily experience on the job, they become 'the way things are done.'"[48]

Implicit in Sigal's emphasis on the role of media practices in the (uncertain) coverage of political news is the notion that humans are "boundedly rational" (to use the term of the economist and Nobel laureate Herbert Simon). Journalists' reliance on these practices would be unnecessary were they certain about their environment and the effects their actions had on it. If journalists had that certainty, individual reporters and editors would simply figure their objectives, determine their choices, calculate the probable effects of their actions, and act to achieve their desired outcomes. Such clarity in goals, alternatives, consequences, and execution would allow them to act in any number of ways, depending on the conditions at hand.[49] However, most of the time, journalists—like other individuals—are faced with imperfect information about themselves and about their environment, as Simon points out. Only sometimes do they actually know their goals. Only sometimes do they know of all the possible alternatives. And only sometimes do they know what effects their actions will have. The result is that journalists are unable to realize their optimal preferences through means-end calculations. Instead, they rely on standard practices.

The sociologist Diane Vaughan's recent observations about the culture at NASA apply equally well to journalism:

> Paradigm obduracy is embedded in institutional forces in environment and organization that go beyond scientific communities and the received wisdom of scientific practice. Most science and technology is done in socially organized settings that can hardly be described as neutral. The professions and organizations that generate scientific and technical work struggle to survive in an often turbulent environment, experiencing competition and scarcity, and thus decisions are governed by other cultural imperatives that coexist uncomfortably with those of scientific practice. This case shows how these imperatives also become part of practitioners' world view, providing additional constraints, blocking opportunities for innovation.[50]

Although I do not emphasize culture, my attention to cognition and taken-for-granted practices is consistent with a cultural perspective. But I follow Gaye Tuchman and others who argue that culture derives from structure—in this case, the structure of journalists' and news organizations' larger environment. In the words of the sociologist Arthur Stinchcombe, "The reason for leaving the culture . . . out of our theory is that culture gets its stability only from the structure of stability of the social organization of which it is part."[51]

In this book, I look at the media practices that derive from news organizations' production of the news. Specifically, I examine the news practices that derive from the media's larger political environment in two different situations: political contests and policy monopolies. The former are occasions of distinct sides competing against each other on an issue or over an office, and the latter, situations in which information with respect to policy (or a person, for that matter) is held confidential and under control. I then look at the environment and practices of producing commercially successful news.

Journalists and news executives experience uncertainty in the production of political news in both realms. In the first instance, journalists are uncertain of their capacity as commentators on and bystanders to political contests such as electoral campaigns and lawmaking. They focus on the strategies of political competitors, evaluate the performance of participants, and try to predict the eventual winners and losers. There is a clear give-and-take: journalists need politicians as sources of stories, and politicians need reporters and news organizations to publicize their appeals to interested parties and their constituents.

A second uncertainty for journalists is simply whether they can secure access to important information about politics and government, given that it may be kept confidential by politicians or government personnel. For information about the presidency, foreign policy, the national economy, and other issues, journalists and news executives may have to depend on a select group of public officials, including the president, top White House aides, departmental secretaries, U.S. senators, congressional committee chairs, and others, who are joined in a policy monopoly. What information will be released to journalists and when are uncertain, regardless of the size of the stakes involved.[52]

A third uncertainty confronting news organizations is the marketplace: whether they can remain highly profitable—or sometimes merely economically viable—in the face of competition from other sources of news and entertainment and in the midst of rapid technological and demographic changes. Even the most successful news organizations operate in an extremely competitive market. And financial officers, chief executives, boards of directors, and shareholders place a premium on corporate earnings. (Suggestive of the stakes involved is the fact that in 1994, the publishing and printing industries combined ranked second among U.S. industries in return on sales, second in return on assets, and eighth in return on stockholders' equity, according to *Fortune*.) The commercial stability of any one news organization is hardly predetermined, as the dwindling numbers of newspapers, the increase in news company mergers, and the turnover among network affiliates attest.

The result of these uncertainties is that news organizations rely on regular "media practices" (what Sigal calls "routines" and "conventions," Tuchman calls "inevitable processes," Gans calls "considerations," and the communications scholar David Altheide calls the "news process").[53] These are the informal rules of news production that have evolved to allow journalists and news organizations to handle their uncertain relationships within the interorganizational field of political communication. The use and adaptation of these routines are especially important for leading news organizations, since they are the ones who largely define the news.

The cumulative and coincident presence of these practices provides news organizations (or at least the several leading news organizations in the United States) with an essential coherence in the production of salient news about American politics and government.[54] The existence of these shared media practices explains how individual reporters, editors and producers at various levels of seniority, and corporate executives are able to transform the complexity of political reality into a limited set of narratives about national politics. These practices constitute the microfoundations of the news media's existence as an aggregate political institution and bridge individual and organizational behaviors and macropolitical outcomes.

For both these reasons—the reciprocal impact of the news media on other political actors and the common practices of news coverage—the news media may be considered a single political institution. The news produced by the major American media exerts widespread effects on both domestic and international politics. Moreover, the news media operate more or less in unison when covering national politics and government. Even so, the news media's institutional status is under threat from technological and social change.

The News Media's Uncertain Future

As we move into the twenty-first century, the news media face a highly uncertain future. One reason for this is the change in the news audience. Fewer Americans read newspapers, as more and more people who grew up with television are now in their forties and fifties. Whereas in 1967, 60 percent of eighteen- to twenty-nine-year-olds regularly read a newspaper, in 1989 only half that percentage, 29 percent, did so. Americans' primary source of news has become television: in 1967, about 20 percent of Americans responded that "television only" was their principal source of news; that percentage rose to 40 percent by 1980 and to about 60 percent by 1991. Meanwhile, those depending on "newspapers only" stayed at 20 percent from 1960 through 1980 and then fell to about 10 percent by 1991.[55] In a world of increasing "aliteracy"—where Americans can read but prefer not to—the dominant position of the *New York Times,* the *Washington Post,* the *Los Angeles Times,* the *Wall Street Journal,* and the wire services in political communication is no longer guaranteed.

Overall newspaper and newsmagazine readership has also been stagnant in recent years. "Nobody picks up a paper and says 'Holy Shit!' anymore. Because they know what's going on," comments David Shribman, the Washington bureau chief of the *Boston Globe* (and a former reporter with the *New York Times* and *Wall Street Journal*). "So we have to give them something different," he adds. Newsmagazines no longer even report the news. Whereas previously they provided weekly summaries of the news for people who did not read a large daily newspaper, now they interpret politics; they "tell you something about it."[56] The role of the newspapers and newsmagazines has inexorably been altered.

The place of the television networks is hardly more secure. The networks lost a third of their viewers in the twenty-five years between 1976 and 1991, and in 1997 more than half of their audience for the evening news shows was age fifty or older. CBS News, NBC News, and ABC News are seeing their viewership eroded by the rise of cable television (which is able to offer specialty programming), the presence of other news programming (e.g., that of CNN, CNN Headline News, CNBC, Fox, MSNBC, and others to come), and the growing leverage of their local affiliates and independent stations. Sixty percent of Americans older than eighteen watched network news programs in 1993, compared with only 38 percent in 1998.[57] In 1997, the three major television networks controlled 62.1 percent of the prime-time audience in the May ratings sweeps, down from 65.2 percent a year earlier; cable channels controlled 32.4 percent, up from 29.5 percent a year earlier. The biggest winner was the upstart Fox network, which added about a half-million viewers, most of whom were in the younger age groups most favored by advertisers. One estimate has it that the total cable audience will exceed the total audience of the top four broadcast networks combined by 2001.[58] There is also more local news on the air (and proportionately less national news), and the network affiliates are increasingly able to pick and choose among networks—and are willing to do so—in order to get more profitable programming.[59]

Network television once provided a foundation of American political and popular culture. What was on television was a cultural constant that united Americans across region, age, race and ethnicity, and income. After the assassinations of President John F. Kennedy and the Reverend Martin Luther King, for instance, the networks became a "common church" for the American people. About three-fourths of viewers watched the miniseries *Roots*, and almost all Americans watched at least part of the Anita Hill–Clarence Thomas hearings and saw video footage of the Persian Gulf War. But unifying events such as these and the Challenger disaster, the fall of the Berlin Wall, and the death of Princess Diana are comparatively few.[60]

The experiences of the television audiences in the United States have become increasingly fragmented. Fewer Americans tune into the nightly network news, much less the annual State of the Union Address or the national party conventions. Cable television does not fill the gap, given the proliferation of cable channels that offer news, sports, syndicated comedies, educational shows, movies, and other niche programming; any single cable channel rarely gets as high as a ten in the ratings. The result is that "network news and all its premises" are being reexamined, observes Penn Kimball, a former journalist and professor emeritus at Columbia University's School of Journalism.[61]

The news cycle has also been transformed. Print and broadcast journalists have tremendous access to news almost wherever and whenever it is made, thanks to all-news television and C-SPAN, as well as the Internet, Lexis-Nexis, the "Hotline" news service, and other news services and databases. "Even if you are not there physically, there are so many things that you can watch take place now," observes David Broder, the writer and columnist for the *Washington Post*.[62]

Creating further uncertainty among news organizations is the spread of the Internet, which is able to offer spot news, longer news articles (equivalent to magazine articles in length), interactive "talk" formats, access to government documents, and other information of political relevance. The number of World Wide Web sites is growing at the rate of 10–15 percent a month, and as of July 1996 there were about 230,000 Web sites in more than one hundred countries around the world; there were as few as 27,000 Web sites in early 1995.[63] As of December 1996, more than one in five of Americans had Internet access at work, in school, or at home—this is double the percentage who had Internet access only fifteen months previously. Twenty percent used the Internet to get news once a week.[64] Although the ultimate scale and political impact of the Internet remain unclear, the place of the major news organizations is also uncertain as the twenty-first century approaches. Most newspapers, newsmagazines, TV networks, and local TV stations offer online services, of course, yet they may be driven more by fear of being left behind and the vague promise of the Internet than by firm expectations of future profitability.

The scope and economics of today's news media are thus highly uncertain at present, a time when the power of microprocessors has doubled about every eighteen months. Nor is it known how these different media will relate to each other and to the new technologies on the horizon. The effects of the media revolution are still unfolding. Ed Fouhy, executive director of the Pew Center for Civic Journalism, comments that for newspapers, the "status quo is very frightening." Mort Pye, the late editor of the *New Jersey Star-Ledger* from 1963 until 1994, calls the future "confounding," noting that there is "such an air of uncertainty" about the newspaper business. What is true about newspapers is true of television and the newsmagazines. The news media in the United States are at a crossroads.[65]

These broader issues facing the news media offer another reason to reexamine the role of the news media in the American political system. Furthermore, a consideration of the daily and the longer-term uncertainties that face news organizations prompts a more basic question about the relationship between the news media and political order. If there are a proliferating number of media channels and ever more fragmentation in political communication, will the media be able to provide a baseline of political order and stability in American politics as they were arguably able to do throughout most of the twentieth century?[66] I return to the question of political order later in the book.

Methods

This is essentially an interpretive project, since there are not good systematic data on many of the phenomena with which I am concerned. There are no systematic data on editors' decisions about what to publicize, on the credibility of politicians and other news sources and how they may retaliate against journalists, or on how top editors, producers, and news executives consider political and economic factors in their production of political news. Nor do we have comprehensive records about how publishers and news executives decide whom to hire and promote. Few authors since Altheide, Argyris, Epstein, Gans, and Tuchman have been able to spend extensive periods within national news organizations, observing the operations of news production firsthand.[67]

My work therefore consisted mostly of synthesizing a large body of existing research done by political scientists, sociologists, and scholars of journalism and mass communication. Fortunately, much of this research directly addresses my concerns and interests.[68] Also, in contrast to most other social scientists writing on the news media, I rely on the work of journalists who have written about American politics, political reporting, and the news process in my synthesis and integration of secondary material. Journalists have actual expertise in the production of political news (which most media scholars do not have). Although there is the chance that practicing journalists (or practicing politicians, for that matter) will be self-serving in their writing and speech, the findings of political scientists, sociologists, scholars of mass communication, and other journalists provide a baseline against which to assess the accuracy and plausibility of any particular claims. Individual journalists also have their own track records as political commentators, as well as their own reputations, at stake.

I also engaged in personal interviews and participant observation—that is, I relied on my own ears and eyes. I interviewed about three dozen persons working in the news business or related fields in the summer of 1995 and spring and fall of 1996. The interviewees are identified in my notes, except for three who wished to remain anonymous. Although the interviewees do not constitute a random sample of Washington journalists, congressional press secretaries, or media consultants, they do constitute a pool of persons who were of different ages, worked in various media and for different organizations, and had varying responsibilities within the sphere of political communication.

As a participant observer, I accompanied reporters on their news beats, attended editorial meetings, and watched a number of reporters and newsrooms in action. Participant observation allowed me to compare and reconcile my own views—acquired from formal and informal study of the news media and from my own (brief) experience at a magazine—with firsthand impressions of the production of political news at several of the leading news organizations in the United States.

This project is "prescientific," then, insofar as I draw on existing scholarship, the testimony of journalists, politicians, and consultants to offer an interpretation of why the news media are an institution within the American political system. To this end, I rely on the words and expressions of those who have participated in political communication: these are the persons (mostly based in the nation's capital) whose perceptions matter. My hope is that future research will be able to develop further the arguments presented here and test hypotheses derived from this work.

Definitions

By "journalists" I mean the reporters, editors, and producers involved in the daily production of the news. By "reporters" I mean the individual men or women researching and (usually) writing the news story, whether for print or for video (i.e., broadcast or cable) media. By "news executives" I mean the publishers, company presidents, and other top executives who are typically removed from the production of the news on an everyday basis but who make the ultimate decisions about what to publish or broadcast and whom to hire, promote, or fire. I use the term "media personnel" to refer to any or all of the above.

By "news organization" I mean the organization or part of an organization that effectively operates a newspaper, newsmagazine, television network, individual television station, or wire service. Thus "news organization" refers to *Newsweek* or the *Washington Post,* and not to the Washington Post Company. When I do refer to parent corporations or holding companies, such as Times-Mirror (the *Los Angeles Times)* or the Walt Disney Company (ABC News), I identify them as "corporations" or "companies," rather than "news organizations."[69]

I generally use "the press" synonymously with "news media" (inclusive of the print and video, i.e., broadcast and cable media), although I sometimes distinguish between the two. When I use "news media" or the "press" I am typically referring to the largest and most prominent news organizations in the United States: NBC News, ABC News, and CBS News, as well as CNN (which is both a cable news channel and the equivalent of a video wire service), *Time, Newsweek,* and *U.S. News and World Report* (*U.S. News* hereafter), the largest national and regional newspapers, such as the *New York Times, Washington Post, Wall Street Journal,* and *Los Angeles Times,* and the Associated Press and Reuters wire services. On occasion I refer to large regional newspapers, such as the *Chicago Tribune,* the *Boston Globe,* and the *Dallas Morning News.*

Not only are these news organizations the analogues to Stephen Hess's "inner ring" newspapers, but politicians, journalists, scholars, and my interviewees consistently referred to these organizations as the news organizations to which they paid most attention.[70] The *New York Times* and the *Washington Post* were constants among the news organizations mentioned by my interviewees, while the *Wall Street Journal,* the *Los Angeles Times,* Associated Press, television networks, and newsmagazines were almost always mentioned by the interviewees. Other news organizations whose names came up were *USA Today* and the *Washington Times.* Smaller newspapers and local television stations do not have the resources to gather and produce political news independently of the major news services (e.g., the *New York Times* and *Washington Post/Los Angeles Times* news services) and the wire services. Only a few organizations have their own news bureaus in Washington, D.C., in other cities around the United States, or in foreign capitals; most newspapers and television stations therefore rely on the major news suppliers.

I also refer less frequently to other newspapers, newspaper groups such as Knight-Ridder, Gannett, and Scripps-Howard, the local network affiliates, cable television, radio, and the alternative press. The local network affiliates are particularly important in an understanding of the news media, given their profitability, their growing independence from the networks, and the fact that many are owned and operated by the networks themselves or by other media companies.

By "politics," I mean not only electoral campaigns and party competition (whether in Congress or nationwide), but also governmental operations (whether public administration, the conduct of domestic and foreign policy, implementation, or the interpretation of law) and issues of economic salience. All of these are implicated in a definition of "politics" as the authoritative allocation of resources over a territory, to follow Lasswell's formulation of politics as the struggle over "who gets what, when, and how."

Overview of the Book

In Chapters 2–7, I elaborate on why the news media are a political institution and what this means to students of American politics. In the second, third, and fourth chapters, I consider the news coverage of the politics and economics of American society—politics and economics within which the news media are embedded. I also describe the political and economic environment within which the news media operate and within which journalists and their organizations exert a reciprocal impact on politicians, public officials, and the political process. I then explore some media practices that have evolved to mitigate the uncertainties that news organizations face in their production of political news.

In Chapter 2, I explore the often tense relationship that exists when journalists cover contests of national politics. Journalists and political officials have essentially distinct interests: the former try to gather information and publicize news that sells; the latter attempt to use information to further their own political objectives. This is the news coverage of political contests—contests evident not only in electoral campaigns, but also in much congressional activity, in executive and legislative branch relations, and in the Senate confirmation of presidential appointees. Coverage of political contests is a delicate task: journalists have to be credible witnesses to and interpreters of these competitions and rivalries, while at the same time needing the information that the politicians have and wanting to avoid being exploited by them. I conclude the chapter by giving instances of standard practices that have emerged to stabilize the potentially volatile relationships between journalists and politicians.

In contrast to their coverage of political contests, journalists and news organizations enjoy much less discretion in covering the executive branch, where there is a sizable arena of information controlled by politicians and government officials. In Chapter 3, I consider the news coverage of this domain of "policy monopoly," where journalists typically depend on information held by political officials, who have the advantage in determining what news gets publicized and what does not. I then look at some of the media practices that have evolved to allow journalists to present political news under these conditions.

In Chapter 4, I consider the commercial pressures that bear on the news media, given the existence of news organizations as large for-profit enterprises, and examine how the commercial aspects of news production affect news content. Financial factors that affect political communication include commercial advertising, market journalism, cost cutting, libel, and political action. After examining some of the practices that news organizations use to fit their commercial objectives into the production of political news, I conclude the chapter by addressing the common claim that news supply follows demand—it does not.

In Chapter 5, I turn to the roles that top editors, senior producers, publishers, and news executives play in producing news that is able to reconcile the several and distinct uncertainties they face on a daily basis. After looking at the hierarchy of news production, which enables news executives to produce accessible and timely news within the various political and economic constraints that confront news organizations, I discuss the insularity of the community that communicates national politics to the American public and touch on the cue taking and use of reference groups that goes on among news organizations. I then explain the evolution of particular "multivocal" news conventions that are able to speak simultaneously to the several uncertainties faced by news organizations and their executives: "balanced" (or "objective") reporting, the use of a limited number of "news frames" for identifying and categorizing the news, reliance on authoritative sources, and maintenance of the "transparent" production of political news (that the news appears to be *un*mediated by organizational processes). The exercise of these multivocal conventions, enforced by ranking media personnel, binds the separate persons and organizations of the news media into a single institution. To conclude the chapter, I summarize why the news media can be conceptualized as an aggregate political institution and reconsider the myth of a liberal news media.

I give examples of the news media's behavior as a political institution in Chapter 6, reviewing five cases in which the news media were seriously deficient in guarding the public interest. I examine the news coverage of international affairs in the instances of the 1991 Persian Gulf War and the 1983 Korean Airlines Flight 007 disaster, the coverage of the political economy in the instance of the savings and loan debacle of the 1980s, and the coverage of public health in the cases of AIDS and the work of Gaston Naessens, a Canadian biologist and inventor who has done original research on human blood and a cure for cancer.[71] In each instance, the news media acted consistently with the institutional framework I describe in the preceding chapters: they had a great impact on national politics, politicians, public officials, and the American public, they reported all five cases similarly, acting in concert, and they betrayed the democratic ideals of a free press and their own stated ethical principles of public service or, in short, the public trust.

In Chapter 7, I propose reforms for the current system of political communication in this country, including changes in public policy, alternative policies that news organizations and news personnel could follow, and initiatives for individual citizens to take. The chapter concludes with a brief discussion of the Internet and other new technologies, given the potential effects of the spread of the Internet on political communication.

MEDIA ATTACK DOGS

Were reporting the simple recovery of obvious facts, the press agent would be little more than a clerk. But since, in respect to most of the big topics of news, the facts are not simple, and not at all obvious, but subject to choice and opinion, it is natural that everyone should wish to make his own choice of facts for the newspaper to print. The publicity man does that.—Walter Lippmann, *Public Opinion,* 1922

Political conflict is not like an intercollegiate debate in which the opponents agree in advance on a definition of the issues. As a matter of fact, the definition of the alternatives is the supreme instrument of power; the antagonists can rarely agree on what the issues are because power is involved in the definition. He who determines what politics is about runs the country, because the definition of the alternatives is the choice of conflicts, and the choice of conflicts allocates power.—E. E. Schattschneider, *The Semisovereign People,* 1960

ONE VIEW OF THE NEWS MEDIA'S COVERAGE OF POLITICS IS THAT JOURnalists are "attack dogs," relentlessly critical of politicians and government officials. Individual candidates, political appointees, political parties, and political consultants alike get torn down and are torn apart by the adversarial news media. Journalists have become more critical of political figures and assert themselves more boldly as political spokespersons in the place of, and at the expense of, politicians, political appointees, and civil servants. Given journalists' prominence in the news and the news media's negative portrayal of politics, the American public has become distrustful of and alienated from national politics. In this view, the news media are "out of order" or on a "feeding frenzy," as the political scientists Thomas Patterson and Larry Sabato title their respective books.[1] Journalists, many claim, bear much of the responsibility for the "dirty politics" of today.[2]

Yet there is an opposing view of the news media and their relationship with politics: that journalists are the "lap dogs" of political insiders. A number of writers, including David Broder, Ted Galen Carpenter, William Greider, Mark Hertsgaard, Howard Kurtz, and Tom Wicker, observe that top Washington journalists largely cooperate with politicians, executive branch officials, and other political figures.[3] Others go further and speak of the hegemony in American politics and the propaganda disseminated by the U.S. news media.[4]

Stephen Hess, a senior fellow at the Brookings Institution and a former speechwriter for President Dwight D. Eisenhower, writes explicitly on the press's dependence on and deference to the government when reporting news about the "Golden Triangle," that is, the White House, State Department, and Pentagon. Studies of government-media relations before and during the 1991 Persian Gulf War suggest the same.[5] The *Wall Street Journal* echoes this view of a compliant media with complaints about how the (other) news media have covered the Clinton administration, particularly the Whitewater affair and the administration's handling of White House lawyer Vincent Foster's death, its breach of confidentiality with respect to hundreds of Republican personnel files, and its political fundraising conducted from inside the White House.

Whether journalists are adversarial or cooperative in their relationship with public officials depends on which of two political situations they are reporting on: they are attack dogs when they are covering political contests, but they are lap dogs, a "handout press," when covering a policy monopoly.[6] In this chapter, I explore the news media's coverage of political contests and the media practices that follow from this coverage. In the next chapter, I discuss the news media's coverage of policy monopolies.

The News Media: Umpires with an Attitude

Reporting on political contests puts journalists in the position of being the unofficial umpires of national politics. This domain includes much, if not most, of national politics: presidential races, battles between members of Congress over legislation, standoffs between the executive branch and legislative branch over matters of policy or prerogative, and clashes between Democrats and Republicans or between contingents within each party, such as during the primary elections or after a loss in general elections.[7] In each of these political contests, it falls to journalists to keep score.

Journalists and their news organizations explain electoral campaigns and track electoral progress; they make guesses as to the outcomes of particular bills or legislative agendas; and they speculate on how Cabinet nominees,

Supreme Court candidates, other presidential appointees, and government treaties will fare in the Senate. Journalists tell the public, politicians and public officials, and each other who or what is ahead, and who or what is behind, just as they pronounce who or what is gaining or losing ground. Journalists may thereby greatly influence who the winners and losers are in these political struggles.

The news media are more than umpires, however; they are critics. Political reporters from both the print and broadcast media have become increasingly judgmental in their stories on presidential electoral politics. The rise in negativity coincides with the adoption of an increasingly interpretive style of reporting, since interpretive news stories easily lend themselves to reportage on politicians and political campaigns that expresses the skepticism of correspondents and columnists. Given their television exposure, which is enjoyed by many of the prominent print reporters as well as television reporters, some journalists rank with cabinet members, film stars, and prominent athletes in terms of public recognition. In fact, more than one observer has noted that the top political journalists have the status of diplomats, on a par with U.S. senators and other top politicians.[8]

Despite sharing celebrity status, politicians and journalists have "competing cultures," as Marvin Kalb, the former CBS correspondent, remarks. The politician is intent on "controlling the message," whereas the journalist is "determined to spot the message, dissect it, and then report it his own way." Leo Rosten's observation from the 1930s still holds: "Officials and newspapermen meet for essentially conflicting purposes. The official wants to present information which will reflect most favor upon him. The newspaperman, motivated by the ancient values of journalism, is interested in precisely the type of news which the official is least eager to reveal."[9] Journalists may be the unofficial umpires of political contests in the sense of interpreting political messages and the statements of public officials, but their refereeing is vulnerable to manipulation by those same public officials. The result is a maneuvering by "journalists and advocates" that creates a "subtly composite product," according to the media scholars Jay Blumler and Michael Gurevitch:

> Each side is striving towards realizing different goals *vis-à-vis* the audience; yet it cannot normally pursue these without securing the co-operation of the other side. Politicians need access to the communication channels operated by media organizations; and they must adjust their messages to the demands of formats and genres that have been devised inside such organizations. At the same time, journalists cannot perform

their task of political reporting without access to politicians for interviews, news and comment.[10]

Journalists seek to maintain their neutrality—and thus their credibility—and at the same time to avoid being manipulated by the political actors on whom they depend for information.

Journalists and public officials are thus engaged in a "dance" to determine who will better achieve their objectives.[11] The dance is particularly evident in the relationship between journalists and politicians in the production of news about presidential election campaigns. It is also evident, if to a less extent, in the news coverage of the presidency, Congress, the Supreme Court, and the federal bureaucracy.

In the following sections, I consider the news media's coverage of presidential elections, the president, Congress, the Supreme Court, and the bureaucracy. In each case, journalists must report without knowing the exact status of the political contest they are covering (since it may be unclear who or which side will win) and without being able to trust the information received from politicians and others in government (since politicians and other interested parties seek publicity that furthers their own ends). I then consider some of the practices shared by journalists in their handling of news of political contests.

Presidential Elections

The Media as Lead in the Dance

BACKGROUND. The news media play a dominant role in contemporary presidential elections in the United States.[12] One reason for this is the reforms passed in the late 1960s and early 1970s, which undermined the importance of political parties and gave a greater role to the news media. The ostensible achievement of the 1969 McGovern-Fraser Commission reforms was to take the nomination process out of the hands of party elders and put it into the hands of the voters. When, as a result of these reforms, a growing number of states decided to hold party primaries rather than caucuses, the news media began to have a much larger role in the nomination process. As the providers of political information for most voters, the print and broadcast media gained considerably more influence over the nomination process, since individual voters, rather than state party elders, now determined who would be selected as delegates to the national convention.[13]

The other legal change was the Federal Election Campaign Act of 1971 (which set the nominal rates of political advertising at the lowest scheduled rates) and the 1974 amendment to the act, coming on the heels of the abuses of the 1972 presidential campaign and the Watergate affair. The new law restricted contributions to $1,000 (individuals) and $5,000 (political action committees) per candidate for each election cycle, specified that politicians had to reveal their funding sources, and set up the Federal Election Commission to monitor the new regulations.[14] The effect of the financial reforms was to shift funding responsibilities from the parties to the individual candidates, who now had to be successful at mass-marketing themselves (and their politics) if they were to win office.

The unintended consequence of the two reforms was that they combined to greatly reduce the role of the political parties in the nominating process and enhance the influence of the news media in this new era of entrepreneurial politics.[15] The new campaign financing laws had the perverse effects of making fundraising more important and increasing the use of soft money, which was not limited by contribution but was restricted to party-building purposes, but in fact may often be dedicated to particular candidates and specific elections. Reporters' and editors' decisions about what and who were newsworthy became of heightened importance.

Another reason for the news media's dominant role in presidential campaigns is television, which, as Douglass Cater, Thomas Patterson, Kathleen Hall Jamieson, and others observe, has led to more interpretive reporting. Members of the media increasingly substitute their own messages for those of presidential candidates and other public figures. In the 1992 presidential campaign, for instance, television reporters spoke six minutes for every one minute that candidates spoke on television. The average length of the sound bites excerpted from the speeches of presidential candidates has shrunk from 42 seconds in 1968 to under 10 seconds in 1992 (7.3 seconds, in fact).[16] Journalists have encroached on the turf of politicians and other public officials, as the pictures, voices, and opinions of reporters (and anchorpersons) receive the dominant share of airtime and newsprint. News stories in both the press and video media have become less descriptive of politicians' messages and political events and more interpretive and analytical.[17]

Television also exerts an effect as an instrument of American political culture. In a nation of 270 million persons, television is the most effective way for political candidates to reach potential voters. The political consultant Mary Matalin ranks the importance of the various media in the 1992 presidential election campaign as follows: "First, the networks—ABC, NBC, CBS, CNN—obviously, because they have the greatest reach and therefore the greatest influence. A good photo op on CNN was worth more than half a page of exposure in *The Washington Post* . . . Next the print guys, the majors: *The Washington Post, The New York Times, The Wall Street Journal*, the *L.A. Times*."[18] And since free television—that is to say, news coverage—is an unpredictable commodity, most candidates must be willing to make extensive media buys. Both free and paid television exposure is necessary for winning elections.

News coverage appears to be partly driven by paid television—advertising—since journalists as well as others consider the ability of presidential candidates to run expensive political advertisements an indicator of their resources and thus a measure of their viability as candidates. Political advertising may even set the news agenda with respect to which candidates to focus on as well as the substance of that focus. Jamieson finds that the television commercials of the 1988 election campaign set the agenda for reporters' coverage of Democratic challenger Michael Dukakis on crime: "The language of a candidate's ads infuses the vocabulary of reporters." She further determines that later exposure to news that relates to the advertisements is able to evoke the whole partisan image in the mind of the viewer.[19]

The consequence of television's pervasiveness in American society has been that the cost of presidential campaigns has steadily risen, with about 60 percent of candidates' campaign funds in the 1992 and 1996 elections going to purchases of political advertising on the news media—by far their biggest single expense. Candidates have to place ads, mostly negative ads, in strategic television markets across the country. As a result, the pursuit of paid advertising and free press "determine[s] how the candidate spends his or her time, how the campaign organization is structured, and what key strategic decisions are made by the campaign," note the political scientists Stephen Ansolabehere, Roy Behr, and Shanto Iyengar. "The necessity of obtaining both paid and free media forces candidates to emphasize fundraising and the creation of newsworthy materials. The system rewards those candidates who have perfected these 'media management' skills."[20]

The political parties have suffered as a result of the media's new importance in national elections. "The press has no time for parties," concludes Thomas Patterson. In fact, research by Michael Robinson shows that "television's portrayal of political parties is overwhelmingly negative." Other research reveals that "70 percent of newspaper stories about parties were unfavorable and that persons exposed to newspapers which had a higher degree of negative criticism directed at politicians and political institutions were more distrustful of government and [had] higher levels of cynicism."[21]

Party identification now exerts less control over electoral outcomes. The percentage of Americans who identified themselves as political independents rose from 20 percent in 1952 to 30 percent in 1990, and the percentage of those who split their tickets, that is, voted for different parties in the same federal election, rose from 29 percent in 1952 to 57 percent in 1980.[22] This means the news media are providing political information to a less partisan electorate that can presumably be more swayed by the news media than a partisan electorate could. This is despite the fact that the elections in the 1990s suggest a renewed importance of parties, in state legislatures as well as in the House and Senate.[23]

Given the status of the political parties, the structural reforms, and the prevalence of campaigning through television, fundraising is paramount for present-day presidential candidates. ABC News's Cokie Roberts observes, "The power of money on politics and television can't be overstated. When you are talking about political campaigns costing millions and millions of dollars and almost all that money goes to television, then it completely changes how politics is operated."[24] The Federal Communications Commission chair, Reed Hundt, makes the same point: "The cost of TV time-buys makes fundraising an enormous entry barrier for candidates for public office, an oppressive burden for incumbents who seek reelection, a continuous threat to the integrity of our political institutions, and a principal cause of the erosion of public respect for public service."[25] Indeed, Ansolabehere et al. find that "most politicians view fundraising as the most distasteful part of their job . . . The system now rewards candidates who are willing and able to devote days to asking strangers for money."[26] This means that politicians have less time for other important activities, such as learning about issues, meeting with constituents, and formulating policy. Simply put, candidates' schedules are driven largely by the pursuit of money and media attention.

These shifts in the electoral terrain have caused a fundamental change in U.S. presidential campaigns. The preprimary period (the "invisible primary") and the early primaries, New Hampshire and Super Tuesday (composed of a number of southern states) have become critical. Whereas the campaigns of old were based on presidential candidates' building a political base and then putting together a coalition of voters and interested groups, today's electoral campaigns are based on an assortment of group and individual donors—without any necessary internal coherence—as well as a demonstrated ability to reach voters through the free and paid news media.[27]

CONTEMPORARY CAMPAIGNS. These changes in campaign rules and the ever-larger place of television in American political culture have amplified the importance of the news media in presidential elections. The news media have been put in the position of being the unofficial umpires of political contests—whether in editorial columns, on TV talk shows, in news analyses, or in simply reporting the news about the presidential campaign. The veteran *Wall Street Journal* reporter John Fialka comments, "You become more like a sports reporter than . . . a serious news reporter. And you are busy handicapping races that haven't happened yet."[28]

Put in the role of umpires or handicappers, journalists rely on whatever indicators they can find to predict the outcomes of political contests. They sift through the clues provided by "public opinion polls, the sophistication of campaign organizations, endorsements by recognized officeholders, support from active interest groups, personal style on television, fundraising success, performance in early primaries and caucuses, accumulated delegates, [and] leadership on public policy questions" to determine candidates' prospects, finds the political scientist Christopher Arterton. The ability to raise campaign funds and attain a good standing in public opinion polls becomes key in the absence of strong national political parties and party identification. So do events such as preprimary straw votes, party caucuses, and, of course, the New Hampshire primary as indicators of candidates' electoral prospects. These indicators provide journalists with at least some guidance when it comes to deciding which candidate(s) to focus on, who (and when) to profile and investigate a candidate, and how to interpret a candidate's political standing.[29]

Amid this ambiguity, the media's umpiring is an art form. ABC News's Hal Bruno cautions that straw polls and fundraising ability may be misleading in the early primary stages: "news judgment," "experience," and "feel" are key.[30] The implication of Bruno's cautionary note—and other political reporters and commentators concede the same—is that the role of individual journalists and their subjective interpretations of presidential candidacies takes on heightened importance. "Informed opinion," as Arterton puts it, or the "Great Mentioner," as the New York Times columnist Russell Baker calls it ("Candidate so-and-so has been mentioned . . . "), can influence other journalists and the public about the election and the candidates. Arterton gives the example of R. W. Apple's article on the front page of the New York Times of January 12, 1976: "A kind of rough standing among the candidates has suddenly started to emerge in the minds of professionals around the country . . . In the group from which the nominee is most likely believed to be selected are . . . In the second, candidates given a conceivable chance of being nominated are . . . ." Although Apple had visited twelve states and had conversations with hundreds of politicians and party activists, he concedes later in the article that "early calculations are highly speculative . . . But early calculations have a life of their own, because they are the backdrop against which politicians and the media tend to measure the performance of the various candidates in their early confrontations."[31] Journalists have to adjust as conditions warrant.

Reporters, sensitive to fluctuations in the possible fates of candidates—given the absence of a strong party system or party bosses to choose the most viable presidential candidate—are quick to indicate changes in political momentum. None want to be wrong, and they all want to have the latest story. Accordingly, they jump on and off candidates' bandwagons with alacrity, depending on whether their performances meet expectations.

Examples of the news media's vacillating behavior are evident in the news coverage that increasingly favored Bill Clinton in the summer of 1992 and Hubert Humphrey in the closing weeks of 1968, when these candidates were "on a roll," and, conversely, the fall in the percentage of favorable coverage devoted to Jimmy Carter when he was "losing ground" in 1976 (although he was still able to defeat incumbent President Gerald Ford). Patterson provides evidence to suggest, interestingly, that the effects of coverage that portrays a candidate as being "on a roll" or "losing ground" are stronger than the effects of news portrayals of a candidate as a "likely loser" or a "frontrunner": examples of the latter categories are President George Bush in the early fall of 1992, George McGovern in the summer of 1972, and Barry Goldwater in 1964 (all "likely losers") and President Richard Nixon in 1972 and President Ronald Reagan in 1984 ("frontrunners").[32]

The former congressman Morris Udall, a candidate for the presidency in 1976 and 1984, comments on the media's volatile role in presidential campaigns: "It's like a football game, in which you say to the first team that makes a first down with ten yards, 'Hereafter your team has a special rule. Your first downs are five yards. And if you make three of those you get a two-yard first down. And we're going to let your first touchdown count twenty-one points. Now the rest of you bastards play catch-up under the regular rules.'"[33] Media researchers Michael Robinson and Margaret Sheehan, Robert Lichter and Richard Noyes, Thomas Patterson, and others also find the presence of a double standard in the media's coverage of frontrunners, especially during the nominating phase, when a candidate breaks out of the pack.[34] In the absence of a party or coalitional basis of political support, there is no stopping the media-induced roller-coaster rides of candidate popularity (e.g., President Carter in the late 1970s and President Bush in the late 1980s). All voters have to go on is the rhetoric of politicians—rhetoric selected, interpreted, and passed on by the news media.[35]

The prominence of journalists in political campaigns accentuates the changes in the candidates' standings. Journalists shift their focus from one candidate to another, revealing past political records and damaging or enlightening personal histories. It was journalists who pointed out President Ford's error in saying that Poland was not controlled by the Soviet Union in his 1976 debate with Jimmy Carter; viewers and listeners of the debate thought Ford had won the debate. It was a journalist, CBS News's Roger Mudd, who in 1980 caught Senator Edward Kennedy with nothing to say when asked why he wanted to become president. It was journalists who in 1984 transformed Gary Hart into an instant frontrunner after his electoral upset over Walter Mondale in New Hampshire (Hart had a plurality of 10,000 votes). Hart made the covers of *Newsweek* and *U.S. News,* and journalists described his candidacy as being "awash in a tidal wave of support for the youthful candidate" and snowed under by an "avalanche of publicity."[36]

Four years later, it was a *Miami Herald* reporter who broke the story that Gary Hart was involved in an extramarital affair with Donna Rice, and it was CBS News's Dan Rather who sparred with Vice President George Bush in a live television interview, in which Bush fought back so as to defy his "wimp" reputation. Also in 1988, journalists trumpeted Senator Joe Biden's unattributed borrowing of speeches by the British Labor Party leader Neil Kinnock, forcing Biden to withdraw from the campaign. And it was journalists who focused overwhelmingly on the Bill Clinton–Gennifer Flowers story in the 1992 election campaign, even though voters expressed other priorities.[37]

Television executive and political consultant Roger Ailes calls it the "orchestra pit theory" of political journalism. "It goes like this: a presidential candidate can give the most important speech of his career on a topic that is the number one priority of the voters[,] but if he falls into the orchestra pit on his way off the stage, all the networks and newspapers will report the stumble and ignore the speech." Research that compared the communication of the media with the messages of presidential candidates in 1992 found that candidates focused much more on domestic policy, economic policy, and foreign policy, whereas the media focused on "nonissues." Similarly, the media covered the campaign horse race at the expense of candidates' voting records and positions on issues.[38]

The news media are like the real estate market in overdramatizing the trend of the moment, underbuying or overselling political candidates. It may be the "big feet" journalists who are the political bosses as the twenty-first century nears.[39]

The Politicians as Lead Partners

Nonetheless, the dance does have two partners. The politicians being covered by the news media are hardly passive in this process; they, too, would like to be the "lead." Politicians seek to use political news for their own purposes, given the significance of news coverage in the legitimization of a candidate for public office and as an indicator of frontrunner or high-momentum candidates. Presidential candidates (and other political actors) try to get *their* news out and to persuade the press corps of the accuracy and legitimacy of *their* views. They therefore hire media and public relations consultants, campaign in states where they think they can win straw votes, caucus elections, or primary elections, and not in other states, and downplay their own chances (even though they might know otherwise) so they can surprise the conventional wisdom.[40]

At times, they go so far as to lie to reporters. Journalists have discovered that politicians lie to them in person, lie to the cameras, and lie to the public. John F. Kennedy campaigned for office on a nonexistent "missile gap" and deceived journalists and the public both with respect to the Bay of Pigs invasion. The Johnson administration gravely misled the public on the involvement of U.S. forces in the Vietnam War in 1964, contrary to Johnson's electoral promise to tell the truth, and it was under Johnson's administration that the term "credibility gap" came into use.[41] President Richard Nixon deceived the press and the public on his involvement in Vietnam and Cambodia. Despite his slogan of 1968, "peace with honor," U.S. troops were not withdrawn from Indochina until 1974, and with dubious honor at that (to distinguish the honor of the United States as a nation from the honor of individual Americans).

Indeed, the Nixon administration perfected the art of media manipulation. President Nixon "used to go into the press room with a statement that was only 100 words long because he did not want [the journalists] editing him," says David Gergen, a political advisor and journalist. "He knew that if he gave them more than 100 words, they'd pick and choose what to use." In Nixon's 1972 campaign against George McGovern, "[Chuck] Colson [Nixon's campaign manager] established a new standard in negative campaigning, using surrogates and the 'line of the day' to put together one of the most effective, sustained and brutal political assaults in American history," according to the political journalist Michael Kelly. One political consultant noted that Colson, Gergen (who learned under Colson), and the Nixon reelection team "charted, about a week in advance, what the attack message was going to be every day, what we were going to hit McGovern with that day and how to mobilize the entire resources of the campaign and even the Administration to focus on that single message and dominate the news." By Kelly's reckoning, "Today's campaigns, dominated by systematic, tightly-planned, character-based attacks, are the direct descendants of the 1972 Colson operation."[42] Indeed, President Bush gave the press little access in his 1992 campaign, and Senator Bob Dole held no press conferences for the last several months of his 1996 bid for the presidency.

Matters have not improved. James Fallows, the former editor of *U.S. News,* writes of former Clinton communications director George Stephanopoulos's telling television interviewers that election night 1994 was "a pretty good night"—referring to a night the Democrats were in full retreat, losing both houses of Congress. "They'll look you straight in the eye and tell you things they don't believe," a CBS News vice president remarks. Adds CBS News's Bill Plante, "I think they all lie to us to some degree."[43]

In short, recent presidents and presidential candidates, from Nixon to Ross Perot to Bill Clinton, have used the strategy of avoiding journalists and reaching the electorate directly through advertisements or public addresses or indirectly through talk shows or the local media.[44] At other times, they lie or dissemble.

Politicians and their aides also increasingly speak and behave like journalists. Their "statements come in one-liners designed to ease the work of newspaper headline writers and to give television reporters pithy 10-second sound bites," reducing journalists "to virtual channels of propaganda." Famous one-liners from candidates include Walter Mondale's query of Gary Hart, "Where's the beef?", Lloyd Bentsen's line during the 1988 vice presidential debate, "Senator Quayle, you're no Jack Kennedy," and George Bush's imperative, "Read my lips!" Politicians and their advisors have become expert at tailoring "their messages to the requirements of journalists' formats, news values and work habits." They have the assistance of "publicity advisors, public relations experts, campaign management consultants, and pollsters"; they have become "source professionals." "Televised politics is survival of the briefest," as George Will comments on Malcolm "Steve" Forbes's campaign for the presidency in 2000.[45]

Candidates also "adapt their behavior to the imperatives of news production," scheduling speeches and appearances so they coincide with reporters' schedules, arranging travel plans for members of the press, providing well-written press releases that they can adapt easily for their own uses, and the like. What candidates do not do is provide specific content for the media to cover. They argue that complex issues cannot be readily communicated through the media, that specific messages are open to attack by reporters, and that voters are not interested in issues, especially complicated and potentially unappealing messages.[46]

Lee Ranie of *U.S. News* notes that "fifty percent of [politicians'] energy goes into [working the news media] and fifty percent goes into 'how can we get our stuff out without having to rely on these bastards?' And the smartest and most innovative and creative politicians are the ones who are devoting increasing time to nontraditional forms of communication." He elaborates,

> Different forms of media are used for different purposes. There is sort of a food chain at work. The smartest people in the public policy realm . . . know that the big four newspapers can truly be agenda setters. And if you get your story on the front page of the *[New York] Times*, the *[Washington] Post*, and to a lesser extent the *[Wall Street] Journal* and the *L.A. Times*,

those four, . . . [there is] every, every chance that all three net[work]s will pick it up that night. I agree . . . that everybody wants to get on TV but there are routes to get there that different people use.[47]

But political reporters and their bosses, having been duped before by Senator McCarthy and Presidents John F. Kennedy, Lyndon Johnson, and Richard Nixon, refuse to play the fools again.[48]

Theodore H. White's *The Making of the President 1960* and successive volumes on the 1964, 1968, 1972, and 1980 presidential campaigns are cited prominently by students of the news media and of presidential campaigns. White gives minute-by-minute insider accounts of what a president, presidential candidate, campaign consultants, and their aides were doing during each campaign.[49] By the end of the 1960s, White's novel-like style became the norm for journalists, and it is now typical of much political reporting.[50] (White later regretted perpetrating this "inside-baseball" journalism, complaining, "You guys in the regular press corps are routinely doing *during* the campaign what I used to do after it was all over.")[51]

White's contribution notwithstanding, Joe McGinniss's book on Nixon's presidential campaign, *The Selling of the President 1968*, may better represent the journalism of today. McGinniss's book contains both the inside story of the minutiae of campaign strategizing and the dismal truth of the political manipulation being conducted by Nixon and his advisors (former advertising executives) via the control of campaign appearances, political ad campaigns, and strategic use of the news media. McGinniss showed the deceit, self-serving quality, and cynicism of Nixon's campaign. The implication for journalists covering other presidential campaigns was that politicians and their advisors and consultants would stop at almost nothing to ensure election (or reelection).[52] The cynicism of today's media practices, as articulated by Christopher Arterton, Michael Robinson and Margaret Sheehan, Kathleen Hall Jamieson, Robert Lichter and Richard Noyes, Thomas Patterson, Matthew Kerbel, and others, reflects the lessons brought home in McGinniss's book.

The importance of the news media to contemporary presidential candidacies and the office of the president has affected who is running for office. Whereas presidential candidates once almost always came from the Senate, candidates now are increasingly outsiders, such as Jimmy Carter, the former governor of Georgia, and Ronald Reagan, the former California governor, movie actor, and radio announcer. Other governors who have been presidential candidates are Bill Clinton of Arkansas, Jerry Brown of California (1988, 1992), and Pete Wilson, also of California (1996). The new breed of presidential candidates even includes persons who have never held public office before, such as Jesse Jackson (1984), Ross Perot (1992, 1996), and Steve Forbes (1996). The role of the news media means that political experience and knowledge of Congress and Washington are less important than they once were; name recognition and fundraising ability matter more. There is, in sum, a marked reciprocal effect of the news media on presidential election campaigns.

The President

The adversarial journalism that characterizes news coverage of political contests is also evident in the coverage of American presidents once they are in office. Much of the news of the president resembles that of the campaign trail, particularly with the advent of the "permanent campaign" being waged from the White House (as well as from Capitol Hill).[53] As President Nixon remarks in his memoirs, modern presidents "must try to master the art of manipulating the media not only to win in politics but in order to further the programs and causes they believe in; at the same time they must avoid at all costs the charge of trying to manipulate the media. In the modern presidency, concern for image must rank with concern for substance—there is no guarantee that good programs will automatically triumph."[54]

The Reagan administration learned from Nixon's lessons. For instance, "each major television appeal by President Reagan on the eve of a critical budget vote in Congress was preceded by weeks of preparatory work," asserts the political scientist Samuel Kernell.[55] He quotes a Reagan administration official as commenting that governing "'amounts to little more than an extension of the campaign.'" Kernell concurs. "President Reagan's conduct of office closely resembled his campaign for it. Both entailed heavy political travel, numerous appearances before organized constituencies, and extensive use of television—even paid commercials during nonelection periods. Moreover, both campaigning and governing required systematic planning and extensive organizational coordination."[56] President Clinton is not much different. He, too, governs in the form of a campaign, to the extent of employing full-time consultants for polling, political strategy, and fundraising while in office.

Modern presidents have to rely on the news media, since they have much less of a party structure to keep them in office. They rely on free media coverage during the campaign and cultivate the media once in office. Presidents take more of their messages to the public, in fact, even as a greater proportion of their appearances are "minor speeches," rather than large national addresses.[57] There is good reason for presidents to conserve the use of national addresses, of course: fewer Americans are tuning in.[58] And in keeping with the permanent campaign, policy serves rhetoric.

Thus presidents in large part govern through their communication, whether it is called "going public" (Kernell), "the sound of leadership" (Roderick Hart), or "the rhetorical presidency" (Jeffrey Tulis).[59] Presidents rule through the strategic use of the media: sometimes they use White House correspondents, sometimes they take their messages directly to the public through radio and television addresses, and sometimes they avoid the major media by using regional and local media or talk shows.

Indicative of the attention the media pay to the president—and the fact that the news coverage has to be managed—is the rise in the number of White House personnel dedicated to the management of the news media or to public relations. The White House has to develop extensive organizations and chains of command to deal with public relations and the news media, as the political scientists Martha Joynt Kumar, Michael Grossman, and John A. Maltese document.[60] In 1995, three of the sixteen highest paid White House staff were directly responsible for communication (the press secretary, the communications coordinator, and the speech-writing and research associate), and most of the other thirteen "had a significant communications element in their work," reports Kumar. Some directly briefed the press, others used publicity in support of the president's initiatives, and others considered the public relations of the First Lady. Kumar concludes that "almost all of the White House senior staff are concerned with presidential publicity." Between the senior staff and their assistants, there are now 430 persons on the White House payroll who deal with the president's public relations. The growth in the staff of the White House's press operations parallels the growth in the ranks of the Washington press corps (print and broadcast combined) from about 1,000 persons in 1960 to more than 3,000 by the 1990s.[61]

Accordingly, says Kernell, White House correspondents "must weigh" the rhetoric of presidents and presidential hopefuls.[62] Journalists are aware that presidents and their staff are often able to use them for strategic purposes and always seem to be calculating their actions for political effect; they see that in large part, presidents govern as they campaign, complete with the use of strategic experts, pollsters, public relations consultants, and the like. Reporters and their editors therefore balance presidential rhetoric with interpretive reporting and independent analysis; they do not hesitate to voice their opinions of the White House.

President Reagan had a rough time of it with the press at the beginning of his eight years in office and in the middle of his second term. His successor, President Bush, was almost always under fire from the news media, except during the Persian Gulf War period of 1990–1991.[63] President Clinton was attacked for his policy proposals almost as soon as he took office in 1992 and has fended off media attacks and investigations throughout his two terms in office. A Nexis search reveals that Whitewater appeared in more than 31,000 news stories, whereas the 1994 health bill was mentioned in only 2,400. Thus despite the fact that presidents stand at the center of it all, where almost anything about them or their family is considered newsworthy by the media, they by no means have a free PR ride. Just as they do to candidates in presidential elections, journalists now challenge, criticize, and condemn American presidents—even those just elected into office—in contrast to the deferential treatment they showed to presidents in the past.[64]

On the other hand, presidents usually enjoy favorable coverage with respect to symbolic acts such as inaugurations, public ceremonies, state dinners, and funerals of former or present heads of state and times of national emergency.[65] There is only one POTUS (as the Secret Service refer to the president of the United States), and there are no rival presidential candidates out in the field. Much of presidential coverage is therefore that of a policy monopoly (see Chapter 3).

Congress

Whether covering which version of a bill will make it into law, the probability of success for the majority party's legislative agenda, or which members of Congress will be awarded senior positions of leadership or committee chairs, the media turn the situation into a political contest.

With the exception of a brief period after the election of the Republican 104th Congress in late 1994 and early 1995, there is generally much less news about Congress and the legislative process than about presidential elections and the presidency. The political scientists Robinson and Sheehan find that senatorial and congressional races are "practically invisible" in the news, combining for about 2 percent of CBS News broadcasts (to use the coverage of one network as representative). Another study shows that in the elections of 1980, more than 93 percent of CBS News coverage concerned the presidential race, as opposed to state races, congressional elections, and the vice presidential competition.[66]

Furthermore, the proportion of news devoted to Congress has decreased in the last twenty years; most members receive virtually no coverage whatsoever in the national media. The television networks' coverage of Congress shrunk by half between 1975 and 1985, and of the one in ten network stories that mentioned Congress, only about 40 percent focused on Congress.[67] Political scientists Stephen Hess and Timothy Cook both note that the only members of Congress to get significant attention in the national media are those in leadership positions, those occupying important committee chairs, and those considered possible presidential material. Despite the fact that

Congress is a wonderful vantage point from which to survey the entirety of U.S. national politics, as the *Washington Post's* David Broder observes (since virtually all political issues make their way through Congress at some time and in some form), news organizations are increasingly choosing not to run stories on Congress.[68]

To the extent that journalists do cover the House and Senate, they typically cast the legislative process as a political contest. "The tendency [is] for television to regard governance as politics and to cover the development of legislation as if it were a presidential campaign," writes the political scientist Matthew Kerbel. "Performance-based standards emphasize the process by which policy is shaped; with the president in the lead, he is evaluated for his capacity to govern in terms of the speed with which the legislative process moves towards approving what is invariably regarded as 'his' program." Kerbel observes that "congressional disagreements with respect to proposed legislation" become "benchmarks" that both the print and video use "for measuring the congressional drive toward the goal and [are] interpreted as if they [are] lost yardage in a football game—as unfortunate movement in the wrong direction."[69]

The media decide how legislation gets defined, and it is typically in terms of the contests between parties, between the legislative and executive branches, or between different societal interests fighting it out on the Hill. Richard Harwood, a former reporter, editor, and ombudsman for the *Washington Post,* elaborates on how journalists treat a piece of legislation, be it a budget, welfare, or trade bill, in terms of its probable victory or defeat for a party or politician: "TV encourages views that a bill is a 'complete sellout' or 'great,' but opponents are trying to sabotage it for political purposes. Sure the opponents are trying to do this, but such reporting does not advance anything. So reporting will be on what has happened [that is] personal, and what 'Joe Jones' says will affect you in this way." Harwood continues, "A disappointment is that the press is so process-oriented—process rather than on the punch line of the environment, taxation, etc. Lobbyists come in here, congressional reporters depend on them for spin on stuff, for the environment they go to the Sierra Club."[70]

The permanent campaign is well evident in both the lower and upper houses of Congress. One reporter's estimate is that from one-third to one-half of legislators' time is spent raising money. (About $230 million was spent on political advertising alone in 1990, for instance—and this in a midyear election.) "Incumbents routinely complain about the time, effort, and indignities associated with asking people for money," one congressional scholar observes. "Personal discomfort figures prominently in how they raise their funds. A fear of defeat and a disdain for fundraising have two principal effects: they encourage incumbents to raise large amounts of money and to place the bulk of their fundraising in the hands of others, mainly professional consultants." For almost any publicly elected office, challengers likewise have to spend most of their time raising money for media buys.[71]

Members of Congress also have to respond to the news generated by the president and the executive branch more generally. Kernell notes that in 1982 House Speaker Thomas ("Tip") O'Neill and the chair of the House Ways and Means Committee, Representative Dan Rostenkowski, both gave public television addresses in response to the public relations strategy of President Reagan with respect to that year's proposed budget and his tax cut. The effect of television is "a Congress that is less likely to get along with itself, more likely to focus on higher office, less likely to behave as a group than as a disjointed collection of individuals," observes Robinson.[72] Television makes members of Congress "far less dependent on their colleagues and party leaders to achieve their objectives" of getting reelected, achieving policy goals, and advancing their legislative careers.[73]

In fact, the ability to attract media attention defines members of Congress much more now than it did in the past. Evidence suggests that "showhorse" members of Congress succeed better than "workhorse" members (who rise by virtue of party networking and legislative achievement); until recently, that had not been the case.[74] With the continued decline of partisanship nationwide—as opposed to the role of the parties in Congress—the ability to get television exposure offers better chances of political success, even if only a handful can ultimately succeed. Recent examples of such media-driven success by members of Congress include House Speaker Newt Gingrich, the current secretary of energy and former U.S. ambassador to the United Nations Bill Richardson, Senator Charles Schumer of New York, the former representative Pat Schroeder of Colorado, and Senators Barbara Boxer of California and Phil Gramm of Texas, among others.[75] In this new political world, the policy and media entrepreneur is better served.

The news media also affect policy making, changing the speed and priority of different legislative actions, as the political scientist Martin Linsky and his colleagues show in their studies of the news coverage of toxic waste in Love Canal, New York, the Carter administration's decision to deploy the neutron bomb in Europe, the efforts to reform the U.S. Post Office, and the Bob Jones University tax case (although some of these cases involved more presidential action than congressional action). Kernell also finds that there is a new politics of policy making evident, one that is faster, less careful, and perhaps less accountable than that of the past. He cites legislation on the savings and loan industry and the legislative success of Mothers Against

Drunk Driving as examples.[76] More recent examples suggestive of the news media's impact on policy making include the quick legislative responses to the Oklahoma City bombing and the explosion of TWA Flight 800: Congress quickly granted the Clinton administration's request to pass new antiterrorist measures giving additional powers to the FBI and further regulating air travel. Then there were the Senate hearings on "Ebonics" in early 1997, in response to widespread (and exaggerated) stories in the national media. News attention and the deliberate use of media campaigns can accelerate the passage of new legislation.

More seriously, the close connection between political fortunes and the news media may mean that members of Congress have further incentive to avoid difficult problems: politicians may shrink from tackling issues involving entrenched or broad-based opponents, given the greater likelihood that they would receive unfavorable publicity on such issues. With the increasing tendency of representatives and senators to adopt an "outsider" strategy and the prominence of publicity-based politics on Capitol Hill, subtlety is lost, notes Timothy Cook.[77]

Like the coverage of presidential campaigns and the presidency itself, too, coverage of Congress has become increasingly negative. Members of Congress typically get news coverage only in connection with scandal, rather than because of their expertise or policy initiatives.[78] Newspaper stories and editorials are disproportionately negative, according to one analysis of 2,300 articles and editorials in ten newspapers over a thirty-day span in 1978.[79] Scandals are the embodiment of political contests, of course, since they pit a member of Congress against his or her peers. Scandals do not become scandals unless publicity is generated by partisan skirmishing and leaks from congressional rivals. Cases in point are the scandals involving former House Speaker Jim Wright, former chair of the House Ways and Means Committee Dan Rostenkowski, former House Speaker Newt Gingrich, Representative Edith Waldholtz (a Republican from Utah), and the "Keating Five" senators (see Chapter 6). The only time incumbents are likely to lose office is if they are involved in a scandal: Rostenkowski lost in his bid for reelection, as did seven-term Congressman Nicholas Mavroules of Massachusetts, who was indicted in 1992 on seventeen federal charges of bribery, extortion, and tax evasion. Wright chose not to run for reelection.[80]

Congress also gets negative coverage because, according to Senate staffer Brad Austin, legislation inherently "is a dirty process. It is a process which is driven by friction. Nothing happens unless you have a positive and a negative fighting it out."[81] With members of Congress strategizing on how to use the press and succeed in the media's eye, journalists, are, again, likely to be highly critical of legislators and the legislative process.

In sum, the news media have, by necessity, become an important part of congressional operations. The 535 members of the House and Senate and their tens of thousands of aides (98% of senators and 76% of representatives have their own press secretaries) release an estimated fifteen thousand press handouts a year to promote publicity favorable to their persons, causes, or parties. Most use their resources carefully, targeting their mailings to specific journalists or news organizations, rather than sending out mass mailings; on average, Senate offices send out ten press releases per month, and House offices between five and six per month.[82] Members of Congress try to get their news in the major media—even though only a few (the most prominent committee chairs, presidential prospects, and those in official leadership positions) actually make the national news with any regularity.

The Supreme Court

Even the Supreme Court gets most of its news coverage in situations of political contest. Ironically, it is in the period immediately after justices have been nominated for the Supreme Court, when they become subject to the approval of the U.S. Senate, that justices and the Court get the most intense news coverage. Senators from the opposition party, professional lawyer associations, advocacy groups, and other interests weigh in on the qualifications and appropriateness of a particular nominee. The political division over a Supreme Court nominee—and there is almost always such a split— is amply covered by the news media.

Most of the Supreme Court's actual work falls below the scope of media attention, however, for several reasons. There are too many cases for media scrutiny, and decisions occur unevenly throughout the year, being lumped at the end of the judicial calendar in late spring and early summer. Moreover, cases are typically complex and decided on narrow legal points, and there are usually several concurring and dissenting opinions in each decision, further confusing the message.[83] One study, using the 1989–1990 term as representative, shows that almost three-fourths of the Court's decisions received no attention at all from the network news programs.[84]

The news media devote much more attention to socially divisive issues, such as civil rights (e.g., affirmative action) or judicial pronouncements on social issues (e.g., abortion), than to judgments on criminal law, property rights, labor law, or other less volatile legal issues. A former CBS News Supreme Court correspondent comments that over the course of the 1980s, his network shifted focus away from reporting on a "broader meaning" of the Court's decisions and "more toward personalities, more toward sensational events."[85] Indeed, the nomination of Supreme Court Justice Clarence Thomas revolved around the allegations of sexual harrassment made by Anita Hill and involved an orchestrated public relations campaign on the part of the Bush administration and its congressional allies. However, the justices may themselves quietly cultivate their reputations by issuing separate concurring and dissenting opinions and occasionally briefing the press and granting private interviews. The Court is a partner to the limited and skewed reporting it receives.[86]

In fact, the Supreme Court is able to maintain its august reputation largely because the justices make no obvious public relations effort; they are not in the business of trying to explain the Court's decisions or putting their own spin on controversial decisions. "The Court's power is preserved by public opinion and therefore the Court's primary objective vis-à-vis the public is to maintain public deference and secure widespread compliance with policy decisions," notes the Supreme Court and media scholar Richard Davis. The Court deliberately positions itself above the fray of everyday politics—outside of the usual political contests—through its complex, technical writing, its ceremonial robes, and its emphasis on precedent and rational argument. It has to, since the Court is the "least dangerous branch" as Alexander Hamilton wrote in *Federalist* paper no. 78, possessing neither the purse nor the sword. The justices prefer it that way: with little news coverage, the Court is better able to maintain its image as being above politics.

The Bureaucracy

Typically, few political contests are revealed in and among the departments, bureaus, and agencies of the federal government. Most of the federal bureaucracy receives almost no media attention. To the extent it does, moreover, it is skewed to the older and more prominent departments: the Department of Defense, the Department of State, the Department of the Treasury, and the Department of Justice. (Most of the coverage of these agencies is discussed in Chapter 3.) The administrative agencies are not usually divided by partisanship or fights between the legislative and executive branches, and news coverage of these government organizations reflects the objectives and priorities of the incumbent administration most of the time. Nor is news of public administration or of the regulatory agencies high among journalists' priorities.[87]

The bureaucracy attracts attention when a major debate emerges, for example, between the Department of State and a presidential administration over a human rights issue, or when a scandal, such as corruption or wrongdoing on the part of a cabinet appointee, erupts (just like the news coverage of Congress). During the first Clinton administration, for instance, Secretary of Agriculture Mike Espy was indicted (later overturned) for misusing government funds and accepting favors from private interests. Surgeon

General Joycelyn Elders made the headlines, the nightly news, and the op-ed pages by discussing the legalization of marijuana. Secretary of Energy Hazel O'Leary released information that the U.S. government had conducted radiation testing on unwitting American citizens. O'Leary also made the news when it was found that she had taken an extensive entourage on expensive trips across the United States and around the world—with taxpayers footing the bill.

The use of the media is part and parcel of the public administrator's job, to be sure. Federal departments and agencies determine public relations strategies, have permanent positions for public affairs officers or press secretaries, and devote considerable time and energy responding to reporter inquiries or to news stories that affect them and their agencies. Each military service, for instance, has "a small army of public affairs officials. About 3,500 such military personnel work for the [Department of Defense] worldwide, including 275 for the Air Force." The department's public affairs offices handle all communications with the outside world, produce videos and magazines, and must clear all interviews of employees by news reporters.[88] Journalists therefore weigh the importance of the agency and the message in prioritizing what to publicize.

IN SUM, JOURNALISTS ARE THE UNOFFICIAL UMPIRES OF POLITICAL contests, contests that include presidential election campaigns, the permanent campaigns now waged from the White House and congressional offices, and even much of the Supreme Court's and the federal bureaucracy's news coverage. Journalists' livelihoods depend on their being able to communicate to their audiences information about important differences in national politics and simultaneously show their independence from their sources—by being critical. Indicative of this combined role of judgment and criticism are "ad watches," whereby journalists at once judge and criticize the political advertisements of presidential candidates.[89]

Journalists therefore are caught up in an ongoing struggle with politicians and members of the government as they attempt to counteract these public officials' attempts to control political communication.[90] Veteran NBC News correspondent John Dancy notes that "you use reporters, reporters use you. A trade-off. And what you try to do is not let too much of your honor and integrity disappear in the bargain." While it may be possible to play off one source with another, says Dancy, "they each have their own spin." Reporters are used to being spun and try to resist it; sometimes they are successful, and sometimes they are not.[91] The result is a tawdry and tainted political system: "Members of Congress fret about the next election. Presidents worry about themselves and calculate each move according to probabilistic estimates of how to increase their popularity. Self-absorbed reporters tell us about everyone else's selfishness," asserts Kerbel. "From this self-feeding process we somehow [are supposed to] govern ourselves."[92]

Media Practices

A number of standard practices have evolved that help the news media mitigate the uncertainties of reporting on political contests. These practices, some formal and others informal, allow for continued reporting on the contests of national politics. I focus on four: horse race news coverage, the provision of balanced news, the dominance of interpretive and negative news reporting, and the definition of politics primarily in terms of elections and clashing persons and parties.

Focus on the Horse Race

The "horse race" aspect of presidential campaigns is remarkably prevalent in contemporary news coverage of national politics. For example, not even a week after the second Clinton inauguration on January 20, 1997, a spate of articles and columns appeared about the prospective Democratic and Republican candidates for the presidency in 2000. As one NBC News executive described the coverage of an earlier campaign, "The only thing that viewers want to know about this election is who will win."[93] The statement is suggestive of the mentality of news organizations.

The language of the political contest, which is often referred to as a "game" or "war," supplants that of the issues or policy. Content, education, implications, and problem solving are of secondary importance, if relevant at all, to the news coverage of the horse race. The focus on the horse race might seem to be detrimental to the campaign process, yet news coverage of the horse race between candidates, parties, or factions cues journalists, politicians, and other politically attentive readers and viewers to the many items along the lengthy campaign trail that lead to one of the candidates' eventually becoming president.[94] Horse race coverage enables journalists to report on the presidential campaigns (and other political contests) with one single approach as well as allowing them to play a dramatic role in determining who gets elected. As James Carville remarks, "What reporter wouldn't rather report on strategy than message?"[95] By focusing on the horse race, the news media avoid the issue of what to report outside the politics and political associations dominant at the time. Horse race coverage sidesteps discussion of the purposes of the different candidates and the implications of their winning, of the impact of legislation's passing, and of the philosophies and potential consequences of the nominees approved by the

U.S. Senate; the horse race is safe turf. Journalists are the expert handicappers; the voters passive spectators on the sidelines of the "game." Reporting about contests, especially elections but also legislative battles, fights over cabinet and Supreme Court nominees, and other political contests, allows journalists to umpire; it becomes an occasion for reporters' reflections rather than those of the candidates, much less the voters.[96]

At the same time, the horse race focus provides presidential hopefuls, legislators, and even cabinet-level or Supreme Court nominees (and their supporters) with clear guidelines by which to use the news media to their own advantage. They know what kinds of indicators journalists rely on and plan accordingly. The dominance and simplicity of the horse race thereby also open the door to the political manipulation of journalists. If winning is everything, the programs and policies not subject to prominent political contests—those of a policy monopoly—get less and *deserve less* media attention, since there will be no obvious winner or loser.

The news media's emphasis on the horse race in politics is a recent phenomenon, dating only from the late 1960s and early 1970s. Patterson's analysis of front-page stories from the *New York Times* shows the coverage of presidential elections to have made the greatest change from a "policy schema" to a "game schema" (i.e., the horse race) between 1968 and 1976.[97] The press's enthusiasm for focusing on the horse race, rather than the substance of political competition, shows no sign of abating.[98]

Balanced Coverage

A second established practice of the news media is the provision of generally balanced coverage of political contests. Reporters (and their editors) are put in the position of having to determine the quality of political information, weigh the merits of different sources, and then interpret their implications for future politics. Journalists have to appear evenhanded in their coverage of presidential election campaigns and other political contests, such as struggles over policy making, budgets, or personnel nominations.[99] There is pressure on journalists to be reasonably fair, given the uncertainty of the outcomes of political contests.

In fact, the major media usually do cite arguments on both sides of an issue or controversy, often alternate front pages with stories on opposing major candidates, and trade off news leads when covering opposing candidates or issues, leading with one candidate or one side of an issue on one night or in one week and leading with the other candidate or the other side of the issue the next.[100] Newspapers and newsmagazines also balance columnists, reporters, and the location of stories partial to one side or the other. Similarly, the TV networks alternate which candidate leads off the news among the likely party nominees or major party candidates, equalizing the time devoted to each. They also take care to rotate the journalists who cover the campaigns among candidates. Editors may even count the number of column inches devoted to particular candidates or parties to ensure evenhanded coverage.[101]

The news media thereby protect themselves against the unpredictability of political contests by relying on what tangible indicators of political performance they can find and being balanced in their treatment of opponents in the contests they cover. By reporting on political issues and the federal government only when fissures appear in political alignments, journalists are able to avoid having to take sides and thereby avoid charges of bias or a loss of credibility.

The practice of balanced reporting is relatively new. The role of journalists as unofficial umpires—the presumption that they can somehow stand apart from politics—is the legacy of the Progressive Era and the professionalization of journalism in the early twentieth century: no longer were reporters and their news organizations to be openly partisan or clearly affiliated with one or another of the political parties. Since then, the norm of impartial reporting has prevailed among most journalists, with the *New York Times* and other respected papers leading the way.

Interpretation and Negativity

A third and increasingly common journalistic practice is the tendency of reporters and their editors to take a critical view of political news. That is, the news media are not merely umpires, but hanging judges.[102] And the more prominent and likely to become president the candidate is, the more prevalent and more serious the criticism. Bill Clinton and Ross Perot found this out in 1992, Gary Hart and Michael Dukakis found this out in 1988, and Walter Mondale and Hart found this out in 1984. Journalists are in the position to interpret politicians and campaigns, in contrast to simply describing them, and they do so with increasing boldness, leveling more and more criticism (rather than being neutral, much less positive, in their reporting). There is a double standard: the proportion of negative reporting rises as the primaries progress and the frontrunners emerge.[103]

By being critical, journalists can signal to a mass audience and to fellow journalists, public officials, and the politically attentive that they know what is going on and are not being taken in. Journalists "make sure that the audience knows that they know that they are being used. They have been fairly good at this," explains Walter Cronkite. When "politicians can predict confidently which events and comments will ring reportorial bells, media professionals are deprived of opportunities to exercise their own judgment.

Yet the routines that open the media to such manipulation cannot be discarded or overhauled without much disruption and cost." Journalists, faced with the professional politicians and news handlers, distance themselves by exposing events as "contrived" and thereby suggest that the news not be taken too seriously. Any change in politicians' positions, Patterson notes, is seen as manipulation.[104]

Negative reporting therefore allows journalists to maintain a constant position that protects them from the machinations of politicians or government officials. Because standard journalistic practice does not permit the reporter to come out and call the source a liar, the journalist offers "an all-purpose sneer" instead, remarks Fallows, "which vents his frustration and sends the viewers a warning that politicians are trying to hoodwink them too."[105] By being critical, journalists are responding to experience.

Politics is uglier now, and the news coverage reflects this. "We cover what's there. Candidates determine coverage," remarks ABC News's Hal Bruno.[106] He may be overstating the case, blaming solely the politicians for what journalists are also responsible for, but journalists' negativity is, I agree, an adaptive response to the last few decades of politicians' and public officials' manipulation of the news media. Journalists have learned to doubt and mistrust virtually all politicians, even duly elected presidents, most of the time. An ABC News correspondent notes, "You can be wrong as long as you're negative and skeptical. But if you're going to say something remotely positive, you'd better be 150 percent right or you're going to be accused of rolling over. I was once told, 'Look, you're never going to get on the air with positive views; do you want to get on the air or not?'"[107] Politicians thus have the worst motives ascribed to their actions, and bad news about politicians and politics drives out the good. Speeches with substance and successful visits to diverse audiences around the country have no integral worth; all are media events. The consequence of this critical attitude has been that attack-dog journalism now extends to much of a legislator's, and president's, time in office, and mistrust of politics and of the potential contribution of the news media is cultivated in the audience.

Again, this criticism and negativity is recent. Patterson uses the proportion of "good" and "bad" stories that ran in *Time* and *Newsweek* from the 1960 election through the 1988 election to show that journalists were far more cooperative with and trusting of public officials before the late 1960s and early 1970s. At the end of the 1960s and the beginning of the 1970s, journalists started to become much more critical and interpretive in their reporting, and top political journalists in both the print and broadcast media began to indulge in irony, smirks, and snide commentary.[108] David Brinkley may be the exemplar of the sardonic and sarcastic commentary, but many network correspondents and news anchors—such as Brit Hume, Dan Rather, Sam Donaldson, and Ted Koppel—routinely engage in editorializing in ostensibly straight, on-air news stories.[109]

The Narrow Definition of Politics

Another standard practice of contemporary reporting is the definition of politics primarily in terms of elections and the competition between persons and political parties, despite the fact that the term "politics" encompasses legislation, policy implementation, lobbying, budgetary and fiscal matters, public relations efforts, and fundraising. The legislative process, public administration, and the budget do not get nearly the media attention given to politics in its narrow definition—the electoral struggle over who gets ahead, whether winning a contest of some kind or getting into office (consistent with the emphasis on the horse race coverage). If politics is the resolution of "who gets what, where, and how," then journalists would presumably cover the politics of the winners and losers in American society other than those running in elections.

Here, too, there is a strong historical dimension to the division of the politics beat into coverage of elections (and some legislative battles and clashes between the executive and legislative branches) and that of Congress, the regulatory agencies, financial news, and other news categories. In the Progressive Era, when the parties dominated national politics, it made sense for news coverage to focus on party competition, since which party came to power significantly determined national policy with respect to agriculture, social welfare, trade, taxation, and other issue areas. However, even though the parties now play a much smaller role in national politics with respect to information, funding, the selection of candidates, and the organization of voters and constituent groups in the aftermath of the 1969 McGovern-Fraser Commission reforms, the passage of the Federal Election Campaign Act of 1971 (and its 1974 and 1976 amendments), and the pervasiveness and power of television, the politics category has not similarly evolved for journalists.[110]

There are other media practices that bridge the relationship between media personnel and politicians and public officials.[111] Some also apply to the coverage of policy monopolies, and I discuss them in the next chapter.

Conclusion

Journalists who work for the leading news organizations in the United States exist in a complex relationship with politicians and government officeholders, one that is simultaneously conflictual and dependent. "Politics, in a sense, has always been a con game," Joe McGinniss points out, just as "advertising, in many ways, is a con game too." No surprise, then, that "politicians and advertising men should have discovered one another. And, once they recognized that the citizen did not so much vote for a candidate as make a psychological purchase of him, [it is] not surprising they began to work together." Journalists have learned, through their own bitter experience, how politicians and their handlers operate. The practice of politics "has deteriorated," ABC's Hal Bruno remarks, even as "political coverage is much more sophisticated than 17 years ago."[112]

"The result is an arms race of 'attitude,'" to use Fallows's metaphor. In this arms race, "reporters don't explicitly argue or analyze what they dislike in a political program but instead sound sneering and supercilious about the whole idea of politics. Public officials become more manipulative and cunning to try to get their message past the hostile press—and the press becomes even more determined to point out how insincere the politicians are. As in a real arms race, neither side feels it can safely disarm."[113] With each passing election, the antagonists acquire more "arms"—the journalists become more adept at revealing and criticizing official practices and the political advocates become more skilled at manipulating political communication through the media and public relations.[114]

Recent examples of politicians' guile come from the 1996 presidential campaign. Twenty minutes before the first debate in Hartford, Connecticut, Clinton staffers distributed a six-page, single-spaced memo to hundreds of reporters detailing what Senator Bob Dole might say and what the facts really were. Less than an hour into the debate and while the debate was going on, aides from the Dole campaign distributed handouts pointing out President Clinton's misstatements. David Broder, a four-decade veteran of election coverage, remarked that "this was the first time he'd ever seen predebate spin."[115] Another example of the arms race was the Clinton administration's brilliant "stealth" media campaign of 1995 and early 1996, whereby the president's reelection team advertised its messages in nonmajor media markets and thereby eluded the scrutiny of the prestige print and broadcast media, located in the largest media markets.

The battle over political communication between political advocates and journalists happens not only with respect to presidential campaigns, of course, but also with respect to coverage of the president, legislative and partisan rivalries, presidential appointments, and particular policy initiatives. Journalists throughout the news media handle the uncertainty of reporting on political contests by focusing on the competition itself—the horse race—by presenting a more-or-less balanced view of these contests, and by covering politicians, government officials, and other political advocates critically, so as to appear wise to the ways of the politician and the "publicity man," to use Lippmann's term from the epigraph to this chapter.

There are many other issues and events, however, where journalists are able to exercise considerable discretion—where they are the "lead" in the dance. Only the most prominent members of Congress receive national news coverage, after all, and only the secretaries of the older departments (e.g., the State Department) regularly command attention from the major media. Even then, the president may not get his way with the news media, should important political contests be involved. In early 1995, for instance, House Speaker Newt Gingrich eclipsed President Clinton and the Republican freshmen of the 104th Congress overshadowed many of their more experienced Democratic colleagues. An undersecretary of state may receive more publicity than the secretary of state, as the attention paid to Richard Holbrooke over Warren Christopher in the first term of the Clinton administration illustrates. Similarly, the FBI director may receive more attention than the attorney general. Political rank does not necessarily dictate officials' relationship with the news media.

The tenor of the particular official-journalist relationship depends on a number of other factors as well, which may on occasion override the effects of structural position. These factors include

- the newsworthiness of the issue in question,
- the official's style and personality,
- the official's administrative goals and public relations strategies, and
- contingent factors, such as the political climate, partisan balance, and additional policy initiatives underway.[116]

Different political advocates may have different communications strategies, but they all have to use the media.

Because the news media have the power to publicize political contests, they are able to exert a considerable influence on who is involved in an issue and how the issue is formulated, to follow the political scientist E. E. Schattschneider's statement in the epigraph to this chapter. The scope of a conflict—the publicity about a person or event involved in a political contest, in this instance—may determine the ultimate winner and loser of that conflict.

The relationship between political figures and journalists is more significant than a dance, however. The presence of the news media has ineluctably altered electoral politics and the political system more generally. The dominance of the news media—television especially, given the new campaign rules, the decline of the parties, and the unfortunate history of American politics in recent decades—in contemporary national politics has affected the criteria for election, reelection, and appointment to public office. It has therefore affected the quality of politicians seeking public office. Present-day politicians and public officials have to be familiar with the needs of broadcast and print journalism. They have to be more articulate, more personable, and more presentable than the persons entering office a generation ago.[117] They also have to be more cautious in their statements and more willing to have their private lives made public. Persons with these media-suitable characteristics are advantaged in both of the necessities of contemporary campaigning: fundraising and appealing to mass audiences.

But the press-politicians relationship becomes a danse macabre when it comes to the news media's coverage of a policy monopoly. In the situation of a policy monopoly, journalists defer to political advocates who control the relevant information and may be able to say what the law is (and be in a position to enforce it). Thus with respect to many political issues and events, the press-politicians relationship is a strongly imbalanced one, and it is not the press who are dancing the lead.

MEDIA LAP DOGS

There is a very small body of exact knowledge, which it requires no outstanding ability or training to deal with. The rest is in the journalist's discretion. Once he departs from the region where it is definitely recorded at the County Clerk's office that John Smith has gone into bankruptcy, all fixed standards disappear. The story of why John Smith failed, his human frailties, the analysis of economic conditions on which he was shipwrecked, all of this can be told in a hundred different ways. . . . He knows that he is seeing the world through subjective lenses.—Walter Lippmann, *Public Opinion,* 1922

American journalism suffers from too many golf players.—H. L. Mencken, *Journalism in America,* 1919

WHEN THERE IS LITTLE OR NO APPARENT DIVISION WITHIN THE GOVernment or among leading national politicians with regard to an issue—that is, when there is a "policy monopoly"—journalists tend to be reserved in their news coverage and reluctant to judge. In this case, public officials (and possibly private-sector actors) control newsworthy information and are agreed on how to handle publicity. A policy monopoly may exist in any agency or policy domain, and it may involve only a handful of members of the executive branch or may span personnel from the White House, several federal agencies, Congress, and the private sector. It could include not only news of the "Golden Triangle"—the White House, State Department, and Pentagon—but also news about the Federal Reserve Bank (and monetary policy), the Department of Energy (and energy policy), the Department of Justice and FBI, Drug Enforcement Agency, and Bureau of Alcohol, Tobacco and Firearms (and domestic security policy), the Department of Agriculture (and farm policy), and other federal departments or agencies (and their respective policies).[1]

Journalists and news organizations rarely bring up political issues if the executive branch, legislative branch, and major group interests, or parts thereof, are already aligned politically. News organizations have little desire to become controversial political actors in their own right (see Chapter 5). This is not to say that newspapers, newsmagazines, the television networks, and wire services do not cover governmental corruption, government contract cost overruns, white-collar crime, or other investigative stories. It is to say that in situations of policy monopoly, news organizations are typically reluctant to investigate and slow to pronounce judgment. Media coverage becomes deferential, in contrast to the zeal for interpretation and criticism that the media show in conditions of contested politics. What explains this caution?

Journalists' deliberation and risk aversion in situations of governmental accord comes from an unsettling and profound uncertainty: should they disseminate news on their own authority, without the support of statements from major political actors, and thereby possibly open an important issue up to public debate?[2] The journalists would themselves become party to a political contest—a previously nonexistent contest—were they to judge or take an independent position on the events or persons at issue. Are they willing to go up against major political and societal actors? Are they willing to report news of social movements, third parties, or minor candidates—issues and persons outside the dominant political associations and political perspectives of the day?

In this chapter, I discuss the media's coverage of policy monopolies and the difficulty of this coverage (as opposed to the coverage of political contests): that is, whether journalists are able to secure access to newsworthy political information when the government (or part of it) has control over this information. When public officials do not discernibly disagree over policy and are able to present a unified front to journalists, they have a decided advantage over the news media. Theirs is the news that gets publicized— if it gets publicized at all. After a discussion of the advantages that political sources have in their relationship with journalists and news organizations in the situation of a policy monopoly, I suggest a number of media practices that have evolved in this environment.

Coverage of Controlled News

Advantages Held by Political Actors

There are a number of reasons why journalists forsake their usual adversary stance toward government and politics and cooperate with officeholders under conditions of a policy monopoly. The top political actors have some advantages.

CONTROL. The essential advantage possessed by political officials—be it the president and his top advisors and staff, the administrators of federal agencies, or members of Congress and their staff (at times)—is the simple *control* of newsworthy information. High-ranking public officials may have in their possession sensitive information about White House strategy, legislative and budgetary planning, national security, trade policy, personnel changes, or other issues that few others in the United States have. These actors may thus have a monopoly, or near monopoly, on important news about national politics and government.

The information from a policy monopoly, whether narrowly or broadly demarcated, can be contrasted with information about Congress and other federal departments and agencies. The latter information is typically dispersed (rather than concentrated), is discussed in open rooms and hallways (rather than kept behind closed doors), and is accessible (rather than kept secret). When covering a policy monopoly, reporters and their news organizations may have to depend on the president and his aides, departmental secretaries, or even some members of Congress for information about stories of future diplomatic summits and peace initiatives, presidential campaign moves, commitments of U.S. troops abroad, presidential policy priorities, legislative agendas, partisan strategizing, or other matters.[3]

EXCLUSIVITY. The numbers also work in favor of the top political actors: whereas there are only a few political officials in possession of important information—one U.S. president, one secretary of defense, one U.S. attorney general, one Speaker of the House, and one Senate majority leader, for example—even in the prestige media there are dozens of newspaper, magazine, and television reporters competing for political information. As one longtime White House correspondent for the *Washington Post* remarks, "There are only six or seven real sources in the White House who know anything. . . . [If former Secretary of State James] Baker has three hundred phone message slips waiting for him, . . . he's going to call back the ones he likes or needs." Another student of Washington reporting notes, "White House leaks go only to a favored few. With some exceptions, foreign policy leaks go to the *New York Times,* domestic policy and political leaks go to the *Washington Post,* and leaks about economic policy go to the *Wall Street Journal.*"[4] Nor are reporters willing to gang up to confront a presidential administration that refuses to explain itself. Defection by any one journalist is too easy, and any collective action by the press makes an easy target for politicians, other journalists, and a skeptical public.[5]

EXPERTISE. Another advantage of the top political actors is their expertise: the vast majority of journalists do not have the depth of knowledge possessed by White House and executive branch officials. Journalists are usually generalists rather than issue experts. Reporters are rarely able to establish independently the validity of the government's information on the economy, the military, science and technology, the environment, or medicine. Public officials, though, are usually themselves expert or have specialized information at their disposal. They are in the position to know what is (and is not) in certain pieces of legislation, what the military did (and did not do), and how U.S. trade partners will most likely respond to a statement by the president.[6] As the political writer Edward Jay Epstein puts it, "A reporter cannot establish the existence of an influenza epidemic, for instance, by conducting medical examinations himself; he must rely on the pronouncement of the Department of Health (a journalist may of course become a doctor, but then his authority for reporting a fact rests on his scientific rather than his journalistic credentials). Whenever a journalist attempts to establish a factual proposition on his own authority, his authority must be open to question."[7] During the Persian Gulf War, for instance, when few journalists had prior combat experience or military expertise, Pentagon officials referred to reporters as "tourists," and a sign in the press room read "Welcome temporary war experts."[8] Journalists often have little recourse but to rely on governmental information.

Even when news correspondents have particular expertise (as do several journalists at the prestige news organizations), there is typically far too much in any one department or policy arena for one or a few journalists to cover. Even the best correspondents can be little more than roving eyes in a vast, complex government; journalists usually have to rely on the interpretation provided by government sources. An example is the two-thousand-page Clean Water Act of 1990: journalists relied on what members of Congress (and lobbyists) said was in the bill. Such reliance also characterizes news coverage of the qualities of particular military aircraft and the details of a certain health policy.[9]

PERSONAL APPEALS. Then there are the personal appeals government officials make to journalists' citizenship, loyalty, responsibility, and patriotism. Politicians and executive branch officials can appeal to the values and identities of journalists, and if journalists print or broadcast material relating to national security that the government and decision makers hold in their own possession—classified or not—they open themselves up to charges of irresponsibility and lack of patriotism. As Leon Sigal observes, "The reporter's conception of himself as a patriot still inclines him to put consideration of national interest ahead of those of the news. 'We are, we believe, good citizens as well as good journalists' says the [former] Washington bureau chief of *Time*, John L. Steele. There are some things you happen on you simply don't report.' What these things are newsmen often let officials determine." The *New York Times, Washington Post,* and *Los Angeles Times,* the television networks, CNN, and the other major media have all cooperated with the U.S. government on occasion.[10]

DISINFORMATION. Journalists are further vulnerable to disinformation, or the reporting of untruths disseminated by political officials. The Senate Select Committee on Intelligence (also known as the Church Committee), under Senator Frank Church of Idaho, "found evidence of more than two hundred wire services, newspapers, magazines, and book publishing complexes owned outright by the CIA. A 1977 exposé in the *New York Times* uncovered another fifty media outlets run by the CIA, inside and outside the United States." The historian William Preston Jr. and the editor Ellen Ray note that such exposures are only the "tip of the iceberg," in view of the fact that much is hidden from both Congress and the news media. Given the number of domestic and foreign news outlets owned by the CIA and the fact that many journalists cooperate with the government, whether voluntarily or for compensation, disinformation is a staple of American government.[11] The military also directly provides the news media with disinformation, as happened during the Vietnam and Persian Gulf wars, for instance.[12]

STONEWALLING. Journalists may also be stonewalled. The Nixon and Ford administrations made it particularly difficult to get information from the White House. Former *New York Times* Washington bureau chief William Kovach reports that the Reagan administration made "a consistent and organized effort . . . to reduce the flow of government information." President George Bush's administration was just as closed. The point is that much information sought by political correspondents is unavailable; reporters too often remain stuck in the briefing room, awaiting an appearance by the press secretary or other briefer.[13]

THREAT OF RETALIATION. Executive and legislative branch officials may retaliate against journalists or news organizations who do not go along with the official line. Presidential candidates, top political appointees, and leading members of the House and Senate may complain to individual journalists or their superiors, or public officials may impugn a journalist's reputation, denigrating his or her integrity, judgment, patriotism, or professionalism. President Dwight Eisenhower and his press secretary, James Hagerty, banned the humorist Art Buchwald from the White House press briefings when Buchwald ridiculed the briefings for their triviality. President John F. Kennedy tried to get the *New York Times* to remove David Halberstam from the Vietnam beat (to no avail). Later, both the Pentagon and the Johnson administration condemned the lack of professionalism of the news reporters who reported unfavorably on the Vietnam War. President Johnson also regularly complained to television network executives, especially CBS News's Frank Stanton. During the Nixon administration, Chuck Colson, Nixon's director of communications, complained to CBS President Bill Paley about the network's story on Watergate, and the second installment of the two-part series on Watergate was shortened by half. Nixon aides tried to get Dan Rather pulled from the White House beat, though they did not succeed.[14]

The journalist Mark Hertsgaard gives the example of the Reagan administration's complaints to CBS executives about the Iran-Contra coverage. Both the State Department and White House also severely criticized Raymond Bonner, who was reporting from El Salvador for the *New York Times*. Bonner was reassigned. The *Wall Street Journal*'s John Fialka tells of his experience when he wrote an unflattering piece about Henry Kissinger's conflicts of interest in U.S.-China policy. "[Kissinger] came back. He probably did the most thorough job of getting back at me. He even told me he was going to do it. He came at all levels of my editors, including the social level. That really bothered me. Then he went to all the people I quoted and tried to get them to say that I twisted their quotes. All but one refused and the one happened to be one of his protégés." Fialka notes that Kissinger "is known for that. I am not the only guy he has tried that with."[15]

Political officials may also retaliate by withholding news from or denying access to particular reporters and news organizations. The media writer Ken Auletta gives an example from the Bush administration:

> The Bush campaign tried to repay Rather and CBS for its take-no-prisoners interview on the Iran-contra scandal by denying interviews to CBS. At one point Rather dispatched his producer, Tom Bettag, to Washington to smooth differences with Bush's campaign chairman, Lee Atwater. Bettag was kept waiting, and then Atwater saw him for only a moment, be-

fore brushing him off on an aide. "It was a clear back of the hand," said Rather, who came to view the press as "spineless" during the campaign, a characterization [CBS News President David] Burke did not disagree with.[16]

A further example comes from the Persian Gulf War, when a journalist released a picture of a wounded soldier's reaction to the death of a close friend in battle. The photo portrayed an intense personal side of the conflict that was at odds with the Pentagon's efforts. The photographer, David Turnkey, was later denied access to press pools in Sarajevo and had problems getting other assignments.[17]

By complaining about individual and organizational news coverage, public officials attempt to influence future coverage, just as ballplayers complain about a ruling, knowing full well that it will not be overturned but hoping to predispose future rulings.[18] For the broadcast media, however, implicit in the complaints is the threat of regulatory action. Auletta tells of NBC's getting pressure from the chairs of the Democratic and Republican national committees, the chair of the House committee overseeing broadcast regulations, Massachusetts Congressman Ed Markey, and other members of Congress to cover a presidential debate rather than the scheduled broadcast of the 1988 Olympics (the other networks were carrying the debate live). The president of NBC News reluctantly caved in to the pressure. Michael G. Gartner, a former president of NBC News, comments:

> The networks have been conditioned like Pavlov's dogs, to react when a Congressman calls. Indeed, just the threat of a call—the rumor from an aide that his boss will soon be calling—or a statement, or, God forbid, a hearing can sometimes force the broadcast industry into submission on a question of policy, programming, or scheduling. Broadcasting today is essentially a public-policy laboratory in which the Congress feels it can play with impunity. For lovers of the First Amendment, it is a nightmare.[19]

This threat of congressional action may be yet another sanction public officials have at their disposal.[20]

Government officials may also use the coercive powers of tax and criminal laws to punish journalists who they feel are prying too much. Tax returns may be audited, as were those of some journalists under the Nixon administration, and reporters may be prosecuted, as were CBS News correspondent Daniel Schorr by the Nixon administration and the writer Samuel Morison by the Reagan administration.[21] The government has also been known to monitor journalists' behavior through police or intelligence agencies, such as the FBI and CIA. The government is assisted by extensive rules of secrecy and information classification.[22]

DEFINING THE NEWS. Most fundamentally, the government has legal and potentially coercive authority to determine what the news is. As the sociologist Mark Fishman observes, it is ultimately government personnel who define what the law is; it is the government's interpretation of political reality that counts in the end.[23] Journalists look to the government for certification or legitimization of political information. Blumler and Gurevitch make this exact point. Government organizations are powerful because

> they can plausibly claim authority over the definition of the issues falling in their spheres . . . the Treasury and the Federal Reserve [Board] are regarded as the authorities to turn to on the state of the economy; the Pentagon is defined as the authoritative voice on defense and military matters; the police pronounce on issues of law and order; and the President is the "primary definer" of what constitutes the "national interest." Not surprisingly, when journalists seek an authoritative perspective on a certain field of issues, they turn to those officials who are defined by their positions as authoritative sources.[24]

The consequence is that the news media rarely do investigative reporting when confronted with a policy monopoly. Challenging political power invites public controversy, and editors are sensitive to what politicians and the public may perceive as intrusive media practices. The result is editorial self-censorship.[25] Although retaliatory action on the part of public officials may be infrequent, they could exert chilling effects that have influence far beyond the actual number of incidents.

USE OF REWARDS. Sanctions may also be positive. Pentagon officials, like other government officials and politicians, reward cooperative reporters: "If you are a kind of good boy and you don't write stories they don't like, there has been a tendency over the years to reward you with little leaks and stuff," comments Fialka. "Television people are most vulnerable to that. If you are going to invade Grenada, say, and you are going to announce it at 3:00 and CBS comes on the air with its exclusive at 2:50, that is an enormous gift to CBS. Somebody has paid for that. And you see that time and again." Tom Wicker, the former Washington bureau chief and columnist for the *New York Times,* concedes, "I have on too many occasions responded like one of Pavlov's dogs when summoned to the august presence of a White House official . . . I usually grabbed and ran [with whatever had been given to him]— motivated more by the reporter's fierce desire for a good story, particularly if it was an 'exclusive,' than by any hard and objective judgment about the material thus foisted on me, or why it had been."[26] What Fialka and Wicker admit, many others experience.

Thus if journalists *are* able to get news on a policy monopoly, there may be a tacit understanding that they will "report the information in a way that will accomplish the objectives of the President" or other public official who leaked the news.[27] Furthermore, if political figures leak information, there is typically a motive behind the apparent largesse: to send up a trial balloon on a program or personnel change, to sink a proposed action, or to attract outsiders to and thus change the dynamics of an issue.[28] In short, the news exclusive—the scoop—is a powerful inducement for journalists to depend on political officials, even if the scoop is obtained only a few minutes before other news organizations receive the news or if the resulting story serves particular personal or political ends.

IN SITUATIONS OF POLICY MONOPOLIES, THEN, JOURNALISTS' COVERage of persons, events, policies, or procedural matters is usually supportive of established policies and persons. This does not mean that government personnel always get the political communication they seek; they have to work to control political communication. Even areas of the government where there is a history of unity and little discernible public dissent are vulnerable to decaying public relations over time. Witness the unfavorable publicity of the later stages of the Vietnam War, NASA after the Challenger explosion, and the CIA after the revelation that Aldrich Ames and Bill Nicholson had been working for the Soviet Union.

Nonetheless, the military learned from its experience in Vietnam, borrowed from the British experience in the Falklands, and repeated tactics used in Grenada in 1983 and Panama in December 1989 in order to carry out the Persian Gulf War in 1991.[29] There is no reason to think that the same has not occurred in the State Department, the CIA, or the FBI. In fact, the promotion of media-savvy Madeleine Albright to secretary of state and the FBI's handling of a Texas independence group in west Texas (in the aftermath of the Ruby Ridge and Waco disasters) suggest that more areas of the government are learning how to use the media for their own advantage.

Journalists' Cautious Response

Politicians and political officials who work within a policy monopoly thus have numerous advantages in getting the information they want to be communicated into the news. Journalists do not want to embarrass themselves or injure their standings in the high-stakes world of unclear and complex politics and government. One veteran Washington correspondent notes that publishing a news story in an area "where no one has written about anything before," where "there is no guideline," was "the toughest moment." The worst part of his job, he says, was to wait for the reaction to "an expose or enterprise" news story. "And it is going to print . . . where have I screwed up? . . . You could get sued . . . You are just sitting there kind of going over it again. That is the scariest part."[30]

The exalted position of the ranking journalists and prestige news organizations makes them risk averse. They are wary of being outliers or outsiders on news stories—more wary of getting a story wrong than attracted to a scoop, in fact. ABC News's Ted Koppel admits,

> We are a discouragingly timid lot. By "we" I mean most television anchors and reporters and most of our colleagues of the establishment press, the big metropolitan dailies and news weeklies. Never mind the self-confident bluster of our headlines; we tremble between daydreams of scooping all of our competitors and the nightmare of standing vulnerable and alone with our scoop for too long. We enjoy being ahead of our rivals, but not too far ahead. An old friend and rival, Bernard Kalb, coined a rule to that effect: "Get it first, but first, get it second." Never, in other words, be too far in front of the pack.[31]

When the *New York Times* published a series of stories about the CIA's activity in Chile and its domestic operations in 1975 (domestic operations that were outside the CIA's official mandate), Washington rumor had it that the investigative reporter Seymour Hersh had overwritten the story and not done his homework and that the *Times* had gone out on a limb (despite the fact that the newspaper had been very careful in its coverage). Wicker remarks that he was ostracized in Washington because of his columns on the Vietnam War.[32] Similarly, the *Washington Post* was greatly relieved when other news organizations picked up the Watergate story. Publisher Katherine Graham recalls asking editor Ben Bradlee, "If this is such a hell of a story, where is everybody else?" Leonard Downie, who was one of several editors working with Carl Bernstein and Bob Woodward, recollects, "We didn't really believe that the president was going to resign . . . We were very concerned about being right all the time. We were very concerned about the judgments we made. And we were a small group of people . . . It was hard." During the period when *Time* was out front on the Watergate story, it, too, was "uneasy about being alone."[33]

When the *Washington Post* ran stories on the Iran-Contra affair in mid-1987, it was again subject to widespread criticism. The *New York Times's* Washington bureau chief, Craig Whitney, joked that "the *Post* often printed the same story three separate times on the front page in the same week," implying that there was nothing new being reported. CBS News's Brian Healy said that the *Post* story of September 6 came "very close to being a made-up front-page story." Joseph Lelyveld, now executive editor of the *New York Times,* called the *Post*'s coverage "tendentious"—printing what the reporters thought had happened "rather than their knowledge of what did happen." The most common complaint was that the *Post* had overplayed the story. The former *Newsweek* and Associated Press reporter Robert Parry was also shunned by his colleagues for his skeptical reporting on the Nicaraguan contras.[34]

In fact, the *New York Times*'s and *Washington Post*'s coverage of the Pentagon Papers and Watergate was both more exceptional and less risky and radical than their actions might appear. The investigation of President Nixon in the Watergate affair was almost abandoned at a number of points, and had it not been for the Oval Office tapes—the "smoking gun"—Nixon may not have had to resign. Nor was the precursor to Watergate, the publication of the Pentagon Papers, by any means a given: the Supreme Court almost ruled against the *New York Times,* and if it had, there is little doubt that the *Times* would have abided by the Court's ruling and not published the papers, as Nixon wished.[35]

Journalists "quickly learn that they frustrate the expectations of their publics at their own peril," one media researcher observes. "That is why a commonly held wisdom forms the boundaries within which reporter and policymaker comfortably operate . . . To be premature or late may be as deadly a sin as getting it wrong."[36] (I return to the significance of the conventional wisdom in Chapter 5.) Given the uncertainty of news organizations in reporting important political news—facing the possibility of sanctions from government officials or ridicule from their peers—the journalists and news organizations that report on national politics are typically cautious. The news media are usually in agreement in their reporting on U.S. government policy or particular administrations or persons; there is little dissent among the national and major metropolitan newspapers, the television networks, or the weekly newsmagazines (consistent with the homogeneity of news coverage as a condition for the existence of an institutional news media). They rarely dare.

The News Media as an Index of Political Contestation

Whether journalists are adversarial or deferential depends on the issue area and politics in question. When there is salient news about national politics, foreign policy, security affairs, or presidential strategy controlled by the

White House or executive branch, the news media may have little option but to report the news on terms favorable to the people and organizations providing the news. We thus see a further manifestation of the institutional media: the reciprocal effect of the presence of the news media on the White House, executive branch in general, or other formal institutions of government being covered. If the news media simply transmitted all political news, we could not meaningfully identify them as an institution. However, because the media are partly adversarial and partly cooperative, and do not distinguish their more usual umpiring and judgmental reportage from their uncritical reportage of information released by political authorities, the occasions of the latter, lap-dog news coverage have that much more of an impact. Reporting on a policy monopoly typically legitimates and validates particular people and offices in government.[37]

This conceptualization of how the news media differentially treat political contests and policy monopoly is consistent with the news media's practice of "indexing," studied by the political scientists W. Lance Bennett and Daniel Hallin, among others. Indexing refers to the news media's tendency to criticize and dissent from the government to the extent that the government is divided and political appointees and members of Congress are critical of the White House or public policy.[38] In other words, the press investigates the government only to the extent that it is not unified. And if there is a policy monopoly, there is little investigation.

To understand how the institutional news media are grounded in individual and organizational actions—the shared practices of news production—it is helpful to examine the media practices manifest in the news coverage of policy monopolies.

Media Practices

A number of media practices help journalists report the news in the face of the uncertainty of securing information that is controlled by politicians or political officials. I discuss three: the press conference, the fixed format journalists use to report on government officials, and the personal interview. Each allows for flexibility in political communication between political figures and journalists, so as to protect the interests of the news media.

The Press Conference

One practice that eases government-journalist relations and allows journalists to be either dominant or quiescent is the press conference. Press conferences are a principal way for the president, members of Congress, departmental secretaries, and agency heads to publicize information. They give reporters access to government officials, and if they are announced in advance, they serve to regularize journalists' uncertain access to public officials (the president especially). "The press conference saves time and energy; it obviates the necessity of several hundred men running around for information which may just as well be given to them collectively. It removes a great deal of tension of covering Washington," Leo Rosten observes.[39] Press conferences allow reporters to question and even challenge public officials at the same time those officials are able to publicize a particular message or interpretation of political information.

The press conference serves the interests of the president or other political actor, then, since he or she can call the meeting, prepare set remarks and stock answers, and even decide which reporters get to ask questions. News organizations, for their part, are able to decide how they want to use the official's statements and answers. They ultimately decide how to interpret news stories and how much prominence to give them; the less prominent the federal official or politician, the more leeway the news media have.[40]

The press conference establishes a forum that permits flexibility and therefore assists both journalists and public officials in doing their jobs. Indeed, press conferences are a staple of government reporting. They can be held routinely (e.g., the daily White House and State Department briefings) or inconsistently or infrequently (by the president or other top government official, such as the vice president or secretary of defense). Some, such as those held by the secretaries of minor departments or bureau chiefs, by many members of Congress, or by third- and minor-party candidates for the presidency, may be ignored by much of the news media.

The use of press conferences has evolved over the course of the twentieth century, from President Theodore Roosevelt's first regular, informal meetings with members of the press, to President Franklin Roosevelt's frequent press conferences (until World War II), to President Richard Nixon's infrequent press conferences. American presidents have also altered the form in which reporters can question them, changed the frequency with which they hold press conferences according to their political needs and personal styles, and influenced the political impact of press conferences by altering the form and frequency of any other meetings with the press (e.g., FDR held much smaller and fewer press conferences during World War II), by permitting direct quotations (President Dwight Eisenhower), by allowing the press conferences to be televised (President John Kennedy), and by holding more joint press conferences with foreign leaders than their predecessors did (an approach favored by Presidents Bush and Clinton).[41]

The Fixed Format for Reporting on Politicians and Officials

A second standard practice of political coverage is the more-or-less fixed format by which journalists receive political information from politicians or public officials: on the record (i.e., all the information can be used and directly attributed to the source), on background (the information can be used but the source remains anonymous), on deep background (the journalist publishes using his or her own authority), or off the record (no information at all can be used). Journalists and politicians then abide by their mutual understanding. By routinizing their relationship, journalists and politicians reconcile their competing interests with respect to access to newsworthy information. Reporters receive access to news in a variety of forms: they may receive current information or confirmation of other news, or they may scoop their competitors with news exclusives as long as they agree to follow the rules. At the same time, elected or appointed officials or their aides are helped by being able to release newsworthy political information in a way that serves their own interests and those of their superiors, their agency, their party, or their presidential administration. The briefing rules at once help public officials further their particular interests and help journalists obtain new or additional information, but neither journalists nor political figures are held accountable for the information that subsequently gets publicized.[42]

Former Senator Alan Simpson of Wyoming condemns the use of anonymous sources as a "web of manipulation." As Simpson sees it, "If you read a newspaper this morning, you . . . were manipulated by journalists, who were in turn manipulated by people whose identities—and more important, biases—were never revealed to you. This web of manipulation was presented to you as unbiased reporting, pure as snow." Simpson views this "common, universally accepted practice" as "lazy, dishonest, and downright dangerous. The anonymous source is introduced to you as the bearer of truth. In fact, he or she is the enemy of truth," for the reason that these persons are typically "people with deeply held biases and hidden agendas who are nonetheless given an extraordinary gift—the ultimate shield of protection for what they say."[43] Yet the politician or political official who is releasing information does not necessarily get the publicity he or she wants. His or her information may be confirmed or denied by other sources; nor is news coverage automatic.

These rules, too, have evolved over time. A 1958 memorandum by the *Washington Post's* managing editor, Alfred Friendly, effectively codified the rules governing "background" briefings, defining (as specified earlier) what it meant to provide information off the record or on a deep background or background basis. Whereas there had once been "considerable friction" over the rules of the game, Friendly's memorandum clarified matters.[44] The rules stuck.

The Personal Interview

A third media practice that eases government-journalist relations amid the uncertainty of reporting on politics is the personal interview. The interview allows journalists access to information proprietary to the interviewee, while allowing that person to communicate to his or her advantage by furnishing previously unknown information or appealing to the understanding and sympathy of the audiences. Reporters rely on interviews to such an extent that in three-fourths of their news stories, they use no documents at all.[45]

The interview situates journalists as the "authoritative mediators between the government and the citizen," though it is designed to appeal more to the citizen audience than to the interviewee. Both the interviewer and the interviewee are positioned to benefit: the journalist and his or her news organization gets the exclusive in a one-on-one setting, and the interviewee gets his or her information or viewpoint across to a wider public. Even as the journalist assumes a controlling role, asking the questions, setting the discussion agenda, and facilitating the communication of news, he or she rarely challenges the interviewee on the subject at hand. "The relative power of the reporter and the source [is] an ever-present consideration," as Michael Schudson notes, and as a rule, the more prominent the interviewee, the more deferential the interviewer: "the power relationship is the central frame of the interaction."[46] Although the interview may allow for a hard-hitting examination of a person or issue, an "act of aggression," it can also lead to a sympathetic discussion. "A conspiracy of the reporter and the source against the audience" may develop, in that the interviewee may forbid direct attribution and the reporter may protect the source from his or her damaging or erroneous statements or may keep to him- or herself many of the confidences of the source.[47]

This form of political communication is an American invention. The use of the interview spread among reporters after the Civil War, as Schudson tells it, and by the 1880s was referred to by European visitors as "a distinctively and sadly American contribution to journalism." The interview was a hybrid. It was neither a transcript of official proceedings nor a speech by a politician (though much in the way of prepared material may be inserted by the interviewee), and it took the reader to be "less a partisan than a witness, a sort of acknowledged eavesdropper."[48] The interview is now taken for granted, of course.

Other Practices

There are other practices that both enable journalists to cover public officials and allow the officeholders to publicize their own messages. One is the
establishment of groups of journalists who meet regularly over meals with
officials to discuss policy on a background basis. Examples are the Sperling
breakfasts formed in 1966 by Godfrey Sperling Jr., the Washington bureau
chief of the *Christian Science Monitor,* and the luncheons hosted regularly by
the *New York Times's* Washington bureau, the *Washington Post,* the *Los Angeles Times,* and other news organizations.

Then there is the convenience of the basic press handout, as Rosten observes:

> The press corps agrees that no correspondent can possibly handle the full
> quantity of news-matter being created day by day in the capital. The
> handout and the press conference have systematized the flow of infor-
> mation; they have offered newspapermen, regularly and efficiently, re-
> sponsible accounts of official acts. The handout has made the life of the
> Washington correspondent immeasurably easier, removing the confu-
> sion and the uncertainty which would exist without some institutional
> link between complex events and overworked reporters.[49]

Another, more formal standard practice is the existence of a standing
White House press corps as well as the House and Senate press galleries.
"Press pools" (of print, television, radio, and photo journalists) have also developed for the mutual convenience of journalists and public officials during special traveling occasions.[50]

Each of these practices enables the interests of politicians' and public officials to be reconciled with the motivations and needs of journalists. By sub-
sidizing the news—inasmuch as they collect and interpret political information for reporters and their news organization—political officials are also
more likely to get favorable news coverage, coverage derived from the press
conference, news leak, interview, breakfast meeting, or handout.

Many of these practices have also become more-or-less taken for granted, even as they continue to evolve, as we see with respect to the press conference (compare the many press conferences of President Franklin Roosevelt, which he gave on his own, with the much smaller number of press
conferences held by President Clinton, many of which he gives jointly with
foreign leaders), the standard format for reporting political communications from politicians or government personnel, the interview (compare the
formality of the interviews conducted by CBS News's Edward Murrow in the
1950s with the conversational and intimate style of ABC News's Barbara

Walters), and, for that matter, the presidential debate. The point is that these conventions are shared among the news media and thereby root the institutional news media in the workaday practices of reporters and their editors and producers.

Conclusion

Whether the news media relate to national politics in attack-dog or lap-dog mode depends on what and whom journalists are covering.[51] These contrasting perspectives on the news media are not the result of opposing tastes (although people have different opinions as to how aggressive or compliant the news media are in any one instance), and neither of the two views is necessarily mistaken (there is much to recommend both). Moreover, journalists' Janus-faced behavior in political reporting is not the result of individual personalities or political climate (although these may be contributing factors). Rather, these two opposing views of the news media are mutually consistent.

Although the adversarial image of the media captures the aggressiveness of journalists when they are covering much of national politics, especially presidential elections, this view misses the deference that the nation's top journalists show to the government when they report on other aspects of national government. The reason for the frequent kid-glove treatment of politics is the fundamental asymmetry in number between the considerable ranks of highly competitive journalists and news organization and the small cadre of potentially unified and powerful top U.S. government officials. The cooperation of the media is evident with respect to much of the news coverage of the president, the older and more prominent departments and agencies of the federal government, and even, at times, Congress. The Supreme Court typically receives either no attention (and thus avoids scrutiny) or a limited amount of favorable attention (as noted in Chapter 2).[52] Reporters are less the adversaries of government officials than their collaborators, as David Broder and the late James Reston (a former *New York Times* reporter, editor, and columnist) observe. No wonder, then, that in reporting much of the activity of the national government, the news media are more compliant than adversarial, more transmitters of political information than independent critics.[53]

"The whole method of news operation tends to give the government the advantage," remarks the journalist and political writer David Wise. A journalist is "far more likely to be sold a self-serving bill of goods" by the White House or executive branch than "he or she is to extract objective information," notes Wicker, formerly with the *New York Times*. In situations where "you are really tied to a source, where there is a lot of breaking news every day and you are sort of feeding off that and you don't have anything else going on, you are really kind of a captive of the person who feeds you."[54] Those who speak and write solely of an adversarial press neglect the extent of journalists' cooperation, much of it implicit, with political officials.

That said, the relationship between journalists and political actors remains somewhat indeterminate. The press conference, the ground rules for using politicians' and officials' statements, and the interview allow for the indeterminacy of political communication: political advocates are able to exert significant control over the form and forum of the interchange, but they have far less control over the eventual news content. Politicians and officials can hold press conferences, determine the timing and significance of backgrounders and leaks, and grant interviews, but correspondents and their editors and producers ultimately choose which information they publicize and how exactly they do so. Sources may be crucial, as Sigal and others emphasize,[55] but sources may be ignored or may be played off each other.

Ultimately it is the journalists and occasionally company executives who decide what they want to cover and how they will do so. They decide the timing, length, prominence, location, and interpretation of news stories, on which politicians and federal agencies greatly depend for their success and legitimacy.[56] Furthermore, the news media may influence whether an official or event is interpreted as good or successful by pointing out a misstatement, or publicizing an obvious falsehood, no matter the other merits of the address or appearance. Former *Washington Post* editor Ben Bradlee comments that the news media "have the power to define reality, to say what was—and what was not—important at any given time . . . The major television networks, in particular, could cause big trouble for the White House [or any other part of national government] virtually anytime they wanted simply by focusing sustained attention on any of the scandals, inequities, dangerous or bankrupt policies or other shortcomings common to every Washington administration."[57]

The news media rarely cause "big trouble," however. One important reason for this deference is money: the leading news organizations have too much at stake in the political economy of the status quo, as I discuss in the next chapter.

MAKING MONEY AND MAKING NEWS

The press has been transformed into an enormous and complicated piece of machinery. As a necessary accompaniment, it has become big business. There is a marked reduction in the number of units of the press relative to the total population . . . The right of free public expression has therefore lost its earlier reality. Protection against government is not now enough to guarantee that a man who has something to say shall have a chance to say it. The owners and managers of the press determine which persons, which facts, which versions of the facts, and which ideas shall reach the public.—The Commission on Freedom of the Press, *A Free and Responsible Press,* 1947

The monopoly publisher's reaction, on being told that he ought to spend money on reporting distant events, is therefore exactly that of the proprietor of a large, fat cow, who is told that he ought to enter her in a horse race.—A. J. Liebling, *The Press,* 1961

THE NEWS BUSINESS HAS NOT ALWAYS BEEN JUST ANOTHER BUSINESS. Almost all newspapers and newsmagazines were once one-person or family firms, and as long as revenues covered expenses with something left over, editorial content could take its own course. The *New York Times* and the *Washington Post,* for instance, could afford "a certain obliviousness" to bottom-line pressures. Even William Paley, the founder of CBS, and Henry Luce, the founder of Time Inc., enjoyed some discretion with respect to the bottom line, autocratic as the owners may have been. News organizations had a "wall of separation" that divided editorial content from business affairs. This was the separation of "church" and "state," as *Time* put it.[1]

Douglass Cater observes in *The Fourth Branch of Government* that news is "big business" and "a commodity that must be purveyed to an ever-expanding audience by increasingly monopolistic distributors. It must be homogeneous for *Homo* genus in the mass." The economics of the "fourth branch" is not Cater's main focus, however, and he develops other points more fully. Sigal, too, remarks that as long "as revenues are sufficient to ensure organizational survival, professional and social objectives take precedence over profits, particularly for the management of firms like the *Post* and the *Times*, where a single family maintains financial control."[2] The implication of the work of Cater, Sigal, and others is that a wall of separation does, in fact, exist in news organizations, dividing editorial content from financial matters. Media researchers can therefore presumably afford to downplay or ignore the commercial dimension of news organizations.[3]

This view of media firms has been out of date for some time. In a celebrated example from 1966, CBS News president Fred Friendly was not allowed to televise a third day of hearings held by the Senate Foreign Relations Committee on the conduct of the Vietnam War; *I Love Lucy* reruns were shown instead. Indeed, commercial considerations have ever intruded on editorial decisions. News organizations, whether for profit or subsidized, are nothing without a minimum of material resources; no news organization can afford to be oblivious of its bottom line.[4] Individual stockholders, institutional investors, employees, managers, and executives in possession of stock (or stock options), and the extended family members pressure news organizations to perform on a yearly or even quarterly basis.

A look at the 1997 economic performances of the leading news organizations suggests their commercial stakes.[5] Among the *Fortune* 500 U.S. companies, the New York Times Company, which owns five network television stations, two radio stations, five forest product companies, twenty-two magazines, twenty-seven newspapers, and information services, ranked 487th in revenues ($2.8 billion), 281st in net profits ($262 million), and 267th in market value ($6.4 billion). The Washington Post Company, which owns *Newsweek,* four network and fifty-three cable television stations, two other newspapers, Kaplan Learning Centers, information services, other media affiliates, and book publishing companies, ranked 628th in revenues ($2 billion) but was 282nd in net profits and 354th in market value.[6] The Dow Jones Company, owner of the *Wall Street Journal* and twenty-three other newspapers, was 520th in revenues ($2.6 billion), lost money in 1997, and was 369th in market value ($5.2 billion). The Times-Mirror Company, owner of the *Los Angeles Times* and seven other daily newspapers, ranked 434th in revenues ($3.3 billion), 289th in net profits ($250 million), and 282nd in market value ($5.7 billion).

Time-Warner, the conglomerate composed of *Time,* Turner Broadcasting and CNN, book publishing companies, two dozen magazines, cable channels, motion pictures, and news media services, among other interests, was 110th in gross sales ($13.3 billion) and 49th in market value ($42.5 billion) in the United States; it was 295th in net profits ($246 million). *Newsweek* is owned by the Washington Post Company, as mentioned, and *U.S. News* is owned by publisher and real estate investor Mortimer Zuckerman (he also owns the *Atlantic Monthly* and the *New York Daily News* as part of his privately held Boston Properties).

Among network television owners, General Electric (GE) owns NBC as well as six television stations, cable channels, electrical equipment, communication satellites, and networking software. GE was 5th in revenues ($91 billion), 1st in net profits ($8.2 billion), and 1st in market value ($260 billion) among U.S. companies in 1997 according to *Fortune*. CBS Corporation has fourteen television stations (almost all in major markets), thirty-nine radio stations, cable interests, and financial services firms. CBS Corporation was 159th in revenues ($9.6 billion), 156th in net profit ($549 million), and 91st in market value ($22 billion). The Walt Disney Company, which bought Capital Cities / ABC for $18 billion in 1995, owns ten newspapers, cable channels, nine television stations (almost all in major markets), and a 14 percent interest in Young Broadcasting (which has eight television stations of its own). Disney ranked 51st in revenues ($22.5 billion), 43rd in net profits ($2.0 billion), and 23rd in market value ($73 billion). In 1995, television and radio profit margins reached 33.2 percent on average, cable TV had a 39.4 percent profit margin, and magazine publishing margins stood at 14.4 percent—their highest level in five years. More than fifty media companies (print, broadcast, and cable) took in more than $1 billion each in annual revenues in 1995.

And the media companies are only getting bigger. Recent evidence of this trend is Time-Warner's merger with Turner Broadcasting, Westinghouse's purchase of CBS for $5.4 billion, Disney's acquisition of Capital Cities / ABC, Gannett's purchase of Multimedia, Inc. (newspapers and television and radio stations) for $1.7 billion, and the New York Times Company's purchase of the *Boston Globe* for $1.1 billion. All of these transactions occurred in 1994–1995 alone, and the acquisition and merger of news organizations are "going to continue to happen," says John Morton, a newspaper industry analyst.[7]

With the increase in size, of course, comes an increase in the number of individuals who have a stake in a company's commercial performance (including creditors to the degree that a company has gone into debt to pay for its expanded holdings), thus making the economic pressures on the major news media even greater. Institutional investors (pension funds, insurance companies, banks, foundations, and endowments) now own 72 percent of Gannett and Knight-Ridder, 57 percent of the New York Times Company, 51 percent of the Washington Post Company, 47 percent of the Times-Mirror

Company, and 43 percent of the Dow Jones Company.[8] With more institutional investors comes a greater demand for stock performance.

The economic pressure on these media companies is "always there," and even the large family owners (i.e., the Sulzbergers of the *New York Times,* the Grahams of the *Washington Post,* the Chandlers of Times-Mirror, and the Bancrofts of the *Wall Street Journal)* are "just like stockholders," comments Richard Harwood. Family firms are "just as focused on economic performance" as other media firms, notes Morton, given the ever-larger number of heirs, the pressures from other stockholders, and the financial incentives of executives. Despite the fact that the New York Times Company and the Washington Post Company have two-tiered stock plans (where family members have one class of voting stock and others may own nonvoting stock only), the commercial pressures on the *Times,* the *Post,* and other family-run firms have only intensified.[9]

These pressures in the production of political news almost necessarily predispose news organizations to give favorable coverage to their own interests and those of corporate America and less favorable coverage to redistributive policies, pro-labor issues, and most political and economic reforms.

How the Business of the News Affects Political Communication

The commercial aspect of the U.S. news media very much affects the quantity and quality of political communication. It does so in several ways: (1) through the effects of advertising, (2) through the rise of market journalism, (3) through cost cutting to raise profits, (4) through the possibility of libel, and (5) through the political action of news corporations. I discuss each in turn and then consider several standard practices that journalists and news organizations have developed to handle the uncertainty of the commercial performance of their company.

Advertising

The news media make most of their money by delivering audiences to advertisers. That is, television broadcasters, newsmagazines, and newspapers sell their product—their audiences—to advertisers, who then "buy" the audience by paying for time or space in which to advertise their goods or services. As former NBC News President Reuven Frank observes, "The product of commercial television is not programs. If one thinks of making goods to sell, the viewers are not the customers, those who buy the product. Advertisers buy the product, pay money for it. Programs are not what they buy. What they buy, what they pay for is audience, people to heed their messages. The bigger the audience, the more they pay . . . Thus seen, the programs are the machinery, that which makes the product."[10] Newspapers make 70–80 percent of their revenues from advertising, magazines make about 50 percent, and over-the-air television stations make all their money from advertising. Cable television, as a class, makes about 30 percent of its revenues from advertising and the rest from subscriber fees.

One obvious result of the news media's reliance on advertising is the presence of advertising itself: about 22 percent of television airtime and two-thirds of newspaper space are filled with commercial advertisements. Indeed, $100 billion is spent in advertising in the United States annually.[11] The message of commercial advertisements is that the viewer or reader can— it is claimed or implied—be more successful, more attractive, more effective, or more personally fulfilled if she or he purchases a certain product or service. It is not a stretch to say that the almost ubiquitous presence of advertising in the United States, where 57 percent of the world's advertising is consumed, creates the culture of consumption.[12] But that is too big a subject to take up here.

Commercial advertisements may relate directly to politics insofar as issue-related or corporate image ads—as distinct from product ads—promote a political climate or policy outcome favorable to the product or image of the corporate advertiser. The corporate sponsorship of National Public Radio and the Public Broadcasting System is to the point. Furthermore, sober editorial-like ads tout the responsibility and contributions of oil companies; glossy pictures of military equipment boast the achievements of particular weapons and defense systems, and upbeat ads polish the reputation of corporations tarnished by political, economic, or environmental scandal. One study finds that fully "one-third of all corporate advertising is directed at influencing the public on political and ideological issues as opposed to pushing consumer goods."[13]

Advertising may affect politics and policy outcomes in another way, too. News company executives may choose not to run some advertisements. In 1986, the television networks refused to run an ad produced by W. R. Grace and Company: "Set in the year 2017, the ad showed an elderly man in a witness cage. The man is being cross-examined by a child who wants to know how the man could have let federal deficits reach $2 trillion."[14] In 1990, the TV networks rejected an ad narrated by the actor Ed Asner: "The murderous civil war in El Salvador has been supported by billions of American tax dollars and by the sale of Salvadoran coffee . . . Boycott Folgers. What it brews is misery and death." Although the ad campaign was supported by the National Council of Churches, most television stations refused to run the advertisement.[15]

More recently, the Military Families Support network, critical of the Persian Gulf War, could not get its thirty-second spot on CNN or, for that matter, on any of the three network stations in Washington, D.C. Similarly, the Los Angeles chapter of Physicians for Social Responsibility was not able to place an antiwar advertisement on CNN or on stations in New York or Los Angeles owned and operated by ABC or CBS. Yet a message supportive of the war was allowed to run on seventeen stations from New York to Los Angeles. (It showed an American soldier at the front writing home to his family and saying "All of the people here are behind us, and I hope the folks back home are, because we deserve their support.")[16] In early October 1997, CNN pulled two advertisements it was going to show that argued against the evidence that there was global warming, claiming that they were inaccurate. "The ads, paid for by the chemical, automobile and oil industries, warn that proposed limits on carbon dioxide emissions could sharply raise prices for gasoline and other goods." A spokesperson for the industries declared that this was "totally a censorship issue," for which Ted Turner and CNN were responsible.[17]

It is clearly in the constitutional rights of publishers and broadcasters to choose the ads they wish to carry. The point is that the commercial notices that are run in the print and video media are precisely that—choices. Company owners and top executives are responsible for and in control of both the news and advertising content of their news organization. Although some omissions might be desirable, such as omission of racist or antireligious advertisements, it is the news executives who ultimately draw the line regarding which advertisements to run and which not to run and who are responsible for the consequences.

The more subtle effect of advertising is its influence on editorial content. Most readers and viewers are at least partially conscious of commercial advertisements, of course, and discount their messages accordingly. "The public pays for the press, but only when that payment is concealed," Walter Lippmann remarks. The indirect impact of advertising on news content is more insidious.[18]

It was in reaction to the "not only perceived but actual appeal to audiences out there" that CNN ran "so much of the O. J. trial," admits CNN's former Washington bureau chief. "You walk a fine line." CNN was apparently able to walk this line: its viewership increased by more than fourfold over the period of the trial.[19] CNN's news decision was hardly distinctive: NBC News and CBS News also ran the O. J. Simpson trial as their biggest news story in 1995. An executive at one of the networks, who prefers to remain anonymous, notes that there was "tremendous stated and unstated pressure [from network executives] to cover O. J. Simpson's trial." Although the trial is an obvious example of the networks responding to ratings pressure, it is by no means unique.

Advertisers may influence news content in several ways. One way is to withhold, or threaten to withhold, advertisements from undesirable programming. In 1970, for instance, when NBC ran a news special on the conditions of migrant workers who picked citrus crops for Minute Maid, Coca-Cola (the parent company) pulled its multimillion-dollar account. For at least eight years thereafter, "NBC [did] not . . . [produce] a documentary on a controversial domestic issue involving an important advertiser." Ben Bagdikian, a former national editor at the *Washington Post* and dean emeritus at the University of California at Berkeley's School of Journalism, provides a further example. In the early 1980s the Mobil Oil Company induced media companies into both withholding stories unfavorable to Mobil and not running corrections, letters to the editor, or other editorial content that would counteract the favorable publicity the oil industry was getting.[20]

Tobacco companies were also for a long while able to suppress unfavorable media publicity on the effects of smoking and on the tobacco industry.[21] More recently, ABC News pulled the plug on a contracted one-hour special on tobacco for *Turning Point,* when Roone Arledge, the ABC News president, got cold feet.[22] ABC News later apologized to Philip Morris (which, through its subsidiary Kraft Foods, is a major television advertiser) for its report on *Day One* about Philip Morris's manipulation of cigarette nicotine levels.[23] In another example, the Chrysler Corporation withdrew advertising from the ABC miniseries *Amerika* because of its "inappropriateness" to Chrysler's "upbeat product commercials."[24] Advertiser pressure on the news media is a "very underpublicized story," writes the journalism professor and former correspondent Doug Underwood.[25]

Advertisers do not have to be heavy-handed about their preferences, as a rule: there is little news critical of business to begin with.[26] Only 6 of the 1,110 members of the Organization of Investigative Reporters and Editors have the corporate world as their beat.[27] The executive editor of the *Washington Post,* Leonard Downie, makes the same point: "few newspapers engage in real investigative reporting, and when they do, private business is almost never examined." A study by the Urban Policy Research Institute found that many publishers allow investigations into "petty payoffs and welfare abuse but draw the line at stories dealing with the institutional foundations of the city or state, the relationships of banks, corporations, elected officials, and—perhaps—newspapers."[28] Michael Schudson notes, too, that "investigative reporting is not a priority" for news organizations today; "nor has it ever been," he adds.[29]

Instead, "the kind of investigative reporting you see doing well is . . . more consumer-oriented and sensationalistic," says Alex Benes, the managing director of the Center for Public Integrity. "It deals with tainted orange juice or OSHA safety in the workplace. None of this is unimportant stuff, but . . . there is not a lot of investigative reporting that speaks to the national interest."[30] CBS's famous 1960s documentaries *The Selling of the Pentagon* and *Hunger* have been cited as exemplars of good television journalism—both stories led to congressional investigations—but they were notable exceptions.[31] Nor is there much incentive for journalists to attack their own (extended) companies.

In short, business—and thus the media industry itself—gets little examination in the major media. As former CBS President Frank Stanton explains, "since we are advertiser-supported we must take into account the general objectives and desires of advertisers as a whole." A top advertising executive underscores the point: "There have been very few cases where it has been necessary to exercise a veto [over the programming content of the television network broadcasters], because the producers involved and the writers involved are normally pretty well aware of what might not be acceptable." News executives, in short, react to their *"perceptions* of what advertisers will tolerate."[32]

This, then, is the media's sin of *omission:* the problem that reporters and their superiors, whether consciously or unconsciously, do not report certain stories because of the perceived impact they would have on advertisers. The omission of news critical of advertisers (but of potential economic and political significance) may occur because of advertiser influence, the lack of investigative resources, and self-censorship on the part of news organizations.

Market Journalism

The converse of the omission of news stories for commercial reasons is the media's sin of *commission* with respect to advertising: the deliberate tailoring of news stories to attract audiences that advertisers seek. This is "market journalism." News organizations that practice market journalism produce stories that create a buying mood—stories that are uplifting or encouraging, rather than somber or depressing.

The premise behind market journalism is that news organizations can be more than simply bearers of ads and can instead actively pursue audiences with advertisers in mind. News organizations can anticipate advertisers' preferences and preempt their complaints. Network executives can "take into account whether they think major advertisers in the aggregate . . . are going to consider a show a hospitable setting for commercials."[33] The executives chase young women—the most desirable of the seven "demos" (demographic groups) into which advertisers break down the audience. Women do more shopping than men, and eighteen- to forty-five-year-old adults have fewer established brand loyalties than do older persons.[34]

The *New York Times, Wall Street Journal,* and *Los Angeles Times* all underwent major redesigns in the 1970s and 1980s to become more reader-friendly.[35] They cut down the number of columns, increased the typeface size, offered more colorful writing, added new graphics, and put in new sections. The newspapers expanded their coverage of lifestyle, food, sports, fashion, furnishings, and the like, with each of the new or expanded sections appealing to distinct (although sometimes overlapping) audiences and connecting to distinct commercial products, whether furniture, garden equipment, computers, sports equipment, cars and automobile products, stereo equipment, clothes, or cookbooks and cookware. The *New York Times,* for example, developed separate "Sports," "Science," "Living," "Home," and "Weekend" sections between 1975 and 1978. With these new sections, the newspaper is able to be different things to different people. As Max Frankel, the *Times's* former executive editor, puts it, "People don't read the paper from start to finish; they dip in and out . . . It's like a supermarket of great riches; you don't expect readers to be interested in everything any more than you expect customers to buy everything in the store." The newspaper's assistant managing editor adds, "We need to be ruthless in admitting how little time readers have for us. If they can't find what they need fast enough or if they get the impression it's just too goddamn much, then they're going to read someone else or not read anything at all."[36]

In the early 1990s, "tie-ins" started making a regular appearance in the *New York Times,* writes Edwin Diamond, the late media critic and professor of journalism. With tie-ins, the *Times* could match "editorial product" with advertising sales: it "polled target constituencies, found out what excited them or *thought* might excite them, and shaped its cultural campaign accordingly."[37] Like other news organizations, the *New York Times* uses its audience—and, hence, their appeal to advertisers—as a guide to its content in the attempt to attract a diverse group of well-educated, high-income readers. "High-ranking editors and business executives often work together at many newspapers, including the *New York Times,* to develop new sections," comments a reporter in the business pages of the *New York Times.*[38] Epitomizing the turn to market journalism is the April 6, 1997, issue of the *New York Times Magazine,* a "special issue" entitled "The Store as Theatre" that contains more than a dozen articles about stores and shopping.[39]

The presence of market journalism in the newsmagazines is evident from the testimony of a former writer and editor for *Time:* "the basic question to be considered" now at the magazine was "doing a cover story because it would sell on the streets." *Newsweek,* too, thoroughly revised its look in the early 1980s by cutting the length of its text by an average of 20 percent, enlarging pictures, headlines, charts, graphs, and excerpts from its articles, and generally simplifying and streamlining the news. One study of the covers of three major newsmagazines—*Time, Newsweek,* and *U.S. News*—based on the notion that the covers are windows into the editors' minds (revealing their primary interests and top priorities), shows that features predominate, analytical pieces are aimed at desirable demographic groups, the magazines emphasize their service to the reader (e.g., personal finance and health care news), and all three magazines address the reader directly. In appealing to demographic segments sought by advertisers, the newsmagazines are following the precedent of other magazines and other media.[40]

A recent and striking example of market journalism comes from the Persian Gulf War. According to the media scholar Edwin Baker, "CBS offered to tailor [its Gulf War] specials 'to provide better lead-in commercials . . . [and] to insert the commercials after segments that were specially produced with upbeat images or messages about the war, like patriotic views from the home front.'"[41] During the Desert Shield and Desert Storm operations of the war, an advertising executive told his clients, "I'm taking a cue from direct marketers who see declines in response rates during times of crisis. While attention to news will be very high, and it seems that's where you should advertise, it will probably be neutralized by the fact that minds will be diverted to very serious things." Market journalism prevails now across all the media, even the prestige press.[42]

The pursuit of market journalism may even cause a news organization to seek a lower circulation base or smaller share of television viewers in order to attract more desirable audiences, contrary to the popular belief that the media wish to reach as many people as possible. Depending on the product(s) being advertised, an audience's demographics may matter more than its absolute size. The *New York Times,* for instance, cut back circulation in Sheepshead Bay and other locations in Brooklyn—Jewish neighborhoods that used to be the bedrock of the newspaper's circulation. On the West Coast, the *Los Angeles Times* "cut back some of [its] low-income circulation" and restricted some of its "country circulation" (the circulation away from the core market of newspaper advertisers), since "the economics of American newspaper publishing is based on an advertising base, not a circulation base," says Bagdikian. Otis Chandler, the head of Times-Mirror and former publisher of the *Los Angeles Times,* admits, "The target audience of the [*Los Angeles*] *Times* is . . . the middle class and . . . the upper class . . . We are not trying to get mass circulation but quality circulation." Reflective of the importance of demographics is the fact that the New York Times has had consistently higher profit margins than the New York Daily News, even though historically it has been significantly outsold by the Daily News.[43]

When eight of the ten largest U.S. newspapers experienced circulation declines in 1993, the New York Times explained the falloff as the result of "price increases and other strategies at big newspapers." Among the other strategies were the tailoring of circulation for "more efficient distribution and shifting [of] more of the cost of newspaper production to readers."[44] In fact, the New York Times posted a net profit of 60 percent in the fourth quarter of 1996 and had a 36 percent annual profit for the year (excluding special one-time write-offs), despite circulation declines at the Times, the Boston Globe (owned by the New York Times Company), and the company's smaller newspapers. "Higher circulation and advertising rates more than offset the decline in circulation." Newsmagazines, too, may periodically run complex or risqué stories "to discourage 'downscale' readers," reports Herbert Gans.[45]

Audience-driven journalism is further characterized by the news organizations' desire not to offend any of their valuable consumer audience. As the New York Times's Craig Whitney explains, if a newspaper forces an opinion or judgment on the public, it "risk[s] losing the trust of people who hold differing views. We sell a million copies of this paper every day. You want both sides of the question to keep reading you and not feel you're shading information one way or another." The managing editor of U.S. News, Lee Ranie, also notes the importance of not alienating any one side of an issue: "one of the things that readers beat the hell out of you for is taking one side of the story." As a result, the magazine is "always thinking about that, because of the criticism you get . . . and our readers are quick to call us on it." U.S. News is "very vigilant" to ensure that different viewpoints get expressed in its stories. Katherine Graham states that she wants the Washington Post to be "a paper for everyone in the [Washington, D.C., metropolitan] area."[46] The outcome of this type of journalism—where audience rather than story substance drives news coverage—is "blandness," remarks the political writer and former Post national editor William Greider.[47]

The importance model of news reporting has given way to an entertainment and service model attendant to audience preferences. Representative of service- and market-oriented journalism is the proliferation of soft-news sections, including even movies and sports sections, in the formerly staid Wall Street Journal, the featured rankings of different financial institutions and investments in U.S. News, and the existence of multiple sections and extensive back-of-the-book (soft-news) material in the New York Times, the Washington Post, and, of course, the three newsmagazines. This may be "news you can use," but "you" may represent a relatively narrow segment of the American public, and the use may be frivolous.[48]

Market journalism has probably most affected television reporting, however, given that television news, with nightly viewership in the tens of millions, is "the principal vehicle by which political and social values are transmitted to a national audience." The economic pressures exerted by television ratings and other market forces are formidable. In the words of Bill Headline, the former CNN Washington bureau chief, if "all the dynamics in trying to wrestle the [CNN] network away from the entertainment folks when there is breaking news . . . used to be difficult," doing so now is "virtually impossible."[49]

With the takeover of the television networks in the mid-1980s, the networks have had to become more bottom-line oriented. The media writer Ken Auletta records how CBS under the management of Lawrence Tisch, ABC under the management of Capital Cities (before its acquisition by Disney) and NBC News under the management of GE fashioned their content to attract the eighteen- to forty-five-year-old female population. Auletta makes it clear that it is market journalism that drives the networks and their affiliates. As one station manager at a network affiliate notes, "It doesn't really matter what kind of news is broadcast—we could have the worst news and the worst working conditions, but *all that really matters is how we look in the ratings.* That's what management looks at in the meetings; that's what's important."[50]

Recent research on network affiliates confirms a picture of ratings-obsessed newsrooms. In his study of four West Coast television stations, the media scholar John McManus finds four general rules of broadcasting to be operative: (1) seek images over ideas, (2) seek emotion over analysis (with corollaries being to avoid complexity and dramatize where possible), (3) exaggerate, if needed, to add appeal, and (4) avoid extensive news gathering. McManus reports that "economics" has "steadily displaced journalism . . . as the primary explanation for news production." The news industry simply "didn't reward good journalism," an assistant news director pointed out; a news director said, "The purpose is to make as much money as possible." The public interest is typically subordinated to the interest of investors, McManus shows. He concludes scathingly, "Television journalists either lack the knowledge necessary to create newscasts that viewers can readily understand to make sense of their environments, or their firms choose not to create such programs."[51]

It is telling that local affiliates have growing influence on the television networks, that the major news companies themselves own many affiliates, and that McManus obtains such unambiguous findings from a study of four separate television stations. The point is that the news gets tailored to the audience. With that comes a probable drop in news quality.

Cost Cutting

Besides meeting commercial goals by heeding advertisers and engaging in market journalism, news organizations may improve their financial performance by cutting operating costs. Yet cost cutting may be achieved at the expense of the quality of political news coverage.

Foreign news, which editors and producers believe audiences care little about, suffers especially (as A. J. Liebling remarks in the epigraph to this chapter). One of the "most serious effects" of this "bottom line thinking" is the closing of so many foreign bureaus, asserts the former journalist Penn Kimball. "There are no permanent American television network correspondents anymore in Africa or Eastern Europe—except when there is a crisis . . . Nor do such capitals as Paris, Rome, and Berlin merit network correspondents these days." Brookings Institution scholar Stephen Hess finds, too, that "the networks are now basically out of the foreign news business" and instead practice "parachute journalism," dropping down where the news is. Indicatively, the total number of minutes devoted to international news ("foreign bureau reports," "foreign policy coverage," and "overseas news" combined) fell almost half for the big three television networks between 1988 and 1996.[52]

Kenneth Walsh, the White House correspondent for *U.S. News,* reports that December 1994 was the first time in memory that no press charter plane accompanied the U.S. president on a trip overseas. President Clinton was going to Budapest for seven hours and then return home. At $10,000 per reporter—and food, ground transportation, and other costs were extra—reporters backed out.[53] What international coverage there is is more than likely to be furnished through arrangements with other news organizations such as Nippon Television (NBC), the BBC (ABC), and Visnet, a British syndicated television service. Furthermore, "both NBC and CBS use material from Britain's Independent Television News, Reuters, and Rupert Murdoch's Sky News," says Hess. The result is that the world is viewed "through a pretty narrow needle."[54]

"This is a very critical matter to the general intelligence provided the American people through their news broadcasts," warns Walter Cronkite. Reflecting on the period after the Iraqi invasion of Kuwait, Cronkite speculates that if the networks "had had bureaus in Baghdad, for instance, or foreign correspondents," or "even a bureau in the Middle East to cover the Middle East thoroughly," then the United States "might not be in the position we are in today" (in the Desert Shield phase of the Persian Gulf conflict in the fall of 1990). Such a situation could readily be repeated, given the unreliability of stringers and other contracted news sources (who may have unanticipated government connections or be otherwise compromised in their ability to provide accurate information). "And the inaccurate information may be far more dangerous than no information at all," Cronkite observes.[55]

Cost cutting hurts the quality of domestic news as well. Whereas each of the three major networks used to have about thirty correspondents in its Washington bureau, ABC News currently has about twenty, and CBS News and NBC News now have only a little more than a dozen each. CBS and NBC now have a combined reporting staff smaller than either the *Wall Street Journal's* or the *New York Times's* Washington bureau. At present, the networks do not have any regular, full-time Supreme Court correspondents, the congressional contingent has been cut in half, and the regulatory agencies receive less news coverage than they once did. The reporters who remain are expected to fold news stories from outside their beats into their normal responsibilities. The effects of cost cutting are such that a "producer doesn't have the time he did in the past to carefully consider a story," notes one assignment editor at a Capital Cities/ABC television affiliate. "There's not sufficient planning—not sufficient time to do stories." All too often, journalists do not have "two days to report" a story and "two days to shoot it."[56]

CNN is the exception. As of midyear 1995, CNN had seventeen crews working out of the Washington bureau alone, doing eight to twelve stories a day. With CNN bureaus in twenty cities overseas and nine cities in the United States, with its news-sharing ties with more than 460 local stations in the United States alone (ones that may also have ABC, CBS, Fox, or PBS affiliation), and with the several versions of CNN in existence (CNN, CNN International, CNN Headline News, CNN Airport News, and CNN for Latin America), the Washington bureau grew fourfold between 1983 and 1995. The bureau now occupies two-and-a-half floors of a new building near Union Station.[57]

Writing about the 1992 presidential campaign, Democratic political consultant James Carville notes, "The real change in media coverage is the emerging power of CNN. CNN has become a very, very important player in presidential campaigns. *Headline News* as much as anything, but certainly CNN [N]ews more than the regular network news." Carville further observes,

> It used to be that the Associated Press had the real effect on campaign coverage. *The New York Times, The Washington Post* and the other majors are all morning papers, while the AP serviced afternoon papers with the

first take on breaking campaign events. They were the first story that other people in the media could see.

But there are fewer and fewer afternoon papers in the country, and CNN is on all day, every day . . . It's now become an article of faith that television is more important than print, so the first television [that reporters see in the afternoon] is CNN.[58]

CNN has changed political reporting, to be sure, but it stands in contrast to the other major news organizations in the United States, and few people watch it on a regular basis.

The imposition of tighter cost controls has also hurt investigative reporting. With fewer reporters on staff (and a low baseline of investigative reporters to start with), there are now only a "few bodies to turn over the rocks," remarks Howard Kurtz of the *Washington Post*. News organizations gamble if they send out a reporter to chase down a story that might not pan out, especially when news stories on some figures, such as a Newt Gingrich or a presidential candidate, are almost certain to make it into print or on the air. As one NBC producer explains, "Investigative reporting involves research, and we don't have the researchers or the time to dig, except on the most important stories."[59]

The decline in newsroom resources has dampened morale in the newsrooms of the three major broadcast networks. According to Kimball, the morale in the Washington bureaus of the three networks is "poor." ABC News, under the cost cutting of Capital Cities (and now Disney), closed its bureaus in Chicago, Atlanta, St. Louis, Miami, Denver, and San Francisco in the late 1980s; its employees are "paranoid" and their morale "terrible." NBC News, under GE, faces a corporate climate where "the pressure by GE is to improve profits," one correspondent remarks. "If you are a professional you feel despised." Other NBC employees note that "you lose your self-respect" in a climate where "nobody cares about quality anymore." At CBS News, "technicians were laid off just after stepping off the plane from Desert Storm and putting themselves at considerable risk." CBS employees say they find the atmosphere to be "unhappy" and that they no longer trust the network.[60]

In all fairness to the new television network executives, Auletta notes the almost incredible extravagance that existed at the networks before financial controls and a focus on the bottom line were imposed. For example, ABC spent $2,000 a week on food for *Good Morning, America* guests, had five private dining rooms, and had limousines available for top executives at all times. Auletta documents that many staff in the television news departments acted imperiously and were impervious to the changes necessary in the face of the declining network viewership and the heightened competition from cable television in general, the Fox network in particular, and the syndicated shows of independent broadcasters.[61]

Jack Welsh, the CEO of GE, asked NBC News executives, "How many stories that are covered actually get on the air? How often is each correspondent on? Why can't we save money by allowing some of the two hundred or so NBC-affiliated stations to cover stories?"[62] Why devote a network crew to a San Francisco or Shanghai office, for instance, if a local affiliate or independent news service can cover any breaking news?

The cost-cutting measures by news organizations have brought about a less centralized and controlled "news net." News organizations rely on a few domestic and foreign bureaus, on the wire services and other news services, on local affiliates, and on independent news contractors (in the case of television) or stringers (in the case of newspapers) to cover news beyond the nation's capital or overseas. The trend may be beneficial in that news companies are willing to go beyond their own organizations and usual affiliates to subscribe to more news services; they might therefore be able to review and present more of the news that is happening at any given time. But there is reason to believe that quality of the news nets has worsened and that there are fewer distinct nets out there to pick up the news from across the United States and from around the world.

An example comes from the *Wall Street Journal.* In the early 1990s, the *Journal* cut back on the number of its Washington editors, with the result that more unedited pieces went directly to New York.[63] Given the different values of the New York newsroom, which is more business oriented and less politically minded, the news stories coming out of Washington did not fare as well in the selection, editing, and layout process as they would have in the Washington bureau.

The American public and the quality of the policy process suffer from the imposition of cost cutting. Without the redundancy afforded by multiple reportage, which allows for comparison and different perspectives, there is a large potential loss of news quality. Moreover, it is not even clear that cost cutting pays; it may be penny-wise and pound-foolish. R. W. "Johnny" Apple, the *New York Times's* former Washington bureau chief, believes that the *Times* has flourished because it has not cut costs to the extent to which the other news organizations have and has therefore been able to keep reporters around and pursue serious stories when they come up. The current publisher of the *Washington Post,* Donald Graham, has also fought against the rising tide of cost cutting. Harwood notes that the *Post* still has tremendous resources (including about $1 million budgeted simply for journalists to take people out to lunch). Kurtz, too, believes that "least common denominator" journalism will fail and more substantive, more passionate reporting—although more costly in the short run—will be the surer path to long-term profits.[64]

In short, cost cutting by news organizations risks the loss of both the quantity and quality of domestic and foreign news.

Libel

The threat or actuality of libel is also an expensive part of the news business, especially for investigative (as opposed to political) reporting. The award of $8.75 million by a Miami jury in 1996 to a banker featured on ABC News's *20/20* is a case in point. Reporters and their editors and producers thus seek to avoid libel suits by following the formulas of objective reporting.[65] *U.S. News*'s Ranie points out,

> Libel is particularly something to worry about when you are an aggressive news organization like this one . . . But to the degree that you put a premium on investigative reporting, as we do, put a premium on getting information first, put a premium on analyzing it and getting behind the scenes and describing motives and stuff, yes, you are taking shots at people, [so] you have to make sure the shots are fair . . . The lawyer guys are worried about it all the time so you just have to make sure you are fair.[66]

The possibility of libel is now an important and inevitable dimension of TV news production as well: "by the late 1980s to the early 1990s, juries were finding against the media about 70 [percent] of the time," the media scholar Dean Alger notes, "although judges have tended to modify or even reverse a number of those verdicts."[67] Even when the news organizations win libel suits on technical grounds, as in the *General Westmoreland v. CBS* and the *Ariel Sharon v. Time* cases, legal action costs them millions of dollars and incalculable losses to their reputation. The consequence of the surge of actual and threatened libel suits is that much does not get publicized out of fear. Potentially troublesome stories routinely go to company lawyers, who are extremely reluctant to risk lawsuits, since even the frivolous ones might cost hundreds of thousands or millions of dollars.

News Corporations' Political Leverage

The scale and profitability of present-day news organizations mean that the media have enormous stakes in public policy. Changes in federal or state regulations, labor laws, or the tax code could greatly affect the sales or profitability of news corporations. The same applies to how federal and state courts interpret the law and how regulations are executed and enforced by the Federal Communications Commission (FCC). Therefore news organizations, like other business firms, try to influence the political system to their advantage. They take political action to mitigate the uncertainty of legislation, the interpretation and enforcement of regulations, or judicial rulings that might harm their interests. Media companies have several ways of influencing policy: financial contributions, lobbying, and the use of their own pages or programs for political ends.

Media companies have the power of the purse. They are able to contribute generously to individual campaigns, political parties, and trade associations. Time-Warner has a political action committee (PAC) in its own name, as does GE. Between 1985 and 1988, the National Association of Broadcasters (NAB), a television trade association, gave more than $300,000 and the National Cable Television Association more than a half million dollars to candidates for federal offices.[68] The top ten "communications and electronics" contributors in the 1991–1992 election cycle included the National Cable Television Association ($644,000), Time-Warner ($583,000), the NAB ($522,000), and Walt Disney ($402,000). The media/entertainment industry contributed $8 million, 32 percent in the form of PAC contributions (72% of which went to Democrats and 28% to Republicans) over the same period. The publishing industry, which includes newspaper and newsmagazine publishing, gave about $3 million, 15 percent from PACs and 55 percent to Democrats. These figures were either comparable to or larger than the political contributions of other industries and industrial sectors (to take the ten highest contributors as indicative), such as agriculture, construction, defense, energy, finance, insurance and real estate, health care, and transportation.[69]

Besides contributing funds, news companies lobby. During the debate over changing telecommunications law in the summer of 1995, the Dow Jones Company lobbied so that regulations protecting newspaper classified ads from other media would be maintained. The *Washington Post,* for its part, sought provisions in the telecommunications bill to favor the broadcast and cable interests of the Washington Post Company's subsidiary, Post-Newsweek.[70] According to Bagdikian, Katherine Graham, the chair of the board of the Washington Post Company and a former president of the American Newspaper Publishers Association, "lobbied personally for legal restrictions to prevent AT&T from competing with newspapers." He adds, "This is a normal activity for the head of any trade organization. She also spoke to the editorial writers and reporters covering the issue for the *Washington Post.* That, too, is normal for trade associations seeking public support. It is not normal that the lobbyist looking for media support is also the employer of the journalists being lobbied."[71]

Bagdikian also tells of when newspaper publishers were dependent on

President Richard Nixon's support for passage of the Newspaper Preservation Act, which would exempt the newspaper industry from antitrust regulations, in 1972 before the November elections. They got it, and after the law was passed, there was surprising silence on the Watergate story in most of the nation's newspapers, Bagdikian observes, despite Nixon's history of hostility to the press. Moreover, the president received the "highest percentage of newspaper endorsements in modern times" in his bid for reelection. Whereas in the previous three presidential administrations, a third of all Hearst papers, a third of all Cox papers, and half the Scripps-Howard papers had endorsed the Democratic candidate, "every Hearst paper, every Cox paper, and every Scripps-Howard paper endorsed Nixon" for reelection once the act passed.[72]

Political scientists Benjamin Page and James Snider make the case that television broadcast owners used both "overt bias" and "covert bias" to ensure their access to the free use of additional broadcast spectrum valued by the FCC at between $11 billion and $70 billion.[73] Snider and Page cite a letter from Nick Evans, a NAB board member, an elected member of the NAB TV board, and president of a television group with eleven stations—including four in Kansas—to Senator Robert Dole of Kansas, a 1996 presidential candidate:

> I hope you take this letter in the spirit for which it is written. It is in no way intended to be disrespectful of you or your position as one of our nation's leaders, and it is not a threat. I simply want to bring a very important issue to light and inform you of our position and intentions if forced to defend what I believe to be the survival and livelihood of free over-the-air television. Personally, I want to support you and vote for you for President. However, my support is waning . . . Your current stance and talk of auctioning [the] spectrum will destroy over-the-air television and America's local television station. I cannot—and will not—sit on the sidelines and allow this to happen. My American and Southern heritage will force me to fight for victory or go down swinging.

Evans then reminds Dole that his company "owns television stations in Kansas, Iowa, South Carolina, Georgia, and Florida" and that he has been a Republican and has personally met the senator. Evans continues,

> This is where the hard part comes into play. If over the next few days your position on the spectrum has not changed and been made public, you will have lost my support. I will be forced to use our resources to tell the viewers in all of our markets of your plan to destroy free over-the-air television. I will be forced to tell the over 700 employees of our company of

your plan and encourage their support of another Presidential candidate. I have spoken with many other broadcasters who feel the same as I do. Without speaking for them, I know that they are making the same plans that I am, while wishing and hoping that they can support your race for the Presidency . . . I believe the spectrum is important to the American people. I hope you will reconsider your views and position. Providing broadcasters a smooth transition to digital is not "corporate welfare." It is good business and a necessity for the American consumer and local broadcasters. My plan is to start our campaign against spectrum auctions and its supporters in the next ten days . . . I hope that you will find a way to be with us so that we can be with you.[74]

Although the extent of NAB cooperation Evans actually had is difficult to know exactly (direct evidence of a jointly organized broadcaster threat is difficult to obtain), the circumstantial evidence is revealing. The NAB board met a week before the letter was delivered to Dole, and Evans, an established member of the board and one with local interests in the key Iowa (and Kansas) markets, was the perfect person to deliver such a message, given the upcoming Iowa caucuses on February 12, 1996. The NAB also maintains a governmental affairs office that keeps contact with its members in each state, runs a toll-free hotline just for congressional contacts, and requests that copies of all congressional correspondence be sent to its headquarters. Two weeks earlier, Dennis Wharton reported in *Daily Variety* that broadcasters were "preparing a grass-roots lobbying campaign to torpedo Dole's digital TV plans. One not-so-subtle strategy call was for TV station execs in key presidential primary states such as New Hampshire to remind the GOP presidential frontrunner of the importance of passing the telecom bill." Shortly thereafter, Wharton left his job at *Daily Variety* to become the spokesperson for the NAB. One week later, Dole caved. He kept the spectrum issue out of the campaign and allowed the telecommunications bill to pass with the spectrum giveaway provision intact.[75]

The very way that the news is communicated (e.g., headlines, layout, and choice of sources), as well as the presence of news editorials, enables media companies to speak to members of the executive branch and Congress and the interested public as no other social actor—political party or other industry—can. In the *Washington Post's* battle against legislation that would have allowed AT&T to set up an electronic Yellow Pages, for instance, the newspaper competed through editorial content as well as through lobbying.[76]

Editor and critic Carlin Romano of the *Philadelphia Inquirer* illustrates how a news organization, in this case the *New York Times,* may influence politics and public policy both in Washington, D.C., and around the country. The *Times* would not admit that it looked favorably on real estate (and media) executive Mort Zuckerman, and it did not report on its support of New York City's controversial Westway road project or the fact that Pulitzer Prize–winning Sydney Schanberg was relieved of his editorial column when he criticized the *Times* for its Westway coverage. Nor did the newspaper acknowledge its favorable treatment of a federal judge who was "a strong advocate of freedom of the press," says Romano. The journalist Tom Goldstein comments that he "was forbidden to write about . . . the close relationship between Irving Kaufman, a Federal Appeals Court Judge, and the *Times* . . . The *Times* flattered him in its news columns and frequently had him write for the paper. The tightness of the bond was well known to many leading lawyers."[77]

Unfortunately, there is little systematic reporting or scholarship on the explicit or implicit editorial positions of news organization (in contrast to studies of the politics and attributes of individual members of the news media). Nor is media corporations' lobbying of members of Congress and the White House much publicized. Even so, as a chair of the House Subcommittee on Communications (and a former journalist) observes, "Every member of Congress is familiar with the special power of broadcasters and publishers. They can make or break you." Arizona Senator John McCain remarks that the NAB "is the most powerful lobby I've run into." A Wall Street investment analyst advised that there were two reasons to buy media company stocks: "profitability" and "influence."[78]

IN SUM, THE MAJOR MEDIA FACE SERIOUS UNCERTAINTIES WITH RE-spect to their economic performance: their dependence on advertisers and, to a less degree, the revenues from their paying audiences of readers and viewers (viewers who may subscribe to cable television), their concern over the internal costs of news production (given the expenses incurred by news operations), the possibility of (expensive) libel suits, and the probability that legislative and regulatory initiatives could have serious effects on present and future profitability. The vested interests that CEOs, publishers, other executives, editors, producers, reporters, and others have in their firm's economic performance make these uncertainties all the worse. Media personnel therefore lobby and attempt to otherwise influence elected politicians, regulatory agencies, judges, other interested parties, and voters to achieve desired policy outcomes.

The news media's commercial operations considerably affect their coverage of important political and economic news. This is evident in the advertising they carry for corporate image and issue-related messages, and for particular products, and in their increased use of market journalism. The commercial existence of news organizations further intrudes on news production in the form of pervasive cost cutting to raise profits. Here, too, the politics in Washington and around the country may be affected by the bottom-line pressures faced by the news media. The existence and threat of libel suits against news organizations—with fundamental bottom-line effects—has further impact on what news ultimately gets printed or broadcast. In short, the huge commercial stakes of the media companies mean that the news media, like other large corporate or societal entities, engage in political action to protect or further their own positions. The effect of the profit motive on news production once more points to the news media's institutional existence.

Not surprisingly, news organizations have developed standard practices by which to handle the commercial pressures on them.

Media Practices

Journalists and news executives have a number of set practices by which to stabilize their positions as journalists and news executives in the commercial marketplace. I focus on a few practices in particular: the lip-service paid to the "wall of separation" between editorial decisions and financial decisions at news organizations, the monitoring of audience preferences, the media's coverage of soft news rather than hard news, the widespread introduction of cost controls, and the distinction made by news organizations between economic or financial news and political news.

The Wall of Separation

One informal norm is the ostensible separation of editorial decisions from financial matters. Reporters, bureau chiefs, and midlevel editors and producers are supposed to keep economic concerns, with the exception of cost controls, separate from their reporting. Indeed, in most instances when reporters produce stories critical of advertisers—stories that could presumably affect the economic viability of news organizations—the stories are nonetheless published or broadcast. But smart reporters, wary editors and producers, and savvy news executives (interested in getting their stories printed or on the air) learn to avoid such stories in the future.[79]

At higher levels, the wall of separation crumbles. The "final responsibility" for newspaper content now, with few exceptions, "rests with the business executive in charge of the company, not the editor," reports James Squires, a former editor of the *Chicago Tribune*.[80] The rising influence of business specialists in news organizations is evident in the careers of such persons as Walt Mattson of the *New York Times* in the late 1980s and early 1990s, or the current publisher of the *Los Angeles Times*, Mark Willes, a business executive hired from General Mills in 1995. Conversely, William Kovach, "an apostle of tough reporting and investigative journalism" as well as an "excellent manager of people," as Edwin Diamond describes him, left his position as Washington bureau chief of the *New York Times* to become editor of the *Atlanta Journal-Constitution*. He then resigned his Atlanta editorship. In both New York and Atlanta, Kovach's news-driven journalism was "not the direction that his bosses wanted to go."[81] Except at the reporter level, the wall of separation has virtually collapsed at the big three television networks, the newsmagazines, and the national and largest regional newspapers.

But the nominal wall of separation is a comparatively recent phenomenon, anyway. Underwood writes that "it was in the 1950s, 1960s and particularly in the 1970s that newspaper after newspaper began to fully professionalize its operations . . . Newspapers that aspired to national stature were no longer run as playthings of their publishers. [And] advertisers seldom controlled content—at least not in the blatant fashion of the past." A former network news executive says he refused to be in the same room as his company's audience researchers; an executive producer for one of the networks says he had a similar policy of "no contact" with market researchers.[82]

Market Research

A second standard practice among news organizations is the widespread introduction of market-driven research: newspapers, newsmagazines, and television broadcasters (both network and local) rely on reader and viewer surveys, focus groups, and consulting firms to learn their audience's preferences. News organizations now determine the day-to-day changes in their desired audience's tastes, socioeconomic standing, and spending habits.

Indeed, the networks and their affiliates are able to get overnight ratings on their performances from the day before, even though the weekly figures and the February, May, and November "sweeps" (when television audiences are measured) matter more. As one television executive puts it, "It's a business tailor-made for competitive human beings . . . Just think about it: you get a little fix every morning when the national overnight ratings come in at 8:30." Virtually all television stations and newspapers with circulations of more than 10,000 have in-house reader/viewer research capability at present, according to one report.[83]

Although the adoption of market-gauging techniques by news organizations was preceded by the use of consulting firms, assistance from trade journals, and the establishment of professional associations for editors, marketers, publishers, and circulation managers, Underwood points to the American Press Institute as being at the "hub of this web." Built in 1974 in Reston, Virginia, for $2.6 million, the institute "is a veritable mecca for editors and other newspaper executives seeking immersion in the latest industry management techniques." The center's "menu of seminars in 1988—the year the marketing and management revolution was beginning to be felt in the furthest corners of the industry—included ones dealing with newspaper design and graphics, the development of management skills, marketing the daily newspaper, management and costs, newspaper production and new technology, human resources management, and cross-training programs for nonnews executives in news-editorial management."[84]

Inclusion of Soft News

A third now-standard media practice is the inclusion of softer, more audience-friendly stories. Television news programs are now expected to close with human-interest or soft-news stories (like the newsmagazines' back-of-the-book sections). Newspapers are expected to offer writing that is funny or light and to use color, bold graphics, and attractive layouts to hold their readers' interest—the "USA Today-ization" of newspapers, Underwood calls it.[85] No major news organization, including the New York Times or the Wall Street Journal, has escaped this trend. Cronkite complains, "I am disturbed, as a matter of fact, by the tendency of the New York Times today to featurize the front page of the newspaper . . . I just wish that the newspapers would stick to giving us the news and let the entertainment . . . leave that to the television networks."[86]

Again, there are precedents. Most significant for the newspaper industry was the case of Al Neuharth and Gannett. In the early 1980s, Neuharth and Gannett bought family-owned newspapers at a premium and then reformatted their newsrooms, news production, and other operations. Neuharth was able to generate profit margins between 25 and 40 percent. The flagship paper of Gannett, USA Today, "is the quintessential product of modern corporation media engineering," reports Underwood, founded after exhaustive research showing that Gannett executives should seek out "a mobile, active, well-paid, well-educated, largely male audience." Almost everything about USA Today was geared to take advantage of the latest in marketing research and communications technology, and the newspaper has had as much of an effect on newsroom management as it has had on news content. Despite reports that former Washington Post editor Ben Bradlee and other prominent editors and publishers have openly scorned USA Today and publicly snubbed

Neuharth, the lessons of *USA Today* in marketing and news presentation have come to dominate newsrooms across the country—even those in New York City and Washington, D.C.[87]

The example in television news was set by NBC when it introduced "Segment 3" of its *Nightly News* in the fall of 1977. "Segment 3" established the daily presence of a five-minute back-of-the-book feature on network newscasts. Although previously the TV networks had usually featured soft news at the end of their evening news, on some days the soft-news feature did not make it on the air because of the judged newsworthiness of the hard news. "Segment 3" incorporated the lengthy soft-news feature as an everyday part of the network news and allowed NBC News—soon to be imitated by CBS News and ABC News—to promote the soft-news segment days before it ran. Henceforth the hard news, not the soft-news feature, would be cut back.[88]

Cost Controls

A fourth practice adopted throughout news organizations—and one integral to the application of efficiency standards and cost-benefit analysis to newsrooms—is the introduction of cost controls. Even the richest and most profitable news organizations no longer allow their personnel to travel as freely and expensively as they had in the past. The "golden age" of television and print media (which were almost as unmindful of costs as NBC had been before its takeover by GE) is over. The most prominent examples of cost cutting are the takeovers of the three major TV networks and the new procedures introduced by Gannett under Al Neuharth.[89]

Distinction between Economic and Political News

A different practice common among news organizations is the peculiar construction of the economics beat, also called the "business" or "financial" beat. It is a low-prestige beat, for one, considered dull and complex by most journalists. And if journalists believe business news to be dull and complex, their reading and viewing audiences will also likely think it dull and complex. Elie Abel, the former dean of the School of Journalism at Columbia University, finds business and economics reporting to be "the most disgracefully neglected sector of American journalism."[90] The economist and former journalist Richard Parker elaborates: business sections

> have surprisingly standard organizational form, despite ever-changing stories. They typically consume a third to half their space (or more) simply publishing financial tables—reporting the activity of stock exchanges, mutual funds, and bond, currency and commodity markets for the previous day. Descriptive reporting concentrates on large, publicly

traded corporations, both local and national—their mergers and acqui-
sitions, quarterly sales data, personnel changes, new product announcements (and, occasionally, legal troubles). Added to that are government
reports—routine announcements of economic data series (unemploy-
ment, housing starts, inflation, trade, etc.), Fed activities, and the like.[91]

Parker observes that although economics coverage (including coverage of
media corporations) has improved, labor issues receive only marginal news
coverage, and "consumer reform-oriented and public interest group-gener-
ated stories are down markedly from the 1970s." Indeed, a recent study of
the news industry shows economic news coverage to be "deeply problem-
atic" for reasons of financial reporters' poor economic training, low experience levels, relatively high reliance on press releases (compared to reporters
overall), and low morale.[92] This is consistent with the lack of investigative
reporting of the corporate world, noted earlier.

Coverage of politics, government, and public policy is curiously divided
for the most part from coverage of economic news, even though the economic news might be every bit as important, if not more important, in its
impact on everyday lives. A staff reporter for the *Washington Post* agrees that
there is a "real wall" between politics and economics reporting. "Those of us
who can converse in both languages are unusual."[93] This division between
economic news and political news is characteristic of most news organizations, of course, not just the *Washington Post*.

In short, business news—including news of media companies—under-
emphasize the political dimensions of economic policy and poorly trans-
lates economics for a general audience. This tendency has been in evidence
for the last half-century, finds Parker. A limited number of audience "frames"
guide viewers and readers through the economic thickets, frames for understanding the political economy that have been relatively consistent
throughout the post–World War II era.[94]

To summarize, the myth of the wall of separation between news organizations' editorial content and financial matters, the monitoring of media
markets with the goal of matching editorial and programming content (and
therefore audiences) with advertisers, the turn toward soft and "feature-y"
news (and away from serious news), the decreasing resources available to reporters, editors, and producers, and the skewed coverage of economic, business, and financial news are media practices found throughout the contemporary United States. These processes and conventions of news
production in relation to the commerce of news production are shared by
the television and print media. Their pervasive presence further suggests the
unity of the news media.

Conclusion

All businesses face challenges, but those faced by the news media are particularly acute. They include the instability of revenues derived from the production of a short-lived and volatile commodity (i.e., the content and programming of newspapers, newsmagazines, and television), the need to create a product that appeals to desired audiences (and therefore is desirable to advertisers), the difficulty of curtailing in-house expenses in an industry with personnel who are difficult to monitor and produce an ephemeral product (news), the possibility of libel suits, and the existence of legislative and regulatory processes where new (or differently interpreted or implemented) laws and regulations may seriously affect the commercial performance of news organizations. All other things being equal, the larger the corporation, the more plentiful the shareholders (both individual and institutional), the greater the number of executives and employees with stock ownership (or stock options), the bigger the debt, and the greater the pressure on company managers.

The pressure on news organizations to reduce daily news expenses is all the more serious in view of the fact that special coverage (e.g., a war or extended congressional hearings) may cost millions of dollars for a newspaper or newsmagazine, and possibly tens of millions of dollars for a television network. If these events have to be covered, given their news value and civic significance, they put even greater pressure on the regular news. "The competitive pressures are so enormous now," remarks Marvin Kalb, the former chief diplomatic correspondent for CBS News and moderator on *Meet the Press.* "I cannot stress enough how tense a newsroom is on a Tuesday morning when the [weekly] ratings come in . . . When the ratings go up, the joy is palpable . . . And if your ratings go up it tends to erase any doubts you might have had about broadcast done that week . . . The networks have always been concerned about profits, but it is more intense now."[95]

With news collection being expensive—television network news divisions cost from $200 million to $300 million a year—the economics of the news business may force media corporations to heed hard news even less. According to Kimball, moreover, federal regulators seem less concerned at present about provision of the news for the "public interest, convenience and necessity" per the Federal Communication Act of 1934 (a relaxing of rules sought by media companies, of course). The concern is now "how the FCC can help preserve 'free TV' against the competitive assault of cable television and liberate the networks from restrictions on producing and syndicating the entertainment shows that they heretofore had been required to buy from independent producers."[96]

A further concern is the greater likelihood of conflicts of interest both within a single (extended) firm and across companies (with interlocking directorships and possible alliances), given the smaller number of media companies in existence. *Time*, for instance, did not report on its parent company's purchase of Warner Communications (the editor said he feared the magazine would appear to be promoting the merger). Later, *Time* featured Warner Brothers movies on its cover (both are parts of Time-Warner, of course). Nor did the magazine refrain from excerpting large sections of former Secretary of State Henry Kissinger's memoirs and putting Kissinger on its cover after the publication of the memoirs by Time-Warner's Little, Brown publishing house. Time-Warner also owns the Book-of-the-Month Club, which made the memoirs a main selection.[97] Even if all of these decisions were made in good faith, the appearance of conflicts of interests is obvious. Media concentration makes such synergies possible and all the more profitable. At the very least, the perception of such conflicts of interest damages the credibility of news organizations.

Additional conflicts of interest are probable in the reporting of foreign news. Veteran TV correspondent Garrick Utley gives some disturbing examples about the implications of news organizations' commercial pressures in reporting on China:

- Disney's Michael Eisner spoke about the synergies possible with the ownership of Capital Cities / ABC: "China, India and other places . . . do not want to accept programming that has any political content. But they have no problem with sports, and they have no problem with Disney kind of programming." But political content, as Utley points out, "is what much of news coverage is about, at ABC or anywhere else."[98]
- China forced NBC to apologize for the following comment that sports commentator Bob Costas made about China during the Olympic Games in Atlanta: "Every economic power including the United States wants to tap into that huge potential market, but of course there are problems with human rights, property rights disputes, the threat posed to Taiwan." A month later, NBC issued its apology for "any resulting hurt feelings . . . The comments were not based on NBC beliefs. Nobody at NBC ever intends to offend anyone."[99]
- Rupert Murdoch purchased Hong Kong's Star TV satellite system in July 1993; Star TV also carried BBC World, the British international television news service. However, because Chinese authorities did not want the BBC's coverage entering China from Hong Kong, Murdoch dropped the BBC from Star.[100]

Conflicts of interest for media corporations also come from interlocks between boards of directors, which are more prevalent when the number of corporations in any one industrial sector shrinks. The media critic Peter Dreier finds "24 news organizations with 447 ties with business organizations, mostly outside directors brought onto newspaper boards." The nation's "'top' newspapers—the *New York Times,* the *Washington Post,* the *Los Angeles Times,* and the *Wall Street Journal*—have the largest number of industry ties."[101] The potential conflicts of interest are obvious.

A CLOSE LOOK AT THE ECONOMICS OF THE NEWS DISPELS THE POPUlar myth that there is a free market of newspapers, newsmagazines, and television channels in which news organizations thrive because they meet the demands of their readers and viewers—and would go out of business if they did not. The truth is that the audience does *not* get what it wants. As long as about three-fourths of newspaper revenues, half of magazine revenues, all of television income, and much of cable revenues come from advertising, the media market is *not* a market where the audience's political news demands are being met by the supply of editorial content. Rather, it is one where news organizations match audiences (determined by their revealed programming and editorial choices) with advertisers (who buy space in a newspaper or magazine or on a television program); it is not the reader or viewer as voter and citizen who determines the economic viability of news organizations, but the reader or viewer as a *potential consumer* of particular goods and services whom the advertisers reach through particular editorial or programming content. The economic basis of the news (with large distinctions among audiences and in audience buying power) is fundamentally distinct from the egalitarian politics of one person equaling one vote.

McManus elaborates on the point that the supply of political news does not match the audience's demand. Citizens are unable to make informed choices about the news they consume because they cannot know whether news stories are in fact accurate or fair (since the news is, precisely that, "new") and because they cannot easily evaluate whether the news of a day's issues and events is, in actuality, the most pressing news (since there is no master list of news with which to compare the news people receive, and a monitoring of all the news stories available would be "extremely burdensome"). Nor is it practical for the overwhelming number of citizens to monitor other media and collect information independently of the one or two sources on which they typically rely.[102]

The news is what economists call a "credence good": a product that has to be consumed on faith, since it is difficult for the customer to evaluate the quality of the commodity, *even after he or she has consumed it.* Medical treatment, automobile and appliance repairs, and a liberal arts education are other examples of credence goods: consumers are typically unable to distinguish high-quality products from low-quality ones at the point of consumption and for a short while thereafter. Individuals cannot inspect the news (unless they are there, in person), and most of the news is beyond their experience (thus they rarely have a real-world comparison for evaluation). They therefore depend on reputation and comparative advantage.

The fact that news is a credence good means that news organizations have considerable latitude in deciding what news to present, subject to their competitive situation, of course. News organizations accordingly define the news largely as the news that sells best: they seek breadth of appeal. News that is rational to produce for commercial reasons (e.g., the O. J. Simpson trial, crime in general, natural disasters, and other sensational stories) can be presented and to some extent accepted as genuinely serious current events. The result, however, is that news sellers are in a position to take advantage of their audience of readers and viewers, who can be misled in the short term.

Known instances of news organizations' misrepresentations that were not corrected until after the important events had occurred include Senator McCarthy's charges of communist infiltration of the U.S. government, President Nixon's denial of Watergate and his bombing of Cambodia, and the quality and degree of the U.S. government's engagement in El Salvador, Guatemala, and Nicaragua, among other countries (see Chapter 6). As McManus summarizes, "The overlap of market and journalistic norms is too small to generate a sufficient volume of the quality of news healthy self-government requires."[103]

As long as advertising supports most of the cost of printing and distributing newspapers, all the cost of "free television," about half the cost of magazines, and a major portion of cable revenues, news organizations will flourish to the extent that they attract the readers and viewers desired by advertisers. These commercially attractive audiences, skewed with respect to income, education, and ethnicity, are unrepresentative of the American population. In tending "to be oriented toward the more affluent," the media stimulate political participation primarily among the more affluent. The advertising subsidy—"subsidy" since the audience does not pay the full cost of the news content—also "quite likely depresses the comparative political participation of the poor."[104] As a result, the subsidy of the news that advertising provides distributes news in a less egalitarian manner than would an open-market system of supply and demand for political news not subsidized by advertisers. Indicative of the possible discrepancy between what viewers and advertisers want on the news is the television coverage of the Persian Gulf War. The war coverage was at once highly rated (a large proportion of the public followed the war both on television and in print) and extremely costly: the big three television networks lost hundreds of millions of dollars on the coverage, because corporate sponsors did not want to run commercial advertisements during the Persian Gulf War.[105]

Why, then, do audiences stay with the news? One reason is that they have little choice if they wish to stay somewhat informed and there is a credible area of intersection between market norms and journalistic values. (The news media do not always pander to profitability: many journalists, from reporters to top editors and producers, work diligently at trying to include serious news where and when they can, as I show in Chapter 5.) Another reason is that individuals may tolerate and even be attracted to much of the sensational material in the news because they are weak-willed: they know what political information is better for them but often fall short of acting on that knowledge. Classic examples of weakness of will (leaving aside the element of chemical addiction) are destructive habits such as smoking and drinking.[106] It may be that individuals want both the hard news of politics as well as the soft news of sports and sex appeal but at any one point in time default to the entertaining and titillating. This does not necessarily mean that audiences want to forsake serious news or have higher overall preference for soft news than for hard news.

The upshot is that advertisers' subsidy of the news is not a "free good." It extracts a serious price on the content of newspapers, newsmagazines, and television news. "There is even a word for consciously selling influence to the advertiser and simultaneously selling purity to the consumer," Edwin Baker remarks. "Fraud." News organizations "purport to give the reader an untainted product under circumstances in which it is difficult for the reader to identify the deception."[107]

THE CHALLENGE BEFORE THE AMERICAN MEDIA "IS NOT TO STAY IN business—it is to stay in journalism," says former journalist Harold Evans. Though the business of the news media is neither easy nor inconsequential, the concern for financial performance has become so dominant that journalism gets neglected for the sake of company profitability.[108] Edward Wyliss Scripps, the founder of the Scripps-Howard newspaper chain, described the duty of journalism as to "comfort the afflicted and afflict the comfortable." A story told by Tim Russert, NBC News's Washington bureau chief, suggests that journalism now does the opposite: When the stock market crashed in 1929, the newspaper reporters at the *Boston Globe* cheered; when the market crashed in 1987, they all ran and called their stockbrokers.[109]

NBC News, for instance, has little sense of "public obligation," reports

Auletta; the network is nothing other than part of GE. "Journalistic responsibility" means nothing to the television networks. An executive at one of the large advertising firms concedes as much: "A network is not in the program business. It's not in the news business or the sports business. It's in the business of selling advertising." The CNN Washington bureau chief concurs that "ratings count more than all of us would like." David Shribman, the *Boston Globe*'s Washington bureau chief, acknowledges, "We are a business."[110]

The former *Washington Post* correspondent Don Oberdorfer comes to a grim conclusion about the condition of the American news media:

> The business of journalism seems to be impinging on the basic functions of journalism in a way that is ultimately dangerous to journalism and perilous to the public interest. Across a broad spectrum of news organizations, the balance between the bottom line and professional news judgments, between journalism's private and public functions, has been tilting toward the forces of the marketplace and maximum return and away from the newsrooms and broadcast studios—and the public interest.[111]

It may be only a slight exaggeration to say, as Kimball notes, that "what is going on . . . is a redefinition of the news, driven by financial considerations and ratings."[112]

Yet the news industry is the only industry with constitutional protection (with the possible exception of firearms manufacturers under the protection of the Second Amendment). Although the First Amendment has arguably served this nation well, one has to wonder about the legitimacy of news organizations' rights "to put vending machines on public streets and in airports, . . . to sit in courtrooms, . . . to see public records, to question the president, [and] to have a front-row seat at the war" if the news is *not* produced in the public interest, if circulation and viewership are being deliberately restricted, if commercial considerations rather than issues or substance drive editorial and programming content, and if news companies exert less effort (and spend fewer resources) to provide news from across the country and from around the world. One may wonder if the First Amendment has become little more than a fig leaf for money making.[113]

ORGANIZATIONAL NEWS, ORDERED NEWS

When on rare occasions, he takes time to review his many mandates, the Washington correspondent is apt to be overwhelmed. His preparation of the news cannot help but be conditioned by the audiences for whom he is writing. Amid competitive and ofttimes contradictory pressures he must somehow achieve skillful equilibrium. And he must do it, quite frequently, in a white heat of creativity, while the waiting presses set the one unyielding pressure.—Douglass Cater, The Fourth Branch of Government, 1959

The essence of a professional man is that he is answerable for his professional conduct only to his professional peers . . . But a journalist still lingers in the twilight zone, along with the trained nurse, the embalmer, the rev. clergy and the great majority of engineers. He cannot sell his services directly to the consumer, but only to entrepreneurs, and so those entrepreneurs have the power of veto over all his soaring fancies . . . His codes of ethics are all right so long as they do not menace newspaper profits; . . . what he faces is not a client but a boss.—H. L. Mencken, Journalism in America, 1919

BECAUSE OF THE UNCERTAINTIES INHERENT IN COVERING POLITICAL contests, accessing political figures and political information, and successfully selling the news as a commodity, the news media are much more restricted in their production of the news than might be thought. The fact that reporters and their bosses have to maintain relationships with politicians, officials, advertisers, and audiences has important effects on the persons and processes of the American political system. This channeling and structuring of politics are accomplished through the practices that journalists and news organizations use to stabilize their positions within their larger environment.

But the problem of coordination remains unresolved: What explains the congruence or consistency of the news media's coverage of political contests and the political economy? How does the cautious coverage of big business or the State Department mesh with the aggressive coverage of presidential candidates and Supreme Court nominees? How do the many practices of news production described in Chapters 2, 3, and 4—for example, horse race news coverage and the separation of political news from economic news— aggregate into a consistent set of media practices? In short, how do we get a single institution out of the effects and practices noted in the preceding chapters?

One way is hierarchy. News stories are the product of reporters and tiers of editors or producers, publishers, and news executives. The hierarchy of news organizations allows the news to be produced in a deliberate fashion, even in the "white heat" (as Cater calls it) of impending deadlines. A second reason for the consistency and congruency of news production among the various media is the fact that political communication takes place within an essentially small world. Political news is typically of, by, and for a small set of players in Washington and in specific policy circles, including politicians, press officers, public relations consultants, and other journalists and news executives. A third way that the complexity of political reality reduces to the same few stories and story lines is the cue taking, or use of reference groups, by editors, publishers, and news executives, as described in Chapter 3. A fourth way the news is produced consistently is the use of multivocal news conventions, which are able to resolve simultaneously the uncertainties of journalists' three relationships in the interorganizational field of political communication: their relationships to competing political actors, those with a policy monopoly of the news, and those responsible for the financial performance of the news organization.[1] And the fact that the news is produced in hierarchical news organizations means that a few persons are in a position to insist that certain news practices be followed and to determine news coverage of salient political issues. After discussing these four means by which consistency is achieved among the news media, I conclude the chapter with a reappraisal of the news media as a political institution.

Hierarchical News Making

Out of the complexity and ambiguity of politics, journalists have to come up with comprehensible, accessible, and, if possible, familiar stories for the nightly, daily, or weekly news. Producing the news "involves choosing and ordering the significant aspects of the data collected about an assigned target," observes Edward Jay Epstein (who studied news production at NBC, CBS, and ABC), given that "surrounding almost any happening is a confusing, confounding blur of information. The journalist—who seldom, if ever, witnesses the entire event—must reconstruct it from a welter of conflicting assertions, fragments of evidence, and possibly some eyewitness accounts." Before information can become news, a reporter has "to at least pretend to make sense out of what he or she is reporting, convincing his or her editor or producer that sense has been made of it. Intelligibility comes first."[2]

The signposts are clearer in other professions, remarks a producer at one of the television networks. In medicine, for instance, the signposts of medical school, internships, and specialization are well marked and acknowledged. The "news is just not that way"; the "definitive signposts" not there. Instead, the news production process is "capricious" and "subject to circumstance." There is uncertainty about both what the news exactly is, and what it means, as Leon Sigal points out.[3] It is up to editors, producers, and their bosses to manage the news process, that is, to make sense of the news and present it to the public.

A news organization is a hierarchy (as Mencken points out in the epigraph to this chapter), and not a collection of professionals, such as lawyers in a law office, stockbrokers in a brokerage house, or architects in a design firm, each with his or her own clients and accounts. Rather, the news media consist of large, multitiered organizations in which top editors and producers fashion the news they want. They edit news stories, place stories in the newspaper or news program as they see fit, and release stories when they decide to. They may also spike (i.e., reject) the work of a reporter or lower-level editor or put a story on hold until a slow news day or the right news peg comes around.[4]

It is up to the top editors and senior producers—and, ultimately, the publishers and company executives—to make the final decisions, even if in each medium they may have to compromise with their reporters and lower-level editors or producers on deciding what the news is. As Herbert Gans finds from his study of CBS News, NBC News, *Time,* and *Newsweek,* "Because news organizations are assembly lines on which people must work together to manufacture a product against a deadline, they almost always generate conformity . . . insofar as news judgment is filled with uncertainty, and top editors must, by virtue of their position, resolve uncertainty and decide which considerations have priority, they also set tones, and sometimes precedents, which then require conformity."[5] The conformity is established by the top editors, who in turn receive their cues from publishers and news executives.[6] These few run the assembly line.

Socialized Reporters

Reporters are not independent observers of the political scene, then, but employees of complex organizations who see their copy go through layers of editors, including occasionally the managing editor and possibly the executive editor. One veteran TV network reporter says his work had to pass through "two, three, four" producers every day in order for it to be cleared—but such layering is characteristic of all the major networks.[7] At the *Wall Street Journal*, to use another example, "more than half the stories proposed for the front or back page are rejected."[8] The newsmagazines, for their part, get far more copy than they can use in any one issue, and their reporters usually have their work rewritten by their section editors and possibly senior editors.

Accordingly, reporters learn what kind of news stories, especially when they are covering salient political and economic issues, will pass through the several screens and be published or publicized. The ability to write compelling stories that get published or broadcast is a developed skill acquired over years of being on the job. The *Wall Street Journal's* John Fialka estimates that it takes four to five years of training for a reporter to "catch on" at newspapers such as the *Journal* or the *Washington Post*. "In the beginning it [story generation] is always top-down. But once you catch on in the business it should be 60 to 80 percent bottom-up."[9] In fact, bureau chiefs, editors, and top reporters at the *Journal*, the *Post*, and the *New York Times* note that they use about 95 percent of their reporters' final copy—a fact that testifies to the learning skills, intelligence, and ambition of their reporters.[10]

Print and broadcast journalists who rate their organizations as "excellent" are "more likely to value media staff for cues on the definition of the news" than are those who rate their organization less highly, media researchers David Weaver and Cleveland Wilhoit report. Reporters, especially younger reporters, pick up what they need to know to get published or broadcast from their editors and producers, respectively, as well as from their colleagues. If reporters are to get ahead, they need the approval and respect of their bosses, and thus successful reporters have to embrace the difficulties and even contradictions of journalism.[11] Even the most talented journalists, who are able to quickly translate and interpret the complexity of political life into accessible news stories while under immense pressure, learn how to "routinize their task to make it manageable," observes Gans. Indicatively, Doyle McManus, now the Washington bureau chief of the *Los Angeles Times*, remarks that he wrote more to "hit editors' buttons" than he did for his peers, sources, or reading audience.[12]

The News of News Executives

Those in charge of the news thus decide what is newsworthy. Top editors, producers, publishers, and news executives are responsible for the continued viability of their news organization; reporters and low-level editors and producers are not. The top executives cannot let their news organization simply report "what happened," but have to be aware of their organization's larger stakes.

For TV producers, the day is "a constant meeting," says the former Washington bureau chief of CNN. "There is constant dialogue between the production side and the assignment side." It starts from the moment "we walk in in the morning and it ends when we walk out at night." In the morning there is a large editorial meeting with Washington and New York on the phone with Atlanta (CNN headquarters), during which participants consult a 20-page document on everything CNN is covering. Yet "there will be stories that Atlanta management feels so strongly should be aired, because of their news value, that there will be a mandate. Usually it's not necessary because stories of that caliber stick out anyway. They are going to get run."[13]

Although CNN may be the extreme case because it provides around-the-clock news, editors and producers in all news organizations have to work out what they think the news is. At the *Wall Street Journal,* editors talk individually with each other and in conference, usually twice a day, to select the news that will come out the following morning.[14] The *New York Times, Washington Post, Los Angeles Times,* and most other newspapers have two scheduled editorial meetings a day, typically one in the late morning and the other in the midafternoon or late afternoon, for the purpose of deciding what to publish and where in the paper to put it.

Top editors look for certain things. One is drama. In the words of Reuven Frank, former NBC president and executive producer of NBC Evening News, "Every news story should, without any sacrifice of probity or responsibility, display the attributes of fiction, of drama. It should have structure and conflict, problem and denouement, rising action and falling action, a beginning, a middle, and an end. These are not only the essentials of drama; they are the essentials of narrative."[15] With 50 percent of Americans relying on television for most of their news (24% rely on newspapers and 14% on the radio), and television being the more trusted medium,[16] the values of video, which are emotional and personal appeal, increasingly dominate over the values of print, which are reflection and dispassion. Even newspapers and newsmagazines choose dramatic news stories and respond to the video media, since it is television that interprets politics for most Americans. Reporters are "filmmakers" as the media scholar John McManus puts it, with the imperative to simplify and to communicate as concisely, cogently and emotionally as possible.[17] The job of producers and, increasingly, editors is to make the news into entertainment, in which drama is the "defining characteristic of the news."[18]

Elaborating on news executives' and producers' assumptions, Epstein explains that one assumption is that "viewers' interest is most likely to be maintained through easily recognizable and palpable images, and conversely, most likely to be distracted by unfamiliar or confusing images." In addition, since the evening news airs at dinnertime, children may be watching. Accordingly, "cameramen, correspondents and editors are instructed to seek out and select pictures that have an almost universal meaning. Hence stories tend to fit into a limited repertory of images, which explains why so often shabbily dressed children symbolically stand for poverty; uniformed police symbolically stand for authority; fire symbolically for destruction, and so forth." A second assumption is that conflict is more compelling than placidity: "News events showing a violent confrontation between two easily recognizable sides in conflict—for example, blacks versus whites, uniformed police versus demonstrators, or military versus civilians—are preferable to ones in which the issues are less easily identifiable. However, even when the conflict involves confusing elements, it usually can be reconstructed in the form of a two-sided conflict." A third assumption is that viewers' span of attention is limited but may be prolonged by action.[19]

Producers' values also influence the mix of stories presented in the news. NBC News's John Dancy explains,

> The producer looks at the day's news as one great picture, and tries to weave the available news into a tapestry that will be interesting and appealing. That means some things get left out. That does not mean simply rank ordering stories in priority from one to ten . . . producers don't think that way. They think about "How can I put on an interesting newscast?" Not too heavily weighted one way or another with a certain type of story. Not all combat, not all from Washington. They want a mixture of stories . . . So what you're fighting is not whether your story is important or not, but if it is going to be part of the "soup" that appears that day.[20]

TV news managers make sure they offer an appealing assortment of news stories to the public. The same may be said of the editors who select front-page stories at the *New York Times* and *Washington Post*, Sigal shows.[21] For reasons both aesthetic and organizational (i.e., that not all news be on one topic from one bureau or division), editors and producers mix the types of stories offered on their front pages, on their television programs, and in their magazines. For instance, depending on the day's anticipated schedule of news stories, a bill being introduced in Congress might be included in or omitted from news coverage.[22] Important or pressing political news might get left out, for reason of the day's "news budget."

The consequence of the hierarchical process of news production is that "the drive toward intelligibility" may "detour through distortion. The news process reduces the complex into the very simple. Under deadline pressure, . . . imposing pattern on observation rarely exposes the heart of the matter," observes Martin Mayer. The dictates of drama and a distribution of news stories matter more.

The "distortion" caused by news "compression may be the biggest single problem with television news, and it clearly affects reporting on politics and public policy." Both correspondents and their subjects become the "victim[s] of sound bite editing" as a result of the correspondents' having "to present a coherent report" with "inadequate time." Presenting the news with a single point of view is difficult to do, however, and thus a "one-time editorial is born" (in that the story presents only one side). Most news stories are, as a result, necessarily partial and incomplete. They cannot do justice to the matter at hand given the shortage of time and personnel. David Altheide gives the example of how the issue of urban transportation in and around Phoenix was simplified into a story about building highways and expanding the bus system. The news media *decontextualize* the news and then *recontextualize* it on their own terms.[23]

Organizational Goals, Organizational Values

Hierarchical control is exerted subtly, with decisions justified on the grounds of space, news balance, or other professional criteria—even if value decisions, possibly of great political significance, are necessarily implicated. Journalism is a "series of anticipations," notes Rosten, with "a subtle ordering implicit in the employer-employee relationship." And with the several layers of editors and producers between them and the reporters, publishers or other top executives do not have to intervene on a regular basis in order to have an effect.[24]

The sociologist Chris Argyris makes these same findings in his lengthy study of the *New York Times:* decisions are made at the top (contrary to the paper's stated practices) and in secret. Argyris further finds that conflict is avoided and covered up (consistent with the conformity noted by Gans) and competitiveness and low trust among the reporters are standard (consistent with the fear that Rosten found to be common among reporters).[25]

Dancy reports that his colleagues had "very high standards. The problem was that they were being constantly disappointed by bosses or other people at the networks. And I say networks because it happened at all three. I remember early on a colleague saying that this was the only business where the employees had higher standards than their bosses." Dancy is unable to explain why "several people" edited his scripts. Many times "the editing appeared to be editing for its own sake" and did not "add anything to the story . . . You're a highly paid professional, you know what's happened, you are on the scene, and some guy in New York is telling you how to do the story." News executives, not required to explain themselves, can keep their subordinates guessing about what will stand and what will be cut.[26]

Yet the hierarchy of news production allows for a settling—or at least temporary reconciliation—of the political and commercial pressures bearing down on news production. Driving editorial decision making is "an important element of business strategy," Paul Weaver points out, given that owners and executives have to meet the commercial objectives of the news organization. News organizations also evidence a political agenda, Weaver observes, inasmuch as editors and their bosses "are always coming from somewhere, politically speaking, and these preferences can have an impact on the news." This "is always concealed and routinely denied, to be sure."[27]

Having tiers of editors and news executives protects lower-level media personnel from the political and economic demands or constraints placed on news organizations. The presence of an organizational hierarchy smooths journalists' political relations to the extent that editors, producers, and executives of the major media may select, edit, schedule, and omit news stories to lessen or avoid political conflict. They respond to, or anticipate, the pressures put on their organizations by presidents, high-ranking White House staff, and the defense and diplomatic community to cut or modify politically sensitive stories (see Chapter 3), even though this political influence is rarely acknowledged within the news organization itself, in the press, or on the small screen.[28]

The hierarchy of news organizations further allows for mitigation of the uncertainties of the media's commercial objectives. Editors, producers, and their bosses carefully scrutinize both the content and the process of news making with an eye toward meeting their financial goals. They run stories in single columns on successive pages (thereby reducing their attractiveness to readers) in order to accommodate large advertisements, they end the news broadcast (or magazine) with a human-interest story to put viewers (or readers) in a more upbeat "buying mood," they prepare the viewers and readers for the programming and content to follow in subsequent days or weeks, they alter the schedule of news programs or news specials to maximize gains or minimize losses for the network and its affiliates—even if the potential viewership of the national news or a news special suffers as a result, and they run material past lawyers to make sure it does not risk legal action. As Doug Underwood remarks, "The focus on managing people and managing resources means a return to the 'strong' editing system in the newsrooms of today's market-oriented newspapers."[29]

Although the desire to improve company stock prices is not new (see

Chapter 4), the attention to bottom lines and to stock performance has intensified. One high-ranking producer at a television network notes that the "ongoing tension is the balance between these degrees: good news judgment versus a rush for ratings." The producer, who wishes to remain anonymous, notes, for example, that "there was tremendous stated and unstated pressure to cover the O. J. Simpson trial." Dealing with the tension between news judgment and commercial considerations was the "most stressful" part of this man's job.

News executives have to ensure the place of their organization in the larger environment in which they operate. Epstein finds that all producers agree that their primary job "is to enforce the standards of the organization for which they work . . . Whereas the correspondent concerns himself mainly with the particular content of an event . . . the producer concerns himself with fitting individual events into a general format." This format "both fulfills the requisites of the program and avoids any violations of the network's policies. As one ABC producer puts it, producers must be more attuned to 'the rules of the game' than correspondents."[30]

In consequence, reporters who write stories that "threaten the institutional interests" of the news organization feel the "invisible hand" of the newsroom's social control—that is, they learn to regulate and censor themselves in order to be successful. As one media researcher points out:

> The reporter who best reflects the interests of the institutions on his or her beat is rewarded with scoops, special interviews, "inside" information, air-time, bylines—and recognitions (or reputation) for being authoritative on these topics . . . Those reporters who most threaten institutional interests are the ones we used to read about. The independent, curious, unafraid investigators who are constantly looking for stories behind the story which may identify the real institutional interests and their activities.[31]

The upshot is that the distinct combination of political and commercial relationships and incentives causes each news organization to have its own news "policy." "Policy is covert," notes Warren Breed, but "every newspaper has a policy, admitted or not." Reporters never get told what the newspaper policy is, though; they have to learn it "by osmosis," as Breed puts it.[32]

The political scientist Benjamin Page finds that news organizations routinely distort the news to their advantage in his study of the coverage of three prominent stories of the early 1990s—the Los Angeles riots, the Persian Gulf War, and the Zoë Baird appointment to attorney general—by the *New York Times* and other news organizations. Page observes that "political points of view are not confined to editorial and op-ed pages but pervade news stories."

The *Times,* the *Washington Post,* and other leading news organizations in the United States had a "whole repertoire of techniques (conscious or unconscious)" for slanting the news on these stories.

The most important technique, "and probably one of the most effective because of its unobtrusiveness, is *to control the prominence"* of stories, says Page. Control is evident in the placement of a story on page 1 above the fold, in the use of "big headlines, backup stories, sidebars, and continuations on the front and inside pages, and follow-up stories over a number of days," and "on television, long and repeated stories and placement as the top news of the day."

Another technique is *"to solicit, select, and shape quotations* around which a news story is built." Although journalists may follow the canons of impartial coverage, "reporters and editors have a great deal of freedom to decide whom to seek out for quotes, which of their words to use (or twist), and which quotations to actually include in the story."

A third technique used by news organizations is

> *to choose which facts to report* so as to advance editorial purposes. Uncertainty over what is true and what false gives media considerable leeway to report varying realities; so does selection among multitudes of relatively uncontested facts. The political beliefs and values of editors and reporters are bound to influence which facts they see as newsworthy and as illustrating the true meaning of events.

In addition, says Page, the media *"frame the meaning of news stories* so as to further the media editors' and owners' political purposes." By framing the news, the media are able to "make the reader or viewer see things the medium's (or a reporter's or source's) way . . . Framing is often accomplished at the very outset of a news story, in an opening interpretive sentence or sentences, organizing the first facts and quotations that are presented" (see Chapter 5 for a discussion of news frames). Finally, "the least subtle" technique, "is *to use overtly evaluative words and statements,"* as in the use of colorful adjectives and punchy verbs.[33]

In short, the hierarchy of news production—Gans's "assembly line"—allows for a series of checks on the news so that news organizations are consistently able (although not always able) to produce a commodity that is politically acceptable and commercially viable.[34] And the promotion and hiring decisions of publishers and company executives, for top editors and producers in particular, are made on the grounds of the candidates' news judgment and understanding of organizational interests.

Yet the editing of television reporters' scripts, newsmagazine text, and newspaper reporting are the consequence of the uncertainties faced by high-level editors and producers and their superiors. They, and not the correspondents, have to reconcile the pressures of arbitrating among political contests, maintaining access to sources of political news, and meeting commercial goals.[35]

Although news organizations have always been controlled by their owners—whether publishers, CEOs, company presidents, or other executives—today they are characterized by the disappearance of the individual leadership seen in the past. Rather than the hands of the Luces, Paleys, Hearsts, Pulitzers, McCormicks, Grahams, Pattersons, and Sulzbergers, among others, we see the explicit application of business management techniques to the process of news production.[36]

In his early experience working at the *New York Times,* David Broder found that "the *Times* editors had a certain few stimuli to which they reacted in a political story: Instances of extremism, either of the New Left or the Radical Right; political action by southern (but not northern) Negroes; Kennedy stories of any variety."[37] But the lesson from Broder's account is that what might be interpreted as the *Times's* whims—its attention to political "extremism," the political action of blacks, and anything to do with Kennedys—may well be hard calculation based on organizational politics and market research. Less of the news is left to chance, discretion, or idiosyncrasy; risk aversion prevails after the changes of the 1970s and the 1980s in the newspaper, magazine, and television businesses.

Of, By, and For a Few

The hierarchy of news organizations is one way that the many reporters, columnists, editors, and producers in the news media aggregate into a much smaller number of effective voices and viewpoints. A second factor that explains the conformity and consistency of political news is the small size of the political universe in which ranking media personnel live. Top editors, producers, columnists, and reporters operate in an insular world, one in which the words and pictures of national politics may have significant consequences not only for political processes and government operations, but for individual careers, the status of particular news organizations, and the reputation of political figures.

Only a few journalists, politicians, political appointees, lawyers, lobbyists, academics, and think-tank researchers follow the twists and turns of any one political issue or career. Only a handful of reporters, editors, and producers are employed by the leading news organizations in the United States and thus are in a position to explain and interpret political reality. These few Washington journalists are the "priesthood" of the political scene, as

Lawrence Grossman, the former president of NBC News, calls them. Broder also points out that "national politics has narrowed to coverage of insiders by insiders, for the insiders . . . In a city where elected powers come and go, the press has become part of the permanent social establishment." ABC News's Washington bureau chief concurs: "Today as never before our reporters are part of the town's elite."[38] Indeed, the more educated and affluent the audience, the more inclined it is to follow the coverage in the prestige media.[39]

An indication of the insularity of the world of political communication is the Washington social scene, where top journalists and news executives move in the same social circles as government officials and politicians, compromising the supposedly adversarial relationship between journalists and officials. "It is hard for Washington journalists to maintain their distance. A lot of the problem revolves around eating," says Broder, explaining that journalists compete to bring the most glamorous public officials to their functions. "The dinner gives the reporters an opportunity to show off in front of their bosses, and the owners have a chance to hobnob with government officials." Rosten remarks, "In Washington, social life and official life are not divorced from each other. The mechanisms of practical politics, the making of 'contacts,' the spinning of alliances, the formulation of political tactics—these germinate in the innumerable 'parties' which characterize life in the capital."[40]

Katherine Graham's dinner parties, when she was publisher of the *Washington Post,* were "the best ticket in town" writes David Halberstam, where "the great men of Washington could socialize with members of the press." But the *Post* also hosts lunches where cabinet officials, other senior officials, diplomats, and others are able to talk to Graham, her son Donald (the current publisher), and about twenty editors and reporters. William Greider notes that "the talk may be bullshit, but it takes on a different meaning when said over the intimacy of the luncheon table. The ambiance is 'We're all insiders here.'" Such lunches take place in the dining rooms of the offices and Washington bureaus of the other leading news organizations, as well.[41]

When President Clinton hosted a state dinner for China's Premier Jiang Zemin, for instance, fourteen of the invited couples were journalists, heads of news organizations, publishers, or CEOs of media conglomerates; only business (eighteen couples) and Congress (twenty-one couples) were better represented.[42] "None of this does much to inspire confidence in the adversary relationship that journalists reflexively point to as their prime reason for receiving special treatment in the Constitution," says Fred Dutton, a Washington attorney and political advisor.[43]

The celebrity of many journalists (see Chapter 2) equals that of all but the most prominent politicians. Thomas B. Rosenstiel of the *Los Angeles Times* gives the example of when Robert Novak, the columnist and participant in CNN's *Crossfire*, was covering Representative Richard Gephardt's (D-Mo.) presidential campaign in Iowa. By Novak's account, "People ignored Gephardt and gathered around me, whose views they hated, . . . It wasn't that they thought I was good, or liked what I said, or defended my right to say it. It was just that I was on TV."[44] ABC News's Sam Donaldson likewise took the spotlight away from Massachusetts Governor Michael Dukakis's 1988 presidential campaign. As one reporter observed, "At virtually every stop, crowds react[ed] more to Mr. Donaldson than to the candidate, cheering and hounding him for photos and autographs." Even Dukakis's press secretary did not know "if people ask[ed Sam] for more autographs or ask[ed] Dukakis for more."[45]

Journalists also identify with fellow journalists and others (e.g., executive branch officials, lawyers, consultants, and lobbyists) in the Washington area. They relate typically to upper-middle-class, politically moderate, pragmatic persons who have official positions and speak standard English. Many journalists and others in official Washington send their children to the same colleges and universities, live in the same communities, eat in the same restaurants, shop in the same stores, and vacation in the same places. And the journalists, like the politicians and the top civil servants and political appointees they report on, are overwhelmingly white. There are few African American (3.7%) or Hispanic (2.2%) journalists in the ranks of American journalists—and almost none among the publishers, top media executives, and senior editors or producers in the leading news media—in comparison to a U.S. population that is about 12 percent African American and 11 percent Latino.[46]

It is also an economically rarified world. In a profession that is notoriously underpaid on a national basis, Washington journalists do quite well.[47] Those who think that journalists are "part of the proletariat are badly out of date," notes Broder. Before World War II, nearly all journalists, "although perhaps white collar by profession, earned blue collar salaries," observes Walter Cronkite. "We were part of the 'common people.'" Now, most Washington journalists "are well paid and have done very nicely." Television news anchors earn in the millions, executive producers and top television correspondents earn in six figures, and editors, producers, and top print reporters are paid in the low six figures.[48]

A handful of star reporters are able to parlay their participation in television talk shows, such as *Meet the Press, Crossfire,* or *The McLaughlin Group,* into hundreds of thousands of dollars in income from speaking appearances. Cokie Roberts of ABC News, Steven Roberts, formerly with *U.S. News,*

Michael Kinsley, formerly with *Crossfire* and *New Republic* (and now with Microsoft's *Slate* online magazine), and Sam Donaldson of ABC News are prominent among these lecturers. Fewer than 10 percent of Americans earn as much as $50,000 a year; meanwhile, the greater Washington area is now the wealthiest metropolitan area in the United States.[49]

Most indicative of the shared world of journalists and public officials is some journalists' switching from positions in the news media to those in the government. "The denizens of government's executive suites and the Washington bureaus of the major news organizations are becoming interchangeable," remarks Stephen Hess. Out of a total membership of about 1,300 in the prestigious Council on Foreign Relations, for instance, "at least 130 persons are or have been journalists, nearly 40 of whom are Washington practitioners." Hess notes that the "distinction of being the first to go from journalism to government to journalism to government to journalism—the true test of the inner-outer—may belong to Eileen Shanahan, whose resume reads: *Journal of Commerce*, Treasury Department during the Kennedy administration, the *New York Times*, Department of Health, Education, and Welfare during the Carter administration, and the *Washington Star*." Hess points out that "at least 11 journalists have served in both the *New York Times*'s bureau and [a] recent presidential administration." Richard Burt, John Chancellor, Leslie Gelb, David Gergen, Tim Russert, Diane Sawyer, Strobe Talbot, Russell Wiggins, Pete Williams, George Stephanopoulos, and Susan Molinari are among those who have cycled between political positions and news organizations. It is "a small world," Hess concludes.[50]

The people who create the public images of elected officials, those to be elected, and high-ranking appointees—that is, the people who do political communication—know each other:

> They interview each other, argue with each other, sleep with each other, marry each other, live and die by each other's judgment. They joust and josh on television together, and get rich together explaining Washington to conventions of doctors and lawyers and corporate executives. Not surprisingly, they tend to believe the same things at the same time. They believe in polls. They believe in television; they believe in talk; they believe, most profoundly, in talk television. They believe in irony. They believe that nothing a politician does in public can be taken at face value, but that everything he does is a metaphor for something he is hiding.[51]

Even if reporters know their sources are lying or know that alternate legitimate viewpoints exist, notes Associated Press (AP) reporter Mort Rosenblum, they rarely get the alternate observations across to editors, because "reason and definition originate in the [Washington] beltway."[52]

Reference Groups

Not surprisingly, then, editors, senior producers, and news executives typically rely on their friends and colleagues to determine what is, in fact, the
news, and what exactly is to be made of it. Editors pay assiduous attention
to their competitors, and especially to the few individuals and news organizations in the "inner ring" of the media, such as the *New York Times* and, depending on the topic, the *Washington Post*.[53] As Gans describes it,

> The *Times* is treated as *the* professional setter of standards . . . When edi-
> tors and producers are uncertain about a selection decision, they will
> check whether, where, and how the *Times* has covered the story; and sto-
> ry selectors [i.e., editors] see to it that many of the *Times's* front-page sto-
> ries find their way into television programs and magazines . . . The role
> of the *Times* extends beyond story selection, however, for at the maga-
> zines, *Times* stories are required reading for writers. Reporters are ex-
> pected to be able to do as well or better than their peers at the *Times,* and
> must be able to defend their files if these conflict with what has appeared
> in the *Times*.[54]

Moreover, the *Post,* the *Los Angeles Times,* and other papers consult the front
page of the *New York Times* when they paste up their own front pages.[55]

As the common denominator among news organizations, AP also helps
to set the news standard. The AP's Washington bureau chief explains:

> The major newspapers all pay attention to us and publish our work even
> alongside their own. We also of course pay attention to their coverage
> and try to complement what others are doing. The broadcast outlets are
> also regularly watching the wire. The broadcast networks and CNN see
> our material and react and follow up and simply use our material every
> day . . . We work for the newspapers and broadcast; a.m. newspapers,
> p.m. newspapers, morning drive time, afternoon and evening news-
> casts.[56]

AP provides this national service through its international, national, and
statewide wire stories, as well as through its "daybook"—a summary of the
political events and appearances for every given day and widely viewed as
the indicator of a day's news. "Ninety percent of the coverage of campaigns
is derivative of what ten percent produce," says the veteran political writer
Jack Germond. "It was ever thus."[57]

The consequence of journalists' use of referents and the resulting "conventional wisdom" is that there is *one* standard, current idea or set of ideas
to be learned about and then publicized. Because journalists rely on each

other amid the uncertainty of political communication, their thinking becomes confined to a "narrow band width" after working in Washington for a while and continually relying on the same sources, remarks AP's Rosenblum.[58]

Of Washington journalists and other image makers, Michael Kelly says, "Above all, they believe in the power of what they have created, in the subjectivity of reality and the reality of perceptions, in image." Yet this "inside-baseball" reporting about national politics and government is often removed from the concerns of everyday American citizens. Indicatively, three well-respected newspaper bureau chiefs admit that they rarely, if ever, watch television. In the words of one, "If you are looking for a portrait of someone who is totally out of touch with mainstream American society, you are looking at him right now."[59]

Granted, extremely busy people cannot be expected to watch a lot of television, but those who report on national politics *are* commenting about politics to an audience that has been reared on the medium. As Page finds from his study of the 1994 Los Angeles riots, the Persian Gulf War, and the Zoë Baird nomination, the mainstream news media—and the officials and experts on whom they rely—are "out of touch with the values of ordinary citizens." Gaps between elite and mass opinion are "not so uncommon," he finds. Similarly, the *Washington Post's* Howard Kurtz comments, "Where once newspapers were at the heart of the national conversation, they now seem remote, arrogant, part of the governing elite." Recent public opinion polls confirm these observations. The public thinks that the media are insensitive to victims' pain (82%), too concerned with the private lives of public officials (75%), too sensational (65%), and too manipulated by special interests (63%).[60]

Multivocal Conventions

In view of the fact that the news is produced by a relatively small number of persons, the news decisions of these top editors, producers, publishers and news executives are particularly important. Their choices matter; those of their subordinates matter less. However, as noted earlier, control is exerted subtly, through decisions based on journalistic principles rather than personalities or politics. Certain news conventions are of particular importance, however, given the need of ranking editors and producers to promote the well-being of their organizations. These are the "multivocal" conventions of balanced reporting (also known as "fair," "impartial," or "objective" reporting), the use of a limited set of news frames in the production of political news, the reliance on authoritative sources, and the transparency of the news media (the fact that news organizations make the news appear as unmediated as possible).[61]

Balanced Reporting

The principle of balanced reporting in relation to the coverage of political contests is almost taken for granted. It is accepted as a matter of faith that there are different perspectives on issues—from those who agree and those who disagree—and that it is appropriate for journalists to present both sides to an issue and not predispose the reader into taking one side or the other. Furthermore, it is assumed that journalists will not show their bias by interjecting their own views into news coverage.[62]

Stories, editorial columns, guest editorials, and letters to the editor are typically balanced (although not exactly), the different sections of newspapers and newsmagazines even out their front-page or front-cover exposure, and newspapers and television networks attempt to reflect a spectrum of opinion in which their position is located between the radical views of the left and the right.[63] Balanced reporting thereby frees reporters, editors, producers, publishers, and news executives from having to determine what stories signify for their audiences. It protects journalists from critics, since it is expected that the news media will express the diversity of American opinion and present contending political claims.[64]

The practice of offering two sides to any given political issue enables journalists to maintain their role as umpire and, since any inference on the part of the reporter is countered by opposing views, to avoid giving offense to news sources (which might reduce their access to future stories). "The real operative word is fairness," one television producer notes. "Is my work fair to a presentation of various views?" Journalists relay what politicians, public officials, and other socially prominent persons write and say and then let readers or viewers draw their own conclusions with respect to a particular controversy or debate.[65] The norm of balanced reporting thus keeps journalists from having to determine the merits of different positions on thorny political questions or difficult issues of economic distribution. Were journalists to take their own position on these issues, they could upset their several audiences (see Chapter 3). The balancing is, in fact, symbolic and formulaic—a "strategic ritual"—since an interpretation of political reality cannot be impartial or value neutral.[66]

Impartial reporting also fits the commercial interests of news organizations intent on reaching a diverse mass audience either within a metropolitan area or nationally. It is good business for news organizations to present information that appeals to the broad middle; impartial reporting militates against the publication or transmission of stories to which members of the audience or advertisers might take offense. It is stabilizing and more profitable for news organizations not to take sides and to avoid controversy, since advertisers want to avoid consumer boycotts and reach as many consumers as possible.[67]

In short, balanced reporting meets the variety of constraints facing news organizations. The "word 'objectivity' is fraught with meaning," as Gaye Tuchman notes,[68] consistent with its multivocality.

The history of the media's adaptation of impartiality (or "objectivity") reflects the multiple purposes of the norm. Objectivity is said to have emerged with the advent of the telegraph and the birth of AP in 1848: the fact that the news produced by AP was used by newspapers in many regions and with many different political leanings meant that it was distinctly balanced, or objective, using a minimum of adjectives and presenting no clearly discernible political positions. "For the early wire services, presenting facts connoted presenting information acceptable to the editorial policies of all newspapers subscribing to the service," explains Tuchman. The diverse publishers constituting AP "had little in common but their shared interest in cutting the cost of newsgathering and assuring their access to telegraphic facilities. They also feared that the telegraph companies might go into the news business and freeze them out entirely." Impartiality spread so quickly as a reporting norm that by the 1890s, the great muckraker Lincoln Steffens could write that journalists "report[ed] the news as it happened, like machines, without prejudice, color and without style; all alike. Humor or any sign of personality in our reports was caught, rebuked and, in time, suppressed."[69]

It was more than the emergence of the telegraph and AP that boosted objective reporting to preeminence, however. The commercialization of the newspapers in the nineteenth century made impartial reporting viable. Since large and diverse populations within and surrounding the growing cities were now reading newspapers (developments in paper, printing, and transmission dropped the cost of getting newspapers to readers), partisanship was bad business. Partisan newspapers could not be "fair and truthful" one *Evening Post* editorial writer argued, and most "editors feared that partisanship would alienate readers and advertisers." Although many newspapers still took partisan positions, to be sure, editors now "approached the world of politics gingerly; they kept their distance from politicians and political parties."[70] Economics took over.

Whereas advertisements had provided 40 percent of newspaper revenues in the 1890s, they supplied 75 percent of their revenues by World War I. "The nature of the news product underwent a corresponding change," reports Paul Weaver. "Advertisers, wanting to reach the largest possible audiences, sought media that evaded audience-limiting points of view and stressed uni-

versalistic, audience-increasing postures. The news media quickly adapted
to the needs of their biggest customer. Thus was born the concept of news
as a story about crisis and of journalism as a purely factual discourse without point of view."[71]

In addition to the wire service and commercial considerations, a change
in politics contributed to the emergence of impartiality as the dominant
norm among elite American journalists. With the rise of progressivism in
the early 1920s came the idea of an independent profession of journalists to
counteract the corruption of partisan politics. The middle class felt skepticism and criticism toward the growing working classes, Michael Schudson
points out. "The professional classes now took public opinion to be irrational and therefore something to study, direct, manipulate, and control.
The professions developed a proprietary attitude toward 'reason' and a pa-
ternalistic attitude toward the public." Public opinion was no longer familiar and trustworthy, but rather something suspiciously different.[72]

"By the mid-thirties, the term 'objectivity,' unknown in journalism before World War I, appears to have become common parlance," says Tuchman. Objectivity became established as method, and the "facticity" (as she
calls it) of the news proper was to be distinguished from the opinion contained on editorial pages.[73] The history of the New York Times is illustrative.
Adolph Ochs bought the newspaper in 1896, when it had a daily circulation
of only nine thousand. The Times was only one small voice in New York politics, given the existence of about fifteen other general circulation newspapers in the city, and a tiny voice in national politics. Not until the 1910s and
1920s did the Times come to enjoy its preeminent political authority and its
impartial style of reporting become dominant. By midcentury, the New York
Times was one of the leading papers in the nation.[74]

By the same token, the separation of straight reporting from editorializing did not always exist. Reporters were not an occupational category distinct from unsigned editorial writers until the late nineteenth century.
Columnists did not appear until the 1920s and did not flourish until the
1930s and 1940s. The op-ed page ("opposite editorial" page) was not introduced in the New York Times until September 21, 1970. With the emergence
of columnists, editorials, and op-ed pieces as distinct editorial content, news
organizations—and their readers, listeners, and viewers—could ostensibly
distinguish between fact and opinion.[75]

News Frames

A second multivocal convention is the use of a limited set of news frames
into which editors put the news into an understandable context. Frames cat-
egorize events, connect present events with those of the past, indicate causal

relationships, and create oppositions. They facilitate familiarity; the new is expressed as the known. Frames enable journalists to identify the particular significance of complex events; they also may contain within them moral judgments and suggested remedies. As the media scholar Robert Entman observes, "Frames call attention to some aspects of reality while obscuring other elements, which might lead audiences to have different reactions . . . Framing in this light plays a major role in the exertion of political power, and the frame in a news text is really the imprint of power—it registers the identity of actors or interests that competed to dominate the text."[76]

Yet the number of frames typically used in news production is limited. Prevalent among the news frames used by the major media are

ethnocentrism and nationalism,
altruistic democracy,
responsible capitalism,
minimal government,
anticommunism and the cold war (through the 1980s),
individualism and personalization, and
moral disorder.[77]

There are others. For example, in research on American public opinion on U.S. foreign policy, Benjamin Page and Robert Shapiro find news coverage to be cast in terms of partisanship and incumbency. Gans notes the presence of "moderatism" in his exploration of enduring news values. The media scholars Russ Neuman, Marion Just, and Ann Crigler report that the frames of "powerlessness" and "human impact" were used to characterize the news of the five political issues they studied.[78]

News frames are multivocal in that they mitigate simultaneously the uncertainties of political reporting, government-media relations, and commercial achievement. With respect to political reporting, the frames orient and limit political and partisan battles. In terms of government-media relations, the casting of news in nationalist, democratic, pro-capitalist, anticommunist, and individualist frames is consistent with the pro-market and strong-defense positions of the U.S. government, Congress, State Department, and Defense Department; these frames are also consistent with the continuation of existing budgets and administrative configurations. With respect to commercial objectives, the pro-market, anticommunist, and individualist news frames are consistent with a corporate- and consumer-oriented society and inconsistent with a regulatory and collectivist society. Not only are the frames relatively enduring, but they are the way that most Americans assimilate new information. Culture itself may even be defined as the set of frames operative within a society.[79]

Consider the personalization frame. In both visual and print media, reporters and their editors use *persons* as the vehicles through which to tell stories about national politics. Even the complex and the abstract are explained in terms of, or reduced to, something more finite and more comprehensible: an individual person. Events and causes are likewise explained in terms of individuals. This is synecdoche, of course: the State Department is Secretary of State Madeleine Albright, Iraq is President Saddam Hussein, Germany was Chancellor Helmut Kohl, and Microsoft is CEO Bill Gates. Personalization makes the news comprehensible and accessible; it allows news organizations to communicate political news in terms of familiar persons, the politicians and other public persons whom we recognize. The news media thereby finesse the problems of trying to communicate abstract, intangible, and complex ideas.

As Roderick Hart points out, the personalization of political news—what he calls "personality politics"—is the legacy of television. Television is a human medium that brilliantly communicates basic emotion. As Hart tells it, not only do we learn about politics by watching television, but we are *television watchers:* who we are as humans is in part defined by the attention that we pay to television. "A truly rich understanding of modern governance must ask what politics feels like when we watch it." The prevalence of television and its impact on the reportage in the print media drive today's personalization of political news. The newsmagazines and newspapers have adapted their news coverage accordingly (see Chapter 2).[80]

Using the dominant news frames serves the interests of the news organizations, allowing them to simultaneously address their political uncertainties and meet their commercial objectives. These few frames have not always dominated the American media, contrary to the popular belief that there is a more-or-less constant "American creed."[81] Much news coverage in the late nineteenth and early twentieth centuries framed political, economic, and social issues in terms of class differences, corporate excess, and the rights of farmers, industrial workers, and miners. At a time when the United States was only one of several major military and economic powers, moreover, news was often framed in isolationist and protectionist terms—i.e., anti-market and pro-government—as in the discussion on tariffs and the American debate over the League of Nations in 1919. In the second half of the twentieth century, the growth of the postwar economy, the triumph of consumer culture, and the ascension of the United States as a superpower, among other factors, have induced journalists to consciously or subconsciously frame the news in terms of individualism and personalization and the other frames listed above.

Authoritative Sources

Being uncertain about the news and how it will play out politically and affect advertisers and paying audiences, journalists rely on societal indicators of achievement: authoritative sources. This is evident with respect to which politicians, political candidates, public officials, business leaders, academics, and others are able to get on the news or are used as sources in printed articles. As we know from our study of presidential campaigns, Congress, and public administration in Chapters 2 and 3, only a few of the many political actors who have something to communicate receive media exposure.

In fact, only a handful of sources dominate the news. A study of ABC News's *Nightline* and the former *MacNeil/Lehrer NewsHour* reveals a concentrated representation of political spokespersons, despite the progressive and generally favorable reputations of the two shows. Political debate was highly circumscribed by virtue of the narrow cast of personnel invited on the programs.[82] At the same time, journalists' circumscribed attention legitimates prominent politicians, certain officeholders, corporate leaders, and experts of various kinds (and, if applicable, that of their organizations). They thereby endorse the prevailing processes and the criteria of such success.[83]

The media's use of authoritative sources coincides with the interests of the politicians and other persons in official positions, authenticates the values of official Washington, and verifies and celebrates the present-day success of particular persons, products, and companies. In addition, it implies a marginalizing of dissidents and those who challenge the status quo and a minimizing of the voices of others less economically potent.[84]

The contemporary news media's reliance on a limited set of authoritative voices is, like its reliance on balanced reporting and news frames, a function of the times—the result of a confluence of political and economic forces. The partisan press of the nineteenth and early twentieth centuries had different definitions of "authority": party officials, political bosses, union leaders, and others received much more publicity than they do today. It was not unusual, for instance, for the leaders of the American Federation of Labor or the Congress of Industrial Organizations to give national radio broadcasts in the 1930s and 1940s, and the yellow press of the late nineteenth and early twentieth centuries gave voice to working Americans and new immigrants.

Transparency

The news media seek to appear "transparent": they give the impression that news making is a frictionless process and avoid acknowledging that political information is actually mediated by organizational employees and intricate bureaucratic practices.[85] When it comes to reporting on the economics of the news business, the mistakes made by journalists, or the news media's direct involvement in the creation of a certain news story, for example, the news media "tend to hide rather than explain these constraints."[86]

One example of the media's pretense at transparency is the fact that the newsmagazines "print a false publishing date on each issue (usually a week after publication). This deception makes it difficult for the reader to ascertain the point when news had to be cut off because of the deadline," explains Epstein. He notes that journalists would greatly enhance the value of news to the public "if news organizations revealed, rather than obscured, the methods by which they select and process reality."[87] A journalist with *Time* gives another example of how the news media deflect attention away from how the news is produced:

> Walter Cronkite, the most respected broadcast reporter of his generation, used to say in nearly every speech and interview that television news was a headline service, utterly inadequate to keep a citizen informed. But he did not express that opinion on the nightly news, where it would have mattered—not even during the most complex periods of Vietnam and Watergate. Cronkite and his colleagues have treated their eminence much as the dog treated the manger: over and over they have absolved themselves of responsibility for directing the public's education, yet have fought for primacy rather than yield that role to any other journalists.[88]

Paul Weaver writes of an all-too-common example of the media's keeping the production of the news away from public view. In the early 1980s, a high-ranking aide to President Reagan who was part of a small cadre of centrists in the otherwise right-leaning administration shared inside information with a White House correspondent for the *New York Times*. The stories "naturally were favorable to the personalities and perspectives of [the aide's] fellow nonconservatives." The *Times* then published a number of articles about the Reagan White House under the byline of that reporter. The articles made no mention of the administration's communications strategy (or that of the administration's nonconservative wing) or of the political context of the articles. "How different the reader's impression would have been," notes Weaver, had the following note been appended: "The subject of this story was suggested by a senior White House aide whom the *Times* has agreed not to identify as a condition of his assistance. The story idea was tendered during a theater-and-dinner party hosted by the aide and his wife; the aide is a non-Reagan loyalist and moderate who is aligned with the Baker-Deaver wing of the staff and who appeared to have been seeking to attract favorable publicity to his allies on the president's ideologically divided staff."[89]

Nor did the major media report the censorship and other constraints imposed on reporting from the invasions of Grenada (1983) and Panama (1989) and the Persian Gulf War (1991). In the coverage of the war, for instance, none of the nation's leading news organizations joined in a lawsuit, filed in January 1991 by the Center for Constitutional Rights on behalf of eleven news organizations and five writers (including *Harper's*, the *Village Voice, Mother Jones*, and *The Nation*), arguing that there is a constitutional basis for overturning of the wartime media controls. The prestige media did not even report the existence of the lawsuit. (Although the *New York Times* at one point mentioned it at the end of a lengthy article datelined Riyadh, Saudi Arabia, the reference misstated the purpose of the lawsuit.)

Democratic political consultant James Carville, who has dealt extensively with the news media in his professional life and counts many journalists among his friends, points out that journalists

> are so into self-justification that they have turned journalism into the one institution in America with the least capacity for self-examination and self-criticism. If a political professional criticizes them they say it's the government that's doing it and hide behind the First Amendment. These people think that the First Amendment belongs to them. It doesn't; it belongs to the American people. The ultimate arrogance is that they view any criticism as some sort of censorship or media-bashing. [We] Democrats have Republicans to criticize us; Republicans have Democrats to criticize them. Ford's got GM, GM's got Ford. But the media, they never criticize each other. Thou shalt speak no evil of another reporter.[90]

The news media typically give their readers and viewers "no hint that the 'news' they are reading has been 'generated,' 'leaked,' provided not by journalistic legwork and thought but by a government handout which is 'not for attribution.'"[91]

If the personalistic and organizational qualities of news production happen to become apparent, as occurred with the "accidental" gas tank explosions engineered by producers at *Dateline NBC*, the *Washington Post's* publication of a Pulitzer Prize–winning story about a nonexistent eight-year-old heroin addict, and the broadcast of a man deliberately setting himself on fire, the media engage in "repair work."[92] More recent examples include the reportage of the *New Republic's* Steven Glass, the *Boston Globe's* Patricia Smith, and CNN/*Time* on the U.S. military's use of sarin gas against U.S. defectors in Vietnam. Editorial writers, prominent journalists, and news anchors point out the exceptional circumstances of the problem at hand, distance their organization from the one at fault, reassure audiences that the problem is under control, and otherwise attempt to restore the credibility of news production.

Transparency thus allows journalists to avoid calling attention to the manufacturing of "photo ops" and other contrived premises of news production—what Daniel Boorstin calls "pseudo-events"—whereby journalists are assisted by public relations personnel who feed them handouts, lines-of-the-day, packaged events, and other serviced or staged news items that convenience news production.[93] The transparency of the news media further allows the print and entertainment industries to escape the economic scrutiny that attends other sectors of the national economy. The greater concentration among news companies facilitated in the 1995 debate over the telecommunications bill, for instance, was covered modestly in the *New York Times, Washington Post,* and *Wall Street Journal* and ignored by the other major news organizations. In fact, in the broadcast media there was a virtual blackout on news of the telecommunications bill, according to Snider and Page's findings.[94] Were these procedures brought to light, the credibility of the media could be endangered. The convention of media transparency is multivocal to the extent that it simultaneously serves the political, governmental, and commercial interests of news organizations.

News organizations used to be more opaque. The partisan press, even if allied with the president and the majority party, was scarcely "transparent" as read by a member of the opposition, a foreigner, or, no doubt, some partisans. That the news was partisan was manifest. The yellow press made no bones about exaggerating and embellishing the truth if it communicated what its publishers believed to be a basically truthful message.[95] In contrast, in the second half of the twentieth century, the standardization of impartial reporting, the professionalization of journalism, and the commercialization of the news have combined to entrench the norm of media transparency in news production. Transparency thus gives the illusion that the news media constitute a disinterested, nonintrusive system for collecting and disseminating political information.

IN SUM, THE PRODUCTION OF POLITICAL NEWS BY THE MAJOR MEDIA manifests what I identify as multivocal news conventions: impartial reporting, reliance on a limited set of news frames, use of authoritative sources, and the transparency of news production. These practices reconcile simultaneously the uncertainties that confront journalists and their news organizations in their larger political and economic environment. They are especially powerful, I submit, because of their multiple functions. They are also especially effective because they are usually taken for granted; they are assumed to be standard (and desirable) professional practices—symbolic, even—and rarely subject to question. Most audiences assume that the news presents both sides, they do not question the frames being used, they accept the sources who are selected to be heard, and they do not wonder about the organizational practices involved in making the news.

The multivocal conventions are informal rules that not only unite news organizations in how they conceive and operationalize their profession, but also anchor the place of the leading news organizations as privileged interpreters of the political world. Like the media practices discussed earlier, multivocal conventions are *constructed* by the media so that they can interpret and communicate political news. Compared with the other media practices, however, they operate on a larger scale: multivocal conventions such as balanced reporting and the use of authoritative sources are more general phenomena than the more specific media practices of negative reporting and the reliance on market surveys.

Conclusion: A Reappraisal of the News Media as a Political Institution

When we consider the other features of the news media, mentioned earlier, along with these multivocal conventions, we begin to see the media cohering into a whole. One feature is the division of labor that exists among news organizations. Although there are important differences among the news media and often vigorous competition between separate organizations (and sometimes individual journalists), there is also a de facto division of labor among the news media: the various media that publish, broadcast, or otherwise disseminate political news exist in more-or-less fixed relationship with each other when it comes to the timing, content, and presentation of the news. The news contained in newspapers is not exactly the same as that on television, for example—indeed, the networks often look to the newspapers or the wire services to indicate what is important[96]—just as the content in the newsmagazines is not exactly the same as that on television or the radio.

Another factor that binds the media together is the limited resources of most newspapers and television and radio stations (see Chapter 1): only a few organizations have a "news net" extensive enough to get information from cities across the United States and capitals around the world. As a result, a limited number of news organizations determine most important political news: the television networks, the national and largest regional newspapers, the three newsmagazines (*Time, Newsweek,* and *U.S. News*), the wire services, and the news services of the prestige press.

The population of newspapers, newsmagazines, broadcast and cable television, and radio broadcasters in the United States thereby constitutes a composite political institution, one that produces remarkably consistent news coverage across separate organizations—no matter the medium. Research on media congruence ("interchannel homogeneity") includes a study of the "student movement" on U.S. television between September 1968 and April 1970, a study of U.S. incursions into Laos during the Vietnam War, and studies of U.S. electoral campaigns. The latter studies found "a high, almost uncanny, similarity in the share of time, attention and of types of news given to the contenders by the three main networks," as well as in the kind of story types broadcast by the networks. Another study shows that the networks duplicate an average of 70 percent of their news stories.[97] Neuman, Just, and Crigler also find a close correspondence of the news media's coverage of five cases from the 1980s.[98]

This similarity in news production is to be expected, of course, given that the mainstream news media exist in the same political and economic environment, journalists share common practices, and most news organizations rely on the same limited cast of sources for political news.

THE TRADITIONAL IMAGES OF HARD-BITTEN, ICONOCLASTIC REporters and chaotic, fiercely independent newsrooms are exaggerations. We might better think of reporters, editors, and producers as organizational employees and of newspaper, newsmagazine, and television offices and newsrooms as places of bosses and subordinates, with induced conformity. In view of the hierarchical production of the news, the shared world of Washington politics, the cue taking prevalent among media personnel, and the use of the same multivocal news practices, it is possible to conceptualize the political news media as an aggregate single actor—an operational component of the American political system, inextricably connected with the formal institutions of government and national politics.

Despite their presence in the politics and policies of national government, the news media occupy a curiously uncertain position: between politicians, the government, and the market, and with constitutional protections but without a constitutional foundation. Accordingly, they continually have to monitor their political ties, maintain their relations with government officials, and reestablish their economic foundations in order to ensure their continued survival as authoritative voices on national politics.

Grant McConnell makes the brilliant point that the autonomy of an organization can actually be a liability:

> On the face of it, it is an enviable situation for any bureaucratic unit; it seems to imply that the agency is at liberty to do as it sees fit. More realistically, however, such liberty is very dangerous to the agency enjoying it and not to be envied in the slightest, for it would expose the bureau to charges of irresponsibility and arbitrariness whenever it could not adduce unassailable criteria for its choices and actions.[99]

Although McConnell is writing about the U.S. Army Corps of Engineers and government agencies in general, his insight very much applies to news organizations: the seeming independence of the media is, in fact, a risky position for them to be in. Without a definitive constitutional status and a certain economic basis, media personnel must maintain tight ties with politicians and government officials and their commercial guarantors (both advertisers and audiences) so as to buttress their positions among the communicators of national politics. It is the top editors and producers, publishers, and news executives who have to decide how to create the news, given the complexity and ambiguity of political news, and thereby reconcile the different political and economic uncertainties in a way that best furthers the interest of their news organizations.[100] As a result, much of the news media's apparent independence and discretion is chimerical.

The other result of the news media's seeming autonomy is that their similar political, governmental, and economics positions effectively bind them together as a single political institution. Institutions are often nested—existing on different, mutually compatible levels, like the Russian wooden dolls. We may think of the institutional news media in the same way. At the level of individual journalists and news organizations, there are the standard practices with respect to their political, governmental, and economic external relations, which along with the help of the hierarchy of news organizations, culminate in the multivocal conventions.

At the level of the population of the news media, there are the limited number of leading journalists and news organizations who report authoritatively on politics for much of the nation. They are watched or read by millions around the country, either directly via the television networks, subscriptions, and newsstand sales or indirectly through newspaper news services and local news programs. The *New York Times,* the *Washington Post,* the *Wall Street Journal,* the *Los Angeles Times,* AP, Reuters, the newsmagazines, ABC News, NBC News, CBS News, and CNN, especially—are viewed as political authorities. Moreover, in any one issue area, a particular organization may dominate: for instance, the *Journal* with respect to economic policy, the

Post with respect to the viability of legislation, or the *Times* with respect to the soundness of a treaty or executive agreement. Furthermore, the top reporters, editors, producers, and news executives of these organizations look to each other for the definition of the news.

Finally, at the macropolitical level of the whole of the political system, the news media exert systematic effects on elections, Congress, the presidency, the federal bureaucracy, and even the Supreme Court and on foreign, economic, and other public policy. Politicians, public officials, and special interests cannot maneuver without factoring in the presence and potential actions of the news media.

The upshot is that these multilayered news media institutions are, by and large, mutually consistent; they cohere into a single actor for most intents and purposes. This is not to say there are not sometimes clashes between economics and politics, occasional differences in the news frames used in reporting, or areas where the news media may exert little or no effect. Even though institutions may abrade each other or be mutually *in*consistent,[101] conflict is mainly obscured, and conformity rules. This is part of the ideal of "objective" news that still prevails—the notion that smart, well-placed journalists and news executives will reach the same conclusions and make the same decisions on political news. In fact, there is strikingly little variation among the news media on salient political issues, as many scholars have already found.[102] The news media are an aggregate actor in the way that six aircraft flying in formation may be considered a distinct entity: bound together by the internal cognitive processes of the different two-person pilot teams, united by training and socialization, and reacting similarly to changes in their environment—weather and visibility, terrain, the approach of an enemy threat, or the need to close in on a desired target.

The news media are not a "fourth branch" in the sense of being part of the government itself; nor are they a "fourth branch" or "fourth estate" in terms of being able to check the excesses of the other three branches of government or serving as a countervailing power to that of business and the government. Instead, it may be that the news media constitute a "fourth corner" in the "iron triangle" model of the policy process: their role in contemporary American politics makes them a party to the threesome of congressional committees (and subcommittees), special interests, and public administrators in an account of policy making and policy outcomes.[103] Whether vocal or silent, the news media play a key part by questioning or validating the policy process and the politics of who gets what from government. The image of an iron square or box perhaps better captures the role and influence that news media exert on regulatory, distributive, and redistributive policies in the United States.

IS THIS A LIBERAL POLITICAL INSTITUTION? THE ARGUMENT IS OFTEN made that the news media are overwhelmingly and typically left of center. Evidence for this view comes from surveys that find that journalists generally support Democrats and Democratic interests. (For instance, of 139 Washington bureau chiefs or correspondents surveyed, 89% said they voted for Bill Clinton in 1992.) Other evidence comes from analysis of the Reagan and Bush years, which shows that the media attacked President Ronald Reagan. Not only was there no "Teflon president" when it came to the publicization of stories critical of him, but the media discriminated against President George Bush in his reelection campaign of 1992.[104] Political journalists also allied early on with the feminist movement, antinuclear advocates, ethnic and minority causes, and the gay and lesbian movement. "In that sense," comments Richard Harwood, "they are anti-establishment and anti-middle class." Rich Oppel agrees: "The reality is that the newsrooms" are "at odds with the people they serve," given that the ranks of journalists include many more skeptics and nonbelievers than does the general populace.[105]

Yet to say the news media have a liberal bias is misguided, and on several grounds. One is that an emphasis on journalists' personal politics slights the fact that they work within hierarchical organizations with established records and organizational "policies." Ambitious and successful journalists, whether in the print or video media, learn what to write about and how to write it (as noted above) in order to please publishers and CEOs, who tend to be considerably more conservative—and they ultimately decide what is to be the news and which reporters are to be hired or promoted. Therefore journalists are liberal in their news coverage to the extent that their executives and owners are. It is a journalist with a short-lived career who regularly lets personal views bias his or her news coverage—hence the importance of the self-censorship reported by Gans and others. Those who claim that journalists' political opinions determine the news need to demonstrate that personal politics trump the organizational and professional factors in journalism today.

Second, journalists who are dependent on the federal government (whether an agency, the White House, or other body) will reflect the dominant foreign policy, national security policy, or economic policy and not offer their readers or viewers any "liberal" alternative to the explicit or implicit agreements that make the consensus among the powerful political and economic interests in the United States. In such cases, the news media may be no more than conduits for the information provided or released by executive branch officials. They cannot be said to be liberal, then, if they more-or-less follow the politics of the executive branch. (Even were the government liberal, it would make little sense to call the media "liberal," since they would not exercise any discretion on their own.)

Furthermore, the commercial pressures bearing on news organizations (and therefore, indirectly, on journalists themselves) lead them to match their news product with their market niche so as to achieve high financial returns. This means, for instance, that the coverage in the *Washington Post* reflects its Washington-area constituency (affluent, socially liberal, pro-government) and that of the *New York Times* appeals to its mostly Manhattan and East Coast readers (wealthy, cosmopolitan, heavily Jewish). The same goes for the *Wall Street Journal* and other news organizations, whether print or video, with respect to their markets. Audiences and advertisers at once guide and constrain the news produced by any one news organization (as noted in Chapter 4).

Interestingly, surveys show that although the public sees the media as being biased (52% agree that being "too biased" is a major problem with the news media), it believes that special interests' manipulation of the media (63%) and the media's penchant for sensationalism (65%) are worse problems. Moreover, when asked about undesirable influences on the news media, the public ranked "media's desire to make profits" as the most serious influence, the "interests of corporate media owners" as the next most serious, followed by "advertisers," "big business," and, last, "elected officials."[106]

In short, reporters' liberal bias is undermined by the facts that the news is produced in hierarchical organizations, that journalists are often dependent on political officials for material, and that commercial considerations dominate (even if some audience market niches are more liberal than others). This is not to say that the news media do not have ideological or partisan effects: the news may often have ideological or partisan repercussions, but it is not so much political belief, partisanship qua belief, or partisanship as the logic of the news organizations as institutional actors.

Rather than a liberal bias, the problem is the "news perspective," the "structural bias," and the "journalistic bias" of the news media.[107] After spending a year watching the news production of the three major television networks, Epstein concluded that the "pictures of reality were systematically distorted by organizational requirements."[108] Media researcher David Altheide similarly found that the "news perspective" was "a more troublesome bias than values and ideology, because fellow journalists, like most of the audience, take the perspective for granted . . . There can be no effective check on the bias of this perspective unless it is articulated and shown to be operative."[109]

TO CONSIDER THE NEWS MEDIA AS A SINGLE POLITICAL INSTITUTION accords with other work on political institutions. Recent research by the political scientists Kent Weaver and Bert Rockman on the effects of political institutions across nations is consistent with the perspective of an institutional news media. Weaver and Rockman describe three "tiers" of institutions and conclude that institutions do, in fact, affect governance across nations. They find that the institutions that matter are not so much the primary institutions of a parliamentary versus presidential system of government, but rather the second tier of institutions, such as "electoral rules and norms," the third tier of institutions, such as federalism, bicameralism, and forms of party discipline, and other "factors" (which they label "noninstitutional"), "such as a society's political culture and its structure of social and political divisions." They determine that overall institutional effects may be "strong, direct, unidirectional, and consistent over time and across policy sectors" when it comes to the impact of second- or third-tier factors, or may be "subtle or indirect and . . . contingent in strength and direction upon the presence of other factors."[110]

The news media fit Weaver and Rockman's findings on institutional effects in that they certainly influence policy making and public opinion— making them third-tier institutions by Weaver and Rockman's criteria. Indeed, although these researchers omit reference to the news media as a potential institution in their discussion of institutional or noninstitutional third-tier factors, the news media readily fit the majority of their conclusions about the effects of institutions on governance:

1. Institutions affect governance, although their effects are contingent on other factors.
2. Specific institutional arrangements create both opportunities and risks for government capacity.
3. Policy-making capability may vary significantly across policy domains.
4. Institutional influences are channeled through the decision-making characteristics of elite cohesion, multiple veto points, elite stability, interest-group access, and elite autonomy from political pressures.
5. Second-tier institutional arrangements influence government capability at least as much as the relationship between executive and legislative power.
6. Neither parliamentary nor presidentialist arguments offer satisfactory explanations of capabilities.
7. Divided party control of the legislative and executive branches of the U.S. government exacerbates problems of governance, especially the setting of priorities.

8. There are direct trade-offs between some institutional capabilities.

9. Governments may gain room to maneuver in policy making by creating countervailing mechanisms.[111]

The news media obviously affect the governance of the United States in crucial instances (point 1), as is seen in the Watergate and Lewinsky scandals. The number, orientation, and technological sophistication of U.S. news organizations clearly create opportunities and risks for political action (point 2). Leaks to the news media may have beneficial (trial balloon) or harmful (endangering or wrecking careers) effects, depending on the array and quality of news organizations in the United States at any one time—or, in comparison to the organizations and traditions of political communication in other countries.

Policy-making capacity, too, is greatly influenced by the presence of the news media (point 3). The coverage of legislation dealing with First Amendment issues, for instance, would enjoy a very different fate from that involving defense budgets or energy policy. Relatedly, the news media have the capacity to paper over or antagonize divisions among political elites, emphasize or downplay particular issues, and amplify some voices and ignore others (point 4). In fact, the premise of this book, as well as others on the news media, is that paying attention only to the formal structure and powers of government is grossly insufficient to account for the American political system (point 6).

In addition, the news media may at times be a decisive tipping factor in the promulgation or rejection of policy initiatives in circumstances of divided government (point 7). It is also clear that the news media's capacity to influence political communication comes at the cost of the ability of politicians, federal departments and agencies, and societal actors to communicate freely with the public. There are often direct trade-offs between institutional capabilities (point 8). Finally, politicians and political interests have indeed learned how to entice or otherwise use the media for their own ends (point 9). As discussed in Chapter 3, political actors have created their own ways to use the new media for their particular ends. We thus see that Weaver and Rockman's conclusions are, with the exception of the fifth point (which does not apply), consistent with the existence of an institutional news media.

In Chapter 6, I examine specific instances of media congruence—the news media acting as a single political institution—in the coverage of several salient issues of national politics. I also show that the media may be considered essentially conservative in the sense of upholding the status quo.

THE WATCHDOGS THAT
DIDN'T BARK

The press is much more frail than democratic theory has so far admitted. It is too frail to carry the burden of popular sovereignty, to supply truth sponta- neously. When we expect it to supply such a body of truth we employ a mis- leading standard of judgment. We misunderstand the limited nature of news, the illimitable complexity of society; we overestimate our own endurance, pub- lic spirit and all-round competence.—Walter Lippmann, *Public Opinion,* 1922

The press does not speak the voice of the nation. It does not even speak the voice of those who write for it.—Fanny Wright, 1829

THE FACT THAT THE NEWS MEDIA ARE A POLITICAL INSTITUTION SYS-
tematically affects what the American public receives as the news. We have seen that the news media's coverage of electoral campaigns and other polit- ical contests, of policy monopolies (especially with respect to the president, foreign policy, and national security), and of their own commercial inter- ests is mutually beneficial to the media and the other parties. We have also seen that ranking organizational executives are able to reconcile the sever- al pressures that bear on news production to create a coherent, attractive commodity that is produced on a weekly, daily, and even hourly basis. The result is that the news is less the product of independent reporters qua indi- viduals than the product of an organizational hierarchy, staffed by tiers of subordinates and superiors. The news first and foremost serves news orga- nizations' own interests, given the uncertain environment. Such a concep- tualization of news production is consistent with the notion of the news me-

dia's "structural bias," or their construction of reality through the process of news production.

This structural bias has some beneficial effects on the news coverage of national politics. The press cover well the stories that match journalists' and news organizations' own incentives and predilections, and there are many such stories. The news media thus ably cover stories that reduce to political contests with two distinct sides (to focus coverage on the competitive process itself, rather than on the substance of the contest), such as general elections, legislative battles, controversial cabinet or Supreme Court nominees, and major court trials.

Persons and events that fit into the prevailing news frames (see Chapter 5) also receive ample exposure. For example, the American pilot whose plane was downed in Bosnia in 1993 and who survived on his own for several days before being rescued by U.S. forces received plenty of attention, his story perfectly fitting the "personalization" and "nationalism" frames. The achievement of universal suffrage in South Africa and the beginning of electoral politics in Russia and other nations of the former Soviet Union are two events that received considerable coverage, given that they fit the "altruistic democracy" frame. The news media also readily report instances of successful business entrepreneurship (the "responsible capitalism" frame), just as they publicize the illegal activities and venalities of government officials or government agencies (the "minimal government" frame), such as the abuses of the Internal Revenue Service and the alleged corruption of Mike Espy, President Bill Clinton's former secretary of agriculture. News stories of the attributes and accomplishments of presidential candidates, film stars, business entrepreneurs, athletes, and other celebrities also abound ("individualism"). Conversely, the news media emphasize the abnormalities or perversions of particular persons, such as terrorists, criminals, and "extremist" politicians ("moral disorder"), examples being Oklahoma City bomber Tim McVeigh, Ted Kaczinski (the Unabomber), mass murderer Jeffrey Dahmer, and racist presidential candidate David Duke.[1]

The news media are also proficient at disseminating stories that originate from official sources. Presidential speeches, the pronouncements of top cabinet officials, and the statements of congressional leaders are typically publicized widely. So, too, are the details about the travels of the president and the campaign activities of the major party candidates. The press is best at covering stories that involve the whole of the government, such as a major war or a presidential assassination, as James Reston observes.[2] The significance and singularity of such stories drown out competing or conflicting news.

The media distinguish themselves, too, when they report on serious divisions within the political establishment, those instances when high-ranking officials are in conflict, breaking a policy monopoly. The television and print media began to communicate the horrors of the Vietnam War once the Johnson administration, the American public, and the military themselves were divided over the war. Similarly, a handful of reporters were able to pursue the Watergate story because members of the Nixon White House, the FBI, and other federal agencies cooperated with journalists (see Chapter 3). The same goes for the investigations into the Clinton administration's fundraising operations: White House aides (Harold Ickes and George Stephanopoulos) from Clinton's first term in office took documents with them when they left office and released them to the press.[3] As noted in Chapter 3, this is the news media's "indexing" of national politics: journalists' criticism of government is an index of internal political dissension within Congress or executive branch. When political sources overtly disagree, there are "two sides of the story"; when they agree, whatever they say constitutes "the facts of the case."[4]

In fact, it is because the news media do so many things well—and communicate the news with vivid images almost instantaneously on our television screens or early the next morning outside our doors—that they are so effective and prominent an actor in the American political system. Other stories get missed, however. The institutional status and standard practices of the news media make for deficient coverage of other political news. "If too much is made of the press's role in elections, too little may be made of its importance of governance, and in particular, in the formation of preservation of oppositions," observes Leon Sigal. "The routines of news gathering and the convention of authoritative sources, when strictly adhered to, do help inoculate reporters from the charlatans and hucksters who vie for attention," he notes. "But they may also silence or distort opposition voices."[5]

Unreliable News: Recent Case Studies

In many instances, the news media are incapable of protecting the public interest against the corrupt and self-interested behaviors of politicians, public officials, political parties, leading businesses, and the major professions. The five cases discussed below are examples of defective news coverage by the American media. Two cases involve crucial events in international relations: the war in the Persian Gulf in early 1991 (and the buildup to the war in the latter half of 1990) and the crash of Korean Airlines (KAL) Flight 007 in 1983. The savings and loan (S&L) crisis of the 1980s, involving hundreds of billions of dollars in taxpayers' money, is the third case. The fourth and fifth cases involve serious issues of public health: the spread of the AIDS epidemic and the development of a diagnosis of and cure for cancer. The cases are from recent history, 1980 to the present, with three taking place concurrently in the first half of the 1980s.

Besides representing diverse matters of importance to the welfare of Americans, the cases show the news media's different approaches to issues. The national media were very much present in the Persian Gulf War and KAL 007 stories. They were inconsistently present in the S&L and AIDS cases. They have been essentially absent in the case of Gaston Naessens's inventions and biological research on human blood (as of this writing). Although I did not choose the cases at random—I sought prominent recent instances of media failure—each case is highly significant in its own right. The analyses in this chapter are consistent with much of social science, then—to provide accounts of important and rare events, analogous to research on world wars or civil wars, social revolutions, nuclear accidents, or spaceship disasters. Although explanations of such events are complex, generalizations may still be possible. My purpose is to see whether the coverage in the five cases is consistent with an institutional perspective of the news media.

In discussing each case, I first summarize the events and then review the news coverage and show how it affected national politics. I then examine whether the media did indeed behave as an institution in covering these stories, that is, whether the cases show hierarchical production of news, the use of multivocal conventions, uniformity of news coverage by the leading news organizations, and the betrayal of journalistic ethics. I conclude the chapter by discussing the news media's place in upholding political order—and the kind of political order they uphold.

The Persian Gulf War

The news coverage of the Persian Gulf War exemplifies the essential cooperation of the press in the coverage of a policy monopoly. In all phases of the war, from just before Iraq's invasion of Kuwait on August 2, 1990, until after the cease-fire upon the expulsion of Iraqi forces from Kuwait on February 27, 1991, the news media more or less accepted what the Bush administration and the Pentagon told them, showed them, or released to them.

The leading news media underplayed the United States's support of Iraq's President Saddam Hussein as a regional power in the years before the invasion of the State of Kuwait. Little context was given for why Iraq might so misconstrue American objectives regarding their threat to invade Kuwait. Indeed, the news media barely noted the fact that it was the Bush administration and Secretary of State James Baker who gave April Glaspie, the U.S. Ambassador to Iraq, the mild message she personally delivered to Saddam

Hussein only days before the invasion of Kuwait. Critics in Congress, the State Department, and the press charged that she was soft, placating President Hussein and implicitly encouraging Iraq to invade.[6]

Journalists also went along with the portrayal of Hussein as another Hitler and did not report on the large public relations campaign being conducted in the United States at the time by Hill and Knowlton, the public relations consultants, on behalf of the Kuwaiti government (through intermediaries). The story about Iraqis killing babies in incubators was planted, for example; the story was not true. Nor was much attention given to the several serious peace options being offered by Iraq and third parties in the Desert Shield phase, after the invasion but before the armed conflict. The news media also underplayed the antiwar movement in the United States.[7]

Once the Iraqis invaded the whole of Kuwait, the news media transmitted, without scrutiny or criticism, the U.S. government's claim that there were 250,000 Iraqi troops massed in southern Iraq. Once again, the story was untrue. The news media also downplayed the horrors of the war and went along with exaggerated claims of the success of the "smart" American bombs and missiles, especially the Patriot missiles.[8] In addition, journalists' film was seized and destroyed by military officials, reporters and photographers were manhandled and detained, and General Norman Schwarzkopf played favorites among those reporting from the Gulf,[9] and yet there were few complaints or reports of these behaviors at the time they occurred.

The leading news media tolerated the censorship and other constraints, including pool arrangements that restricted the movement and access of reporters from different media, imposed by the Bush administration and Department of Defense to the extent that they declined to participate in a lawsuit filed by eleven other media organizations (including *Harper's, Village Voice, The Nation,* and *Mother Jones*) against the U.S. government for its suppression of the press. Despite the media censorship during the war, a Times-Mirror poll found that 57 percent of the survey respondents "thought the military should exercise *more* control over how the news groups report about the conflict."[10]

The news media's subordinate position during the war was captured in a skit on *Saturday Night Live* on February 9, 1991. The skit made journalists the targets of ridicule, showing them repeatedly asking the same stupid questions of the military briefers; it left the Bush administration and the military—and their heavy-handed treatment of the press—alone. It could be argued that the news media would have treated the Bush administration and the government differently had there been thousands or tens of thousands of U.S. casualties, or if the ground war had lasted for months or years instead of one hundred hours, but the fact remains that it was a short war.

Once the war ended, though, representatives of the major media changed their minds about the Department of Defense's treatment of the media during the conflict. A group of Washington bureau chiefs from major U.S. news organizations determined that "the combination of security review and the use of the pool system as a form of censorship made the Persian Gulf War the most uncovered major conflict in modern American history." The fifteen bureau chiefs agreed that the military had repressed the media: "The flow of information was blocked, impeded or diminished by the policies and practices of the Department of Defense. Pools did not work. Stories and pictures were late or lost. Access to the men and women in the field was interfered with by a needless system of military escorts and copy review. These conditions meant that we could not tell the public the full story of those who fought the nation's battle."[11]

Instead, the American news media had essentially communicated what President Bush, National Security Advisor Brent Scowcroft (a former Air Force general), Defense Secretary Richard Cheney, General Schwarzkopf, Defense Department spokesperson Pete Williams, and General Colin Powell, chairman of the Joint Chiefs of Staff, wanted them to. American journalists were overwhelmingly loyal to the war effort: only five of the tens of thousands of stories being sent from the Gulf had to be cleared in Washington. The worst censorship was self-censorship, concludes the media critic Jim Naureckas after a review of the testimony and writing of leading Washington reporters, columnists, editors, and news anchors: journalists consistently edited their own reports.[12]

Although the U.S. and allied forces prevailed easily, the war nevertheless cost billions of dollars and tens of thousands of Iraqi lives, and President Saddam Hussein and his dictatorial government were left standing. The American economy continues to be dependent on Gulf-imported oil, and therefore the United States remains vulnerable to events in the Middle East. In addition, the United States arguably ended up with worsened diplomatic relations with the emerging nations and Islamic states. Although it is not to be expected that freedom of the press will fully prevail in wartime, the journalists of the major media were severely constrained in their reporting of the events leading up to the war and of the war proper—and they went along with it.[13]

For all the attention paid to CNN correspondent Peter Arnett's reporting from Baghdad, there was scarcely any attempt by other journalists in the major media to warn their viewers or readers that they were receiving a far from open-minded presentation or discussion about the U.S. intervention in the Persian Gulf.[14] Nor was there any suggestion in the news that the major media were acting more as an adjunct to the government than as an independent voice capable of challenging the actions of the Bush administration in late 1990 and early 1991.

Irrespective of what one thinks of the merits of the Persian Gulf War, the Bush administration was clearly successful at using the news media to obtain public support—whether one thinks of it as implementing public diplomacy or using propaganda—and this public support was crucial to the war effort.

The Crash of Korean Airlines Flight 007

A second example of the news media's failure to serve as a guardian of the public trust or watchdog over the government is the coverage of the crash of KAL Flight 007 in the early morning hours of September 1, 1983. Since the known facts of the case—and much remains unknown, as of this writing—clash with the conventional reports of the crash, I provide more description of the case.

KAL 007 was en route from Anchorage, Alaska, to Seoul, South Korea, when it apparently went off course and lost contact with air traffic control. Later that morning, Secretary of State George Shultz charged that the Soviets had shot down the Korean airliner. Shultz said the airplane had unwittingly gone off course and, after crossing the Kamchatka Peninsula and Sea of Okhotsk, had been intercepted by a Soviet fighter plane over Sakhalin Island and hit by an air-to-air missile. He expressed "controlled fury" over the fact that the Soviets had shot down in cold blood a commercial airliner full of innocent civilians. President Ronald Reagan and U.N. Ambassador Jeane Kirkpatrick likewise condemned the crash, to the outrage of their national and international audiences. Both *Time* and *Newsweek* had the airplane on their covers that week.[15]

The downing of KAL 007 marked one of *the* high-stress moments of the cold war (the Cuban missile crisis being the outstanding example of the superpower rivalry). The crash represented the largest loss of human life in the history of the direct confrontation between the United States and the Soviet Union in the postwar years. In the aftermath of the crash of KAL 007, the U.S. Congress passed a defense budget of $187.5 billion (despite a projected overall budget deficit of $189 billion);[16] the incident undermined the antiwar and the antinuclear movements in the United States, collapsed the European opposition to the United States's installation of Pershing II missiles, and cast a dark shadow over the pending INF (intermediate-range nuclear forces) talks and START (strategic arms reduction talks) negotiations between the United States and Soviet Union. Some in the United States, including the political commentators George Will and Pat Buchanan and the scholars Richard Pipes and Robert Conquest, called for the United States to respond more vigorously to the Soviets' "unconscionable" action of shooting down a passenger plane that had "innocently" strayed into their airspace. Despite the fact that the U.S. government was restrained in its response, the incident gave President Reagan a powerful short-term boost in public opinion polls.[17] Later, the *New York Times, Washington Post,* and other news organizations reported that the Soviets may not have known that the plane was a commercial airliner and thus may have unwittingly killed the 269 civilians on board KAL 007.

Yet the evidence available as of this writing suggests that the foregoing account of the plane crash is mistaken in most important respects.[18] Recent work by a French aviation expert, Michel Brun, and a retired Foreign Service officer, John Keppel, shows that in all likelihood the Korean airliner did *not* enter Soviet territorial airspace at either Kamchatka or Sakhalin, but rather flew through the Kuril Islands over water, crossed the Sea of Okhotsk, and passed through the straits between Sakhalin and Kamchatka. The evidence, Brun and Keppel write, indicates that KAL 007 then flew south off the coast of Hokkaido and Honshu for at least another forty-five minutes before it was destroyed by means and for reasons that remain obscure. At the same time the Korean airliner crossed the Sea of Okhotsk, however, so did a number of U.S. military aircraft. When these aircraft entered Soviet territorial airspace at Sakhalin, a two-hour air battle ensued in which some ten U.S. Air Force and U.S. Navy aircraft were shot down by Soviet interceptors and about thirty U.S. servicemen were killed.[19]

There had already been two instances in April and June 1983 in which U.S. carrier aircraft had made prolonged and provocative flights over Soviet territory in the Kurils. That the Soviets did not respond to either incident may have led U.S. military strategists to believe that the Soviets would not respond vigorously to a larger-scale and deeper incursion. The next penetration would show that the Soviet Union could not control the air over one of its most sensitive strategic areas. Brun and Keppel also argue that the August 31 flights over Kamchatka and Sakhalin may have had other, more strictly military purposes, including the use of satellites to gather and transmit intelligence information in "real time" (i.e., instantaneously).

Evidence from the several crash sites, area shorelines, electronic transmissions, and other sources suggests that what happened off Sakhalin Island was not the crash of the Boeing 747 jumbo jet, but an air battle that resulted in a number of separate U.S. military aircraft being shot down. The U.S. government, or part of it, appears to have used a civilian airliner to gather an "intelligence bonanza" on the Soviets' electronic and aerial defenses, a mission that somehow went horribly wrong. Secretary Shultz's statements to the news media on the morning of September 1, 1983, charging that the

Soviets had deliberately shot down a commercial airliner, suggest that from the moment the plane was first overdue in Seoul, the U.S. government began a massive and orchestrated cover-up of the catastrophe.[20]

The evidence for the fact that an air battle took place over Sakhalin Island is extensive:

- There were multiple crash sites on and around Sakhalin Island and Moneron Island (a small island next to Sakhalin). Brun writes that at least ten U.S. aircraft were shot down, including an RC-135 (a Boeing 707 adapted for gathering communications and electronic intelligence) and two EF-111s (supersonic electronic warfare aircraft) or, less probably, F-111s (strike/attack aircraft).[21]
- The Soviet interceptors, Nos. 805, 121, and 163, whose pilots' voices are recorded on the tape Ambassador Kirkpatrick played to the U.N. Security Council, were only three among a much larger number of Soviet aircraft employed during the air battle of Sakhalin. They included two battlefield surveillance aircraft (Soviet AWACs) and additional interceptors, probably MiG 31s, flown over from the mainland during the battle. During the naval search off Sakhalin, the Soviets recovered a number of different black boxes at the various crash sites they explored.[22]
- The debris removed from the crash sites and from the water was from a military aircraft (an ejector seat and a part of flap of a moveable wing aircraft, most likely an EF-111A). Neither piece is consistent with the equipment of a Boeing 747.[23]
- The Japan Maritime Safety Agency (JMSA) reported that it collected fifty-four pieces of floating aircraft debris in international waters north of Sakhalin and west of Moneron Island. The JMSA stated that none of the items came from KAL 007. Tags on the pilot's ejection seat and the EF-111 wing flap bore numbers from the JMSA number series.
- *Izvestiya's* series on the KAL 007 disaster—which in general presented evidence in support of the single-intruder, single-shootdown, and single-crash scenario—contained statements from witnesses at the crash sites who found "no baggage, not even a carry-on bag" but did find "computers," "recording machines," "kilometers of tape," "cameras," and "electric cables connected to consoles."[24]
- A throttle quadrant from a two-engine jet and an engine cover with a Pratt and Whitney logo—a logo that does not match the much larger Pratt and Whitney logos on KAL 007's engines—were found on the shore of Hokkaido.
- Transcripts of Soviet military communications published with the second International Civil Aviation Organization (ICAO) report (June 1993)

contain language indicating at least nine interceptions of U.S. aircraft over Sakhalin, as well as coded identifications of incoming aircraft meaning "probably hostile."[25]

- The air battle (and multiple-crash) scenario makes sense of a variety of confounding information, including whether the KAL 007 lights were on or off, whether the plane responded to Soviet communications, what models of interceptors the Soviets were flying, the oddity that two different names have been given for the pilot who shot down the Boeing 747 (Major Vasily Kasmin initially and Lieutenant Colonel Genady Osipovich later), the inconsistencies among the altitudes and courses taken by the intruding aircraft, and the discrepancies in the precise time of the shootdown.

The evidence that KAL 007 actually crashed off Honshu and about twenty-five miles west of Narita in the Sea of Japan, rather than off Sakhalin Island, is also compelling:

- Parts of KAL 007 were found on the western coast of Japan and off the northern island, Hokkaido (debris painstakingly collected by Brun in hundreds of miles of waterfront search). The flow of the ocean currents in the Sea of Japan and around Sakhalin Island means that the debris from KAL 007 that Brun picked up could not have floated to where it was found unless the plane crashed about four hundred miles south of the alleged crash site.[26]

- Not until September 10 did debris identified as that of KAL 007 appear off Sakhalin in the Sea of Okhotsk. Had KAL 007 "crashed north of Moneron, no part of its vertical fin could have reached the Hokkaido beach," says Brun, again, because of the existing ocean currents in the area. A JMSA admiral in charge of the search told Brun that he was of the same opinion. Other pieces of the aircraft (floating aluminum honeycomb) were found on the northern, western, and southern shores of Hokkaido and along the western shore of Honshu. Some pieces had Korean markings and paint coloring consistent with Korean Airlines; others did not explicitly identify KAL 007 but were identified as pieces of a large commercial aircraft. But no other aircraft of that kind is known in recent history to have gone down in that part of the Sea of Japan.

- Transmissions were received from KAL 007 as long as forty-five minutes after the official account of events claims that the airliner was shot down. Spectroscopic and voice-print analyses have identified the transmissions as coming from the airliner. The latest transmissions by KAL 007 were sent by very high frequency, which has line-of-sight characteristics and thus has a range limited by the curvature of the earth. That they were recorded at Toyko's Narita Airport indicates that KAL 007 was at altitude and off Honshu at the time they were sent.

- Pieces of the vertical fin of KAL 007's tail that bear the aircraft's registration number (HL7442) were found on a Hokkaido beach by the Japanese, and other fragments were found off Sakhalin by the Soviets. These pieces had drifted north from the airliner's crash site by the current, where the current splits at the strait between Sakhalin and Hokkaido.
- The surfaces of the vertical fin were bowed outward. This appears to be inconsistent with the effects of an air-to-air missile, which would have exploded outside the airliner. It suggests internal pressure from an explosion inside the fuselage at the base of the fin, where the black boxes are located.[27]

The clear implication is the black-box tapes that the Russians produced were either *forgeries* or *edited compilations* of military aircraft flight data recorders. Keppel's analysis, aided by electronics experts, points to this probability:

- The tape from the digital flight data recorder has the aircraft transmitting on five radios simultaneously; KAL 007 was able to transmit on only three radios at the same time.
- The landing and taxiing sequence of the plane landing in Alaska does not fit the design of the Anchorage International Airport.[28]
- The flight recorder tape lasts twenty-seven hours; the tape aboard KAL 007 could last only twenty-four hours and forty-eight minutes.
- The flight recorder tape the Russians gave the ICAO shows that the plane followed a constant magnetic heading of 245 degrees—a heading that would have taken it over Sapporo or southern Hokkaido, not Sakhalin.
- The tape ends with an 18:27 Greenwich Mean Time transmission "descending to one zero thousand." The air traffic control recording made at Narita Airport and released in the Japanese diet in 1985 had the transmission ending with the phrase "bloodbath, really bad."[29]

Other evidence points to the multifaceted ability of the U.S. military to collect, record, and transmit data concerning Soviet air defense actions, radar operations, and communications during the overflights. *The U.S. government was gathering intelligence from the flight of KAL 007.*

- Electronic monitoring by U.S. equipment in the air (the RC-135 aircraft), on the water (the U.S.S. *Observation Island,* which is used to monitor electronic signals and missile testing and was reported to be somewhere in the "North Pacific" that evening), and on the ground (the very large "Cobra Dane" phased-array radar at Shemya and the Air Force's Electronic Security Group at Misawa air base in northern Honshu) would have put KAL on the electronic "center stage," as the electronic communications expert and sociologist David Pearson puts it. There were also the National Security Agency stations in Korea, a number of U.S. "ferret" satellites in orbit capable of picking up signal intelligence from the Soviets, and possibly the space shuttle Challenger overhead—in a position to monitor Soviet communications between the Far East and Moscow the night of August 31 and September 1. Other U.S. reconnaissance planes were also nearby. "To postulate such a simultaneous failure of independent intelligence systems operated by the Navy, Army, Air Force, N.S.A., C.I.A. and the Japanese Self-Defense Forces is hardly credible," comments Pearson. There was in fact one warning issued by air traffic controllers to the military post monitoring the KAL 007 flight: "You guys got someone bumping into the Russians' air defense over here . . . A person should warn him." The fact that KAL 007 was not warned—and the pilots could have been warned—suggests that the plane was doing exactly what it was supposed to.[30]

- Captain Chun Byung-in of KAL 007 left a copy of his flight plan in Anchorage, with the notes "ETP 1501 NM 3 HR 22 MIN" and NEEVA "250 NM" handwritten on it. When KAL 007 flew 1,501 nautical miles from Alaska on its actual flown course, the plane reached the edge of Soviet airspace in Kamchatka; 250 nautical miles after the waypoint NEEVA was passed, a beam would have also taken KAL 007 to the Kamchatka airspace; and ETP could stand for "estimated time of penetration."[31]

- The United States and Soviet Union had a long tradition of "tickling" each other's defenses, intruding each other's airspace, and using commercial aircraft for espionage and electronic intelligence. The direct precursor of KAL 007 was KAL 902, which on April 28, 1978, was forced to land in Soviet territory.[32]

- Captain Chun had flown other such missions, and he told his wife that "the next flight will be particularly dangerous" and that he "might not return." Chun was extremely well qualified and well respected. Just before the flight, his wife took out extra life insurance; his son was the named beneficiary.[33]

- KAL 007 carried unexplained extra weight. An unconfirmed report has it that the airliner had recently been seen on the Navy side of the field at Andrews Air Force Base outside Washington, D.C., where special equipment may have been installed.[34]

- National Security Advisor Judge William Clark, one of President Reagan's closest and longest associates, resigned suddenly six weeks after the disaster, and with little explanation; the mission would have been under his

control. Clark next served briefly as secretary of the interior, and then retired from public office.[35]

Throughout the history of the KAL 007 incident, the major news media
have essentially cooperated with the government's official story. The news
media have on occasion carried challenges to the U.S. government's position, however, and they did provide places for government critics to express
themselves. The *New York Times* broke the story that the Soviets may not
have known that they were shooting down a passenger plane. A little more
than a year after the incident, the *Times* published a column by Tom Wicker pointing out gaps in the government's account of the KAL 007 disaster.
The *Washington Post* also condemned the political damage caused by the al-
legation by those in the Reagan administration that the Soviets knew they
were firing on a civilian airliner when, in fact, there was "no indication that
Soviet air defense personnel knew the plane they were firing at was a commercial airliner."[36]

The television media, too, publicized stories that questioned the official
position. Judy Woodruff, then with PBS, moderated a discussion on the *Mac-
Neil/Lehrer NewsHour* between Keppel (formerly on the Soviet desk of the
State Department's Bureau of Intelligence and Research) and Lawrence Eagleburger (the undersecretary of state for political affairs at the time) on the
discrepant accounts of KAL 007. ABC News's *Nightline* also devoted a portion of the show on May 22, 1991, to the KAL 007 incident, with Ted Koppel moderating a discussion among Keppel, Pearson, Alexander Shalnev of
Izvestiya, and James Oberg, a senior engineer at NASA.

In general, however, the U.S. "media did a grossly inadequate job of covering the downing of Flight 007," reports Pearson. "Instead of addressing the
inconsistencies and questioning dubious assertions in the official versions
of events, instead of actively investigating the downing, journalists in the
fall of 1983 simply reported what officials said." Typical were the editorials
in the *Washington Post* in the months after the disaster. The editorials accepted the official story of the shootdown of KAL 007 as a given. Later, on
the first anniversary of the crash, the *New York Times* ran a story by Assistant
Secretary of State Richard Burt—a former *Times* reporter—that ridiculed
"conspiracy buffs" and "spy plane theorists" in defense of the U.S. government. Burt called Pearson's work "pure baloney."[37] Both Burt and *Time* held
that criticisms were the product of the Soviet Union's "massive overt disinformation campaign." The editors of *U.S. News* responded to Pearson's article in the August 1984 issue of *The Nation* by saying that their examination
of the evidence cited in Pearson's article showed the facts to be "planted by
the Soviets." Administration officials, former U.S. government officials, and

prominent journalists all castigated the *Nation* article as well as Wicker's column questioning the U.S. government's story.

Nor did any of the major media pick up a well-researched series on KAL 007 in the widely read German newsmagazine *Der Spiegel*. The *Spiegel* series, written by the investigative journalists William Bittdorf and Anthony Sampson, established the National Security Agency's ability to track KAL 007 and communicate what was happening back to Washington in real time, it noted that American leaders had decided to use the Soviets' actions as a political weapon, and it wrote that U.S. leaders contacted Japanese and Soviet leaders through back channels in order to coordinate a cover story. The series—translated and delivered to all the major news organizations in the United States—was ignored.[38] Moreover, since the release of the forged flight data recorder tapes in late 1992, there has been no further clarification or investigation into the KAL 007 incident.[39]

Part of the reason for the media's quiescence lies with the U.S. government, to be sure: the Reagan administration extended American secrecy laws and powers to new domains (under Executive Order 12356), restricted Americans' travel abroad, heightened the classification restrictions on potentially sensitive information, and refused to share information with Congress.[40] It similarly used confidentiality laws to fend off journalists' questions.[41] Left on their own, journalists have limited abilities to analyze and sift through bits and pieces of information (as noted in Chapter 3). "Complex stories requiring a great deal of digging, synthesis, and expense are less likely to be fully investigated," says Jacques Ellul, a writer on propaganda.[42]

Yet the nation's leading news organizations supported the Reagan administration and the federal agencies involved in the case: they scarcely questioned official accounts of the airliner disaster, they did not conduct independent investigations of the incident, and they chose not to pick up the news story in *Der Spiegel* (unlike their later follow-up of the revelation of the Iranian arms-for-hostages deal in a much more obscure Lebanese publication).[43] This lack of inquiry speaks volumes about the American media's willingness to go along with the Reagan administration and the U.S. government.

The implication of the KAL 007 case and the news media's coverage of it is that the U.S. government placed unknowing Korean and American civilians in mortal danger for the sake of a military intelligence mission (a mission that went by the code name "1010 Delta," it appears).[44] Although the mission may have arguably been desirable, given the Soviet Union's new phased-array radar complex at Krasnoyarsk, its missiles stationed in eastern Siberia, and the existence of the cold war, it is difficult to argue that it was absolutely necessary for the country's survival. It seems impossible to justify such a mission with any circumstances other than an immediate threat to the survival of the United States.[45]

Another implication of this history is that the air battle in the Soviet far east, taking place amid an already highly tense U.S.-Soviet relationship, made for a plausible chance of a third world war.[46] Just before the KAL 007 incident, the United States led a large military exercise in Europe, "Able Archer," which the Soviets perceived as highly threatening. Furthermore, the evidence from the Soviet pilots and the multiple crash sites points to the probability that a second wave of military aircraft attacked the Soviets on Sakhalin Island, aircraft most likely sent by the commander in chief of the U.S. Pacific fleet an hour after the first wave (possibly explaining some of the time discrepancies), in response to the fact that the earlier planes met unexpected resistance. That resistance may have been caused by the deployment of still-secret MiG 31s—a fact that neither the Soviet/Russian government nor the U.S. government has yet admitted. In fact, the Japanese Air Defense Forces declared a Defcon 3 alert for the Northern Command that evening—one level short of general mobilization.[47]

Furthermore, to the extent that the denial and cover-up by the U.S. government are exposed in the case of KAL 007, the U.S. government faces a further erosion in its credibility among Americans who already view it with suspicion. The existence of a long-term and systematic cover-up by the U.S. Navy, the National Security Agency, the CIA, the State Department, and Presidents Reagan, Bush, and Clinton points to the conduct of high crimes at the core of American government. The KAL 007 case contains the implicit message that other such acts by the U.S. government—ostensibly in the interest of American security—could and did occur.

If the national government (or part thereof) is able to seriously violate federal and constitutional law with impunity—violations such as the withholding, misrepresentation, and destruction of evidence and the deliberate furnishing of false information to Congress, victims' next-of-kin, judges in federal courts of law, journalists, and the American public—the KAL 007 incident throws into serious question the notion of responsible government in the United States.[48]

THE PERSIAN GULF WAR AND KAL 007 CASES ARE NOT UNIQUE WITH RE-spect to the major media's coverage of international affairs. The Tonkin Gulf incident, which the major media accepted the Johnson administration's official line on, was the key to expanded American involvement in Vietnam. The news media likewise reported late and partially on U.S. aid to Nicaraguan contras (American complicity that contradicted the mandated policies of Congress, i.e., the Boland amendments), and the prestige media reported little on U.S. aid to the governments in El Salvador and Guatemala (which, like the contra involvement, resulted in thousands of deaths). More recently, the news media has presented a one-sided and an "oversimplified picture of naked Serb aggression" in the former Yugoslavia. Much has gone unquestioned, and many journalists have framed Serbia in terms reminiscent of Nazi Germany and the Soviet Union during the cold war.[49] None of these are trivial examples, given the lives, money, precedents, and principles at stake. There are others.[50]

In sum, the U.S. government appears to be able to use the news media as a conduit for its own purposes when it comes to some crucial events of international affairs. It is aided, of course, by secrecy laws and the coercive powers inherent in the national government.[51] But as Sissela Bok, the philosopher of ethics, comments with respect to government lying about the Vietnam War, governmental deception "strikes at the very essence of democratic government. It allows those in power to override or nullify the right vested in the people to cast an informed vote in critical elections. Deceiving the people for the sake of the people is a self-contradictory notion in a democracy, unless it can be shown that there has been genuine consent to deceit."[52] No wonder, Bok continues, that the trust in government has declined so sharply.

The Savings and Loan Collapse

The record of the news coverage, or the lack thereof, of the S&L scandal of the early and middle 1980s offers a third example of the media's silence as a watchdog over business and government. Estimates of the total cost of the S&L disaster are between $500 billion and $1.5 trillion (including interest on the government's expense), making the S&L disaster the worst financial scandal in American history—worse than the Teapot Dome scandal of the Harding administration and the Credit Mobilier scandal of the Grant administration. By the end of 1987, almost a third of the nation's S&L establishments were effectively insolvent: 435 thrifts had less cash on hand than regulators stipulated as the absolute minimum of safety, and more than 500 thrifts were insolvent under any measure—they were the "living dead" or "zombies."[53] Whereas there were 3,262 federally chartered thrifts in the United States in 1985, there were only 1,436 S&Ls by midyear 1996.

Both boards regulating the S&Ls would also be shut down as a result of the scandal: the Federal Home Loan Bank Board (FHLBB), responsible for promotion and oversight, and the Federal Savings and Loan Insurance Corporation (FSLIC), the insuring agency.[54] Finally, the government bailout was provided through the establishment of an off-budget government corporation, able to hide the actual cost of the S&L debacle.

The news media did run stories about the S&Ls when the thrifts first came under serious pressure in the middle and late 1970s, when the average interest rate earned by depositors fell below the most conservative measures of the nation's inflation rate. However, the most prominent political journalists and news organizations never pulled the story together or paid sustained attention to the deregulation and then abuse of the thrifts that was happening across the whole country, from Massachusetts to California. Instead, news stories were sporadic and unrelated to each other. To the extent that the S&Ls were covered, they were typically featured in the business or financial sections of newspapers rather than placed with political news in the front sections of newspapers. Not until the end of the 1980s did the news media pick up on what was happening with the S&Ls.[55] The press simply missed "the debacle of the savings and loan crisis," remarks the veteran journalist Haynes Johnson of the *Washington Post*. "We didn't report on it. We didn't talk about it. We didn't prepare the country for what was happening in the financial system . . . I once went back to the *Post* computer files after Milken was about to be indicted and . . . I don't think there was a single entry on Michael Milken. Who was he?"[56]

The financial writer Martin Mayer suggests why. "The years 1980–89 witnessed an irrepressibly powerful confluence of the interests of fast-growing S&Ls, Wall Street brokers/dealers, gargantuan law firms, and elephantine accounting firms—all pressing to maintain and extend the incentives to waste and fraud implicit in what the government had done."[57] Journalists would have had to tackle many of the most prominent private law firms, investment companies, and individual investors in the entire United States were they to find out what was happening with the S&Ls.

Among those working with the failing S&Ls were some of the top law firms in the United States—Jones Day Reavis & Pogue of Cleveland, Baker & Botts of Houston, Akin, Gump, Strauss, Hauer & Feld of Dallas, Sidley & Austin of Chicago, Fulbright & Jaworski of Houston, Kaye Scholer Fierman Hays of New York, Paul, Weiss of New York, and Hogan & Hartson of Washington. The law firms charged millions of dollars in fees to handle S&L transactions and advocate the interests of the thrifts in Washington and the courts. The major investment houses were also making millions by trading for the S&Ls, not only Michael Milken's Drexel Burnham Lambert, but also older, established firms such as Merrill Lynch, Solomon Brothers, Kidder Peabody, and Shearson Lehman. The big accounting firms profited, too, among them Ernst & Young (later, Arthur Young), Touche Ross, Coopers & Lybrand, Deloitte Haskins, and Arthur Andersen. In addition, the largest individual investors in the country, such as Ron Perelman, Saul Steinberg, and the Bass brothers, were making hundreds of millions of dollars from their investments in the thrifts. Also participating were the nation's largest commercial banks, including Bankers Trust and Citicorp.[58] Even Alan Greenspan, an economic consultant at the time, wrote letters to the FHLBB of San Francisco on behalf of Charles Keating and Lincoln Savings.[59] Indicative of the "powerful mix of economics and politics in the S&L fiasco" is the fact "that the families of both President Clinton and former President Bush have been implicated."[60]

In the period when the S&Ls were growing astronomically in size, the fee-charging professionals who certified, represented, and traded with them stood to do quite well. Some Texas S&Ls grew up to 1,250 percent a year, for instance, and the assets of Silverado Savings and Loan (where George Bush's son, Neil Bush, was a director) increased from $250 million in 1982 to $2.7 billion in 1988. At the same time the S&L owners were making money hand over fist, so too were the individual investors, the investment banks, the lawyers, and the accountants. Kitty Calavita, Henry Pontell, and Robert Tillman determined that

> In the first quarter of 1984, 721 thrifts grew at an annual rate of 25 percent or more and 336 grew at an annual rate of more than 50 percent. The fastest growers reported the highest profits, the highest net worth, and the most nontraditional assets. By the second quarter of 1984, California and Texas had respectively 74 and 62 thrifts growing at 50 percent annually, totaling over $75 billion in assets. A study of the so-called Texas 40 (forty of the worst thrift failures in Texas) found that on average they had grown 300 percent between 1982 and 1986—more than three times the rates of other thrifts in Texas and more than five times the general industry average.[61]

Mayer estimates between one-tenth and one-third of the disaster to be the result of out-and-out theft or fraud and the single biggest winners in the S&L scandal to be the investment houses. In their study of the S&L crisis, Calavita et al. present a convincing case that "crime and fraud" were "central ingredients in the collapse" of the S&Ls.[62]

Congress was an all-too-willing partner in the S&L disaster. Congress and the Reagan White House—far more so than the FSLIC, the Federal Deposit Insurance Corporation (FDIC), the FHLBB, and the Resolution Trust Corporation—were responsible for what happened. Federal policies made a bad situation much worse. As one member of the Securities and Exchange Commission observes, "An industry that garners the support of a geographically dispersed, ideologically neutral, monied constituency that is not asking for a direct handout can cut through Congress like a hot knife through butter."[63] With the money solicited from the S&Ls and accepted by the members of the House and Senate, Congress was deeply compromised.

It was members of Congress who in 1980 lifted "Regulation Q," which fixed the interest rate that S&Ls could offer depositors. It was members of Congress who passed the Garn–St. Germain Act, which deregulated the thrifts by uncoupling the ratio between how much an S&L could lend to a developer and how much the development was appraised for and allowing developers to buy S&Ls; the act also completely deregulated the interest rate that S&Ls could offer on short-term deposits. It was members of Congress who agreed to increase the FSLIC's maximum protection to $100,000, up from $40,000 (and, four years before that, $25,000)—although the average depositor had only $6,000 in savings deposits. It was members of Congress who changed the rules and allowed the thrifts to be owned by just one stockholder: before 1981, S&Ls had to have at least 450 stockholders, with at least 125 of them residing in the community served by the S&L in order to qualify for federal loan guarantees; nor could any individual own more than 10 percent of the stock or any "control group" own more than 25 percent.[64]

It was the "Keating Five"—Senators Alan Cranston of California, Donald Riegle of Michigan, and Dennis DeConcini of Arizona, John McCain of Arizona, and John Glenn of Ohio—who pressured Ed Gray, the chair of the FHLBB, to lay off the S&Ls and who covered for Charles Keating and his Lincoln Savings, thanks to Keating's generous campaign donations.[65] And it was Speaker of the House Jim Wright and Democratic House majority whip Tony Coehlo who passed the Competitive Equality Banking Act in 1987, which rescinded measures that the FHLBB could use to cope with fraud and "starved" the FSLIC by not providing it with the funds necessary to restore it to solvency. Wright and Coehlo were also friends and beneficiaries of the S&L owners.[66]

In short, Congress threw the doors wide open for fraud and abuse: How could S&L owners—whether investors, builders, developers, or friends—go wrong if their money was protected by the FSLIC as long as it was bundled in $100,000 pieces? As the financial journalist James Adams asks, "What happens if elected representatives develop vested interests separate from, and even opposed to, the interests of the taxpayers who elected them?"[67] A letter from former Senator William Proxmire of Wisconsin to Gray describes the legislative system. The system operated on

> thinly concealed bribery that not only buys [senators'] attention but frequently buys their vote. The special interests that make these contributions know exactly what they are doing. They know just what changes they want to make . . . A little change can make it possible for them to make or lose millions while the taxpayers make nothing but can lose bil-

lions. The S&L and bank lobbyists know that. Here is precisely why they raise millions of dollars for campaign contributions.[68]

The executive branch was no better. The Reagan administration and the Treasury Department either neglected or were openly hostile to concerns about the solvency and integrity of the thrift industry. Reagan was elected on antigovernment ideology, and once in office, he and his aides pursued deregulatory policies. His secretary of the treasury, Donald Regan, opposed maintaining the S&L regulations. Regan and the other advocates of financial deregulation perceived the government to be coddling an old-fashioned industry, one encumbered by a number of outdated regulations and protected by too many out-of-touch bureaucrats and businessmen. Nor did the budget director, David Stockman, pay attention to the S&Ls. The Reagan administration simply did not take the S&L crisis seriously. It saw the S&Ls as a minor problem that plagued some individual thrifts amid the larger overall benefits of deregulation. Indicatively, the president never once met Ed Gray while Gray was chair of the FHLBB.

President Reagan's first appointee to the Federal Bank Board, Dick Pratt, oversaw the deregulation of the thrift industry encoded in the Garn–St. Germain bill. Pratt, an economist by profession and a protégé of Senator Jake Garn (D-Utah), went ahead with the bill, despite the fact that Congress—because of the political leverage exacted by the Savings and Loan Association League—would not go along with the provisions to omit deposit insurance or give up the traditional role of the thrifts (i.e., portfolio home lending). With deposit insurance in place and without a new role being found for the S&Ls, the mortgage market would be unable to function—even though the whole point of deregulation was to allow market forces, rather than the government, to allocate financial assets across the United States. Pratt had little sense of the complexities of the situation; he was a "bull charging ahead," unaware of the subtleties of S&L policies, says Mayer, who sees Pratt as the single biggest cause of the S&L disaster.[69]

Ed Gray, who for all his faults was one of the few heroes of the S&L crisis, was either ignored or harassed by others in the Reagan administration. Gray came to realize the extent of the thrifts' problems only some time after his appointment in 1982, and his late warnings were ineffective. In fact, the U.S. League of Savings Institutions and many S&L owners viewed Gray as a traitor, members of Congress and their staffers saw him as being uncooperative, and Treasury Secretary Regan and others in the Reagan White House saw him as not "being on the team." Gray therefore came under heavy fire from Keating, other thrift owners, and members of Congress, on the one hand, and from Regan and others in the Reagan administration, on the other hand.

The upshot was that Gray's efforts on Capitol Hill and in the state capitals and his attempts to persuade the Reagan White House of the seriousness of the S&L problem were futile. "In every way that one can be right in an argument and the other can be wrong, Gray was right and Pratt was wrong," as Mayer puts it. "In every way that one man can win an argument and the other lose it, Pratt won and Gray lost."[70]

Gray's successor, H. Danny Wall, also played a key part in the S&L disaster. Wall, an inveterate optimist, helped write the legislation of the Garn–St. Germain bill and then, as chair of the Bank Board, was little more than an advocate for the thrifts. He put a good face on the S&L crisis (including a show of support for Keating's Lincoln Savings) and refused to confront the seriousness of the S&L situation and to consider what solutions were called for. Wall protected many of the S&L owners and did little to stop the abuse of government policies.

Later, FDIC chair and then Resolution Trust Corporation (RTC) chair William Seidman allowed government-owned banks and thrifts to adopt risky strategies, protected banks from lawsuits, and tolerated a poor administration of the shutdown of the S&Ls in the late 1980s. Seidman succeeded in expanding his jurisdiction such that the FDIC took over the FSLIC and the RTC became responsible for selling the assets of the failed thrifts, something for which it was ill-suited both bureaucratically and culturally. The result was that whereas assets should have been sold as expediently as possible, and the S&Ls should have been liquidated in whatever form brought in the most money for the federal government, the FDIC kept the S&Ls intact and was "supercautious" in selling the government's newly acquired assets. In his defense, Seidman felt that he was doing what he could in a politically and economically intractable situation.[71]

In short, none of President Reagan's appointees displayed the independence, administrative competence, and outspokenness necessary to deal with the S&L disaster. The federal agencies in fact cooperated with the thrift industry and most members of Congress by hiding the extent of the damage from the deregulation (or, better, the "unregulation") of the S&Ls: as the regulators nominally in charge, they would look bad if the extent of the failure and fraud of the S&Ls were publicized. Nor did the Reagan administration seem to care. The S&L disaster was the distinct product of the appointees, oversight, legislation, and ideology of the two-term Reagan administration. It happened on President Reagan's watch.[72]

The news media did not seize this opportunity to exploit a split in a seemingly unified Reagan administration. Rather than investigating Gray's charges (and thereby reporting that Gray had good cause to be concerned about the health of the S&Ls), the news media highlighted his own venalities. To the extent that Gray received news coverage, it was publicity of such things as his spending tens of thousands of taxpayer dollars to redecorate his office, traveling at S&L expense, forgetting the cars he parked at airports, and throwing lavish parties at a time when the industry under his jurisdiction was facing collapse. In the face of his own bad publicity, Gray's objections to the deregulation of the S&Ls were discounted by members of the press.

A statement by *Washington Post* reporter Kathleen Day exemplifies journalists' attitude. Day reports that Gray was "not taken seriously" in Washington. By "Washington," Day means Washington *journalists;* Gray *was* taken seriously by the S&L industry (which was extremely concerned about what he would do), members of Congress (who were embarrassed and angered by his testimony), and Regan and others in the Reagan administration (who wanted to loosen the controls on the thrift industry). But it was the perception of Washington journalists that mattered most when it came to the news about the S&Ls.[73]

There was also a split in Congress. Here, journalists were apparently distracted by the chair of the House Banking Committee, San Antonio Congressman Henry Gonzalez, who they viewed as old-fashioned, given to rambling digressions, and even somewhat cartoonish.[74] By so characterizing Gonzalez, journalists allowed personal image to drive news coverage and to obscure the larger issues at stake. Given the opportunity of Democrats taking on other Democrats in congressional hearings, another chance to explore what was happening in the S&Ls, the news media passed it over. They did not use the hearings as a peg for their own investigations of the thrift industry.

Even the 1988 presidential election campaign did not serve to raise the S&L issue, despite the fact that the news media ran several stories on the thrifts in 1988. The one time that Massachusetts Governor Michael Dukakis brought up the S&Ls in the 1988 presidential campaign, Vice President George Bush observed that the Democratic Congress had a role in the problem and ridiculed Dukakis for wanting to raise more taxes.[75] Nor did the news media take the opportunity of the 1988 campaign to highlight what was happening with the S&Ls, despite the fact that, as the political writer William Greider comments, "Everyone—the press, the lawmakers, the candidates' handlers—knew that members of Congress had papered over the S&L crisis with an $8.5-billion bailout designed solely to get them past the election."[76]

To put it simply, the condition of the S&L industry—and the billions of dollars at stake—was not a priority of top editors, top producers, newspaper or newsmagazine publishers, or television news executives. This despite the fact that "it was happening in fucking broad daylight in the Congress. The stuff was all available," as Greider points out. The news media had little reason to engage in investigative reporting, according to Greider. "It's easier [for journalists] . . . if the authorities say there's no problem, until events blow up in your face."[77]

When House Speaker Jim Wright was exonerated by the House Ethics Committee on the charges that he "exercised undue influence" over the FHLBB, for instance, the *Washington Post* "trivialized" the incident according to the financial journalist James Adams. The newspaper noted that "in the absence of any financial interest by Wright in the thrifts, committee members argued that the speaker's conduct was proper and consistent with his role as a member of Congress, sources said." The *Post's* only comment was that Wright may have been "intemperate."[78]

Meanwhile, the *Post's* Howard Kurtz noted that the *New York Times* commented favorably on Keating. The *Times* reporter wrote that although Keating's methods were controversial, he was able to transform "Lincoln from a money loser into a profitable institution." Keating was, of course, doctoring the books. On other occasions, the investigative journalist Michael Binstein was unable to get his stories about Keating and the S&Ls in the *New York Times* or the *Los Angeles Times*. Nor would any of the leading newspapers run "a huge front-page series" or the equivalent on the "big, big, black bottomless pit" of the S&Ls and the likely price tag in the billions of dollars, as did the *Chicago Tribune*. The author of the *Tribune's* series remarked that because his paper was not read in Washington, it could not set the political agenda.[79]

The media also consistently lowballed the cost of the S&L disaster. Adams reports that the *Wall Street Journal* and the *New York Times* continued (as of late 1990) to stick to a cost figure of $180 billion, despite the fact that a General Accounting Office report informed Congress that the S&L rescue cost would exceed $325 billion, "excluding general Treasury financing costs." More recently, a *New York Times* story of December 1996 listed the cost of the S&L disaster to taxpayers at $132 billion. Not only does this figure represent an extremely low estimate of the actual bailout cost of the insolvent thrifts, but the figure ignores the carrying-costs of the debt, since Congress and the public are not going to pay for the bailout out of current tax revenues.[80] If the funds are not going to be raised from taxes, the government has to borrow them at market rates.

Finally, business is a low-prestige beat (as noted in Chapter 4); according to one study, it ranks eleventh in prestige among the major thirteen news beats in Washington. Immediately below the economics beat come the regulatory agencies, and the lowest-ranking beat is regional reporting.[81] All three of the lowest-ranking news beats in Washington were thus involved in reporting on the S&Ls: coverage of business and finance, coverage of the regulatory agencies (the FHLBB, FSLIC, FDIC, and RTC), and coverage of regional politics. Nor do political reporters follow or even understand finance, as a rule; they cover the political process, rather than the substance of politics, as noted in Chapter 2. Bureau chiefs, top editors and producers, publishers, and news executives do not seem to care. As Seidman remarks, "There were a few good early stories when the problems started to unfold, but they did not comprehend the size of the problem and there was little of the follow-up that would have been essential to keep the story alive . . . But the media didn't stay with it, and therefore neither did the public." Seidman adds, "More could be said, but I have made it a lifelong principle never to make war with someone who buys ink by the barrel." Political and financial reporters did not seem to be immune from the 1980s Zeitgeist of government deregulation.[82]

The little and late attention the thrifts did receive has been to a large extent because of the persons involved: Charles Keating and Michael Milken. The S&L disaster has been personified by the controversy over Keating and his subsequent sentence to 12.5 years in federal prison. Keating's sentencing in early 1992 was preceded in 1989 by Milken's being charged with ninety-eight counts of securities fraud and fined $2 billion. (Milken's firm, Drexel Burnham, had to spend $650 million to settle charges and went bankrupt in February 1990.) Other than the attention paid to Milken, Keating, and Neil Bush, the thrift industry, Congress, the Reagan administration, the Wall Street investment houses, the nation's leading law firms, the big eight accounting firms, and the most prominent individual investors received little scrutiny.[83] For most of the story, the news media had "no prominent villain," and they were afraid that coverage of the S&L disaster would "move the [financial] markets." So they went along with the assurances of Danny Wall and others that no bailout would be needed.[84]

Mayer summarizes the S&L debacle as follows:

> The S&L story is desperately important not for reasons usually given but because its development, maturity, and crisis raise profound questions about American society. In the light of this bonfire, *we must ask whether our great professions are still capable of self-regulation, of giving honest service, and of accepting fiduciary duties* in an age when all costs and benefits are reduced to monetary measurements and all conduct that is not specifically prohibited has become permissible.[85]

Journalism is not one of the professions Mayer has in mind, but his comment applies.[86]

AIDS

Coverage of AIDS in the early 1980s provides another instance of the media's deficient coverage—here, with respect to the epidemic that was spreading among gays and intravenous drug users. In covering the story, the media pulled their punches. Journalists were squeamish about revealing the details of how AIDS was transmitted. They were also wary of sensationalizing the story and causing panic among their audiences: they did not wish to hype a disease that few knew much about.[87] So news stories conveyed a generally optimistic tone, suggesting that medical science would soon provide an AIDS vaccine, when in reality this was far from the case.

To some degree, the "defects of AIDS coverage," which ended up costing thousands of lives and hundreds of millions of dollars, were due to "the tried-and-true responsible methods of journalism as an institution," asserts the political scientist Timothy Cook.[88] For one, there was the media's reliance on official sources. The chief counsel for the House Subcommittee on the Health and Environment, Tim Westmoreland, remarked on the press's gullibility: "It was as if the initials M.D. or M.P.H. after these officials' names had conferred upon them the credibility of Moses. Didn't reporters know how to ask that tough second question? Or was it the more likely scenario, that they simply did not care?" The late journalist Randy Shilts himself commented that "reporters were willing to believe any story handed to them in a press release without the slightest inclination to discover whether the reported facts were true." It was handout journalism at its worst.[89]

As David Colby, with the Physician Payment Review Commission, and Cook comment,

> Journalists converged upon agreed-upon experts and authoritative sources; they presented ostensibly balanced reports . . . they moved away from repetitive "old news"; they sought to avoid subjects that seemed peripheral to their imagined audience or that presented too many problems for how that audience might react. Each of these strategies is a rational adaptation to journalists' uncertainty and vulnerability when trying to figure out what's news. Arguing that the media should have been more objective or rational overlooks the possibility that objectivity and rationality led us precisely to the incomplete image of AIDS that television news presented.[90]

Colby and Cook are surely right to focus on the news media's cautious strategy in the face of uncertainty about how audiences might respond to the AIDS story, but they neglect to point out the lack of investigative will revealed in the news media's early attention to AIDS. Not only were the "agreed-upon experts" hardly neutral in the matter, but news organizations shunned AIDS stories for reasons of convention and organizational hierarchy. There simply was not much news of any kind being reported on AIDS, and the reason for this was not only journalists' reliance on authoritative sources.

Dr. James Curran of the U.S. Centers for Disease Control (CDC) notes that media attention was critical to mobilizing resources for finding the cause of AIDS, but

> the *New York Times* had written only two stories on the epidemic [by the end of 1981], setting the tone of noncoverage nationally. *Time* and *Newsweek* were running their first major stories on the epidemic now, in late December 1981. There was only one reason for the lack of media interest and everybody in the task force knew it: the victims were homosexuals. Editors were killing pieces, reporters told Curran, because they didn't want stories about gays and all those distasteful sexual habits littering their newspapers.[91]

The *New York Times,* despite its resources, its scientific expertise, its reputation, and its location in New York City, was especially slow to cover AIDS. Shilts compared the news coverage on AIDS in the *San Francisco Chronicle* and the *Times* between June 1982 and June 1985: whereas the *Chronicle* printed 442 staff-written stories on AIDS, of which 67 made the front page, the *Times* printed 226 stories, of which 7 made the front page. The *Chronicle* framed AIDS news as public policy; the *Times* framed it as a medical phenomenon "with little emphasis on social impact or policy." The *Washington Post* did worse yet, "a deplorable job in covering federal AIDS policy" in the early and middle 1980s, by Shilts's reckoning.[92]

The organizational culture at the nation's leading newspapers was inhospitable to gay issues. "Newspapers like the *New York Times* and *Washington Post* solemnly insisted that they did not discriminate against an employee on the basis of sexual orientation," Shilts writes. "In practice, however, such papers never hired employees who would openly say they were gay, and homosexual reporters at such papers maintained that their careers would be stalled if not destroyed once their sexuality became known." The view was that gays could be drama critics or food reviewers, "but the hard-news sections of the paper had a difficult time acclimating to women as reporters much less inverts [i.e., homosexuals]. Few in the business ever talked about it." This was true for the *New York Times* and the other prestige newspapers, as well as the wire services, newsmagazines, and television networks.[93]

AIDS stories made the news only if they featured heterosexuals. As Dan

Rather admitted in the summer of 1982, "You rarely hear a thing about [AIDS]." Yet as the managing editor of CBS Evening News, Rather was someone who could have spread the word about AIDS. Throughout the 1980s, in fact, the networks did not provide much coverage of AIDS, in accord with the rest of the mainstream media's avoidance of the subject.[94]

The major media were consistent, too, in overreporting the number of researchers working on AIDS and underreporting the funding problems that beset this research. Even though the number of AIDS cases was rising rapidly throughout the mid-1980s, the Reagan administration planned to cut the 1986 budget for AIDS research by $10 million. The 1985 hearings in one House subcommittee revealed "in excruciating detail" the extent of the rivalry among government agencies working on AIDS, the government's failure to formulate a long-term plan to fight and prevent AIDS in the future, and the Reagan administration's lack of concern about AIDS (despite its words to the contrary). The *Washington Post* made no mention of a devastating report about the lack of progress of AIDS research released by the Office of Technical Assessment; the *New York Times* put out the story four days after the report was released, and on page 14 at that.[95]

There was "media non-reaction to stories of deceit at the highest levels of Washington's AIDS bureaucracy," comments Shilts. The media refused "to devote serious investigative journalism to federal AIDS policy," a resistance that Shilts sees as "downright astounding" in view of the seriousness of the epidemic. "Network television coverage, meanwhile, was little more than a diary of the obvious. No television network had assigned a reporter full-time to cover the unfolding story, and none of the networks' already overworked science correspondents had demonstrated either the background or the disposition to challenge the administration's official press releases."[96]

Again, the government was complicit in the media's lack of attention to AIDS and to the misleading information that was being publicized about the epidemic. Members of Congress were hardly outspoken in their support for more AIDS funding, and the Reagan administration simply wanted the problem to disappear. The 1988 presidential election was no help; AIDS was barely mentioned in the campaign. Reporters did not bring it up, and presidential candidates skirted the issue. Neither the Democratic nominee, Michael Dukakis, nor the Republican nominee, George Bush, offered any specific plans on what his administration would do with respect to AIDS once he was in office. Congress, the White House, and the National Institutes of Health all did little.[97] So did the news media.

The news media systematically deemphasized the seriousness of AIDS. If no major news organization picked up the story, neither did less prestigious news organizations. The story did break through to national attention in early 1983 during the first wave of AIDS hysteria and then in 1985 with the death of Rock Hudson. In early 1985, AIDS stories were 10 percent of health stories; after Hudson's death, they constituted 55 percent. It was still not until 1987 that the news media started to bring consistent pressure on the government and the health professions began to do much more about the AIDS epidemic. In 1987, AIDS stories peaked at 3.3 percent of national news volume.[98]

Interestingly, in the early 1990s the news media's coverage of AIDS erred in the other direction, systematically exaggerating and distorting the dangers of AIDS for the heterosexual population as a group (deriving possibly from the earlier inattention to AIDS and from the fact that heterosexual news was more compelling to editors). Although heterosexuals are at risk when exposed to the population of intravenous drug users and when engaged in (male) homosexual relationships, they are far less at risk absent those conditions. In fact, the CDC admitted that it had overstated the risk of heterosexual AIDS as a necessary evil to protect the funding for AIDS research, programs for HIV testing, and social programs for education on and prevention of AIDS. The *Philadelphia Inquirer*'s David Boldt notes, "From the *New York Times* and network news to *Money, Dance,* and *Skin Diver,* practically every news outlet helped propel the story onward."[99]

In short, as Colby and Cook comment, the top journalists in the United States do not "reflect a democratic variety of voices," but instead reflect the authoritative voices of political leaders and governmental agencies. "NIH officials were often the *only* people quoted [and] had the propensity not to tell the truth," and some journalists were little more than transmitters of the government's testimony.[100] The Reagan administration paid little heed to AIDS at first, and those in the CDC who were working on AIDS received little support from the National Institutes of Health or the Department of Health and Human Services. Nor were members of Congress as a class attuned to what was happening, and the medical profession itself was slow to respond.

In the absence of official voices speaking out on AIDS, the news media did little. It took the actor Rock Hudson, as well as eleven-year-old Ryan White and the tennis star Arthur Ashe, both of whom died of AIDS after contracting HIV from blood transfusions, for the nation to become aware and concerned about the epidemic. The lost years exacted their toll on the millions of Americans who became infected with HIV and the well over one hundred thousand who died as a result.

Gaston Naessens

Another example of the news media's failure to report on fundamental issues of public health is their coverage of a Canadian biologist's research on subcellular organisms in the blood and his development of a cure for cancer. If there were any subject on which we might expect full and timely news, it would surely be the advancement of medical science regarding cancer. Yet the media have been silent on the topic of Naessens's revolutionary research at the foundations of human life.

Naessens, a biologist and mechanical inventor born in France in 1924 and a resident of Quebec, has spent his life researching what had once been thought of as strange and unexplained material in human blood.[101] Believing that such "dross" might have biological significance, Naessens was able in the 1950s to build a microscope capable of viewing living tissue. What distinguishes Naessens's microscope from others is that it uses laser and ultraviolet technology to produce indirect light that illuminates cells and subcellular material. The microscope's ability to make the specimen appear light against a dark background resembles what is called a "dark-field microscope."

Unlike conventional light microscopes, Naessens's microscope allows magnifications up to 30,000 times—more than 10 times the power of other light microscopes. Unlike electron microscopes, which magnify up to 500,000 times and require that tissue be killed and prepared, Naessens's microscope enables the viewer to look at living tissue only minutes after it has been taken from the body. Finally, the microscope has a resolution of 150 angstroms, in comparison to a standard light microscope's resolution of 30 to 50 angstroms.[102]

Naessens's microscope allowed him to find small bodies moving around in the human blood, which he called "somatids" (meaning "little bodies"). The somatids are "pleomorphic," meaning that they take a variety of biological forms. They are also almost indestructable, surviving fire at 200° centigrade and exposure to fifty thousand rems of radiation (more than enough to kill other living organisms). In healthy persons, the somatids take three forms after their creation in red blood cells: somatic, spore, and double-spore. In unhealthy blood, the somatids take thirteen additional forms, for a total of sixteen. Using his microscope, Naessens has been able to identity somatid phases 4–16, indicators of a weakened immune system.

The presence of such bodies in human blood—bodies that are essentially electrical, according to Naessens—runs contrary to standard scientific textbooks, which do not recognize or attempt to explain this phenomenon. Oncologists hold that microbes have little to do with the onset of cancer, even as Naessens himself has made videotapes and taken pictures of changes in the blood microbes—that is, of the somatids—that indicate cancer.

Naessens has developed a treatment based on a camphor-based compound that he calls 714-X, which may be injected directly into the lymph nodes. The cancerous cells appear to feed off the nitrogen in the camphor-based solution, and thus the injection of 714-X allows the other cells and the immune system to recover. Naessens's 714-X treatment has been able to arrest cancers in more than a thousand cases worldwide—many cases in which other medical professionals gave up on a cure. Yet medical doctors have said that Naessens's injection of his camphor-based serum is physiologically impossible.

Naessens's discovery of the somatids is not new, interestingly enough. More than a century ago, Antoine Bechamp, a contemporary and rival of Louis Pasteur, held that the cause of disease lay within the entire system of the body. Bechamp, with much cruder instruments than Naessens uses, then proceeded to observe tiny particles in the blood, which he called "microzymas." These, Bechamp concluded, were the most fundamental form of living matter and were essential to any form of life.[103]

In the 1920s and 1930s, Royal Raymond Rife, an American, constructed a microscope capable of magnifying from five thousand to fifty thousand diameters (conventional microscopes at the time could magnify only up to about two thousand times). Made out of 5,682 parts and 14 lenses and prisms, Rife's microscope allowed the viewer to look at organisms visible only under specific frequencies of light or by specific parts of the light spectrum. (*Science* referred to Rife's microscope as a "supermicroscope," and the *Journal of the Smithsonian Institution* and the *Journal of the Franklin Institute* published articles describing the innovations of Rife's microscope.) Rife, too, identified sixteen separate and distinct subcellular organisms, contrary to the notion that the cell is the most basic building block of life. Rife also identified the microorganisms as being pleomorphic and came to the conclusion that human disease "is not always caused by bacteria invading a person's body from the outside, but instead is just as often caused *when certain bacteria found inside the human body begin to change form in order to adjust to disruptions in the body's internal environment* which may be the result of stress or other problems."[104]

Rife proceeded to develop a unique electromagnetic device able to destroy the bacteria that he believed to cause cancer. At the conclusion of tests at the University of Southern California, "fourteen of these so-called hopeless cases [out of sixteen] were signed off as clinically cured by a staff of five medical doctors and the pathologist for the group. The treatments consisted of three minutes duration . . . at three-day intervals. It was found that the elapsed time between treatments attains better results than cases treated daily." Dr. Arthur Yale reported to his colleagues that "when using Rife's device, cancerous masses 'have disappeared . . . so far with no reoccurrences.' He stated at the time that he was making his own results public because 'the treatment and results have been so unique and unbelievable.'" Rife's work was rejected by the medical establishment, his microscopes were disassembled, and his research files and documentation have since disappeared.[105]

Naessens's work has its predecessors, then. Despite this fact and the prominence of the subject, Naessens has received almost no attention in the leading American news media. Several factors contribute to this. One is that Naessens does not speak English and is little interested in self-promotion or money (although he has kept proprietary rights to the Somatoscope and has manufactured and sold a "condenser" that allows ordinary microscopes to similarly use light to illuminate tissues). More significantly, Naessens has not yet conducted the randomized, double-blind, controlled experiments that would confirm his research to the scientific community. As a result, he has not contributed to scholarly journals. These have all hurt his cause.

Nonetheless there is ample basis for Naessens's work to attract significant national and international media attention:

- Several U.S. news organizations, including *USA Today,* and Associated Press, have run stories in 1995 and 1996 on Naessens and 714-X.[106]
- Naessens's research has been written up in a number of periodicals, attesting that a number of editors and publishers have found his work to be both newsworthy and credible (given that their own reputations are at stake).[107]
- Naessens's work is featured in a number of books.[108]
- Naessens has been subject to criminal charges. In 1989, the Quebec Corporation of Physicians (the Canadian medical profession's licensing body) indicted him on three interlocking sets of charges: one sixty-three-count charge of "illegal practice of medicine," a second charge of medical fraud (defined legally as "extracting of money for false pretenses and subterfuge"), and a third charge of negligent homicide—that Naessens's intervention "led to the deaths" of two Canadian women. Naessens was arrested and put in jail; had he been found guilty, he would have had to serve a life sentence. After dozens of witnesses attested to the beneficial effects of 714-X, Naessens was acquitted on all counts. (He did have to pay a single fine of $5,000.) After the trial, Health and Welfare Canada allowed for the legal distribution of 714-X under the Emergency Drug Relief Program for those with terminal cancer only.[109] In a related matter, in November 1994, Charles R. Pixley, the director of Writers & Re-

searchers, Inc. of Rochester, New York, and the author of *Do No Harm* (about 714-X) faced a nineteen-count federal indictment for the alleged distribution of an unapproved drug (714-X) after an FDA raid of July 12, 1994, since the importation and distribution of 714-X are still illegal in the United States.

■ Naessens's work has been recognized publicly by other scientists: Thomas G. Tornabene, director of the School of Applied Biology, Georgia Institute of Technology, Professor Vitaly Vodyanoy, Department of Physiology and Pharmacology, College of Veterinary Medicine, Auburn University, Rolf Wieland, senior product specialist, Microscopy, Carl Zeiss, and Walter Clifford, a former U.S. Army Laboratories bacteriologist based in Natick, Massachusetts. When Naessens first settled in Canada, his research was funded by the MacDonald Stewart Foundation of Canada, a prominent and prestigious source of funding for medical research.

The major American news media have ignored Naessens's work. An exception is a July 1995 article in *U.S. News* that dismisses his research as "wackiness," refers to it as one of several "dubious treatments," and uses ironic quotation marks to refer to Naessens's cure. The article follows the line of the National Council Against Health Fraud, which refers to 714-X as the illusion of "desperate patients and ding-a-ling freelance writers who spin yarns about the grand medical conspiracy," and that of the American Cancer Society, which listed Naessens's work as one of sixty-three "unproven methods."[110]

Naessens has not been mentioned in most of the leading U.S. media, however. There has been nothing, in fact, from July 1995 through December 1996, despite the billions that have been spent on cancer research, and despite the fact that in the face of the medical community's devoted resources and dedicated expertise, the incidence of viral and bacterial disease has scarcely abated over the last few decades. The story of Naessens's inventions and discoveries would appear to be worth mentioning.

In sum, the late coverage of AIDS and the lack of coverage of Naessens's research illustrate the narrow field of news that is reported in the American news media. These are both political issues (AIDS more so, Naessens less so) under the definition of politics I use here—that is, how scarce resources, be they human health and human life or funds for medical research, are authoritatively allocated. Once more, the media's reporting, or rather nonreporting, of AIDS in the early years and of Naessens's work has had considerable implication for the welfare of the American public.

THE PRECEDING CASE HISTORIES SUPPORT THE CONTENTION THAT THE top news organizations in the United States inadequately cover political news that is not subject to political contest. Furthermore, they do not challenge policy monopolies and poorly cover news stories that are unrelated to or threaten economically desirable audiences (and therefore are irrelevant to or in conflict with advertisers' interests). The prestige media have slighted news about marginal persons such as foreign nationals (the Persian Gulf War and KAL 007 coverage), about ethnic, sexual, and religious minorities (e.g., early AIDS coverage), and about the general populations of present and future taxpayers, travelers and tourists, and the sick (coverage of the Persian Gulf War, KAL 007, the S&L debacle, and Naessens's cancer research).[111]

These cases further show that the news media act as an institution, to the detriment of the public interest.

Defects of the Institutional Media

First, the hierarchical organization of news production is evident in all cases. Each reveals the priorities of the leading news media and the striking absence of investigative effort and commitment of investigative resources. It is difficult to conclude anything other than that the news coverage of the five cases was what publishers, company executives, senior editors, and producers wanted. Reporters are not simply free to write whatever they want (as noted in Chapter 5). Not only do they partly depend on the resources and assignments bestowed by their bosses, but they learn from how their past stories were handled and from their colleagues and superiors which stories and story angles will be well received and which will not. They are restricted in their reportage, even if the restrictions are typically inferred rather than decreed.

The case histories show, second, that top editors and producers relied on the multivocal conventions I discuss in Chapter 5, that is, the use of balanced reporting, a limited set of news frames, authoritative sources, and transparency.

These news stories were ostensibly balanced in that charges against the government or attacks on policy were matched against the rival claims of government spokespersons. In the case of the Persian Gulf War, news organizations nominally balanced their coverage by publicizing the debate in Congress, publishing editorials and letters to the editor that called for the further use of economic sanctions, and running stories critical of the procedures followed by the Bush administration.[112]

In the case of KAL 007, the media ran stories and testimonies critical of the U.S. government's account of the plane crash, and they publicized both challenges to and defenses of the Reagan administration. Thus the questions raised by Keppel were counteracted by Lawrence Eagleburger, then under-secretary of state for political affairs, and ABC News's *Nightline* matched the testimonies of Pearson and Keppel against the counterclaims of NASA's James Oberg.[113]

In the S&L case, editors paired the bad news about the S&Ls with the optimistic claims of the S&L owners, White House officials, and members of Congress from both sides of the aisle. The AIDS news coverage was also balanced: discouraging news about AIDS and criticism of the Reagan administration's handling of the epidemic were typically countered by reassurances from government scientists. Naessens, of course, received virtually no coverage in the first place.

Journalists also relied on a limited set of news frames in each of the cases. The Desert Shield phase of American intervention in the Persian Gulf was characterized by the use of World War II frames, with Saddam Hussein portrayed as the equivalent of Hitler and the United States's inaction as the equivalent of appeasement. The war itself was framed in terms "invoking symbolic patriotic values that equated attachment to country, national unity, and collective interests with conformity to majority sentiment." Support of the war was framed "as indisputably good and wise," and dissent as "hostile." Supporters of the war were shown being quiet and in the act of prayer, whereas dissenters were framed as "untrustworthy, disheveled, nonconforming 'others' who personify threatening strangeness."[114]

Once the war started, a "military-linguistic" frame became popular: the use of technological jargon (e.g., "sorties" and "collateral damage") by military commentators (thirty-eight commentators in all were used by U.S. news organizations) and soon thereafter by the regular correspondents of CNN, NBC, and the other networks. The antiseptic high-tech jargon sanitized the war: U.S. ordnance "killed" enemy tanks (not troops), and "smart bombs" and "tightly controlled" targeting would, by implication, miss Iraqi civilians and infantry forces.[115]

The news media characterized the crash of KAL 007 as the result of the inhumanity of the Soviet Union, President Reagan's "evil empire" of the Soviet Union made manifest. Another frame was the backwardness and incompetence of the Soviet air force and government—How could they be so stupid as to shoot down a civilian airliner and mistake a Boeing 747 for a Boeing 707? How could they so botch their public relations effort about KAL 007 in the aftermath of the crash?—compared with the technological, diplomatic, and moral superiority of the United States. Later, when questions arose about the U.S. government's story, the government and many in the media applied a frame of communist deviousness and duplicity: challenges to the Reagan administration's story were a Soviet plot, the fruits of Soviet disinformation.[116]

The collapse of the S&Ls was portrayed as the necessary cost of desirable deregulation: though errors and excesses would occur, they were the unfortunate accompaniments to the conversion of government regulation to a market system. Relatedly, the blame for those problems that did emerge could be laid at the feet of individual S&L owners in Texas, Florida, Kentucky, Colorado, California, and other states. The implied frame was a contrast between the sophistication of economists and financial experts in New York and Washington (who knew what was good for the national economy and for the S&L industry in particular) and the moral and intellectual deficiency of the S&L owners in the hinterlands.

The AIDS story was characterized as a homosexual disease for a long while. AIDS was associated with "the lifestyle of some male homosexuals," as NBC's Tom Brokaw once put it. One prominent early frame was that homosexuals brought the disease on themselves. The difficulties of AIDS research were framed as road bumps or twists and turns in the path of scientific progress, where American expertise and ingenuity would eventually triumph against irrational nature. To the extent that the Naessens story has been framed in the major media (*U.S. News*), it has been portrayed as quack medicine, beyond the pale of respectable medical practice.[117]

The use of these news frames, although not identical to the most common news frames, such as individualism, mentioned in Chapter 5, allowed for difficult and complex news to be accessible and acceptable to political sources and political insiders, as well as to advertisers and consumers. Yet not only did the frames distort the record in each case, but after being used once, the frames tended to perpetuate themselves, irrespective of what the existing and subsequent information indicated.

The use of authoritative sources, especially governmental sources, is also clearly evident in the cases. The news media consistently deferred to the White House, executive branch officials, members of Congress, established professionals, and prominent academics. There was little independent journalism that considered those who suffered as a result of the government's action or inaction. The few independent media that did report contrary news on the Persian Gulf War, KAL 007, the S&Ls, AIDS, and Naessens's research were ignored, condemned, or ridiculed.

With respect to the transparency of the news media, the news organizations mentioned in the above cases have generally been successful at avoiding scrutiny. The media have engaged in some self-examination of their coverage of the Persian Gulf War and, to a lesser degree, the S&L case (as noted earlier), but not of their coverage, or lack thereof, of the KAL 007 crash, the spread of AIDS, and alternative medicine in the pursuit of a cure for cancer. "Nobody goes back to the *Washington Post* and the *New York Times* and says, how come you didn't do this?" remarks William Greider in reference to the news media's coverage of the thrifts.[118] No one holds the bureau chiefs and editors of the *Wall Street Journal* and *New York Times*, or, for that matter, the top editors at *Time, Newsweek,* and *U.S. News* accountable for what they missed in the S&L scandal—or in any of the other cases.

In short, the news media's treatment of the above cases was consistent with the multivocal conventions of the institutional perspective of political communication presented here. Nor did any of the major news organizations in the United States deviate from the news coverage provided by the other major players. All went along with the Bush administration's handling of the Persian Gulf War (the only exceptions were two regional newspapers, the Denver *Rocky Mountain News* and the St. Petersburg *Times),* and all followed the Reagan administration's line on the KAL 007 crash. Then, when the *New York Times* broke the story that the Soviets may not have known that KAL 007 was a civilian airliner, the other media reported the identical story.

None of the networks, newsmagazines, and national newspapers—not even the *Wall Street Journal*—led their news with stories about the condition of the S&Ls throughout most of the 1980s. None paid much attention to AIDS until the death of Rock Hudson in 1985. Even then, the attention was brief, and it would not be sustained until after 1987 and the death of Ryan White. Likewise, with the exception of *U.S. News's* dismissive story, none of the media have covered Naessens's work on the somatids and his 714-X cure for cancer.

In each of the five cases, we see the actions of an institutional news media in the sense that the major news organizations all covered the news similarly and operated under more-or-less set guidelines. We do not see evidence of guarding the public interest. In fact, the leading news organizations subverted the ethical code of the Radio-Television News Directors to "gather and report information of importance and interest to the public accurately, honestly and impartially" in each case, just as they betrayed the Society of Professional Journalists' responsibility to "serve the general welfare." The following are the ethical principles of the American Society of Newspaper Editors: (1) responsibility to serve the "general welfare" by informing people and enabling them to make judgments about contemporary issues, (2) freedom of the press, (3) independence from vested interest, (4) truth and accuracy, (5) impartiality, in particular a clear distinction between news and opinion, and (6) fair play—respecting the rights of those in the news, observing standards of decency, giving opportunities for reply, and respecting confidentiality.[119] The media did not adhere to these ethical codes with regard to the five stories.

There was little thorough reporting about the context and motivations for American intervention in the Persian Gulf. The major media did not protest the violations of freedom of the press at the time of government suppression. They also showed little independence from the Bush administration and the American military. There was little reporting, too, of arguments against armed engagement made by those who opposed the war.

Similarly, although the media expressed concern for the KAL 007 crash victims, they did not thoroughly investigate the case and showed no independence from the Reagan administration and the intelligence community when reporting on the crash and its aftermath. Nor was much truth or accuracy evident in the news coverage; rather, news stories themselves contained much disinformation and opinion disguised as fact. Although some news organizations ran stories or presented viewpoints that questioned the government's position, most news coverage—even by those same organizations—supported the government's position and attacked those who questioned it.

Regarding the S&L collapse, the media conducted just as little investigative reporting and showed even less concern for the victims, the taxpayers who would end up picking up the gigantic tab. They showed little detachment from the interests of the Reagan administration, the ranking members of Congress, the S&L owners, and the legal, accounting, investment, and banking professions. Nor did journalists give a fair hearing to key actors such as Ed Gray and Representative Henry Gonzalez. Conversely, they gave favorable hearings to Charles Keating, other S&L owners, and their collaborators in Congress, the White House, and the regulatory agencies.

The coverage of AIDS was, again, hardly in the service of the "general welfare." The major news media severely underreported a story affecting a portion of the American public: homosexual males who engaged in unprotected sex and intravenous drug users who shared hypodermic needles. Then, at the end of the 1980s and after years of neglect, the media exaggerated the possibility of heterosexuals getting AIDS. Moreover, they showed little interest in the individual victims of AIDS, in contrast to their coverage of Legionnaire's disease, for example.[120] The news media were hardly independent investigators of the AIDS epidemic and Congress's and the Reagan administration's response to it.

As to the work of Gaston Naessens, there has been virtually no coverage by the major news media. The general welfare of the American public and the advancement of biological science and medicine have been neglected.

THESE FIVE CASES OF UNRELIABLE MEDIA COVERAGE REPRESENT MORE than episodic errors.[121] Rather, they reveal that "mistakes are socially organized and systematically produced," as Diane Vaughan puts it in the conclusion of her comprehensive study of the Challenger space shuttle disaster. The case studies I have presented suggest that even in periods of "politics as usual," as Russell Neumann, Marion Just, and Ann Crigler describe 1985 through 1988, the late 1980s *were* a remarkable period: the cold war came to an end (with the KAL 007 incident playing a small part), the S&L industry collapsed (causing immense economic damage and taking billions of taxpayers' dollars with it), AIDS spread, and cancer remained a terrible killer in American society.[122]

Meanwhile—and possibly contributing to the passivity of the news media—there was a great growth and consolidation of both print and broadcast media firms across the United States. It is not clear that the coverage of another war or of another complex political, economic, or medical phenomenon would be so different. I do not deny that individuals construct meaning according to their own experiences, as has been argued by, for example, Neumann et al. and Diane Mutz. My point is that not only does news coverage legitimate personal experience and possibly turn individual perceptions into political attitudes, to follow Mutz, but also individuals crucially depend on the news media for information remote from their own experiences: this includes almost all of foreign policy information, most information of a highly specialized or technical nature, and information on the experiences or behaviors of marginal populations and those in remote regions.[123]

The major media have not owned up to their deficient reporting regarding the Persian Gulf War, KAL 007, AIDS, and Naessens's cancer research; the leading news organizations in the United States do not even publicly acknowledge their mistakes. Yet they are very much mistakes to those who expect them to follow the ideals of journalism: conscience, integrity, and public service. We expect the media to cover news that matters—news on important national issues that affect many or most American citizens. We expect the news media to be forthcoming. We expect to learn why wars started and why they are necessary. We want to know the reason for the loss of hundreds of lives from an air disaster and for an escalation in hostility between superpowers. We seek answers for the failure of hundreds of financial institutions and the loss of hundreds of billions of taxpayers' dollars. We want to learn about the emergence and spread of a deadly national epidemic. We expect to be informed about potentially revolutionary advances in science and a cure for cancer. This information is what Walter Cronkite, Dan Rather, Brit Hume, and other correspondents, editors, producers, and publishers reassure us we get—and it is what the codes of ethics of news organizations promise.[124]

Then there is the pathology of the news media's coverage of presidential elections and other political contests: the news media are destructive of the health of the electoral, legislative, and governing processes (as noted in Chapter 2). Politicians are misrepresented, messages are truncated and taken out of context, voters do not learn what matters, and the enormous attention paid to the preprimary period and the earliest primaries undermines the "one-person, one-vote" basis by which citizens presumably elect the president.[125]

News organizations and their spokespersons talk of the public's "right to know," proclaim the First Amendment's protection of a free press, and say they act on behalf of the American public. They do not speak of the restrictions on reporting, the conflicts of interest present in news production, or the commercial motives that drive the production of political news. The news media obscure the fact that their news coverage is compromised by the predictable ways in which they respond to the constraints and incentives they face on a daily basis in their uncertain larger environment.

Conclusion

Journalists' activities and news organizations' operations are responses to the uncertainties fundamental to their occupation. To overcome these possibly destabilizing external relations, news organizations develop various standard routines. Given their status and their intention to stay among the prestige news organizations in the United States, the behavior of the major news media is essentially self-protective. The nation's leading news organizations would, in fact, hurt their own interests and risk their privileged positions in the American polity were they to take chances in their coverage of national politics and the government and with their bottom lines. It is also not in their best interests to expose the extent to which their practices are systematically constrained by these uncertainties of news production.

The consequence is that the news media discourage outspokenness, initiative, and revelation in the coverage of national politics. They thrive on telling stories about new persons, new events, and even new ideas, but they interpret the new information in known terms and perspectives. The cost of this "routinizing the exceptional," as Gaye Tuchman puts it, is that the news media seldom go beyond familiar interpretations of politics and government; they are conservative in the sense of referring to and building on the known, the familiar, and the established. Only when fundamental political interests are not at stake (as in pointing out the errors and flaws of presidential candidates, top cabinet appointees, and leading members of Congress), and only when political elites are themselves sharply divided, are the news media capable of serving as public guardians. But on most issues, even the most serious of issues, the news media operate conjointly with the dominant political actors, the prevailing economic interests, and the professions.[126]

The news media are partners in "an alliance of powerful groups." Even if there is indeterminacy in news production—news being "negotiated among sources, editors, and reporters," news frames clashing with each other, news values being reconciled with commercial interests—the news production of the major media is predisposed in the ways elaborated above. Journalists are often unconscious or only semiconscious of the practices and conventions of news production, as the sociologist Todd Gitlin notes. "Journalists indeed occupy a vulnerable position" in relation to "specific, focused pressures."[127] It is the presence of this vulnerability across multiple dimensions that makes the resultant journalistic practices crucial to an understanding of the news media's role in the United States. The media *are* able to provide a degree of order throughout a huge, geographically dispersed, multiethnic, multiracial, and multireligious society.

Unfortunately, it is a particular kind of order the media provide, one that advantages the powerful and wealthy and disadvantages the many. The American public increasingly senses this. Public opinion polls suggest that a large proportion of citizens already think that the news media do not protect or act in the broad public interest. Even journalists themselves are concerned. In early 1997, the Joan Shorenstein Center on the Press, Politics and Public Policy at Harvard University's John F. Kennedy School of Government sponsored a National Press Club conference entitled "Is American Journalism in Crisis?" Later that year, a group of twenty-eight prominent journalists led by William Kovach, curator of the Nieman Foundation at Harvard University, and Tom Rosenstiel, director of the Project for Excellence in Journalism, announced a schedule of eight meetings as "a call by journalists for a period of reflection about the troubled state of our profession."

The political scientists James March and Johan Olsen observe that dominant institutions "create environments to which others must respond, without attending to the others." As March and Olsen warn, "The ability to ignore others can lead to long-term failure. Powerful institutions and individuals in them find it less important to monitor and learn from experience and thus become less competent at doing so." The result is that "there is some chance that a powerful institution will become dependent on its capability to enact its environment and consequently be unable to cope with a world in which it does not have arbitrary control."[128]

This may be happening to the news media, which appear to be paying less attention to whether they are relevant than to denigrating the intelligence and judgment of the American public. Typical is a story in the 1996 year-end issue of *Newsweek* entitled, "Conspiracy Mania Feeds Our Growing National Paranoia," with the word "paranoia" spanning the entire page. The authors of the article satirize news reports about aliens, the CIA and the crack cocaine trade, military secrecy, and other topics. Only in the last few sentences do the authors admit that, given the Watergate scandal, the U.S. government's reluctance to acknowledge the Gulf War syndrome that has afflicted troops who served in the war, the revelation that radiation experiments were conducted on unwitting Americans as late as 1974, and the recent documentation of the brainwashing of Korean soldiers, there might be some basis to Americans' "paranoia."[129]

Granted, the implications of this public skepticism are bleak. As Tuchman points out,

> Challenging the legitimacy of offices holding centralized information dismantles the news net. If all of officialdom is corrupt, all its facts and occurrences must be viewed as alleged facts and alleged occurrences. Accordingly, to fill the news columns and air time of the news product, news organizations would have to find an alternative and economical method of locating occurrences and constituent facts acceptable as news.[130]

No wonder few journalists or social scientists want to look too deeply into such matters: the loss of the credibility of the political process would be immensely destabilizing to news organizations, as well as to the American public.

Yet holding political leaders and the news media accountable may be the necessary first step to recovering credible and legitimate government. E. E. Schattschneider's words in *The Semisovereign People* are still relevant:

> The system operates largely through processes of which people are unaware. Stratification and isolation and segregation are to a great extent the unconscious or semiconscious by-products of the way the social system operates to organize the community . . . The point is that *the process is automatic, unconscious, and thoughtless.* People reconcile their democratic faith and their undemocratic behavior by remaining comfortably unaware of the inconsistency of theory and practice.
>
> The sixty million [who are politically attentive] share the same values and play the same game; they participate in politics the way they participate in the life of the community and . . . compete for goods and power. Unfortunately this is not a game in which the whole nation seems to

participate . . . The contradictions in the political system have produced a party system that is able to exploit some kinds of issues but not other kinds. Whatever the cause, the present boycott of the political system [by a large portion of the electorate] has brought the political system *very near to something like the limits of tolerance of passive abstention*.[131]

The civil rights movement, the riots in the inner cities in the middle and late 1960s, and the protests of the 1960s and early 1970s revealed that "the limits of tolerance of passive abstention" had been reached for many blacks, poor, and youth in the United States.

Indeed, the news media are integral to the maintenance of Schattschneider's game: it is Washington journalists, politicians, and lobbyists who see policy and elections as a "game" and all "image," and not the public at large, who face real problems and confront the consequences of economic and political policy on a daily basis. As the journalist Michael Kelly comments, the relative few who are involved professionally in crafting public images of elected officials "believe in the extraordinary! disastrous! magnificent! scandalous! truth of whatever it is they believe in at the moment. Above all, they believe in the power of what they have created, in the subjectivity of reality and the reality of perceptions, in image." These few, Kelly writes, are the "Insiders." They speak a language that is "self-referential, self-important, self-mocking and very nearly (if subconsciously) self-loathing. It is deeply cynical." In the current political system, Kelly concludes, "to be knowing [of Washington politics] is to admit the fraud of one's functions in the act of performing them."[132]

We may once again have reached the limit of our tolerance of passive abstention. Even if not, we can ill afford to venture close to it.

REFORMING POLITICAL COMMUNICATION

One of the agreeable spiritual phenomena of the great age in which we live is the soul-searching now going on among American journalists. Fifteen years ago, or even ten years ago, there was scarcely a sign of it.—H. L. Mencken, *The American Journalist,* 1919

As the reporters in Washington survey the product of all their labor, the honest ones sometimes feel despairingly that more and more is being written about less and less. Despite the size of the press corps, the vast paraphernalia at its disposal, and all the government facilities for dispensing information, there is a growing awareness of the perilous state of our communications. Yet hopefully, there is also a new sense of awareness that our very survival as a free nation may depend on the capacity of reporters to relate the essential truth and "make a picture of reality on which men can act."—Douglass Cater, *The Fourth Branch of Government,* 1959

THROUGHOUT MOST OF ITS HISTORY, THE UNITED STATES HAS BEEN A singularly fortunate nation. It has been blessed with an abundance and diversity of natural resources, relative security from foreign attack, and a flexible and adaptable political system. The luxury of politics in the United States throughout most of the post–World War II era has been the fact that many citizens—excluding most African Americans, women, and other marginalized groups, to be sure—could afford to ignore politics beyond the minimum participation of periodic voting. A large portion of Americans did not have to become involved in politics: the economy was flourishing, cities were growing, water was running, sewers were draining, and the roads were new and clean, or being built.

This has changed. Many if not most of the streets and highways are crowded with cars and in disrepair, the population of America's big cities is stagnant, large sections of most cities are in ruins, and the tap water in many areas is not reliably safe. In almost any sector of the American economy, economic growth does not necessarily translate into job security, higher incomes, or even a well-paying position. Many whites have fled the cities to live in the suburbs, and many of the more affluent have retreated to gated communities or the distant countryside.

Most seriously, citizens' trust in national government is severely strained: not only do Congress and the presidency suffer from poor reputations (a majority of parents now do *not* want their children to grow up and become president of the United States), but more than 75 percent of Americans surveyed in 1992 said that they "never" or only "sometimes" trust the government. In 1962, fewer than 25 percent said they did not trust the government.[1]

Moreover, few Americans believe that the news media can be depended on to attend to the issues meriting deliberation and resolution. In a 1994 Times-Mirror survey, 71 percent of Americans said they think the news media get in the way of solutions, and only 25 percent said they believe the news media help.[2] "Washington has become the saddest dateline in journalism," comments one reporter for a popular weekly magazine. "Important stories are missed or misinterpreted. Reporters who lament the intrusion of entertainment values into journalism audition for talk shows and try out for cameo roles in [movies like] *Dave*. Transparent flattery, social bribery and vengeance seem perfectly acceptable journalistic ethics among the White House press."[3] The news media are not well regarded by the public: a majority of citizens see the media as legitimating a status quo that they do not believe is fair.[4] No wonder so many Americans, the young and the less advantaged in particular, care so little about politics.

And yet the information communicated by the news media is indispensable to an understanding and the operation of national politics: news provides citizens with knowledge about what is happening in their locale, across the United States, and around the world. It allows individuals to make decisions about the kind of political community in which they will live. It is no exaggeration to say that the news media are intimately and inextricably linked to the issue of legitimacy itself, that is, the extent to which Americans have confidence in the persons, policies, and processes of national government. Yet the news Americans receive may be insufficient for self-rule.[5]

Even though most Americans recognize that politics is too important to be left to politicians, political parties, and special-interest groups, this recognition is taking place to a large degree *outside* the news furnished by the leading media organizations in the United States. The surge of talk radio in the last ten years—exemplified by the programs of Rush Limbaugh, Don Imus, Gordon Liddy, and other talk shows—is indicative of the return to politics (the number of U.S. radio stations in the "News, Talk, Business, and Sports" category soared from 405 in 1990 to 1,262 in 1996). It is a comment on journalism and the limited scope of current mainstream party politics that so many Americans turn to controversial talk shows to air their views. Indeed, the decline in the proportion of persons who read the national newspapers and watch the network news, and the drop in the audience for news of party conventions, presidential speeches, and other political events speaks to the diminishing relevance of contemporary political communication.

Is it possible to have a more meaningful communication about national politics? How does political communication get beyond the institutional constraints discussed in Chapters 2 through 5? How can the adverse effects of an institutional media noted in Chapter 6 be avoided?

In this chapter, I consider ways in which political communication in the United States might be improved. As with most serious issues, there is no magic bullet. The problem has to be tackled from several directions at the same time: by national policy makers, by news professionals (journalists as well as non-news corporate executives), and by individual citizens (as both news consumers and voters). There is pressure, however. Arthur Stinchcombe notes that "an institution has authority when it is regarded as inevitable,"[6] but with the proliferation of cable television, the exponential growth of the Internet, the rise of "civic journalism" (discussed later), and the existence of the alternative press (of whatever political slant), there are more and more challenges to the dominance of the prestige and mainstream news media in the United States.

I suggest several possible public policy reforms, some media reforms—civic journalism in particular—and then a few individual-level reforms. I conclude the chapter with a brief account of the Internet and its likely impact on national politics. The several reforms I propose promote more open debate over political ideas, lessen the commercial pressures on news production, and encourage sophistication on the part of journalists in the production of the news and of audiences in the consumption of political news. It may be possible to have political communication in the United States that better represents the interests of the whole of the American public, rather than catering to politically and economically privileged audiences.[7]

Public Policy Reforms

First, if advertisers' subsidy of the news (discussed in Chapter 4) were reduced, advertising would have less of an effect on the news. As the media scholar Edwin Baker recommends, Congress could levy a tax on media advertising and then use the same funds to subsidize news organizations on the basis of their reader-generated circulation revenue (or viewer-generated television audience). Assuming a 10 percent sales tax on media advertising and assuming that three-quarters of newspaper revenues come from advertising, this policy would reduce advertising revenues by 10 percent and increase circulation revenues by 30 percent (given a 3:1 ratio of advertising income to circulation revenues). The reform would explicitly reward news organizations that attracted readers (and viewers)—no matter their circumstances or political positions—and comparatively penalize publications with lower circulation and more advertising revenues or, in the case of the video media, lower viewership and heavily advertised television and cable channels.[8] Although the technology may not yet be in place for such a reform to go immediately into effect for the video media (not to mention the controversy over the accuracy of the Nielsen ratings), the imminent marriage of the television and computer may allow development of a device that would let the news marketplace to function more efficiently, one that neutralizes the advertiser subsidy by helping news organizations with content that reaches wide audiences less attractive to advertisers and that takes away some of the advantage of profitable programs with content that reaches narrower but more advertiser-friendly audiences.

This reform would facilitate communication that attracted readers and viewers, rather than advertisers. The attention of audiences as readers or viewers could function as the equivalent of a voucher that rewards communication with popular appeal, irrespective of advertising revenues. Such a change would alter the current logic of news production.

A second policy reform addresses the economic subsidies of the news, one of which is the government's subsidization of magazines' and newspapers' second-class postage. Although this subsidy enhances the flow of information desirable in a democratic society (especially in an earlier era, when newspapers were more likely to be weeklies and published at some distance from the recipient), it takes away "the natural cost advantages of sparse, light publication and magazines," as Paul Weaver points out. If newspapers and magazines are made heavy by dozens or hundreds of pages of advertisements, the price of these publications should more fully reflect this burden on the postal system.[9]

The other economic subsidy is the legacy of "scarce airwaves." (I use "legacy" because with 70 percent of American households now hooked up to cable television, the scarcity lies much more with the limited capacity of the local cable companies than with the constraints of the television broadcast spectrum.) The subsidy is the easy and inexpensive criteria by which Federal Communications Commission (FCC) licensees—owners and operators of the television networks and other media—are able to renew their lucrative broadcast franchises.[10] Current license-holders have also received for free the additional broadcast slots to be gained from the digitally expanded broadcast spectrum (see Chapter 4). As it is, many affiliates and other local broadcasters as well as network-owned and -operated stations have, through the cooperation of the FCC, almost a right to print money. The FCC (and, by implication, Congress and a series of presidential administrations) has been acting in the interests of an already-prosperous few companies, rather than in the interests of the broader range of American businesses, much less the public at large. Congress could revive the market on both license renewals and the disposition of the new frequencies.

The reduction, if not elimination, of these two news subsidies would make the relationship between circulation and viewership more direct and would reduce the need for editorial content to be so profitable. The politics of news communication would be less entangled with the commerce of news production.

A third policy reform is to encourage an increase in the number of effective news organizations in the marketplace of ideas. With every decade there are fewer different media owners across the United States, and the existing news companies have an ever-larger stake in the status quo. ABC News is only a small part of Disney, NBC News represents just a fractional interest of the appliance manufacturer and defense contractor General Electric, and CBS News until recently was owned by Westinghouse, a media, electronics, and engineering company. All four large newspaper companies also have extensive holdings in other print and television media (see Chapter 4). Indicatively, the eleven major news organizations in this country—the *New York Times, Washington Post, Wall Street Journal,* and *Los Angeles Times,* the four television sources (ABC, CBS, NBC, and CNN), and *U.S. News, Time,* and *Newsweek*—are owned by nine companies (since the Washington Post Company also owns *Newsweek* and Time-Warner owns both *Time* and CNN). Yet it is contrary to common sense to expect news organizations to promote conflict with their own (extensive) interests.

The public would be well served by the presence of as many news organizations as possible: with more voices, there is a greater probability of more distinct political voices, consistent with John Stuart Mill's marketplace of ideas. "Few developments could be more subversive to established doctrines of freedom of the press than the trend to monopoly, concentration, and centralization in the mass media, especially in print," remarks the legal scholar Benno Schmidt. The American polity is best served through diversity and competition, whereas "most newspapers are now monopolies, more and more newspapers and broadcast stations are parts of chains, and the bulk of news in newspapers and on the radio comes from the two national wire services."[11] Restrictions on the number of television stations that a person or entity may directly or indirectly own, operate, or control have been eliminated as long as all the stations of one owner do not together reach more than 35 percent of the national audience. There are no longer any restrictions on the number of AM or FM radio stations that may be owned or operated by one entity nationally. Most worrisome is the effect of broadcast monopolies (or oligopolies) in smaller markets and the cross-ownership of newspapers and broadcast channels. "Right conclusions are more likely to be gathered out of a multitude of tongues," the great jurist Learned Hand observes, "than through any kind of authoritative selection"—whether the authority be political or of the marketplace.[12]

The concentration of media ownership could be reversed. As recently as 1984, public policy restricted media owners to seven FM stations, seven AM radio stations, and five TV stations nationally—rules that had been in place since 1953. Newspaper companies were not allowed to own television stations in the same market.[13] Recent legislation, the result of pressure on Congress from media companies and investors, eroded these restrictions. Now, for example, in the nation's third largest market, Chicago, the Tribune Company owns the *Chicago Tribune* as well as WGN, Channel 9 (IND/WB), and the radio station WGN-AM 720. In Atlanta, the nation's tenth largest market, Cox Enterprises, Inc., owns the *Atlanta Journal-Constitution* as well as WSB-TV, Channel 2 (ABC), and the radio stations WSB-AM 750 and WSB-FM 98.5.

Interestingly, more than fifty years ago the Commission on the Freedom of the Press, known as the Hutchins Commission, came to the same conclusion about the desirability of facilitating more vibrant political discourse. According to the law professor Zachariah Chafee, the commission "was conscious of the growth of vast enterprises in the communications industries, the large sums now required to enter those industries, and the methods often used by the bigger units to discourage competition." The words of one commission member are still relevant:

> Much of the inadequacy of the existing service of information is attributable to conditions which the present owners of the press cannot change without ceasing to be owners—or at least without ceasing to be owners at the existing level. It is because the press has become big business with its policies directed by its owners as owners that information has turned to "news" and to "stories"; that much important and relevant information is suppressed by the press itself; and that the vehicles of information have changed, for the most part, into vehicles of entertainment. It is because the number of owners has decreased, and control has

centered in fewer and fewer hands, that competition in the presentation of opposing views has broken down, and the worst of all monopolies— a monopoly of information—has been effectively established not only in isolated communities but in numerous and extended areas across the country.

This last and most obvious evil can probably be corrected by legal action under existing statutes without risk to the principle of freedom of the press. The only difference between monopolies of meat or sugar or of steel or of oil, on the one hand, and monopolies of fact and opinion, on the other, is that monopolies of fact and opinion are infinitely more mischievous. The only difference between the ownership of a security company by a bank, or of a steamship company by a railroad, on the one hand, and the ownership of a radio station by newspapers or motion picture theaters by motion picture companies, on the other, is that combinations in transportation or in money are less harmful than combinations in ideas.[14]

The 1996 Telecommunications Act scuttled many of the recommendations of the Hutchins Commission (and subsequent regulations): the FCC's limitations on the ownership of chains of television stations and ownership of stations by newspapers were removed, the recommended "vigilant observation" of "cross-channel purchases" by news organizations that form "communications empires" has virtually ceased, and the FCC's policy "to maintain local competition, prevent discrimination, and regulate central producing units," per the commission's recommendation, has been severely compromised. The only restriction left is that a single media owner cannot have an audience reach that is more than 35 percent of the national market.[15] Although Chafee recognized that further decentralization was possible (he also recognized that there was no single remedy), he was not optimistic that the Department of Justice would use the Sherman Anti-Trust Act against news organizations, given the department's poor record on changing the concentration of ownership in other industries.[16]

Two broader policy recommendations follow from the above analysis. One is for campaign finance reform in both congressional and presidential campaigns. Congress is the best place to enhance debate within the government, being the first branch of politics and the one charged with the oversight of the federal agencies and departments. Given the prominent role of money in Congress, however (in large part the result of the expense of modern media-driven campaigns, as I discuss in Chapter 2), members of Congress are too busy raising funds for office and too beholden to interest groups. It is not likely that most members of Congress will unnecessarily expose themselves to political risks (since most see Congress as a career) under the current set of political incentives they face. Significant campaign finance reform that allows a level playing field between incumbents and challengers is in order and could foster more public debate.[17]

Given the dominant role of money in contemporary politics and the fact that most of that money goes to media buys, a crucial aspect of campaign reform is to lessen the fundraising pressures on incumbents and challengers alike by ensuring free or low-cost television time to qualifying politicians, promoting longer advertisements that present more than a sound bite from a candidate, or publicly funding electoral campaigns. Removal of restrictions on contributions or spending (since money will find ways around contribution limits) combined with public funding to a modest level of only those candidates who meet a threshold of voter appeal (e.g., as indicated by numbers of signed petitions or performance in past campaigns) would allow for a modicum of name recognition for challengers and relieve some of the pressure for early money. This would to some extent free candidates and officeholders from obligations they might otherwise incur.[18]

Changes in how presidents and members of the House and Senate achieve and stay in office would necessarily affect how politicians and their advisors use the media and, in turn, how journalists report national politics.[19] At this point, the news media are the conduits, interpreters, and critics of news about an essentially corrupted and corrupting electoral system, which drags them down along with politicians and the political process in general.

The other broad policy reform I propose is reform of primary and secondary education. What news organizations are able to communicate depends to a large degree on the education of the audience. As long as school boards, local, state, and national policy makers, and the American public are willing to tolerate mediocre education for many of this country's youth, there will be a poor general audience for sophisticated and nuanced reporting of news about national or international politics. For example, most Americans receive only slight exposure to foreign languages—and thus to foreign cultures and the wider world around them—and their lack of knowledge facilitates the oversimplification of political news communicated by politicians and the media.[20] The poorer the education, the more vulnerable many citizens are to the distorted and stereotyped presentations of the news media.

Media Reforms

More Substantial Coverage of Campaigns

One reform that could positively influence how the news media cover national politics is for journalists to cover political contests as though there were something actually at stake besides the name and party of the winner.[21] Although politicians, like other persons, usually act in their own self-interest, self-interest need not be seen as the sole motivating cause for their actions and as inconsistent with a larger good. Political journalists could choose to be less cynical and more constructive when reporting on politicians and the promise of political action. Of course, they would have to risk being seen as a sucker for political strategizing.[22]

When covering presidential campaigns, news organizations overload their audiences with information that is often unhelpful to voters, shallow information oriented to the election "game" and diverging from the concerns of the voters and politicians alike. The Republican 104th Congress was sincere about reducing the federal budget in 1995, for instance, no matter what one might think about its chosen means. Yet the seriousness of its intent hardly came out in the news media. Newspapers (and other media) "must resist the cynical impulse," notes Jack Fuller, the president and publisher of the *Chicago Tribune*.[23]

A More Aggressive Approach toward Policy Monopolies

Journalists could turn a more scrutinizing eye toward the policies of the executive branch and other parts of government to detect fractures, such as conflict between personnel, in what might appear to the public to be a solid policy monopoly. (See Chapter 3 for a discussion of the lunches the major newspapers regularly host for government officials.) Whistleblowing and other acts of courage and dissension by government officials could be routinely viewed as opportunities for more investigative journalism (as they infrequently are at present). Similarly, when the U.S. government (or some subset thereof) represses speech, the news media could better publicize such restrictions. When CIA Director John Deutch revoked the security clearance of a senior State Department official who had given Congress information about a CIA-paid informer implicated in the killing of a Guatemalan, for instance, there was almost no publicity.[24] No journalists expressed public outrage over the fact that the government was effectively overturning the moral of the Nürnberg trials of Nazi war criminals at the end of World War II: that duty to God and country took precedence over duty to a specific presidential administration or government agency.

By the same token, the major media should avoid the worst behavior of the lap-dog press, that is, simply repeating official sources on important and controversial matters. The case studies in Chapter 6 are to the point. Kenneth Walsh of *U.S. News* writes of CNN's susceptibility to being spoon-fed by the Clinton White House, given its 24-hour news programming: press secretary Dee Dee Myers would simply go directly to CNN's Wolf Blitzer, who would then put the news (with some qualification) on the air. In Tom Rosenstiel's words, "CNN has become a means to communicate to the press corps without having to hold briefings or face reporters en masse." CNN may serve as a bulletin board for the White House.[25]

Another example is a *New York Times* story in late 1996 that took the whole top of a page to report General Norman Schwarzkopf's emphatic denial that chemical weapons were the cause of the Gulf War syndrome among the thousands of veterans stricken with undiagnosed illnesses. The story simply reported what General Schwarzkopf, speaking by telephone from Colorado, had told the *Times* reporter.[26] The reporter did not refer to sources critical of Schwarzkopf's position or undertake to analyze or interpret Schwarzkopf's assertions, despite their dubiousness (given the sixty-three thousand veterans afflicted). (To its credit, the *New York Times* later printed stories by the same reporter to the effect that American soldiers had not been warned of the chemical dangers that might result from blowing up an Iraqi ammunition depot.)[27]

More Detailed Coverage of Political and Economic News

It would also be a step in the right direction if journalists covered political news more comprehensively and commented less exhaustively on crises. (Crime stories, like fire stories, may be considered as mini-crisis stories.) Reporters and their superiors could cover the more complex economic and political stories in greater detail and with more thoughtfulness. Programs such as *Dateline NBC*, ABC News's *Prime Time*, and CBS News's *60 Minutes* could intersperse more stories about serious political issues with the celebrity-driven or sensationalist "gotcha" investigations that they overwhelmingly carry at present.[28] Journalists could frame the news in more complex ways and present a more nuanced picture of the world to their reading and viewing audiences. The news could be less stereotyped and less shaped into a complete drama and be communicated in a more qualified and provisional manner instead.

Honesty from Journalists about Their Roles

Journalists and their news organizations could also stand to be more forthcoming about their roles as political communicators. CBS News's switch from Walter Cronkite's legendary sign-off "And that's the way it is" to Dan

Rather's "That's part of our world tonight" is a step in the right direction. The *New York Times* could drop the pretension of its slogan "All the News That's Fit to Print" and its present advertising campaign, which claims, "We bring you the world" (for reasons obvious from the preceding chapters). News organizations could also be more explicit about their errors and mistakes. Newspapers and newsmagazines often simply print letters to the editor that point out the mistakes and inaccuracies of news stories (as though the letters were somehow a substitute for editorial acknowledgments of error). Similarly, journalists could admit their own roles in defining the news, an admission that is typically avoided at present (see the discussion of transparency in Chapter 5).[29]

Bolder Coverage of Political News

Finally, there are opportunities for the established news organizations of today to be bolder and more creative in their coverage of political news, just as the alternative press of newspapers, journals, and the occasional cable programs and documentaries—spanning the left and right of the political spectrum—may evolve into more mainstream publications or news programs. There is promising movement here. Since 1990, the number of alternative newspapers has risen from 68 to 111, total revenues of alternative papers have doubled, and circulation has grown from 3 million to almost 6.4 million. In only two years, one of the two national advertising groups that represents 95 such newspapers has experienced sale growth from $250,000 to $6.5 million.[30] Alternatively, some journalists currently working for well-established news organizations could break off and start their own online or cooperative ventures, ones that remove reporters and editors from the hierarchical and commercial pressures of the leading news organizations. In either case—whether journalists, politicians, and the public begin to pay more attention to alternative publications or programs or established news organizations reform how they cover national politics—political communication might be able to reduce the distance between coverage of the politics of K Street and coverage of the politics of Main Street.

Civic Journalism

The most important reform for the news media is the pursuit of what is called "public," "civic," or "community" journalism, which may be seen today in the *Dayton Daily News*, the *Wisconsin Free Press*, the *Charlotte Observer*, the *Rochester Democrat*, the *St. Paul Pioneer Press*, and other newspapers (often in conjunction with local television broadcasters and radio stations). As the media scholar Jay Rosen puts it, "Journalism cannot remain valuable unless public life remains viable. If public life is in trouble in the United States, then journalism is in trouble." The duty of the press is to support public life, "help citizens participate, and take them seriously when they do . . . Most important, perhaps, journalists must learn to see hope as an essential resource that they cannot deplete indefinitely without tremendous costs to us and them."[31] There are several components to civic journalism (as I shall call both the concept and the movement among journalists nationwide).

One is that the journalism engages the audience—be it a local community, a city, a county, a state, or the nation—and does not reflect simply the concerns of political leaders or other authoritative sources. This is especially important when there is a significant gap between official pronouncements reported by the major media and the concerns expressed by the public at large. Fuller quotes approvingly from one study that found a large appetite for "coherence" in news reporting: "More attention is paid to the quantity and newness of information than to its quality; indeed, people are bombarded daily with bits of facts and figures, revelations about old news, conflicting or unconnected statements about a public concern. People often cannot make sense of all this information—it lacks coherence." Fuller argues that "people want knowledge, not just facts or data . . . people still passionately believe in meaning." Ed Fouhy of the Pew Center for Civic Journalism also finds that journalism has not been "serving the citizen."[32] Civic journalism attends to the concerns of everyday Americans; it is more populist than most of present-day journalism.

Civic journalism is also problem-centered. It is cognizant of issues that need to be addressed and attempts to attend to the concerns revealed in community polls, focus groups, and even specific incidents (e.g., the murder of two policemen in one town and the decayed inner neighborhoods in another city). This means that reporters, producers, editors, executives, and publishers have to heed their audiences' own concerns and anxieties, interests and sensibilities, and worldviews (albeit with varying degrees of sophistication and complexity). The challenge for journalists is to listen and to uncover these concerns, sensibilities, and worldviews, even though they may be at some remove from their own concerns as political correspondents. It is especially important that the journalists do this if politicians and other authorities are not addressing what appear to be important public issues.[33]

The new journalism is therefore more proactive and less passive than traditional journalism. The Hutchins Commission made the same point in 1947:

> To protect the press is no longer automatically to protect the citizen or the community . . . Freedom of the press means freedom from *and freedom for*. The press must be free from the means of external compulsions

from whatever source. To demand that it be free from pressures which might warp its utterance would be to demand that society should be empty of contending forces and beliefs. But persisting and distorting pressures—financial, popular, clerical, institutional—must be known and counterbalanced. The press must, if it is to be wholly free, know and overcome any biases incident to its own economic position, its concentration, and its pyramidal organization.

The press must be free for the development of its own conceptualization of service and achievement. It must be free for making *its contribution* to the maintenance and development of a free society.

This implies that the press must also be accountable. It must be *accountable to society* for meeting the public need and for maintaining the rights of citizens and the almost forgotten rights of speakers who have no press.[34]

The commission's statement, which was unpopular among the leading news organizations of the 1940s, describes with remarkable prescience the problems faced by the U.S. news media of today. The media are partially accountable to politicians, public officials, and business, as we have seen, but they are not accountable to the public at large, whom they are supposed to serve according to their stated ethical principles and their privileges under the First Amendment.

Third, civic journalism is a catalyst for popular action and problem solving. This does not mean that newspapers or television stations advocate particular solutions, support particular politicians, or back specific political parties (contrary to many reports of civic journalism). It does mean that news organizations are in a position to be an agent for community mobilization and popular engagement, instead of being a partner in fostering feelings of powerlessness and passivity among viewers and readers. Civic journalism benefits especially the discussion and communication within a community fostered by discussion groups, Web pages, and e-mail facilitated by the new technology of the Internet. Experiments underway in Tallahassee, Florida, Rochester, New York, and San Jose, California, suggest the possible community-building benefits of the use of the Internet for localized problem solving.[35]

Civic journalism also calls for journalists to care seriously about their mission: to take to heart their stated ethical codes that they "report information of importance and interest to the public accurately, honestly, and impartially" and "serve the general welfare." Civic journalism calls for reporters and their bosses to be self-conscious of their limitations, clear about their own visions and versions of a free society, and accountable even to those who do not have other representation in the body politic (consistent with the findings of the Hutchins Commission).

This requires a reorientation of news values for the prestige media.[36] Editors of both the print and video media make decisions all the time, and accompanying those decisions—whether explicitly or implicitly—are values. Consider, for instance, the values revealed in the five case studies reviewed in Chapter 6:

- the news media not only condone but facilitate action that results in the deaths of tens of thousands of Iraqis (people who, like the residents of China, Cuba, or the former Soviet Union, cannot be held responsible for the actions of their government),
- for the United States to improve its position vis-à-vis the Soviet Union during the cold war is worth any price in lives, dollars, credibility, or national integrity,
- bilking hundreds of billions of dollars from taxpayers and the U.S. government is "politics as usual,"
- a fatal disease is somehow less important if it involves marginal populations, and
- medical and scientific breakthroughs, and even a cure for cancer, are less important than the preservation of current medical practices.

Rather than offering any resolution to the pressing political issues at hand, traditional journalism has developed a "culture of lying" instead. Reporters and their bosses print and publicize stories they know to be untrue. Paul Weaver gives the example of the *Washington Post*'s printing a story about the Carter administration's bugging the Blair House, where the Reagans were staying. Although the story was just a rumor, the *Post* explained its behavior by saying that the rumor was an important one and in the public domain and therefore should be published. The *Post*'s editorial defense was an "Ur-moment for the modern information business," as the media scholars Edwin Diamond and Robert Silverman call it, a moment that revealed the moral emptiness at the core of the modern news business. Another example comes from the late 1980s, when President George Bush announced a cancellation of all exchanges with China after the Chinese government's massacre of student protesters in Tiananmen Square. Less than a month later, the president sent National Security Advisor Brent Scowcroft and Deputy Secretary of State Lawrence Eagleburger to Beijing. President Bush was also ready to look the camera in the eye and say, in reference to the nomination of Clarence Thomas to fill Justice Thurgood Marshall's vacancy on the Supreme Court, "The fact that he is black and a minority . . . has nothing to do with this sense that he is the best qualified at this time."[37]

The American news media knowingly pass these fabrications along to their national (and international) audiences.

To repeat and disseminate a falsehood to the public is not value-neutral. Rather, media attention validates and legitimates information.[38] To publicize wrong information is to aid and abet falsehood. If the *New York Times*, ABC News, or *U.S. News* decide to print or broadcast information, it has made a decision that the information being disseminated is important for citizens to know. By repeating stories that are untrue or are likely to be untrue, journalists are implicated in the degradation of national politics.

It cannot be said that journalists do not know what is going on. They figure things out pretty soon, as Weaver observes. Rather, what he calls the "culture of lying" is a product of the self-censorship of reporters, editors and producers, and news executives who fail "to tell stories that adequately reflect their experience as observers of events and gatherers of information." To eradicate this culture of lying would "entail no radical remaking of the journalist's skill or knowledge," by Weaver's account. "It would demand only the rediscovery of the journalist's God-given need to be true to himself and a redoubling of his commitment to telling the story that is present in his experience."[39]

Ben Bradlee reaches the same conclusion: "There's no question, in my mind, that a vigorous uncovering of lies in government is essential, it must continue and must be a major element of what the press does. But I do think we have to go a step farther, which is to replace the lies that we uncover with some form of truth, and therein lies the difficult part." Civic journalism suggests an answer: that the truth to be told is that of news organizations as keepers of the public trust, where the government is the representative of and steward for the public well-being. This means that the news media may sometimes have to take sides.[40]

Not surprisingly, the leading news organizations shy away from such responsibility. Their reaction to civic journalism has been hostile. The executive editor of the *Washington Post*, Leonard Downie, describes civic journalism as antithetical to good journalism. (Downie himself takes impartiality—or the appearance of it—to the extreme of refusing to vote.) Similarly, the editorial page editor of the *New York Times*, Howell Raines, writes that the prescription of public journalism is "dangerous nonsense" and an "insidious danger." To Raines,

> the wisdom of democracy is forged in the rowdy ceremonies of the campaign trail, and that the public gets its education through the vitality of unrestrained debate. The participation of mainstream print journalists in this process as skeptical observers, critics and analysts is a high, ven-

erable and independent calling. Mr. [James] Fallows's case [in *Breaking the News*] for abandoning that calling may be well intended, but it is poisonous to the values of the newsroom.[41]

Neither editor explored the serious issues lying behind Fallows's advocacy of civic journalism. Each sought to discredit the messenger instead. They did not bother to consider, at least in public, why an author and journalist of Fallows's stature would call for civic journalism in the first place.

Richard Oppel, the editor of the *Austin American-Statesman* and former editor of the *Charlotte Observer* and Washington bureau chief for Knight-Ridder, notes that the leading news organizations' hostility to civic journalism is "pretty obvious. They benefit most from an elitist approach to dictating the political dialogue. They are in control . . . The White House is a transient organization, [but] the *Washington Post* is a permanent organization. The White House has a 4–8 year reign, [but] the *Washington Post* is a dynasty." Implicit in the major news media's acceptance of traditional journalism is acceptance of the status quo. As the editor of the *Wichita Eagle* puts it, "Public Journalism had had journalism done to it."[42]

The new attention being paid by a few in the news industry to news that matters means a reattachment of journalists to their communities. Already there are signs that civic journalism is losing its (unhelpful) label and instead becoming more a realization of "news values." David Broder has spoken favorably of the movement, and the *Tribune*'s Fuller is candid that journalism has to reform, "to help create public discussion." Fuller cites the *Charlotte Observer* as a case in point and writes of the promise of the "emerging interactive electronic medium."[43]

There is already early evidence that newspapers and television stations that feature civic journalism do better at attracting audiences than ones that stay with traditional journalism.[44] It is entirely conceivable that some newspapers and a number of television stations or cable channels reorient themselves toward coverage of popular concerns and genuine problems at the same time that the prominent television networks, newsmagazines, and newspapers continue along their traditionalist path.

Implicit in these suggested reforms is the assumption that journalists have the time and wherewithal to reflect on news stories, explore their complexities and ambiguities, and marshal the resources needed to do a more thorough job. This takes us back to the economics of the news business, to the changes necessary at the level of the incentive structures facing editors, producers, publishers, and news executives and to the reasons why it would be in their interest to spend more money, hire more personnel, and desensationalize the news.

As the networks continue to see their dominance of American political culture ebb, there may be a basis for innovation and experimentation. It was the competition between the *Washington Post* and the *New York Times,* perhaps as much as anything else, that motivated Katherine Graham and her executive and managing editors to support two young metro desk reporters in their pursuit of the Watergate story. It was through the proliferation of cable television that CNN and C-SPAN, both useful additions to news programming, became possible. Now that the networks are under severe pressure from the proliferation of cable channels and there is stagnation in newspaper readership, it is possible that important change will take place among news organizations at the advent of the twenty-first century.

Individual-Level Reforms

Although public policy changes and new approaches within journalism are fundamental to the reform of political communication, changes in how individual viewers, readers, listeners, and consumers relate to the news media are also needed.

One thing that individuals can do is to be more self-conscious about their media consumption. Readers and viewers can learn to recognize the stereotypes, the stock words and images, the storytelling devices, and the news frames being used by journalists. Words such as "terrorist" and "extremist" are cases in point, being value-laden terms for action that, depending on the circumstances, could be called "heroic" or "avant-garde" instead.[45] Individuals can realize the effects that the brevity of a two-minute narrative has on what is being communicated, especially if the subject is a complex one. They can also notice stray facts and images that do not fit the news story being presented. By recognizing appeals to sentiment and familiar phrases or images, individuals can be emotionally and rhetorically smart.[46]

Canny news consumers may take into account and discount the presence of the institutions of news production and thereby get a more accurate picture of national politics. "It is essential that we learn to watch the news defensively, in order to know which questions to ask and how to be critical," David Altheide writes. "Once viewers acquire this competence, distinctions can be drawn between sound and distorted reports." These comments apply to reading or listening just as well. Viewers and readers "can demystify news production through the recognition and understanding that the news is a product of practical tasks designed to resolve organizational problems. Clarifying the way news gets done, its objectivity, adequacy, and social usefulness, cannot be accomplished without considering what these practicalities contribute to the news."[47] This is partly my purpose in writing this book, of course.

Individuals can also become less dependent on the major news media by becoming more active news gatherers. They can talk to friends, coworkers, roommates, neighbors, and family about politics and economics, they can try out the alternative press, the foreign press, and other available news sources, and they can use the Internet (see below).[48] Finally, individuals can take the time to read books and additional accounts about particular events, persons, or political phenomena.[49]

In short, people can exert more control over what political communication they are exposed to. There is less of a problem of information overload than of individuals putting themselves in situations in which they receive more information—often trivial information—than they can meaningfully use. Most persons are scarcely affected by most news, even the "hard news," they receive. As U Thant, the former secretary general of the United Nations, pointed out in the early 1960s, we may need only to skim headlines or hear a news synopsis to learn what we need in order to function as citizens, parents, students, or wage-earners on any given day. In the television era, citizens need to discover discipline, asserts Roderick Hart. They need to "just turn it off."[50] Were individuals to exercise more discipline over their exposure to the news media, they would create more time to view and read other material of longer-term and possibly more serious political impact. Citizens can be more strategic in their use of the news media.

Cyberspace

What of the new, computer-based communication technology, the popularity of which is spreading rampantly? Already more than one in four American households have access to the Internet, and about two in five have computers.[51] Will the politics and political processes of American government be affected by the Internet and the World Wide Web in the near future? Barely.

The Internet will increase the availability of news about political candidates and their background, issue positions, legislative or professional records, personal histories, and the like, to be sure. It will also facilitate political discussion among citizens about federal elections, presidential and Congressional candidates, and governmental policies and regulations (to keep to the level of national politics). Even with the advent of the Internet and smart television sets and the availability of hundreds of cable channels, television advertisements will likely play much the same roles in the electoral campaigns of the foreseeable future as they play in current campaigns. Nor is it likely that the new technology itself will reexcite Americans about national politics or presidential elections or that the Internet will change the qualifications or selection criteria for candidates to public office (as television, arguably, has done). The news media will remain the arbitrators of political information.

Other politics will also be minimally affected. Although the Internet allows for mass responses to pending legislation and congressional hearings and expressions of approval or disapproval of cabinet or Supreme Court nominees, it is not clear that the Internet, the World Wide Web, and e-mail make these citizen responses qualitatively different from those now communicated via the telephone, personal letters, personal contacts, group-sponsored initiatives, or financial contributions.

Moreover, the new technology will not greatly affect the role of journalists' political reporting. The Internet and other new technologies, such as online information services, facilitate reporters' and editors' news gathering and story writing, allowing them to be more productive. The new technology may also allow for more individual feedback on the news stories or editorials of at least some journalists. But the proliferation of news sources means that readers and viewers will look to journalists even more for a handle on the news that affects their lives, since the Internet does not itself communicate the significance or insignificance of any one piece of information or sort the thousands of pieces of political information available (as users well know). For the foreseeable future, the prioritization and selection of political information will remain the province of the more respected news organizations. Only a few persons will become "shadow journalists" (as I call them), providers of information who, over time, become reliable sources for a portion of the Internet-using public. The number of individuals who will occupy this category is small compared to the number of salaried journalists with formal affiliation.[52]

That more politically relevant information will be received over wires and through cables rather than over the air or on bleached wood pulp is much less significant than that persons employed in large, profitable, and hierarchical news organizations will still be mediating the political information the public receives. Few individuals will have the time or political expertise to "de-mediate" the news, that is, take the news organizations out of political communication by themselves collecting news about persons and events of political relevance.[53]

Preventing the new technology and the Internet from being more profound influences on political communication are three factors. One is *money*. As long as profits are not being made widely, dependably, and securely on the World Wide Web, the Internet and the Web will have a limited impact on political communication. Perceptions are, of course, as important as reality. The book purchases, travel plans, stock transactions, other sales, and advertising that have become staples of Internet use for some may be signs that money can be made through the Net. Yet the Internet economy is still minuscule, and commerce is far from the main reason why most use the Internet.[54] Even when the Internet eventually does become an economic powerhouse, it remains unclear how politics would be affected.

A second problem is *numbers*. At this point, there appears to be an insurmountable imbalance between the possible quantity of citizens interested in any particular policy, politician, or government organization, and the numbers of politicians, political appointees, civil servants, and staff able to respond to their queries. For all the interactive promise of the Internet, there seems little way for individual citizens to receive personal feedback with respect to their questions about particular candidates, issues, or laws. Even with search engines differentiating and prioritizing among kinds of questions received by a member of Congress, the White House, or a federal department or agency, there is still too little time and too many hits and e-mail messages for the Internet to transform political communication between individual citizens and politicians and administrators. The Web sites now available for members of Congress, political candidates, and government departments and agencies are the equivalent of glossy promotional brochures: public relations tools with typically little substance or depth.[55]

Nor will the presence of the Internet alter the *government's fundamental advantage with respect to many topics and in many policy domains*. The news media (and therefore almost all of the public) will remain dependent on the government for news as long as much political information is still controlled by and proprietary to the government or a presidential administration. The "technologies of freedom" are less liberating for individual citizens and more constraining in their political impact than most perhaps realize. The new technology will facilitate the further invasion of privacy and the greater surveillance of individuals by government (and private) organizations perhaps as much as it will encourage individual communication and expression.[56]

Information controls are technically feasible with the software applications and computers that are now available. For computers able to process huge amounts of data, analysts can develop software or write programs that would flag the profiles of illegal or suspicious activities. It also appears likely (although still to be determined, as of this writing) that the government will be able to regulate private encryption. Other governments (e.g., the French and the Russian) already regulate encryption. Furthermore, the day may not be far off when video surveillance in public and private spaces alike, now common, is almost omnipresent and linked with computers, databases, and communication monitors.

Video and photographic surveillance (through satellite cameras, cameras installed in offices and public spaces, and virtually unnoticeable miniaturized cameras) will make it possible for governments to use advanced technologies for the purpose of securing a more ordered society. This will be possible through examination of electronic communications, monitoring of vehicular traffic, workplace surveillance, and financial record-keeping. Although such a centralization of information control may not be in place at present in the United States, it already happens on a case-by-case basis in the offices of the FBI and National Security Agency (which monitors telecommunications transmissions).

The 178 largest U.S. federal agencies maintain almost two thousand databanks with a total of 3.5 billion records on military service, tax records, social security information, customs files, FBI investigations, and so forth. Through computer matching it is possible for government agencies to connect databanks to catch people who, for example, are delinquent on their student loans or illegally collecting federal benefits. According to former CIA Director James Woolsey, the CIA already uses "artificial intelligence, expert systems software and digitalization" to monitor suspicious activities.[57]

Contrary to former President Ronald Reagan's statement that "more than armies, more than diplomacy, more than the best intentions of democratic nations, the communications revolution will be the greatest force for the advancement of human freedom the world has ever seen," it is perhaps equally plausible that advanced technology will be used to promote enhanced government censorship and social control.[58] President Reagan ignored George Orwell's message in *Nineteen Eighty-Four* that advanced communications technology could be a force for oppression. There are, in short, serious grounds for pessimism about the transformative effects of the Internet or other new technologies for the facilitation of individual expression and the promotion of political liberty.

In fact, business as well as the government may threaten individuals' liberty. Employers are already able to monitor employees' electronic communications (including e-mail), and computers are currently capable of interpreting visual images and comprehending audio communications. Prodigy now scans all texts for the presence of offensive words and has censored online discussion about sexual preferences. America Online has restricted members' access to UseNet discussion groups and terminated a feminist discussion group. Some American colleges and universities have attempted to restrict access to sexually explicit material on the Internet. Indeed, 98 percent of American companies report using some form of electronic supervision of their employees.[59] And virtually all individual commercial preferences, health choices, and financial data are either known or may readily be known to corporate vendors in the near future.

The silver lining behind these dark clouds may be that the Internet allows for more effective public administration, especially in smaller communities and in narrower policy domains. The beneficial aspect of the new technology is the attention that can now be paid to the execution, implementation, and reception of policy initiatives.

OVER THE LONG TERM, THE INTERNET AND RELATED COMPUTER TECH-nologies will no doubt exert a revolutionary impact on political organization and social mobilization. The Internet transforms how people interact with each other and, ultimately, how they perceive themselves and their political attachments. It facilitates the meeting of people who may be separated spatially, socially, economically, or ethnically; people are no longer bound by geography, social status, or life history.[60] The Internet is "dialogical," allowing for two-way communication (similar to telephones and the mail), in contrast to the one-way flow of information in the news media. Not only can persons communicate more easily and cheaply over the Internet, but they can also organize and establish a basis for future action (which is why the debate about encryption and government access to encryption keys is so important).

While the Internet may be amoral—among the groups on the Internet are neo-Nazis and white supremacists, people who deny that the Holocaust occurred, the Hamas, and pro-life groups that advocate the killing of abortion providers—the point is that these groups, other associations, and even third parties can form much more readily than they could before the Internet existed. This is especially true for more narrowly defined groups and for persons in the same locale or profession, for whom the Internet can augment face-to-face meetings and telephone conversations. The community networks and community-based information networks already in existence in many cities and states across the United States point to the promise of the new technology.

In the more distant future, the Internet *will* fundamentally transform American politics. The child or teenager growing up now with the Internet will be socialized politically in a far different manner than the adult in her mid-thirties has been and is being politically socialized or how the retiree was exposed to politics. Just as television altered the boundaries between children and adults, citizens and politicians (or celebrities), and professional behavior and private action, so, too, are the possibilities of the Internet.[61]

The status differences of official position, office space, and living conditions may be mitigated by the Internet, and personal identity may be wholly redefined, given the new ties and new attachments now possible within communities of various sizes—neighborhood, county, region—and within niche groups of expertise and interest.

If knowledge is power, the Internet may change the role that information has played in determining human relations and demarcating social order. A vista has appeared of an open world, one more open than even the freedoms provided by the telegraph, the telephone, the radio, and the television. The technologies of more cable channels, the merger of computers and televisions, videoconferencing, mobile digital communications, and other developments add to this promise.

The likely long-term impact of the Internet makes the work of political scientist David Truman once more of great relevance. Truman, known for his articulation and analysis of the American political community in his 1951 book *The Governmental Process,* emphasized the fundamental importance of the stability of pluralist politics. He attributed this stability to the many overlapping group memberships among Americans, the "balance wheel in a going political system." Crucial to Truman's vision of a functioning pluralist United States was his notion of "potential groups," associations that, even if not in existence at any one moment, *had the potential to form* and then take political action. The latent power of these unformed political organizations could serve as a supplement to and a check on the influence of existing groups and overlapping group memberships. Potential groups could be a corrective to what E. E. Schattschneider called the "flaw in the pluralist heaven": the fact "that the heavenly chorus sings with a strong upper-class accent."[62]

Truman's pluralist argument has been overshadowed in recent decades by the logic of collective action. The late economist Mancur Olson reasoned that collective action was disproportionately possible for those with greater resources, specifically those organizations or individuals that could offer side-payments (or, "selective incentives"), given the costs of organizing individuals for collective action. Olson's basic point was that it makes no sense on a cost-benefit basis for individuals to join large groups. Individuals, instead, tend to "free-ride," to reap the benefits from a public good that others had to organize to provide.[63] But with the minimal transaction costs involved in the use of the Internet, potential groups could mobilize easily. Latent groups might be capable of complementing, moderating, and perhaps upending the power of the established pressure group system. Truman's argument regains salience.

These observations lead me to suggest one more policy reform: that access to the Internet, and to computer information more generally, be available to as many Americans as possible—in schools, in kiosks in libraries and other public places, in workplaces, and in the home. If speech, and political speech in particular, is increasingly communicated electronically, the American political community is best served by having such speech be as widely available as possible. Currently, studies show, people using the Internet are not representative of the public at large. They are younger, more often male (just under two-thirds of users), richer (the average household income of Internet users was $48,200 in 1996, compared with the general population's $44,400 average), and better educated (57% of Internet users have gone to college, compared with 44% of the public at large). People who use the Net are also more likely to be white. Among households with annual incomes below $40,000, whites were six times more likely than blacks to have used the World Wide Web in the previous week. For the one-third of black households with incomes above $40,000, only 29 percent had a computer, compared with 44.3 percent of white households at this income level.[64] This is one domain where Vice President Al Gore and former House Speaker Newt Gingrich agree: all Americans should have access to computers and therefore to the Internet.

IN SUM, NEWS ORGANIZATIONS ARE IN THE AWKWARD POSITION OF having to serve several masters—their competitive goals (hence the skepticism about the promise of politics and politicians), their political authority (hence the willingness to relay falsehoods and hearsay without question), and commerce (hence their compromises in pursuit of high returns)—rather than the public interest. I have therefore proposed a number of policy reforms, journalistic changes (especially a reorientation towards public journalism), and measures that individuals can take to improve political communication.

These reforms are not unrealistic: the evidence from the preceding chapters suggests the artificiality of much of what is assumed about the news media and how they operate, and we see how the different media practices have evolved to take their present form. Change may take time, but the journalistic and corporate practices of the moment are under considerable pressure, with the declining legitimacy of politicians and the federal government among the American public, the diminishing audience for newspapers, newsmagazines, and network television, and the rising challenge posed by new technologies.

IN 1922 WALTER LIPPMANN MADE THE CLAIM THAT THE NEWS MEDIA are no substitute for institutions. About fifty years later, Katherine Graham, the chair of the board of the Washington Post Company and then the publisher of the *Washington Post,* made the exact same claim. Commenting on the Watergate scandal, Graham said that the press cannot hope to do the work of the representative bodies of government. Many prominent journalists and acclaimed media scholars have expressed the same view.[65] I argue that *the news media already are an institution.* There is no going back.

It is therefore up to the American public, organized interests, and national policy makers to decide how they are going to reform political communication—and American politics in general—to reclaim a political community where institutions work, a political community where the news media are able to present a picture of reality that men and women can consult to better guide their own destinies.

Preface

1. Michael Kinsley, "In Defense of Matt Drudge," *Time*, February 2, 1998, 41. See Steven Brill, "Pressgate," *Brill's Content*, August 1998, 123–51.

2. Evan Thomas, *Newsweek's* editor, has said that Drudge's report merely pushed up the story by a couple of days and that the story would have broken soon, anyway ("The Clinton Crisis: News and Rumors," C-SPAN, February 18, 1998).

3. In a Harris Poll conducted February 18–23, 1998, 84 percent of respondents agreed with the statement "The media have given far too much attention to the Monica Lewinsky affair." In a poll conducted jointly by Gallup, CNN, and *USA Today*, 73 percent of respondents disapproved of how the news media "has handled the controversy over Clinton and Monica Lewinsky." A survey by Princeton Survey Research Associates for the Pew Research Center found that 80 percent of respondents believed "there has been too much . . . discussion about this issue by commentators and analysts on television and radio." At the same time, CNN reported "higher viewership spurred by coverage of the Monica Lewinsky affair" (John Consoli, "An Affair To Re-

member," *Mediaweek*, March 2, 1998, 9), and a manager of *Time's* Web site reported that the Monica Lewinsky news spurred "record traffic" on major and minor Web sites. The hit rate at *Time's* site doubled, and the number of hits at the *New York Times's* site reached a new record at 2.5 million (Joshua Quittner, "All Monica All the Time," *Time*, February 9, 1998, 23).

4. Max Frankel, "Testing the Tasteless," *New York Times Magazine*, February 15, 1998, 18.

5. Bartholomew H. Sparrow, *From the Outside in: World War II and the American State*, Princeton Studies in American Politics (Princeton, N.J.: Princeton University Press, 1996).

6. See Walter Lippmann, *Public Opinion* (New York: Free Press, 1922), 18.

7. The direct predecessor with respect to the news media is Thomas Patterson's *Out of Order* (New York: Knopf, 1993). Patterson writes about the dysfunctional behavior of the news media with respect to the U.S. presidential election campaigns, whereas I attempt to write about the entire political system.

8. Grant McConnell, *Private Power and American Democracy* (New York: Vintage, 1966); Theodore Lowi, *The End of Liberalism*, 2d ed. (New York: Norton, 1979). For macroscopic criticism of the pro-business bias of the American political system, see Charles Lindblom, *Politics and Markets* (New York: Basic Books, 1977). For criticism of the Supreme Court and the subordinate federal courts—the third branch of government—see Gerald N. Rosenberg, *The Hollow Hope: Can the Courts Bring About Social Change?* (Chicago: University of Chicago Press, 1991).

9. McConnell, *Private Power and American Democracy*, 5–6.

10. Lowi, *The End of Liberalism*, 58–59, 63.

11. Ibid., xvi.

ONE Introduction

1. See David Halberstam, *The Best and the Brightest* (New York: Dell, 1972); David Wise, *The Politics of Lying* (New York: Vintage, 1973); Tom Wicker, *On Press* (New York: Viking, 1975); Michael Schudson, *Discovering the News* (New York: Basic Books, 1978); William A. Gamson, *What's News? A Game Simulation of TV News* (New York: Free Press, 1984); Daniel Hallin, *The "Uncensored War": The Media and Vietnam* (New York: Oxford University Press, 1986); Walter Cronkite, *A Reporter's Life* (New York: Knopf, 1996).

2. See Harrison Salisbury, *Without Fear or Favor* (New York: Times Books, 1980); David Rudenstine, *The Day the Presses Stopped* (Berkeley: University of California Press, 1996); Wicker, *On Press*.

3. See David L. Altheide, *Creating Reality: How TV News Distorts Events* (Beverly Hills, Calif.: Sage, 1974), 155. According to Ed Fouhy, the executive director of the Pew Center for Civic Journalism, "Vietnam broke the bonds of trust, and the press corps was conceited enough that it could find the truth, could find out the plan, the secret plan of Nixon's. They had the conceit that he had gotten away with it. With Watergate, too, there was the conviction that we had failed to report the character issue" (interview by author, September 7, 1995).

4. On the Murrow-McCarthy interchange, see Fred Friendly, *Due to Circumstances Beyond Our Control* (New York: Random House, 1967); Gamson, *What's News?* 67–69. All three networks covered the first week of television hearings live, but only ABC (in

last place among the networks at the time) continued daytime programming of the McCarthy hearings.

5. See Paul Weaver, *News and the Culture of Lying* (New York: Free Press, 1994), 169.

6. Tom Wicker, *Tragic Failure: Racial Integration in America* (New York: Morrow, 1995), 80; Robert J. Donovan and Ray Sherer, *Unsilent Revolution: Television News and American Public Life,* Woodrow Wilson Center Series (New York: Cambridge University Press, 1992), 3–22. The Supreme Court's ruling in *New York Times v. Sullivan* (1964) also fostered the image of the press as a political watchdog.Only if actual malice were proven could those hurt by media coverage sue successfully for libel. The *Times* was therefore exonerated in running an advertisement attacking a Birmingham sheriff involved in the civil rights struggle.

7. Other coverage of the possible abuse of power by the Clinton administration has included stories on Paula Jones, the handling of White House lawyer Vincent Foster's papers after his death, the campaign fundraising from the White House, and the receipt of campaign contributions from foreign sources.

8. James Baker, "Report First, Check Later," interview by Marvin Kalb, *Harvard International Journal of Press/Politics* 1, no. 2 (1996): 3; Thomas E. Patterson, *Out of Order* (New York: Knopf, 1993), 26; Doris Graber, *Mass Media and American Politics,* 5th ed. (Washington, D.C.: CQ Press, 1997), 3; also see S. Robert Lichter and Richard E. Noyes, *Good Intentions Make Bad News,* 2d ed. (Lanham, Md.: Rowman & Littlefield, 1996), 5–8.

9. The Code of Broadcast Journalists is cited in John H. McManus, *Market-Driven Journalism: Let the Citizen Beware?* (Thousand Oaks, Calif.: Sage, 1994), 24–25; the Code of Professional Journalists is cited in Pamela Shoemaker and Stephen Reese, *Mediating the Message: Theories of Influences on Mass Media Content,* 2d ed. (White Plains, N.Y.: Longman, 1996), 95–96.

10. Journalism scholars David Weaver and Cleveland Wilhoit surveyed more than a thousand journalists in 1992 and found that 67 percent of respondents said that to "investigate government claims" was extremely important, and 69 percent said that to "get information to public quickly" was extremely important. Thirty-nine percent said that to "discuss national policy" was extremely important, and 21 percent said that to "serve as adversary of government" was extremely important (David H. Weaver and G. Cleveland Wilhoit, *The American Journalist in the 1990s* [Mahwah, N.J.: Erlbaum, 1996], 136). All four categories of the news media—newspapers, magazines, television, and radio—and not simply the "adversarial press" are implicit in the concept of the "fourth estate."

11. Roper Center, "News Junkies, News Critics," survey. Arlington, Va.: Newseum, 1997, available at http://www.newseum.org; Media Studies Center/Roper Center Survey, cited in Kenneth Dautrich and Jennifer Necci Dineen, "Media Bias: What Journalists and the Public Say about It," *Public Perspective,* October/November 1996, 12. This is not to say that the survey respondents were not critical of the press. On public attitudes toward the news media, see Times-Mirror Center for the People and the Media, *The People, the Press, and Their Leaders* (Washington, D.C.: Times-Mirror Center for the People and the Media, 1995). The Times-Mirror polls indicate a broad acceptance of the press's coverage of Whitewater and the Clinton administration in general—coverage consistent with the guardian or watchdog image.

12. Herbert Gans, *Deciding What's News* (New York: Vintage, 1980), 205–7; Austin

Ranney, *Channels of Power* (New York: Basic Books, 1983), 52–55. Gans calls the Progressive values contained in journalism a "paraideology."

13. Dan Rather and Walter Cronkite quoted in Lucas A. Powe, *The Fourth Estate and the Constitution* (Berkeley: University of California Press, 1991), 242, 289. Powe observes that Rather did not point out the advantages that freedom of the press provided for reporters or media owners. Brit Hume is quoted in Larry Sabato, *Feeding Frenzy* (New York: Free Press, 1991), 4. Horatio was the Roman general who, on a narrow bridge, single-handedly fought off the invading Etruscans. Sabato also quotes Hume's former ABC colleague Sander Vanocur as saying that he sees "among some young reporters a quality of the avenging angel: they are going to sanitize American politics."

14. Denis McQuail, *Media Performance: Mass Communication and the Public Interest* (Newbury Park, Calif.: Sage, 1992), 85–86; Powe, *The Fourth Estate;* Stephen Ansolabehere, Shanto Iyengar, and Roy Behr, *The Media Game* (New York: Macmillan, 1993); John Zaller, "Negativity and Bias in Media Coverage of Presidential Elections, 1948–1992" (paper presented at the annual meeting of the American Political Science Association, San Francisco, August 1996). Also see Weaver and Wilhoit, *The American Journalist in the 1990s,* for a breakdown of media roles and journalists' conceptions of themselves.

15. Fred Dutton, a prominent Washington attorney and the campaign manager for Robert Kennedy in 1968 and George McGovern in 1972, makes the same point: "The limitations [on the news media] are much more serious and fundamental than people realize" (interview by author, July 18, 1995). For other discussions of the distinct limitations of the news media, see W. Lance Bennett, *News: The Politics of Illusion,* 3d ed. (White Plains, N.Y.: Longman, 1996); Ben Bagdikian, *The Media Monopoly,* 4th ed. (Boston: Beacon Press, 1992); Ted Galen Carpenter, *The Captive Press* (Washington, D.C.: Cato Institute, 1996); Gaye Tuchman, *Making News: A Study in the Construction of Reality* (New York: Free Press, 1978); Michael Parenti, *Inventing Reality: The Politics of the News Media,* 2d ed. (New York: St. Martin's Press, 1993); Todd Gitlin, *The Whole World Is Watching* (Berkeley: University of California Press, 1980); Jay G. Blumler and Michael Gurevitch, *The Crisis of Public Communication* (New York: Routledge, 1995); McQuail, *Media Performance;* Alan K. Simpson, *Right in the Old Gazoo: A Lifetime of Scrapping with the Press* (New York: Morrow, 1997).

16. W. Richard Scott, *Institutions and Organizations* (Thousand Oaks, Calif.: Sage, 1995), 56. Also see Daniel Katz and R. L. Kahn, *The Social Psychology of Organizations* (New York: Wiley, 1966). On organizational approaches to understanding the news media, see Edward Jay Epstein, *News from Nowhere: Television and the News* (New York: Vintage Press, 1974); Leon V. Sigal, *Reporters and Officials: The Organization and Politics of Newsmaking* (Lexington, Mass.: D.C. Heath, 1973); Paul M. Hirsh, "Occupational, Organizational, and Institutional Models in Mass Media Research: Toward an Integrated Framework," in *Strategies for Communication Research,* Vol. 6, Sage Annual Reviews of Communication Research, ed. Paul M. Hirsh, Peter V. Miller, and F. Gerald Kline (Beverly Hills, Calif.: Sage, 1979), 13–42. Also see Tuchman, *Making News,* and "The Exception Proves the Rule: The Study of Routine News Practices," in *Strategies for Communication Research,* Vol. 6, Sage Annual Reviews of Communication Research, ed. Paul M. Hirsh, Peter V. Miller, and F. Gerald Kline (Beverly Hills, Calif.: Sage, 1979), 43–77.

17. I am referring to mainstream news organizations, ones that seek a relatively large, general audience rather than a narrow, politically defined market.

18. Thomas Carlyle is quoted in Powe, *The Fourth Estate,* 261; Jefferson is quoted in Frank Luther Mott, *The News in America* (Cambridge, Mass.: Harvard University Press, 1952), 5; Madison is quoted in Timothy B. Dyk, "Newsgathering, Press Access, and the First Amendment," *Stanford Law Review* 44 (1992): 959.

19. Douglass Cater, *The Fourth Branch of Government* (Boston: Houghton-Mifflin, 1959), 42, 157, 65–67, 168. Bruce E. Gronbeck tells of how the 1952 Eisenhower campaign—the first presidential election of the television era—spent more than ten times the $77,000 spent by Democrat Adlai Stevenson and how Eisenhower used music by Irving Berlin, animation by Disney, and words crafted by the advertising firm BBDO ("The Presidency in the Age of Secondary Orality," in *Beyond the Rhetorical Presidency,* ed. Martin J. Medhurst [College Station: Texas A&M Press, 1996], 33).

20. Timothy E. Cook, "The Fourth Branch and the Other Three: The Washington News Media and the Politics of Shared Power" (paper presented at the annual meeting of the American Political Science Association, New York, September 1994); Bruce J. Evensen, *Truman, Palestine, and the Press* (New York: Greenwood Press, 1992); Graber, *Mass Media and American Politics;* Matthew Kerbel, *Edited for Television* (Boulder, Colo.: Westview Press, 1994); John Nerone, *Violence against the Press: Policing the Public Sphere in U.S. History* (New York: Oxford University Press, 1994); Powe, *The Fourth Estate;* Hedrick Smith, *The Power Game* (New York: Random House, 1988); James Squires, *Read All About It!* (New York: Times Books, 1993); Wicker, *On Press.*

21. See Paul Lazersfeld, B. Berelson, and H. Gaudet, *The People's Choice* (New York: Columbia University Press, 1944); Joseph Klapper, *The Effects of Mass Communication* (New York: Free Press, 1960). See Christopher Simpson on the interrelationship between psychological research on media effects and the politics (and federal funding) resulting from the cold war (*The Science of Coercion: Communication Research and Psychological Warfare 1945–1960* [New York: Oxford University Press, 1995]).

22. Cohen quoted in Stephen Hess, *News and Newsmaking* (Washington, D.C.: Brookings, 1996), 9; Maxwell E. McCombs and David Shaw, "The Agenda-Setting Function of the Press," *Public Opinion Quarterly* 36 (1972): 176–87; James Winter and Chaim Eyal, "Agenda Setting for the Civil Rights Issue," *Public Opinion Quarterly* 45 (1981): 376–83; Shanto Iyengar and Donald Kinder, *News That Matters* (Chicago: University of Chicago Press, 1987); Hans Bernd Brosis and Hans Mathias Kepplinger, "The Agenda Setting Function of Television News: Static and Dynamic Views," *Communication Research* 17 (1990): 183–211; Shanto Iyengar, *Who's Responsible?* (Chicago: University of Chicago Press, 1991); Maxwell E. McCombs and Donald L. Shaw, "The Evolution of Agenda-Setting Research: Twenty-five Years in the Marketplace of Ideas," *Journal of Communication* 43, no. 2 (1993): 58–67. An exception on the coverage of presidential election campaigns is the work of Thomas Patterson and Richard Davis, "The Media Campaign: Struggle for the Agenda," in *The Elections of 1984,* ed. Michael Nelson (Washington, D.C.: CQ Press, 1985).

23. As Colin Seymour-Ure remarks, Lasswell's series of questions have distinct fields of analysis: control, content, medium, audience, and effect. Seymour-Ure also points out that this is a relatively narrow research agenda, one that neglects questions of intention, frequency, reciprocity, and cumulative impact. Hence the "hypodermic syringe" image: a message is "jabbed" into an audience, which is then quickly affected by the injection (*The Political Impact of the Mass Media* [Beverly Hills, Calif.: Sage, 1974], 42).

24. Graber, *Mass Media and American Politics,* 15; McQuail, "The Influence and Ef-

fects of Mass Media" in *Media Power in Politics*, 2d ed., ed. Doris Graber (Washington, D.C.: CQ Press, 1990), 32. Despite the high quality of the experimental work on media effects (e.g., Iyengar and Kinder, *News That Matters*, 1987), the external validity of the experimental findings remains in question.

25. Cater, *The Fourth Branch*, 13; Doris Graber, "Political Communication: Scope, Progress, Promise," in *The State of the Discipline*, ed. Ada Finifter (Washington, D.C.: American Political Science Association, 1992), 305–32.

26. John Zaller, *The Nature and Origin of Mass Opinion* (Cambridge: Cambridge University Press, 1992), 315, 319; see Sigal, *Reporters and Officials;* Altheide, *Creating Reality;* Wicker, *On Press;* Tuchman, *Making News;* David Halberstam, *The Powers That Be* (New York: Knopf, 1979); Gans, *Deciding What's News;* Mark Fishman, *Manufacturing the News* (Austin: University of Texas Press, 1980).

27. Sigal, *Reporters and Officials,* 187. Roshco (*Newsmaking*) argues that news production (or "newsmaking") is a social process, the premise being that "social structure is the major influence on the content of the press." He, too, is concerned with "input" (the production of political communication) rather than "output" (the effect of political communication on the audience). Roshco stresses the structural forces and the historical development that led to the prominence of "objectivity" and its successor, "impartiality," in the production of news about politics and government. Roshco offers an analysis of what is considered the "news" and how the constraints imposed on journalists by the needs of their media shape the content of the news media.

28. McQuail, *Media Performance,* 99–100, 112–13, emphasis added.

29. At least three writers are explicit that the news media *cannot* be viewed as a political institution: Patterson (*Out of Order*), Hess (*News and Newsmaking*), and Howard Kurtz (*Media Circus: The Trouble with American Newspapers* [New York: Times Books, 1993]). By "political institution," however, Patterson means a formal institution, one designed with political functions in mind (*Out of Order,* 21).

30. McQuail, "Influence and Effects of Mass Media," 33.

31. As Altheide puts it, "events become news when transformed by the news perspective, and not because of their objective characteristics. A related point is that news practices can significantly alter one event by either predefining what is most important about it or by retrospectively connecting it to other events" (*Creating Reality,* 173).

32. Douglass North, *Structure and Change in Economic History* (New York: Norton, 1981).

33. Sven Steinmo and Kathleen Thelen, *Structuring Politics: Historical Institutions in Comparative Perspective* (Cambridge: Cambridge University Press, 1992), 2. Whereas many political scientists use the term "political institution" to refer to societywide political phenomena such as the three branches, federalism, elections, voting, and the like (e.g., R. Kent Weaver and Bert A. Rockman, eds., *Do Institutions Matter? Government Capabilities in the United States and Abroad* [Washington, D.C.: Brookings, 1993]), other political scientists, especially those working on economic models of institutions (e.g., William Riker, Kenneth Shepsle, Terry Moe, Mathew McCubbins, and Terry Sullivan), use the term to refer to congressional rules and procedures.

34. This is not to say that political institutions are immutable, but they do systematically affect the actions of others. At the same time, they themselves may be altered by individual or collective action.

35. In other words, there is a nesting of institutions: micro-level phenomena (e.g.,

a handshake or gesture), existing within and complementing global-level phenomena (e.g., capitalism or Roman Catholicism). For an explication of institutional levels, see Scott, *Institutions and Organizations*, and Ronald Jepperson, "Institutions, Institutional Effects, and Institutionalism," in *The New Institutionalism in Organizational Analysis*, ed. Walter W. Powell and Paul J. DiMaggio (Chicago: University of Chicago Press, 1991), 143-63.

36. James G. March and Johan P. Olsen, *Rediscovering Institutions: The Organizational Basis of Politics* (New York: Free Press, 1989); idem, "The New Institutionalism: Organizational Factors in Political Life," *American Political Science Review* 78 (1984): 734-49. Mathew McCubbins and Terry Sullivan write that institutions are "rules of the game that constrain individual choices and provide incentives for individual action" (*Congress: Structure and Policy* [Cambridge: Cambridge University Press, 1987], 3). For an overview of the institutional literature, see, among others, Scott, *Institutions and Organizations;* Powell and DiMaggio, eds., *The New Institutionalism in Organizational Analysis.*

37. Richard Rubin cited in Martha Joynt Kumar, *Wired for Sound and Pictures: The President and White House Communications Policies* (Baltimore: Johns Hopkins University Press, forthcoming); Michael McGerr, *Decline of Popular Politics: The American North, 1865-1928* (New York: Oxford University Press, 1986). Also see Edwin Emery and Michael Emery, *The Press and America: An Interpretive History of the Mass Media,* 5th ed. (Englewood Cliffs, N.J.: Prentice-Hall, 1984). For a similar presentation of the historical role of the press in American political history, see Edwin Diamond and Robert A. Silverman, *White House to Your House* (Cambridge, Mass.: MIT Press, 1994).

38. See, for example, Betty Houchin Winfield, *FDR and the News Media* (New York: Columbia University Press, 1994); F. B. Marbut, *News from the Capital: The Story of Washington Reporting* (Carbondale: Southern Illinois University Press, 1971); Frank Luther Mott, *American Journalism,* 3d ed. (New York: Macmillan, 1962). There remains some debate about the role of the press in the Spanish-American War. A number of media scholars (e.g., Michael Schudson) and historians (e.g., Lewis Gould) have argued that the press played little role in causing American intervention in Spanish-Cuban affairs in the late 1890s. However, conventional wisdom has it right: the yellow press, and the competition between William Randolph Hearst and Joseph Pulitzer in particular, was instrumental in getting Congress and the McKinley administration to go to war against Spain (see Bartholomew H. Sparrow, "Strategic Adjustment and the American Navy: The Spanish-American War, the Yellow Press, and the 1990s," in *The Politics of Strategic Adjustment,* ed. Emily Goldman, Ed Rhodes, and Peter Trubowitz [New York: Columbia University Press and Social Science Research Council, 1998], 139-75).

39. See Mary Ann Watson, *The Expanding Vista: American Television in the Kennedy Years* (New York: Oxford University Press, 1990); Donovan and Sherer, *Unsilent Revolution,* 42-46, 225-26; Colin Seymour-Ure, *The American President: Power and Communication* (New York: St. Martin's Press, 1982), 128-29, and *The Political Impact of Mass Media* (Beverly Hills, Calif.: Sage, 1974), 61-62; Matthew R. Kerbel, *Remote and Controlled: Media Politics in a Cynical Age* (Boulder, Colo.: Westview Press, 1995).

40. See Stephen Hess, *The Government/Press Connection* (Washington, D.C.: Brookings, 1984), David Morgan, *The Flacks of Washington* (Westport, Conn.: Greenwood Press, 1986), and Doris Graber, *Public Sector Communication* (Washington, D.C.: CQ Press, 1992). On the State Department and the news media, see Bernard Cohen,

The Press and Foreign Policy (Princeton, N.J.: Princeton University Press, 1963); Sigal, *Reporters and Officials;* Wicker, *On Press;* William O. Chittick, *State Department, Press, and Foreign Policy* (New York: Wiley-Interscience, 1970). On the Defense Department, see Robert B. Sims, *The Pentagon Reporters* (Washington, D.C.: National Defense University Press, 1983); Hess, *The Government/Press Connection.* On the CIA and the news media, see Salisbury, *Without Fear or Favor;* Malcolm W. Browne, *Muddy Boots and Red Socks* (New York: Times Books, 1993); Howard Bray, *Pillars of the Post: The Making of a News Empire in Washington* (New York: Norton, 1980).

The writer Martin Mayer points out the intimate relationship between the press and the FDA in the case of the Tylenol scare. Mayer also notes how NASA used the press after the Challenger disaster of 1986 (*Making News* [Boston: Harvard Business School Press, 1993], 279). Many agencies suffer in relative obscurity, of course, agencies such as the Department of Veterans Affairs, the Bureau of Indian Affairs, and the Bureau of Land Management. But even the agencies less heeded by the major media may be greatly affected by infrequent bursts of news—whether positive or negative.

41. See James Fallows, *Breaking the News: How the Media Undermine American Democracy* (New York: Pantheon, 1996); Theda Skocpol, *Boomerang: Clinton's Health Security Effort and the Turn against Government in U.S. Politics* (New York: Norton, 1996), 9–17; David Broder and Haynes Johnson, *The System: The American Way of Politics at the Breaking Point* (Boston: Little, Brown, 1996); Henry J. Kaiser Foundation, "Media Coverage of Health Care Reform: A Final Report," *Columbia Journalism Review* 35 (March/April 1997): Supplement; Kerbel, *Remote and Controlled,* 107–09; Jim Naureckas and Janine Jackson, eds., *The FAIR Reader: An EXTRA! Review of Press and Politics in the 1990s* (Boulder, Colo.: Westview Press, 1996), 157–70. The media scholar Kathleen Hall Jamieson notes that the news media's minimal reportage of the single-payer plan "did a serious injustice to the political process" ("The Annual Theodore H. White Lecture with Cokie Roberts" [Joan Shorenstein Center on the Press, Politics and Public Policy, John F. Kennedy School of Government, Harvard University, Cambridge, Mass., 1994, bound transcript], 66–67). Media analysts Diamond and Silverman further point out that the news media (and the Clintons' courting of the "Big Feet" top political journalists) played an important role in building public and inside-Washington expectations for health care reform (*White House to Your House,* 56–67).

42. See Richard Parker, "In Reforming Social Security, What Role Does the Press Play? A Critical Look at Early Coverage of the 1997 Advisory Council Report," Project on Economics and Journalism, Joan Shorenstein Center on Press, Politics and Public Policy, Kennedy School of Government, Harvard University, 1997.

43. See Weaver and Wilhoit, *The American Journalist of the 1990s.*

44. On the external pressures bearing on U.S. news organizations, see G. R. Carroll, *Publish and Perish: The Organizational Ecology of Newspaper Industries* (Greenwood, Conn.: JAI Press, 1987); Shoemaker and Reese, *Mediating the Message;* Weaver and Wilhoit, *The American Journalist in the 1990s;* Sigal, *Reporters and Officials;* Gans, *Deciding What's News.*

45. See Lynne G. Zucker, "Introduction: Institutional Theories of Organizations—Conceptual Development and Research Agenda," and Paul DiMaggio, "Interest and Agency in Institutional Theory," in *Institutional Patterns and Organizations,* ed. Lynne G. Zucker (Cambridge, Mass.: Ballinger, 1988), xiii–xix, 3–21. As the former Senator Alan Simpson puts it, "The mainstream media are forever trying to distance themselves from the tabloids—the *Star,* the *National Enquirer,* the *Weekly World News,* and

so on." Simpson goes on to note how blurred that line has become (*Right in the Old Gazoo*, 103).

46. According to former Secretary of State James A. Baker, "The 'CNN Effect' has revolutionized the way policymakers approach their jobs, particularly in the foreign policy arena, and it started frankly only about 1987 or '88, whenever CNN began their CNN International program. We learned very early, in 1989, that the best way for us to get a message to a foreign head of state was to get on the tube, to get out there on CNN . . . You didn't send a message to the embassy or an ambassador; that delayed it a lot" ("Report First, Check Later," 7).

47. The history of Pulitzer's *New York World* further illustrates the vulnerability of any one newspaper of influence. A revolutionary and extremely profitable newspaper in the 1880s and 1890s, the *World* began to steadily lose money in the early twentieth century and in the 1930s had to merge with the *New York Telegram*.

48. Sigal, *Reporters and Officials*, 1–3, 34, 46, 53–54, 66, 68, 92, 133, 180–81, 191. Cater briefly notes the uncertainty of news reporting (*The Fourth Branch*, 170–72). Others who mention the uncertain character of news production include Jeremy Tunstall, *Reporters at Work: Specialist Correspondents: Their News Organizations, News Sources, and Competitor Colleagues* (London: Constable, 1971), 21; Edward Jay Epstein, *Between Fact and Fiction* (New York: Vintage Books, 1975), 3–8; David Paletz and Robert M. Entman, *Media Power Politics* (New York: Free Press, 1981), 20–21; Gitlin, *The Whole World Is Watching*, 258–67; Timothy Cook, *Making Laws and Making News: Media Strategies in the U.S. House of Representatives* (Washington, D.C.: Brookings, 1989), 8; Thomas E. Patterson, *The Mass Media Election: How Americans Choose Their President* (New York: Praeger, 1980), 130.

49. The exception may be the purchase of consumer durable goods such as electronic equipment, automobiles, clothes, home furnishings, and toys. When people buy these items free of significant time constraints, they are typically able to research the product's attributes, compare prices with substitutable products, check warranties, and so on in their pursuit of a rational purchase.

50. Diane Vaughan, *The Challenger Launch Decision: Risky Technology, Culture, and Deviance at NASA* (Chicago: University of Chicago Press, 1996), 402.

51. Tuchman, *Making News;* Arthur L. Stinchcombe, *Information and Organizations* (Berkeley: University of California Press, 1990), 352.

52. Journalists include columnists or "pundits," some of whom occupy a category of their own. Most columnists are household names and have far more leeway in voicing their opinions and shaping political information. Yet they still depend on government officials for their material. However newsworthy, their material would be worthless in the absence of the politics and political processes already in place.

53. See Sigal, *Reporters and Officials;* Tuchman, *Making News;* Gans, *Deciding What's News;* and Altheide, *Creating Reality*.

54. This is not to say that these practices are all consistent with each other or that they all share the same degree of informality. They may be disjointed; they may abrade each other; they may even be taken for granted (but the product of human artifice nonetheless). See Karen Orren and Stephen Skowronek, "Beyond the Iconography of Order," in *The Dynamics of American Politics*, ed. Lawrence C. Dodd and Calvin Jillson (Boulder, Colo.: Westview Press, 1994); March and Olson, "The New Institutionalism"; Powell and DiMaggio, "Introduction," in Powell and DiMaggio, eds., *The New Institutionalism*, 1–38.

55. Roper Organization, *America's Watching: Public Attitudes Toward Television, 1991,* Figure 3.1, "Americans' Primary Sources of News, 1959–1991," quoted in Ansolabehere et al., *The Media Game,* 43; David Shaw, "For Papers a Generation Is Missing," *Los Angeles Times,* March 15, 1989, part 1, 14, cited in Donovan and Scherer, *Unsilent Revolution,* 305. Shaw adds: "Study after study has shown that they do not consider a daily newspaper either essential or relevant." Also see Michael X. Delli Carpini and Scott Keeter, *What Americans Know about Politics and Why It Matters* (New Haven, Conn.: Yale University Press, 1996), 113.

56. David Shribman, interviews by author, July 7 and 18, 1995; Bill Headline, interview by author, July 28, 1995; Donovan and Scherer, *Unsilent Revolution,* 306; Mort Rosenblum, *Who Stole the News?* (New York: Wiley, 1993).

57. Pew Research Center for the People and the Press, quoted in Robert J. Samuelson, "No More Media Elite," *Washington Post,* July 8, 1998, A17.

58. Bill Carter, "The Networks Lose Viewers to Cable, Again," *New York Times,* May 22, 1997, B3; David Lieberman, "Media Forecast: Strong Spending Picture," *USA Today,* July 25, 1997, B1.

59. On the leverage of the network affiliates, see Epstein, *News from Nowhere;* Altheide, *Creating Reality;* Penn Kimball, *Downsizing the News: Network Cutbacks in the Nation's Capital* (Washington, D.C.: Woodrow Wilson Center Press, 1994); Ken Auletta, *Three Blind Mice: How the TV Networks Lost Their Way* (New York: Random House, 1991); McManus, *Market-Driven Journalism.* Evidence suggests that local affiliates have only grown in their influence over the networks. McManus notes that in 1988, network television news was seen by 76 million people, whereas local news was viewed by 80 million people (*Market-Driven Journalism,* 10).

60. Auletta, *Three Blind Mice,* 570. Other recent moments of television-mediated events of universal political culture include the Tiananmen Square massacre, and Boris Yeltsin's defiance of a right-wing coup in Russia.

61. Kimball, *Downsizing the News,* 10, 22; Auletta, *Three Blind Mice,* 366–73.

62. David Broder, interview by author, June 23, 1995. The "Hotline" is a daily digest (about 20–30 pages in length) of American political news from newspapers, newsmagazines, and television coverage around the United States.

63. *Wired,* March 5, 1995, 47.

64. Pippa Norris and David Jones, "Editorial," *Harvard International Journal of Press/Politics* 3, no. 2 (1993): 1; Pew Research Center, quoted by Samuelson. Also see Mark A. Thalheimer, "If We Build It Will They Come? Profiling the News Consumer of the Future," *Communication,* October 1996, 20–28.

65. Ed Fouhy, interview by author, September 5, 1996; Mort Pye, interview by author, December 8, 1996. The *Star-Ledger* is the nation's fourteenth largest daily newspaper and, as of early July 1995, had a daily circulation of 460,000 newspapers throughout New Jersey. Diamond and Silverman (*White House to Your House*) note the rise of television culture, the existence of a virtual political world, the prevalence of television talk shows, and the attention paid to celebrity by the news media, at the expense of substance.

66. McQuail, *Media Performance,* 68, 73–77. McQuail does not seek to answer this question. Rather, his intention is to diagnose the separate elements of "order" (cohesion) as it relates to the news media: social order (articulating intrasocietal relations) and cultural order (symbolic meanings).

McQuail also points out that the impact of the news media on society may be centripetal (centralizing and unifying) or centrifugal (differentiating and individualizing). The news media may also exhibit a top-down perspective (portraying disorder and deviance negatively) or a bottom-up perspective (emphasizing solidarity, voluntary attachment, and pluralism) (74–76).

67. Tuchman, *Making News;* Altheide, *Creating Reality;* Chris Argyris, *Behind the Front Page: Organizational Self-Renewal in a Metropolitan Newspaper* (San Francisco: Jossey-Bass, 1974); Gans, *Deciding What's News;* Epstein, *News from Nowhere.* All did their fieldwork in the 1970s. Two recent exceptions, although with less prominent news organizations, are Fishman (*Manufacturing the News*) and McManus (*Market-Driven Journalism*).

68. I also borrow freely from earlier work of mine: "Getting What It Wants: Media Practices and Political, Economic, and Technological Reforms" (paper presented at the annual meeting of the American Political Science Association, Washington, D.C., August 1997), "The News Media and the American Polity: Uncertainty and Institution" (paper presented at the annual meeting of the Midwest Political Science Association, Chicago, April 1995), "Thirty-five Years of *The Fourth Branch:* Revisiting the News Media as a Political Institution" (paper presented at the annual meeting of the American Political Science Association, New York, September 1994), and "The News Media, the Executive Branch, and the Gulf War: An Institutional Perspective" (paper presented at the annual meeting of the American Political Science Association, Washington, D.C., September 1993).

69. I use the term "news organization" (and not "news department," per McManus in *Market-Driven Journalism*) for the reason that newspapers, newsmagazines, and television stations are first and foremost *news* communicators. Entertainment and other programming may be (and often are) interrupted for serious or emergency news announcements. Consider that the networks had three days of non-stop reporting—with no advertisements—after the 1963 Kennedy assassination. Recall, too, the coverage of the Challenger disaster in 1986, the Persian Gulf War in early 1991, and the occasional congressional hearings: news organizations in each case preempted their scheduled programs or regular news coverage in order to run special news reports. Newspapers and newsmagazines, too, may employ numbers of reporters to work on the same big story and omit advertising from special issues for the purpose of including more hard news.

70. See Stephen Hess, *The Washington Reporters* (Washington, D.C.: Brookings, 1981), 106–7; Crouse, *The Boys on the Bus* (New York: Random House, 1973), 73; Gans, *Deciding What's News,* 180–81; Halberstam, *The Powers That Be,* 528; Mark Hertsgaard, *On Bended Knee: The Press and the Reagan Presidency* (New York: Farrar, Straus & Giroux, 1988), 196, 339; Kumar, *Wired for Sound and Pictures;* Sigal, *Reporters and Officials,* 47; Wicker, *On Press,* 179.

71. For other writings that argue for the limited capacity of the news media to act as a watchdog, see J. Herbert Altshull, *Agents of Power* (White Plains, N.Y.: Longman, 1984); Bennett, *News: The Politics of Illusion;* David Broder, *Behind the Front Page* (New York: Simon & Schuster, 1987); H. Corbett, *American Public Opinion: Trends, Processes, and Patterns* (White Plains, N.Y.: Longman); David Croteau and William Hoynes, *By Invitation Only* (Monroe, Maine: Common Courage, 1994); Robert A. Hackett, "Decline of a Paradigm? Bias and Objectivity in News Media Studies," *Critical Studies in Mass Communication* 1 (1984): 229–59; Epstein, *News from Nowhere;* Kurtz, *Media Circus;* Fallows, *Breaking the News;* Roshco, *Newsmaking;* and Wicker, *On Press.*

TWO Media Attack Dogs

1. Thomas E. Patterson, *Out of Order* (New York: Knopf, 1993); Larry Sabato, *Feeding Frenzy* (New York: Free Press, 1991).

2. Kathleen Hall Jamieson, *Dirty Politics: Deception, Distraction, and Democracy* (New York: Oxford University Press, 1992); Matthew R. Kerbel, *Remote and Controlled: Media Politics in a Cynical Age* (Boulder, Colo.: Westview Press, 1995); Patterson, *Out of Order;* Sabato, *Feeding Frenzy.*

3. David Broder, *Behind the Front Page* (New York: Simon & Schuster, 1987); Ted Galen Carpenter, *The Captive Press* (Washington, D.C.: Cato Institute, 1996); William Greider, *Who Will Tell the People: The Betrayal of American Democracy* (New York: Touchstone Books, 1992); Mark Hertsgaard, *On Bended Knee: The Press and the Reagan Presidency* (New York: Farrar, Straus & Giroux, 1988); Howard Kurtz, *Media Circus: The Trouble with American Newspapers* (New York: Times Books, 1993); Tom Wicker, *On Press* (New York: Viking, 1975). Wicker also refers to this as "handout" journalism (interview by author, December 6, 1996). John Zaller recognizes the possibility of this discrepant media treatment of public officials at the end of *The Nature and Origins of Mass Opinion* (Cambridge: Cambridge University Press, 1992). Stephen Ansolabehere, Shanto Iyengar, and Roy Behr also acknowledge this alternative perspective in the last chapter of *The Media Game* (New York: Macmillan, 1993).

4. Allan Rachlin, *News as Hegemonic Reality: American Political Culture and the Framing of News Accounts* (Westport, Conn.: Praeger, 1988); Edward S. Herman and Noam Chomsky, *Manufacturing Consent: The Political Economy of the Mass Media* (New York: Pantheon, 1988); Michael Parenti, *Inventing Reality*, 2d ed. (New York: St. Martin's Press, 1992); Edward S. Herman, "Diversity of the News: 'Marginalizing' the Opposition," *Journal of Communication* 35, no. 3 (1995): 135–65.

5. Stephen Hess, *News and Newsmaking* (Washington, D.C.: Brookings, 1996), 33–45, *The Ultimate Insiders* (Washington, D.C.: Brookings, 1986), 105–7, and *Live from Capitol Hill!* (Washington, D.C.: Brookings, 1991), 102. For an application of the "Golden Triangle" concept to the Persian Gulf War, see Timothy Cook, "Domesticating a Crisis," in *Taken by Storm*, ed. W. Lance Bennett and David L. Paletz (Chicago: University of Chicago Press, 1994), 105–30. Also see the discussion of the Persian Gulf War in Chapter 6.

6. The phrase "policy monopoly" makes no claim with respect to partisanship.

7. Patterson refers to journalists as "adjudicators" in *Out of Order.*

8. Michael Baruch Grossman and Martha Joynt Kumar, *Portraying the President: The White House and the Media* (Baltimore: Johns Hopkins University Press, 1981), 14, 147; Don Campbell, *Inside the Beltway: A Guide to Washington Reporting* (Ames: Iowa State University Press, 1991); also see Patterson, *Out of Order;* Robert J. Donovan and Ray Scherer, *Unsilent Revolution: Television News and American Public Life*, Woodrow Wilson Center Series (New York: Cambridge University Press, 1992); James Fallows, *Breaking the News* (New York: Pantheon, 1996).

9. Marvin Kalb, *The Nixon Memo: Political Respectability, Russia, and the Press* (Chicago: University of Chicago Press, 1995), 189; Leo Rosten, *The Washington Correspondents* (New York: Arno Press, 1974 [1937]), 65. One could argue that press secretaries straddle these cultures and that the increasing number of persons going back and forth between political work and journalism bespeaks a common culture. I nonetheless maintain that journalists or public officials are unable to serve two mas-

ters and the interests of journalists and public officials are necessarily and crucially distinct.

10. Jay G. Blumler and Michael Gurevitch, *The Crisis of Public Communication* (New York: Routledge, 1995), 32–33, 103. Blumler and Gurevitch note that the relationship is more than one of exchange, although there is clearly an element of exchange in it (29–31).

11. Herbert Gans, *Deciding What's News* (New York: Vintage, 1980), 116; Ansolabehere et al., *The Media Game*, 234; Mary Matalin and James Carville, *All's Fair: Love, War, and Running for President* (New York: Random House and Simon & Schuster, 1994), 427. The political scientist Timothy Cook refers to this process as the "negotiation of newsworthiness" (*Making Laws and Making News: Media Strategies in the House of Representatives* [Washington, D.C.: Brookings, 1989]; Timothy E. Cook and Lyn Ragsdale, "The President and the Press: Negotiating Newsworthiness at the White House," in *The Presidency and the Political System*, 4th ed., ed. Michael Nelson [Washington, D.C.: CQ Press, 1994]; Cook, *Governing with the News: The News Media as a Political Institution* [Chicago: University of Chicago Press, 1998]).

12. See, for instance, Jamieson, *Dirty Politics;* Kerbel, *Remote and Controlled;* S. Robert Lichter and Richard E. Noyes, *Good Intentions Make Bad News*, 2d ed. (Lanham, Md.: Rowman & Littlefield, 1996); Patterson, *Out of Order;* Sabato, *Feeding Frenzy;* Kenneth T. Walsh, *Feeding the Beast: The White House Versus the Press* (New York: Random House, 1996). I discuss presidential elections almost exclusively; congressional races and gubernatorial elections typically receive little attention from the national news media (as I note in the section on Congress).

13. The percentage of delegates selected by primary elections rose from 38.3 percent in 1960 to 79.4 percent for the Democrats in 1992 and from 38.6 percent in 1960 to 81.2 percent in 1992 for the Republicans (Ansolabehere et al., *The Media Game*, 75). On the McGovern-Fraser reforms, see William G. Mayer, "The New Hampshire Primary: A Historical Overview," in *Media and Momentum: The New Hampshire Primary and Nomination Politics,* ed. Gary R. Orren and Nelson W. Polsby (Chatham, N.J.: Chatham House, 1987), 17–18; Patterson, *Out of Order*, 31–34, 212–15.

14. See Ansolabehere et al., *The Media Game*, 76–77; William Corrado, "The Changing Environment of Presidential Campaign Finance," in *In Pursuit of the White House,* ed. William G. Mayer (Chatham, N.J.: Chatham House, 1996); Mayer, "The New Hampshire Primary," 18–19.

15. David Broder, *The Party's Over* (New York: Harper & Row, 1971); Lichter and Noyes, *Good Intentions Make Bad News,* 2–3; Patterson, *Out of Order;* Nelson W. Polsby, *The Consequences of Party Reform* (New York: Oxford University Press, 1983); David Price, *Bringing Back the Parties* (Washington, D.C.: 1984); Frank J. Sorauf and Paul Allen Beck, *Party Politics in America,* 7th ed. (New York: HarperCollins, 1992); Martin P. Wattenberg, "From Parties to Candidates: Examining the Role of the Media," *Public Opinion Quarterly* 46 (1982): 216–27.

16. Patterson, *Out of Order,* 74–75; Lichter and Noyes, *Good Intentions Make Bad News,* 235–36.

17. Patterson, *Out of Order;* John Zaller, "Strategic Politicians, Public Opinion, and the Gulf Crisis," in *Taken by Storm,* ed. W. Lance Bennett and David L. Paletz (Chicago: University of Chicago Press, 1994), 250–74; Lichter and Noyes, *Good Intentions Make Bad News;* Kerbel, *Remote and Controlled.*

18. Matalin and Carville, *All's Fair,* 195. Matalin also "almost always called the

Washington *Times* pretty early because they were the least likely to attack President Bush."

19. Jamieson, *Dirty Politics*, 125–29; Patterson, *Out of Order*, 163–65. Also see F. Christopher Arterton, *Media Politics: The News Strategies of Presidential Campaigns* (Lexington, Mass.: Lexington Books, 1984); Dean E. Alger, *The Media and Politics*, 2d ed. (Belmont, Calif.: Wadsworth, 1996).

20. Ansolabehere et al., *The Media Game*, 77–78. Although the authors use these words to describe congressional candidates, they also apply to presidential candidates. Presidential candidates, as a result, have had to raise increasing amounts of money each time they run for office (see Stephen Ansolabehere and Shanto Iyengar, *Going Negative: How Attack Ads Shrink and Polarize the Electorate* [New York: Free Press, 1995]). The total cost for the 1996 Dole campaign was about $75 million, for example, with $62 million being raised by the Dole campaign itself and the remainder by the Republican National Committee.

21. Patterson, *Out of Order*, 227; Michael J. Robinson, "Media Coverage in the Primary Campaign of 1976," in *The Party Symbol*, ed. William Crotty (San Francisco: W. J. Freeman, 1980), 187; Arthur H. Miller, Edie N. Goldenberg, and Lutz Erbring, "Type-Set Politics: Impact of Newspapers on Public Confidence," *American Political Science Review* 73 (1979): 67–84, cited in Patterson, *Out of Order*, 227. Also see Benjamin Ginsberg and Martin Shefter, *Politics by Other Means* (New York: Basic Books, 1990), on how partisan politics in Washington is dominated by issues of political communication.

22. Ansolabehere et al., *The Media Game*, 132; Martin Wattenberg, *The Decline of Political Parties, 1952–1980* (Cambridge, Mass.: Harvard University Press, 1984), 21. Also see Walter Dean Burnham, *Critical Elections and the Mainsprings of American Politics* (New York: Norton, 1970); Steven Rosenstone and J. Mark Hansen, *Mobilization, Participation, and Democracy in America* (New York: Macmillan, 1993).

23. See, for example, Walter Dean Burnham, "Introduction," in *The Election of 1996*, ed. Gerald M. Pomper (Chatham, N.J.: Chatham House Press, 1997), 1–20. Consider, too, the partisan changes in the South: in 1990, Republicans filled six of twenty-two Senate seats; in 1998, they filled fifteen of those seats. In 1990, the GOP was the majority party among state congressional delegations in only Virginia; eight years later, it sent a majority of members of Congress in seven states.

24. Cokie Roberts quoted in "The First Annual Theodore H. White Lecture with Walter Cronkite" (Joan Shorenstein Barone Center on the Press, Politics and Public Policy, John F. Kennedy School of Government, Harvard University, Cambridge, Mass., 1990, bound transcript), 43.

25. Reed Hundt quoted in Fred Wertheimer, "TV Ad Wars: How To Reduce the Costs of Television Advertising in Our Political Campaigns" (paper presented at the Joan Shorenstein Center on the Press, Politics and Public Policy, John F. Kennedy School of Government, Harvard University, Cambridge, Mass., December 1996), 1.

26. Ansolabehere et al., *The Media Game*, 77.

27. Arterton, *Media Politics*, 202–5; Orren and Polsby, eds., *Media and Momentum;* Emmett H. Buell Jr., "The Invisible Primary," and Michael G. Hagen, "Press Treatment of Front-Runners," in *In Pursuit of the White House*, ed. William G. Mayer (Chatham, N.J.: Chatham House, 1996), 1–43, 190–219; Larry J. Sabato, "Presidential Nominations: The Front-loaded Frenzy of 1996," in *Toward the Millennium: The Election of 1996*, ed. Larry J. Sabato (Boston: Allyn & Bacon, 1996), 93–120. The Democratic nominations of Jimmy Carter in 1976 and Michael Dukakis in 1988 are cases in point.

28. John Fialka, interview by author, June 29, 1995. Also see Michael Robinson and Margaret Sheehan, *Over the Wire and On TV: CBS and UPI in Campaign '80* (New York: Russell Sage Foundation, 1983); Patterson, *Out of Order;* Kerbel, *Remote and Controlled.*

29. Arterton, *Media Politics,* 52–54, 142–43, 159–73, 193; Alger, *The Media and Politics,* 306–10; Patterson, *Out of Order.* On the use (and misuse) of polls, see Alan K. Simpson, *Right in the Old Gazoo: A Lifetime of Scrapping with the Press* (New York: Morrow, 1997), 230–33.

30. Hal Bruno, interview by author, July 21, 1995.

31. R. W. Apple quoted in Arterton, *Media Politics,* 161.

32. Patterson, *Out of Order,* 116–25. Also see Matalin and Carville, *All's Fair,* 450–51.

33. Morris Udall quoted in Samuel L. Popkin, *The Reasoning Voter: Communication and Persuasion in Presidential Campaigns* (Chicago: University of Chicago Press, 1991), 117–18.

34. Robinson and Sheehan, *Over the Wire and on TV,* 116; Lichter and Noyes, *Good Intentions Make Bad News,* 165–76; Patterson, *Out of Order,* 125.

35. Kerbel, *Remote and Controlled,* 103–4; Theodore J. Lowi, *The Personal President: Power Invested, Promise Unfulfilled* (Ithaca, N.Y.: Cornell University Press 1985).

36. Alger, *The Media and Politics,* 309–10; Lichter and Noyes, *Good Intentions Make Bad News,* 10–11.

37. Simpson, *Right in the Old Gazoo,* 102–3; Patterson, *Out of Order,* 55, 166–67; Alger, *The Media and Politics,* 157. Patterson lists a number of blunders and political events that became "blunders" and "events" only because of the news media. Some of the episodes may easily have been tipping factors in presidential races, swinging momentum and possible outcomes in one direction rather than another (*Out of Order,* 39–42, 151–53). Lichter and Noyes (*Good Intentions Make Bad News,* 105–28) and Matalin and Carville (*All's Fair,* 125, 449) also remark on occasions when the actual character of an event or a day on the campaign trail was a far cry from what ended up being reported in the media. Also see Donovan and Scherer, *Unsilent Revolution.*

38. Roger Ailes quoted in Ed Fouhy, "Some Editors are Saying 'No,'" *Civic Catalyst,* June 1995, 1; Center for Media and Public Affairs, cited in Bruce Buchanan, *Renewing Presidential Politics: Campaigns, Media, and the Public Interest* (Lanham, Md.: Rowman & Littlefield, 1996), 135–58.

39. The term "big feet" comes from a reference to Hedrick Smith's large (size 13) feet, which he used to stick out in the airplane aisle while covering the 1972 presidential campaign for the *New York Times.*

40. Arterton, *Media Politics;* Doris Graber, *The Mass Media and American Politics* (Washington, D.C.: CQ Press, 1997), 269–88; also see Matalin and Carville, *All's Fair,* 431–32, 443.

41. See, for instance, Seymour Martin Lipset and William Schneider, *The Confidence Gap: Business, Labor, and Government in the Public Mind* (New York: Free Press, 1983).

42. David Gergen and David Keene quoted in Michael Kelly, "David Gergen, Master of the Game," *New York Times Magazine,* October 31, 1993, 69.

43. Joe Peyronnin quoted in Fallows, *Breaking the News,* 63; Bill Plante quoted in Walsh, *Feeding the Beast,* 287. On the Clinton administration's dissembling and manipulation, see Walsh, *Feeding the Beast,* and especially Howard Kurtz, *Spin Cycle: Inside the Clinton Propaganda Machine* (New York: Free Press, 1998).

44. As Mary Matalin notes, "Reporters understand that partisans are always only going to give them a one-sided view" (Matalin and Carville, *All's Fair*, 425).

45. Blumler and Gurevitch, *The Crisis of Public Communication*, 103; George Will, "Aiming for the Top Spot: Sense of History Fuels Forbes' Foray into Politics," *Austin American-Statesman*, October 9, 1997, A15.

46. Arterton, *Media Politics*, 81, 206–7.

47. Lee Ranie, interview by author, August 2, 1995. Ranie adds, "It filters down; interest groups are doing the same." Also see Matalin and Carville, *All's Fair*.

48. On the fundamental changes in political reporting that have occurred since the 1960s and 1970s, see Patterson, *Out of Order*, 19, 79, 204; Kerbel, *Remote and Controlled*, 44–45, 56–57; David Morgan, *The Flacks of Washington* (Westport, Conn.: Greenwood Press, 1986), 23–24; Samuel Kernell, *Going Public*, 2d ed. (Washington, D.C.: CQ Press, 1993), 231–32; Broder, *Behind the Front Page*, 154–75.

49. Alger, *The Media and Politics*; James David Barber, *The Pulse of Politics: Electing Presidents in the Media Age* (New York: Norton, 1980); Timothy Crouse, *The Boys on the Bus* (New York: Random House, 1973); Patterson, *Out of Order*; Robinson and Sheehan, *Over the Wire and on TV*.

50. Marlin Fitzwater, the White House press secretary under President Reagan and President Bush, refers to White's inside account of campaigns as "tick tock" journalism (*Call the Briefing! Reagan and Bush, Sam and Helen: A Decade with Presidents and the Press* [New York: Times Books, 1995], 282–83).

51. Crouse, *The Boys on the Bus*, 37; Theodore White quoted in Stan Cloud, "Teddy White Would Have Approved," *Civic Catalyst*, October 1995, 1.

52. Joe McGinniss, *The Selling of the President 1968* (New York: Trident Press, 1969). For an application of McGinniss's findings to the 1992 campaign, see Matalin and Carville, *All's Fair*.

53. Sidney Blumenthal, *The Permanent Campaign*, rev. ed. (Boston: Beacon Press, 1982); Roderick Hart, *The Sound of Leadership* (Chicago: University of Chicago Press, 1987); Kernell, *Going Public*.

54. Richard Nixon quoted in Colin Seymour-Ure, *The American President: Power and Communication* (New York: St. Martin's Press, 1982), 131. Also see Gladys Engel Lang and Kurt Lang, *The Battle for Public Opinion: The President, the Press, and the Polls during Watergate* (New York: Columbia University Press, 1983), 146–48.

55. Kernell, *Going Public*, 148; Hertsgaard, *On Bended Knee*; Kelly, "David Gergen."

56. Kernell, *Going Public*, 148.

57. Ibid., 149, 91–99. President George Bush was somewhat of an exception. He had more of an "inside" strategy of governing, relying more on personal contacts and developed networks than on "going public" (although he did have many informal press conferences). The Bush administration brought in Roger Ailes to handle public relations during Desert Shield and Desert Storm, however, and once the war started, "White House, Pentagon, State Department, and CIA officials" met every morning "before dawn to plot the 'spin' for the day." Every morning the administration settled on a "message of the day" and faxed out "talking points" to friendly party leaders, business executives, and religious leaders (Ann McDaniel and Howard Fineman, "The President's Spin Control," in *The Media and the Gulf War*, ed. Hedrick Smith [Washington, D.C.: Seven Locks Press, 1992], 154–55).

58. Kernell, *Going Public*, 114.

59. See Kernell, *Going Public*; Jeffrey Tulis, *The Rhetorical Presidency* (Princeton, N.J.:

Princeton University Press, 1987); Hart, *The Sound of Leadership*. Admittedly, these are not exactly the same arguments. Also see Ansolabehere et al., *The Media Game;* Cook, *Governing through the News;* Richard Davis, *The Press and American Politics: The New Mediator,* 2d ed. (Upper Saddle River, N.J.: Prentice-Hall, 1996); and Mark A. Peterson, *Legislating Together: The White House and Capitol Hill from Eisenhower to Reagan* (Cambridge, Mass.: Harvard University Press, 1990).

60. Martha Joynt Kumar, *Wired for Sound and Pictures: The President and White House Communications Policies* (Baltimore: Johns Hopkins University Press, forthcoming); Grossman and Kumar, *Portraying the President;* John Anthony Maltese, *Spin Control: the White House Office of Communications and the Management of Presidential News* (Chapel Hill: University of North Carolina Press, 1992).

61. Kumar, "The President and the News Media," in *Guide to the Presidency,* ed. Michael Nelson (Washington, D.C.: CQ Press, 1996), 852, 850; Kernell, *Going Public,* 69.

62. Kernell, *Going Public,* 233, 244.

63. See Fitzwater, *Call the Briefing!*

64. Paul Begala, "It's the Media, Stupid," *George,* October/November 1995, 138; Douglass Cater, *The Fourth Branch of Government* (Boston: Houghton-Mifflin, 1959); Morgan, *The Flacks of Washington,* 10. For a brief history of president-media relations, see Broder, *Behind the Front Page.* Also see Kumar, *Wired for Sound and Pictures.*

65. See Engel Lang and Lang, *The Battle for Public Opinion,* 247.

66. Robinson and Sheehan, *Over the Wire and on TV,* 172–73; Harold Stanley and Richard Niemi, *Vital Statistics in American Politics* (Washington, D.C.: Congressional Quarterly Press, 1988), cited in Kerbel, *Remote and Controlled,* 64; also see Graber, *Mass Media and American Politics,* 271, 290.

67. Hess, *Live from Capitol Hill!;* Davis, *The Press and American Politics,* 244–45; Norman Ornstein and Michael J. Robinson, "Where's All the Coverage? The Case of Our Disappearing Congress," *TV Guide,* January 11, 1986, 5, cited in Cook, *Making Laws and Making News,* 58.

68. Hess, *The Ultimate Insiders* and *Live from Capitol Hill!;* Cook, *Making Laws and Making News;* Broder, *Behind the Front Page.* Most members of Congress, without presidential ambitions, untainted by scandal, and with little hope of making the national media, attend to their local media, which are much better guarantors of their name recognition and reelection chances (Hess, *The Ultimate Insiders* and *Live from Capitol Hill!;* Cook, *Making Laws and Making News*).

69. Kerbel, *Remote and Controlled,* 104, 119; James Fallows, "The Presidency and the Press," in *The Presidency and the Political System,* 2d ed., ed. Michael Nelson (Washington, D.C.: CQ Press, 1984).

70. Richard Harwood, interview by author, July 18, 1995. Danny Weiss, assistant to Congressman George Miller (D-Calif.), notes that the Clean Water Act "was basically written by the chemical industry and the National Association of Manufacturers and others." That outside organizations write legislation is commonplace, but what is different now is that the hearing and mark-up process has been shortened. "There is less debate over the substance of the bill. That is a big change. The access for lobbyists now is 'What do you need, just give it to us, and we will take care of it.' Not like, 'What are your thoughts on this?'" (interview by author, July 24, 1995).

71. Paul S. Herrnson, *Congressional Elections: Campaigning at Home and in Washington* (Washington, D.C.: CQ Press, 1995), 133, 142–45.

72. Kernell, *Going Public*, 134–37, 230–31; Robinson quoted in Davis, *The Press and American Politics*, 249. Also see Hess, *The Ultimate Insiders;* Cook, *Making Laws and Making News*, 97–100; Alger, *The Media and Politics*, 197–99.

73. Ansolabehere et al., *The Media Game*, 121.

74. Cook, *Making Laws and Making News;* Hess, *The Ultimate Insiders* and *Live from Capitol Hill!*

75. See, for example, Tim Curran, "Top Ten Publicity Hounds," *George,* June/July 1996, 79–80. Also see Cook, *Making Laws and Making News*, 155–65.

76. Martin Linsky, *Impact: How the Press Affects Federal Policymaking* (New York: Norton, 1986); Kernell, *Going Public*, 235–38.

77. Cook, *Making Laws and Making News*, 160–66.

78. Benjamin Ginsberg and Martin Shefter, *Politics by Other Means: The Declining Importance of Elections in America* (New York: Basic Books, 1992); David Paletz and Robert M. Entman, *Media Power Politics* (New York: Free Press, 1981), 79–98; Hess, *The Ultimate Insiders* and *Live from Capitol Hill!;* Cook, *Making Laws and Making News.*

79. Graber, *Mass Media and American Politics*, 297.

80. Herrnson, *Congressional Elections*, 193–94. The same holds for Fernand Germaine, representative from Rhode Island, seeking reelection in 1984.

81. Brad Austin, interview by author, July 12, 1995.

82. Danny Weiss, interview by author, July 24, 1995; Brooke Anderson, interview by author, July 31, 1995; Hess, *Live from Capitol Hill!* 78; Cook, *Making Laws and Making News*, 72–75.

83. The political scientist H. W. Perry notes that the coverage of the Supreme Court tends to be divided into that by a rare few expert reporters (e.g., Linda Greenhouse and Nina Totenberg) and the rest (personal communication, November 25, 1997). The national print and radio reporters are helped, of course, by having a larger news hole, in comparison to the opportunities for local and regional newspapers and television stations.

84. Elliot S. Slotnick, Jennifer A. Segal, and Lisa M. Campoli, "Television and the Supreme Court" (paper presented at the annual meeting of the American Political Science Association, New York, 1994), cited in Alger, *The Media and Politics*, 214.

85. Davis, *The Press and American Politics*, 272; Alger, *The Media and Politics*, 214–15; Fred Graham quoted in Alger, *The Media and Politics*, 216.

86. See Ansolabehere et al., *The Media Game*, 119–20; Paletz and Entman, *Media Power Politics;* Richard Davis, *Decisions and Images: The Supreme Court and the Press* (Englewood Cliffs, N.J.: Prentice-Hall, 1994), and *The Press and American Politics;* Cook, *Governing with the News.*

87. See Stephen Hess, *The Government/Press Connection* (Washington, D.C.: Brookings, 1984); Doris Graber, *Public Sector Communication* (Washington, D.C.: CQ Press, 1994).

88. Dana Priest, "Air Force Flew Loose With 'Facts': Reporters Were Misled about General's Trip," *Washington Post,* July 5, 1995, A15. Also see Hess, *The Government/ Press Connection;* Graber, *Public Sector Communication;* Morgan, *The Flacks of Washington.*

89. Lichter and Noyes, *Good Intentions Make Bad News*, 131–61. Lichter and Noyes further point out that news organizations ran "ad watches" selectively.

90. Blumler and Gurevitch, "Politicians and the Press," in *Handbook of Political Communication*, ed. D. D. Nimmo and K. R. Sanders (Beverly Hills, Calif.: Sage, 1981),

467–93; Robinson and Sheehan, *Over the Wire and on TV;* Arterton, *Media Politics;* Patterson, *Out of Order;* Fallows, "The Presidency and the Press." The political scientist Larry M. Bartels makes an ambitious and interesting attempt to find the causal relationships in the "dance" or "chess game" between politicians (Congress and the executive branch) and the press (ABC News, the *New York Times,* and local newspaper coverage) from 1993 through 1995 ("Politicians and the Press: Who Leads, Who Follows?" [paper presented at the annual meeting of the American Political Science Association, San Francisco, September 1996]).

91. John Dancy, interviews by author, September 9, 12, and 18, 1996; Hal Bruno, interview by author, July 21, 1995.

92. Kerbel, *Remote and Controlled,* 124.

93. NBC News executive quoted in Blumler and Gurevitch, *The Crisis of Public Communication,* 106. The executive was referring to the 1984 election, but there is no reason to believe that the 1984 election was exceptional in this regard. On the dominance of the horse race, game, and sports metaphors, see Patterson, *Out of Order;* Matthew Kerbel, *Edited for Television* (Boulder, Colo.: Westview Press, 1994); Marion Just, Ann Crigler, Dean Alger, et al., *Crosstalk: Citizens, Candidates, and the Media in a Presidential Campaign* (Chicago: University of Chicago Press, 1996); Fallows, "The Presidency and the Press"; Thomas E. Patterson, *The Mass Media Election: How Americans Choose Their President* (New York: Praeger, 1980); Thomas E. Patterson and Robert D. McClure, *The Unseeing Eye: The Myth of Television Power in National Elections* (New York: Putnam, 1976).

94. Jamieson, *Dirty Politics,* 185–87; Just et al., *Crosstalk,* 239–44; Arterton, *Media Politics,* 44, 143–45; Jamieson, *Dirty Politics,* 169–88; Patterson, *Out of Order.*

95. Matalin and Carville, *All's Fair,* 427; Arterton, *Media Politics,* 47, 161–65.

96. Patterson, *Out of Order;* Kerbel, *Remote and Controlled,* 72–76, 86–88; Jamieson, *Dirty Politics,* 185–86.

97. Patterson, *Out of Order,* 74. Also see Stanley and Niemi, *Vital Statistics in American Politics,* cited in Kerbel, *Remote and Controlled,* 69–71; Bruce Buchanan, *Electing a President: The Markle Commission Research on Campaign '88* (Austin: University of Texas Press, 1991). Unclear is whether the application of the horse race metaphor to news coverage of the presidency, Congress, and the Court and cabinet nomination processes coincides with the timing of the horse race coverage of presidential elections.

98. For reports on the horse race coverage in the 1996 elections, see Sabato, "Presidential Nominations," 78–79; Diana Owen, "The Press' Performance," in *Toward the Millennium: The Election of 1996,* ed. Larry J. Sabato (Boston: Allyn & Bacon, 1996), 213–15.

99. C. R. Hofstetter, *Bias in the News: Network Television Coverage of the 1972 Election Campaign* (Columbus: Ohio State University Press, 1976). As Paul Weaver points out, however, there may be bias, but it accords with journalistic bias rather than partisan bias ("Is Television News Biased?" *The Public Interest* 27 [1972]: 69). See Patterson (*Out of Order,* 104–111) for a discussion of the journalistic bias as it affected the Bush, Carter, and Dukakis candidacies. Also see Chapter 5.

100. See Denis McQuail, *Media Performance: Mass Communication and the Public Interest* (Newbury Park, Calif.: Sage, 1992), 225–26; Patterson, *Out of Order,* 104–5.

101. Patterson, *Out of Order,* 124; Robinson and Sheehan, *Over the Wire and on TV;* Graber, *Mass Media and American Politics;* Ansolabehere et al., *The Media Game;* Tom Wicker, interview by author, December 6, 1996. There are, of course, many ways to

measure bias in coverage, but if the reality is highly imbalanced, as a result of a better campaign organization or a vastly more popular candidate, there is little reason to expect that media coverage would be balanced.

102. See Fallows, *Breaking the News;* Patterson, *Out of Order;* Ken Auletta, "Annals of Communication: Inside Story," *New Yorker,* November 18, 1996, 44–60.

103. See Patterson, *Out of Order,* 211; Lichter and Noyes, *Good Intentions Make Bad News,* 166–67.

104. Walter Cronkite quoted in "The First Annual Theodore H. White Lecture with Walter Cronkite" (Joan Shorenstein Barone Center on the Press, Politics and Public Policy, John F. Kennedy School of Government, Harvard University, Cambridge, Mass., 1990, bound transcript), 13; Blumler and Gurevitch, *The Crisis of Public Communication,* 104; Patterson, *Out of Order,* 87.

105. Fallows, *Breaking the News,* 63.

106. Hal Bruno, interview by author, July 21, 1995.

107. ABC News correspondent quoted in Walsh, *Feeding the Beast,* 241.

108. Patterson, *Out of Order;* Just et al., *Crosstalk;* Kerbel, *Remote and Controlled;* Walsh, *Feeding the Beast,* 241–42; Ed Fouhy, interview by author, September 7, 1995; Bartholomew H. Sparrow, "The Attenuation of the State: Soldiers, Money, and Political Communication in World War II, Korea, and Vietnam," manuscript.

109. See Robinson and Sheehan, *Over the Wire and on TV;* Patterson, *Out of Order;* John Dancy, personal communication, November 1996. Edward Jay Epstein notes that NBC cultivated the contrasting images of Chet Huntley and David Brinkley as network anchors, promoting the latter as an "anti-establishment maverick" (*News from Nowhere: Television and the News* [New York: Vintage Books, 1974], 202). Tom Brokaw, Bernard Shaw, Christianne Amanpour, and others, to be sure, are much less ironic or sarcastic in their reporting.

110. Carl Leubsdorf, the Washington bureau chief of the *Dallas Morning News,* mentions another standard practice of political news coverage: the habit of journalists in weekend talk shows to define politics and political achievement in terms of "how the president did this week" or in terms of how a political candidate, Congress, or a federal department performed that week—as though a week-by-week accounting makes any sense as a criterion by which to judge national politics or political leadership (interviews by author, August 4 and October 9, 1995).

111. Another standard feature in the news media's coverage of political contests with respect to the campaigns for the office of the president and vice president is the holding of presidential (and vice presidential) debates. These have been regular (and expected) features of presidential campaigns since 1977 (although presidential debates may be conducted without the participation of journalists themselves and only with the camera crews and necessary logistics present to transmit the sound and pictures). The Commission on Presidential Debates has been established precisely to monitor and regularize the debates among candidates for the presidency at both the primary and general-election levels. See Ansolabehere et al., *The Media Game,* 85–86; Alger, *The Media and Politics,* 299–302, 345–52; Davis, *The Press and American Politics,* 203–4.

112. McGinniss, *The Selling of the President 1968,* 26–27; Hal Bruno, interview by author, July 31, 1995.

113. Fallows, *Breaking the News,* 63. The philosopher of ethics Sissela Bok calls the politician-press relationship a "vicious circle" (quoted in Patterson, *Out of Order,*

162–63). Also see Arterton, *Media Politics;* Matalin and Carville, *All's Fair;* Walsh, *Feeding the Beast.*

114. Donovan and Scherer, *Unsilent Revolution;* Kelly, "David Gergen"; Kelly, "The Campaign Trail: Running On," *New Yorker,* September 23, 1996, 55–57; Ansolabehere et al., *The Media Game;* Kerbel, *Remote and Controlled.*

115. Ken Auletta, "Inside Story," *New Yorker,* November 18, 1996, 58–59; also see Matalin and Carville, *All's Fair,* 393–95.

116. Hess, *The Washington Reporters;* Kumar, *Wired for Sound and Pictures.*

117. Alan Ehrenhalt downplays the importance of television and the news media in explaining the changes in who runs for political office in the United States (*The United States of Ambition: Politicians, Power, and the Pursuit of Office* [New York: Times Books, 1991]). Yet the "talent" that Ehrenhalt observes as leading to electoral success happens to be the abilities and skills that translate well over the media.

THREE Media Lap Dogs

1. This distinction provides a means by which to separate Daniel Hallin's "sphere of consensus" from his "sphere of legitimate controversy" (*The "Uncensored War"* [New York: Oxford University Press, 1986], 116–17); also see Pamela Shoemaker and Stephen Reese, *Mediating the Message: Theories of Influences on Mass Media Content,* 2d ed. [White Plains, N.Y.: Longman, 1996], 227–28). Whereas Hallin (and Shoemaker and Reese) suggests that content is the key to where an issue is located, I argue that the politics operative within Congress and government at any given time determine in which sphere an issue is located. Dividing news coverage into these different spheres, as these other writers do, omits the facts that issues may not always belong in the same spheres, that there are different techniques by which controversy is either fostered or suppressed (see my discussion below), and that journalists and news organizations are themselves complicit in determining into which sphere an issue falls. Ideology in the United States is frequently open to definition or subject to cross-cutting cleavages.

2. Individual editorial writers, columnists, and contributors of op-ed pieces may, of course, speak out on particular issues that are agreed on by the government or else simply not addressed in political discourse.

3. Stephen Hess, *The Ultimate Insiders* (Washington, D.C.: Brookings, 1986), 105–7, and *Live from Capitol Hill!* (Washington, D.C.: Brookings, 1991), 102; Douglass Cater, *The Fourth Branch of Government* (Boston: Houghton-Mifflin, 1959), 20, 44–45, 112, 138; Tom Wicker, *On Press* (New York: Viking, 1975), 76–77. The Supreme Court has by and large deferred to the executive branch's prerogatives, especially with respect to national security. Moreover, protecting the president and his top appointees are secrecy laws and classification guidelines, impenetrable to those outside government or, of course, to political journalists. See Harold Hongju Koh, *The National Security Constitution: Sharing Power after the Iran-Contra Affair* (New Haven, Conn.: Yale University Press, 1990).

4. Lee Lescaze cited in Mark Hertsgaard, *On Bended Knee: The Press and the Reagan Presidency* (New York: Farrar, Straus & Giroux, 1988), 55; Don Campbell, *Inside the Beltway: A Guide to Washington Reporting* (Ames: Iowa State University Press, 1991), 145.

5. Timothy Crouse, *The Boys on the Bus* (New York: Random House, 1973), 232–33; Wicker, *On Press,* 98; Robert Parry, *Fooling America: How Washington Insiders Twist the Truth and Manufacture the Conventional Wisdom* (New York: Morrow, 1992). The very

credibility of journalism would be in question should reporters or news organizations attempt to join together.

6. See Edward Jay Epstein, *Between Fact and Fiction* (New York: Vintage Books, 1975), 3–7; Wicker, *On Press,* 174; David Wise, *The Politics of Lying* (New York: Vintage, 1973); Mark Fishman, *Manufacturing the News* (Austin: University of Texas Press, 1980). The asymmetry of information and the resultant dependence of journalists are also results of organization practices: the stability of news production requires that reporters be trained to cover any number of beats. Such flexibility also promotes the reporter's ability to engage the audience and not be overly influenced by the language or worldview of those he or she is covering. See Gaye Tuchman, *Making News: A Study in the Construction of Reality* (New York: Free Press, 1978).

7. Epstein, *Between Fact and Fiction,* 7.

8. Robert Denton, "Introduction," in *The Media and the Persian Gulf War,* ed. Robert Denton (New York: Praeger, 1992), 36.

9. Richard Harwood, interview by author, July 18, 1995.

10. Leon V. Sigal, *Reporters and Officials: The Organization and Politics of Newsmaking* (Lexington, Mass.: D.C. Heath, 1973), 84; Wicker, *On Press,* 187, 217–35; Hertsgaard, *On Bended Knee,* 225–26; Ted Galen Carpenter, *The Captive Press* (Washington, D.C.: Cato Institute, 1996); Harrison Salisbury, *Without Fear or Favor* (New York: Times Books, 1980); Wise, *The Politics of Lying.* For a contrasting view, see the testimony of CBS News's Mike Wallace and ABC News's Peter Jennings with respect to how they would cover a hypothetical ambush on U.S. troops (James Fallows, *Breaking the News* [New York: Pantheon, 1996], 10–16). But the proof is in the practice, and in two recent military engagements, the 1989 invasion of Panama and the 1991 Persian Gulf War, American journalists overwhelmingly exhibited patriotic, even jingoistic behavior (consistent with Sigal's writing), rather than the "news-at-all-costs" ethos articulated by Wallace and seconded by Jennings.

11. See William Preston Jr. and Ellen Ray, "Disinformation and Mass Deception," in *Freedom at Risk: Secrecy, Censorship, and Repression in the 1980s,* ed. Richard O. Curry (Philadelphia: Temple University Press, 1988), 203–23. Although Preston and Ray overstate some of their claims (at least in relation to the evidence they present in their chapter), their general thesis merits attention. Also see John H. McManus, *Market-Driven Journalism: Let the Citizen Beware?* (Thousand Oaks, Calif.: Sage, 1994), 66–67.

12. On the Persian Gulf War, see the discussion in Chapter 6; on the Vietnam War, see William A. Gamson, *What's News? A Game Simulation of TV News* (New York: Basic Books, 1978); Hallin, *The "Uncensored War";* David Halberstam, *The Best and the Brightest* (New York: Dell, 1972); Wicker, *On Press.*

13. Quoted in David Broder, *Behind the Front Page* (New York: Simon & Schuster, 1987), 186. On the life of the White House press corps in the early Clinton administration, see Jacob Weisberg, "The White House Beast," *Vanity Fair,* September 1993, 166ff.

14. Colin Seymour-Ure, *The American President: Power and Communication* (New York: St. Martin's Press, 1982), 32; Crouse, *The Boys on the Bus,* 175; David Halberstam, *The Powers That Be* (New York: Knopf, 1979), 446–48, 656–57; Wise, *The Politics of Lying,* 369–72, 379–82.

15. Hertsgaard, *On Bended Knee,* 28–31, 186–91, 196–200; W. Lance Bennett, *News: The Politics of Illusion,* 3d ed. (White Plains, N.Y.: Longman, 1996), 104–6; Carpenter, *The Captive Press,* 142–45; Edwin Diamond, *Behind the Times: Inside the New*

New York Times (New York: Random House, 1993), 244–45; John Fialka, interview by author, June 29, 1995.

16. Ken Auletta, *Three Blind Mice* (New York: Random House, 1991), 536–37; Sigal, *Reporters and Officials*, 54–55; Wicker, *On Press*, 241; Wise, *The Politics of Lying*, 353–56. Richard Harwood de-emphasizes the role of sanctions, saying they have an "insignificant amount of impact." The Nixon years were "an aberration," he asserts. Harwood sees Washington journalists as "spoiled and very privileged" (interview by author, July 18, 1995). Yet sanctions may be very important, *even if* they are used sparingly and are less important and less common in recent years than during the Nixon administration. Nor is the fact that the top Washington journalists are, as a rule, privileged members of American society inconsistent with the fact that government officials sometimes resort to sanctions.

17. Mort Rosenblum, *Who Stole the News?* (New York: Wiley, 1993), 84.

18. See Wise, *The Politics of Lying*, 369–72; Wicker, *On Press*, 241.

19. Gartner, "Buncombe, Broadcasters, and the First Amendment" (speech given before the Practicing Law Institute, New York, November 19, 1988), cited in Shoemaker and Reese, *Mediating the Message*, 203; Wicker, *On Press*, 240. Gartner's words should be taken with a grain of salt: also see the discussion of the political power of the National Association of Broadcasters and other media lobbyists in Chapter 4.

20. Auletta, *Three Blind Mice*, 543–44. Also see Wise, *The Politics of Lying*, 369–70, 401–2.

21. See Crouse, *The Boys on the Bus*, 225; Hertsgaard, *On Bended Knee*, 223–25; Wise, *The Politics of Lying*, 369–70; Wicker, *On Press*, 240. For a further discussion of the Morison case, see Chapter 5.

22. See David Paletz and Robert M. Entman, *Media Power Politics* (New York: Free Press, 1981), 117–21; Carpenter, *The Captive Press*, 142–45; Wise, *The Politics of Lying*.

23. Fishman, *Manufacturing the News*.

24. Jay G. Blumler and Michael Gurevitch, *The Crisis of Public Communication* (New York: Routledge, 1995), 102.

25. Rosenblum, *Who Stole the News?* 113; Herbert Gans, *Deciding What's News* (New York: Vintage, 1980).

26. John Fialka, interview by author, June 29, 1995; Wicker, *On Press*, 79.

27. Morton H. Halperin, *Bureaucratic Politics and Foreign Policy* (Washington, D.C.: Brookings, 1974), 175.

28. Stephen Hess, *The Washington Reporters* (Washington, D.C.: Brookings, 1981); Sigal, *Reporters and Officials;* Halperin, *Bureaucratic Politics*, 173–95.

29. Everette Dennis et al., *The Media at War: The Press and the Persian Gulf Conflict* (New York: Gannett Foundation Media Center, 1991), 8–16, 41–42; Walter Cronkite, *A Reporter's Life* (New York: Knopf, 1996), 267.

30. See Sigal, *Reporters and Officials*, 92; Chris Argyris, *Behind the Front Page: Organizational Self-Renewal in a Metropolitan Newspaper* (San Francisco: Jossey-Bass, 1974), 47–48, 236–37; Fallows, "The Presidency and the Press," in *The Presidency and the Political System,* ed. Michael Nelson (Washington, D.C.: CQ Press, 1984), 266; Michael Baruch Grossman and Martha Joynt Kumar, *Portraying the President: The White House and the Media* (Baltimore: Johns Hopkins University Press, 1981), 182; Doug Underwood, *When MBAs Rule the Newsroom* (New York: Columbia University Press, 1993), 22–25; John Fialka, interview by author, June 29, 1995.

31. *Nightline*, September 27, 1989 (transcript), cited in Timothy Cook, *Governing*

with the News (Chicago: University of Chicago Press, 1998), 78. Also see Salisbury, *Without Fear or Favor,* 534; Michael Schudson, *The Power of the News* (Cambridge, Mass.: Harvard University Press, 1994), 144, 147; Halberstam, *The Powers That Be,* 668; Hertsgaard, *On Bended Knee,* 338–39.

32. Tom Wicker, interview by author, December 6, 1996.

33. Salisbury, *Without Fear or Favor,* 534; Graham and Downie quoted in Schudson, *The Power of the News,* 144, 147; Halberstam, *The Powers That Be,* 668.

34. Hertsgaard, *On Bended Knee,* 338–39; Parry, *Fooling America.* Few journalists are willing to do the kind of reporting that will isolate them from their fellow journalists—as George Seldes and I. F. Stone did throughout most of their careers.

35. See David Rudenstine, *The Day the Presses Stopped: A History of the Pentagon Papers Case* (Berkeley: University of California Press, 1996); Salisbury, *Without Fear or Favor;* Schudson, *The Power of the News,* 142–65; David Croteau and William Hoynes, *By Invitation Only* (Monroe, Maine: Common Courage, 1994), 11–12; Gladys Engel Lang and Kurt Lang, *The Battle for Public Opinion: The President, the Press, and the Polls during Watergate,* 262–64; Tom Wicker, interview by author, December 6, 1996. The Pentagon Papers case is the first and only time that the U.S. Supreme Court has ruled against the national government in a matter involving U.S. national security.

36. Bruce Evensen, *Truman, Palestine, and the Press* (New York: Greenwood Press, 1992), 5. To its credit, the *Wall Street Journal* often avoids stories that other newspapers or news organizations run (Alan Murray, interviews by author, July 14 and 28, 1995). On the other hand, a low percentage of the feature stories in the *Journal* cover national politics, and the paper has a small news hole for covering politics (about "30 to 40 percent" of pages 2–4 and the back page of the first section of the paper). As a senior reporter at the *Journal* remarks, the front page of the *Journal* "fights against the flow of the news a lot of the time. Not all the time." Instead, "we do an awful lot of off-beat reporting, off the news cycle . . . All it has to do is interest your editors in New York" (John Fialka, interview by author, June 29, 1995).

37. Others who have argued that the news media have a role in legitimizing the political system are Todd Gitlin, *The Whole World Is Watching* (Berkeley: University of California Press, 1980); Tuchman, *Making News;* Bennett, *News: The Politics of Illusion;* Croteau and Hoynes, *By Invitation Only;* Edward S. Herman and Noam Chomsky, *Manufacturing Consent* (New York: Pantheon, 1988); Michael Parenti, *Inventing Reality: The Politics of the News Media,* 2d ed. (New York: St. Martin's Press, 1993).

38. W. Lance Bennett, "Towards a Theory of Press-State Relations in the United States," *Journal of Communication* 40 (1990): 103–25; Hallin, *The "Uncensored War";* Fishman, *Manufacturing the News;* John Zaller, "Strategic Politicians, Public Opinion, and the Gulf Crisis," in *Taken by Storm: The Media, Public Opinion, and U.S. Foreign Policy in the Gulf War,* ed. W. Lance Bennett and David L. Paletz (Chicago: University of Chicago Press, 1994), 250–74; Epstein, *Between Fact and Fiction.*

39. Leo Rosten, *The Washington Correspondents* (New York: Arno Press, 1974 [1937]), 60.

40. See Stephen Hess, *The Government/Press Connection* (Washington, D.C.: Brookings, 1984).

41. See Sigal, *Reporters and Officials;* Grossman and Kumar, *Portraying the President;* Samuel Kernell, *Going Public,* 2d ed. (Washington, D.C.: CQ Press, 1993); Martha Joynt Kumar, *Wired for Sound and Pictures: The President and White House Communications Policies* (Baltimore: Johns Hopkins University Press, forthcoming). The first two prac-

tices described here are not wholly distinct, of course: entire press conferences or smaller meetings between political figures and journalists may be on background, deep background, or off the record.

42. Sigal, *Reporters and Officials,* 111–15; Bernard Roshco, *Newsmaking* (Chicago: University of Chicago Press, 1975), 87–93.

43. Alan K. Simpson, *Right in the Old Gazoo: A Lifetime of Scrapping with the Press* (New York: Morrow, 1997), 144–45.

44. Sigal, *Reporters and Officials,* 112–14.

45. Hess, *The Washington Reporters,* 18, 52. See Schudson, *The Power of the News,* 72–93.

46. Schudson, *The Power of the News,* 75. Schudson observes, "The news interview has at least three parties, not two; it is a triadic relationship in which an unseen public is an 'overhearing audience.'"

47. Ibid., 87, 85.

48. Schudson, "What's Wrong with the Ideal of the 'Informed Citizen'?" (paper presented at the Joan Shorenstein Center on the Press, Politics and Public Policy, John F. Kennedy School of Government, Harvard University, Cambridge, Mass., October 1996).

49. Rosten, *The Washington Correspondents,* 72.

50. See Shoemaker and Reese, *Mediating the Message,* 135. For histories of political reporting in the nation's capital, see F. B. Marbut, *News from the Capital: The Story of Washington Reporting* (Carbondale: Southern Illinois University Press, 1971); Rosten, *The Washington Correspondents;* Kumar, *Wired for Sound and Pictures.* For the history of the congressional press gallery see Timothy Cook, *Making Laws and Making News* (Washington, D.C.: Brookings, 1989); Hess, *Live from Capitol Hill!*

51. James Fallows also remarks on the difference between coverage of "scandal, dissension, gaffes, and horse-race politics," where reporters have the confidence to report on their own authority—as third-party observers and commentators, presumably—and coverage of "what the government actually does," where the "White House controls the topics of the news" ("The Presidency and the Press," 276).

52. For example, David J. Garrow, "The Rehnquist Years," *New York Times Magazine,* October 6, 1996, 64ff.

53. Broder, *Behind the Front Page,* 149; Reston, *The Artillery of the Press,* 64. Blumler and Gurevitch make the point that to define the news media as an "adversary" does not do much: it is a "narrow" ethic that reveals nothing about matters of access, judiciousness, fairness, or honest reporting; it is blind to the cooperation that exists between journalists and public officials; and were it to hold true, the adversary ethic would be unsustainable—genuine adversaries destroy each other, and hence the ethic would be self-destructive for journalists and political officials both (*The Crisis of Public Communication,* 26–27).

54. Wise, *The Politics of Lying,* 452; Wicker, *On Press,* 78–79; John Fialka, interview by author, June 29, 1995.

55. Leon V. Sigal, "Sources Make the News," in *Reading the News,* ed. Michael Schudson and Karl Manoff (New York: Pantheon, 1986), 9–37; Sigal, *Reporters and Officials.*

56. Sources are important, to be sure, since journalists rely on other individuals for the news; rarely are journalists themselves present when something happens, as many have noted. Rather, they need to reconstruct what happened through the testimony

of others. I would note, however, that the source issue may be secondary to the matter of a political contest and who the opponents are in that contest.

57. Quoted in Hertsgaard, *On Bended Knee,* 54.

FOUR Making Money and Making News

1. David Halberstam, *The Powers That Be* (New York: Knopf, 1979), 582. Marvin Kalb, the former CBS News correspondent and the current director of the Joan Shorenstein Center on the Press, Politics and Public Policy at Harvard University, tells a story related to this point: "At the end of 1962 during a dinner in Paris, [William] Paley told his foreign correspondents what his plans were for CBS in 1963. [Correspondent] Charley Collingwood said: 'Bill, that's going to cost you a lot of money.' And Paley said: 'You guys cover the news, I've got Jack Benny to make money for me'" (quoted in Dean E. Alger, *The Media and Politics,* 2d ed. [Belmont, Calif.: Wadsworth, 1996], 119).

2. Douglass Cater, *The Fourth Branch of Government* (Boston: Houghton-Mifflin, 1959), 2–3, 6, 171; Leon V. Sigal, *Reporters and Officials: The Organization and Politics of Newsmaking* (Lexington, Mass.: D.C. Heath, 1973), 8.

3. Emblematic of the wall of separation was the fact that the elevator to the *Chicago Tribune's* newsroom in the Tribune Building stopped at no other floors, just as the other elevators did not stop on the newsroom floor.

4. Fred Friendly, *Due to Circumstances Beyond Our Control* (New York: Random House, 1967). On the profit-maximizing constraints on news organizations (especially television broadcasters), see David L. Altheide, *Creating Reality: How TV News Distorts Events* (Beverly Hills, Calif.: Sage, 1974); W. Lance Bennett, *News: The Politics of Illusion,* 3d ed. (White Plains, N.Y.: Longman, 1996); Edward J. Epstein, *News from Nowhere: Television and the News* (New York: Vintage Books, 1974); John H. McManus, *Market-Driven Journalism: Let the Citizen Beware?* (Thousand Oaks, Calif.: Sage, 1994); Ben Bagdikian, *The Media Monopoly,* 4th ed. (Boston: Beacon Press, 1992). This does not mean that news organizations have to be profitable. Some may be subsidized for ideological reasons (e.g., the *Washington Times,* by the Reverend Moon) or during an incubation period while they grow market share (e.g., *USA Today,* by Gannett).

5. Michael Shain, "TV, Print Coming Up Roses," *Mediaweek,* November 25, 1996, 9 (the author's figures are from the annual Veronis, Suhler Communications Industry Report); "The *Fortune* 500," *Fortune,* April 27, 1998, F1ff. The other figures come from this same source, except for the market value figures for the Washington Post Company and Dow Jones, which are from "The *Forbes* 500," *Forbes,* April 20, 1998, 246ff. In 1989, the networks had a profit margin of 10 percent, but the network affiliates had a profit margin of 38 percent, and cable television had a profit margin of 42 percent (Ken Auletta, *Three Blind Mice* [New York: Random House, 1991], 560).

6. Neither the New York Times Company nor the Washington Post Company separated the earnings of their flagship newspapers from the earnings of their other newspapers in their most recent annual reports.

7. John Morton, interview by author, July 11, 1995. For overviews of the media-business connection, see Bagdikian, *The Media Monopoly;* Edwin Baker, *Advertising and a Democratic Press* (Princeton, N.J.: Princeton University Press, 1994); Doug Underwood, *When MBAs Rule the Newsroom* (New York: Columbia University Press, 1993); James Squires, *Read All About It!* (New York: Times Books, 1993); Michael Parenti, *Inventing Reality: The Politics of the News Media,* 2d ed. (New York: St. Martin's Press,

1993); Alger, *The Media and Politics,* 87–98. An issue of the *Nation* entitled the "National Entertainment State" (June 3, 1996) inexplicably leaves out newspapers and newspaper chains and therefore the newspapers' ownership of network affiliates, magazines, and, of course, other newspapers. Nor are newspapers included in almost an identical issue of *Extra! The Magazine of FAIR* (November/December 1995).

8. John Soloski and Robert G. Picard, "The New Media Lords: Why Institutional Investors Call the Shots," *Columbia Journalism Review* 35, no. 1 (1996): 11–12.

9. Richard Harwood, interview by author, July 18, 1995; John Morton, interview by author, July 11, 1995. Sigal later observes that both companies "are nonetheless economically vulnerable" (*Reporters and Officials,* 8–9).

10. Reuven Frank, *Out of Thin Air* (New York: Simon & Schuster, 1991), 333.

11. McManus, *Market-Driven Journalism,* 61.

12. See Stuart Ewen, *All-Consuming Images: The Politics of Style in Contemporary Culture* (New York: Basic Books, 1988), and *Captains of Consciousness: Advertising and the Social Roots of the Consumer Culture* (New York: McGraw-Hill, 1977). Also see Michael Schudson, *Advertising, the Uneasy Persuasion: Its Dubious Impact on American Society* (New York: Basic Books, 1984).

13. Baker, *Advertising and a Democratic Press,* 45; also see Pamela Shoemaker and Stephen Reese, *Mediating the Message: Theories of Influences on Mass Media Content,* 2d ed. (White Plains, N.Y.: Longman, 1996), 186.

14. Kathleen Hall Jamieson and Karlyn Kohrs Campbell, *The Interplay of Influence,* 4th ed. (Belmont, Calif.: Wadsworth, 1997), 201. Jamieson and Campbell also use the example of Anheuser-Busch's ads that successfully fought a rise in the beer tax. The ads showed how Americans, already paying $3 billion in excise taxes on beer, would be asked to pay more. Jamieson and Campbell also point out that only CNN—and none of the broadcast networks—was willing to broadcast advocacy ads for health care reform.

15. When WHDH in Boston broadcast the ad, Procter & Gamble pulled all its advertising from the station—advertising that had amounted to $1 million a year (Baker, *Advertising and a Democratic Press,* 54).

16. Gene Ruffini, "Press Failed to Challenge the Rush to War," in *The Media and the Gulf War,* ed. Hedrick Smith (Washington, D.C.: Seven Locks Press, 1992), 282–87. The commercial was paid for by a group called Coalition for America at Risk.

17. Associated Press, "CNN Pulls Ads against Pact on Global Warming," *Austin American-Statesman,* October 3, 1997; John H. Cushman Jr., "CNN Halts Companies' Ads Attacking Administration on Warming Treaty," *New York Times,* October 3, 1997. The *Wall Street Journal* reported that Chrysler sent a letter to *Esquire* and 100 other magazines informing them, "In an effort to avoid potential conflicts, it is required that Chrysler Corporation be alerted in advance of any and all editorial content that encompasses sexual, political, social issues or any editorial content that could be construed as provocative or offensive." *Esquire* subsequently canceled a scheduled story with a gay theme after receiving Chrysler's letter ("Magazine Advertisers Demand More Notice of 'Offensive' Articles," *Wall Street Journal,* April 30, 1997, 1).

18. Walter Lippmann, *Public Opinion* (New York: Free Press, 1922), 206. The effects of advertising on editorial matter varies according to the medium, of course, given that television does not have classified ads and that newsmagazines and newspapers get a smaller percentage of their revenues from advertisers than do television broadcasters. It is nonetheless possible to make some general statements that apply across

media, given the commercial pressures faced by all the major news organizations.

19. Bill Headline, interview by author, July 28, 1995.

20. Les Brown, "Sponsors and Documentaries," in *The Commercial Connection: Advertising and the American Mass Media,* ed. John W. Wright, 265, quoted in Baker, *Advertising and a Democratic Press,* 48. Also see Herbert Gans, *Deciding What's News* (New York: Vintage, 1980), 256; Bagdikian, *The Media Monopoly,* 58–65. A vice president at Coca-Cola explained, "It's a Coca-Cola corporate policy not to advertise on TV news because there's going to be some bad news in there and Coke is an upbeat, fun product" (quoted in Baker, *Advertising and a Democratic Press,* 63).

21. Bagdikian, *The Media Monopoly,* 168–173; W. L. Weis and C. Burke, "Media Content and Tobacco Advertising: An Unhealthy Addiction," *Journal of Communication* 36, no. 4 (1986): 59–69; Baker, *Advertising and a Democratic Press,* 65–66, 63.

22. Rick Young, interview by author, July 27, 1995.

23. Mark Crispin Miller, "Free the Media," *The Nation,* June 3, 1996, 10.

24. Nor would advertising agencies recommend that their clients purchase time during a CBS movie in 1980 about an Auschwitz survivor, the reason being the film's "utterly depressing nature" (Baker, *Advertising and a Democratic Press,* 65–66, 63).

25. Underwood, *When MBAs Rule the Newsroom,* 141. In 1977, for instance, the School of Journalism at the University of Missouri found "dozens of examples of journalists punished for upsetting advertisers."

26. Gans notes that when he examined instances of companies pulling their ads, he found no cases of where particular news content was the factor for such a withdrawal. In explaining their decision, the companies cited general characteristics of the programming, such as liberal bias, unsuitable audiences, and the like (*Deciding What's News,* 254). Yet even if a company did not like a news program and wanted to penalize the news organizations, it would be unlikely that company executives would specify in public that it was a particular program that they protested. It is much more likely that company executives voice their complaints in vague and mild terms.

27. Bagdikian, *The Media Monopoly,* 56.

28. Underwood, *When MBAs Rule the Newsroom,* 47; Epstein, *News From Nowhere,* 34.

29. Michael Schudson, *The Power of the News* (Cambridge, Mass.: Harvard University Press, 1994), 158. Schudson agrees with Stephen Hess that investigative journalism became fashionable for a short time only, and that, in the main, editors shy away from investigative journalism.

30. Alex Benes, interview by author, August 2, 1995.

31. Gans, *Deciding What's News,* 256; Bagdikian, *The Media Monopoly,* 218. This is not to deny that those documentaries were path-breaking; it is rather to point out the rarity of television network documentaries that contain critical commentary on contemporary social, political, and economic reality. There have also been a number of documentaries on smoking and tobacco companies that attacked the tobacco industry—the most heavily advertised industry in the United States.

32. See Erik Barnouw, *The Sponsor* (1978), 57, and James Aronson, *Deadline for the Media* (1972), 144–45, quoted in Baker, *Advertising and a Democratic Press,* 49; Todd Gitlin, *Inside Prime Time* (1985), 253–54, quoted in Shoemaker and Reese, *Mediating the Message,* 197, emphasis in original. One "prominent" media effect, as the political scientists David Paletz and Robert M. Entman note, is to insulate "many power

holders from public accountability"—including large corporations (*Media Power Politics* [New York: Free Press, 1981], 250).

33. Shoemaker and Reese, *Mediating the Message*, 197.

34. Auletta, *Three Blind Mice*, 302.

35. This market-driven research is also prevalent at regional metropolitan newspapers. See Underwood, *When MBAs Rule the Newsroom*; Squires, *Read All About It!* The *Austin American-Statesman* relies on reader surveys to guide its news coverage, as does the *Dallas Morning News* (Carl Leubsdorf, interviews by author, August 4 and October 9, 1995; Rich Oppel, interviews by author, May 3 and June 9, 1995).

36. Underwood, *When MBAs Rule the Newsroom*, 18.

37. James Devitt, "The Daily Newspaper Unbundled," in *The Future of News: Television–Newspapers–Wire Services–Newsmagazines*, ed. Philip Cook, Douglas Gomery, and Lawrence Lichty (Washington D.C.: Woodrow Wilson Center Press; Baltimore: Johns Hopkins University Press, 1992), 138–39; Edwin Diamond, *Behind the Times: Inside the New New York Times* (New York: Villard Books, 1994), 162–66, 310–11. In the mid-1970s, the *Times* was also facing deteriorating profits and greater regional and national competition.

38. Iver Peterson, "At Los Angeles Times, a Debate on News-Ad Interaction," *New York Times*, National Edition, November 17, 1996, C1.

39. "The Store as Theatre, Taste Machine, Billboard: A Special Issue," *New York Times Magazine*, April 6, 1997.

40. Don Oberdorfer, "A Journalist to His Profession: 'I am Deeply Worried,'" *Harvard International Journal of Press/Politics* 1(4): 149; Milan J. Kubic, "Foreign News: How Newsweek Has Changed," and Byron T. Scott and Walter Seiber, "Remaking *Time*, *Newsweek*, and *U.S. News and World Report*," in *The Future of News: Television–Newspapers–Wire Services–Newsmagazines*, ed. Philip Cook, Douglas Gomery, and Lawrence Lichty (Washington D.C.: Woodrow Wilson Center Press; Baltimore: Johns Hopkins University Press, 1992), 218, 202–3.

41. Baker, *Advertising and a Democratic Press*, 65–66. Indeed, CBS News's decision to generally devote the last five minutes of the twenty-two-minute news program to "back of the book" material reflected a decision to compromise with an automobile manufacturer's wish to advertise in a soft news section. For a general account of market journalism in local television markets, see McManus, *Market-Driven Journalism*.

42. R. Rothenberg, "Crisis Raises TV News Audience," *New York Times*, January 12, 1991, A46, cited in McManus, *Market-Driven Journalism*, 79; Halberstam, *The Powers That Be*, 713; Squires, *Read All About It!* 62; Underwood, *When MBAs Rule the Newsroom*, 77–83, 130–47.

43. Bagdikian, *Media Monopoly*, 116; Diamond, *Behind the Times*, 90; John Morton, interview by author, July 11, 1995. The *Chicago Tribune* also shed some of its urban Chicago and (distant) northeast Indiana audience in order to boost profit margins.

44. William Glaberson, "8 of 10 Largest U.S. Papers Have Declines in Circulation," *New York Times*, National Edition, April 30, 1994, C17. This logic also holds with respect to television audiences: the second leading news show in Dallas is more profitable than the most widely watched news program by virtue of its superior audience demographics (and therefore the advertising rates that can be charged).

45. Floyd Norris, "NYT Co. Posts a 60% Rise in Net Earnings," *New York Times*, February 6, 1997, D9; Gans, *Deciding What's News*, 219.

46. Mark Hertsgaard, *On Bended Knee: The Press and the Reagan Presidency* (New York: Farrar, Straus & Giroux, 1988), 340–41; Lee Ranie, interview by author, July 21, 1995; Katherine Graham quoted in Chalmers Roberts, *In the Shadow of Power* (Washington, D.C.: Seven Locks Press, 1989), 479. It should be noted that the *New York Times* and the *Washington Post* have distinct audiences beyond the geographic differences: the *Times* appeals to a small percentage of well-educated and affluent Americans, principally in the huge New York greater metropolitan area (two-thirds of circulation) and along the Northeast corridor (about one-third), as well as nationally. The *Times* is unabashedly elitist "in the best sense of the word," noted a former *Times* editorial-page editor (Diamond, *Behind the Times*, 283). The *Post* reaches almost half the households in the greater Washington, D.C., metropolitan area and surrounding counties, and with its comics, editorial cartoons, and extensive sports coverage, is a full-service newspaper.

47. William Greider, interview by author, August 24, 1995.

48. See Penn Kimball, *Downsizing the News: Network Cutbacks in the Nation's Capital* (Washington, D.C.: Woodrow Wilson Center Press, 1994), 48; Alicia Shepard, "Walking the Walk," *American Journalism Review*, November 1996, 40.

49. Bill Headline, interview by author, July 28, 1995.

50. Auletta, *Three Blind Mice;* Altheide, *Creating Reality,* 54. As Altheide finds, one staff member at a television network affiliate "was vaguely aware that [the rating] numbers affected advertising revenue, but they were more conscious of the impact of low ratings on their budget, pressure from the front office, and the news director's moodiness." That is to say that the concern—and uncertainty—over ratings (and hence over advertiser bookings and profits) caused stress in the newsroom (43).

51. McManus, *Market-Driven Journalism,* 162–63, 181, 187–89. Recent findings confirm the movement toward "scandal, celebrity, gossip, and cutesy animal stories" among local television newscasts. Indeed, viewers learn little from television news, and this finding is more the result of the news department than either the medium itself or the audience (which differs from the print audience). The memoirs of news executives (e.g., Frank, *Out of Thin Air,* and Friendly, *Due to Circumstances Beyond Our Control)* are also consistent with McManus's findings.

52. Kimball, *Downsizing the News,* 142; Hess is quoted in *The Media and Foreign Policy in the Post–Cold War World,* ed. M. FitzSimon, cited in Shoemaker and Reese, *Mediating the Message,* 52. On cost-cutting at CBS, see Auletta, *Three Blind Mice,* 276.

53. Kenneth T. Walsh, *Feeding the Beast: The White House Versus the Press* (New York: Random House, 1996), 250. In October 1995, the three networks refused to pay their bills for traveling to Asia with President Clinton during the preceding summer until they received an explanation of their bills. A month after Bill Headline, the TV pool chair and CNN's Washington bureau chief, had asked for an explanation, the White House still had not provided one (Ellen Edwards, "Networks Balk at White House Bills," *Washington Post,* October 20, 1995, B1).

54. *Tyndall Report,* quoted in Garrick Utley, "The Shrinking of Foreign News," *Foreign Affairs* 76, no. 2 (1997): 5.

55. Walter Cronkite quoted in "The First Annual Theodore H. White Lecture with Walter Cronkite" (Joan Shorenstein Barone Center on the Press, Politics and Public Policy, John F. Kennedy School of Government, Harvard University, Cambridge, Mass., 1990, bound transcript of conference), 63–64. Richard Harwood, former na-

tional editor of the *Washington Post*, points out that during the Vietnam War no *Post* journalists spoke Vietnamese (interview by author, July 18, 1995).

56. Kimball, *Downsizing the News*, 25–26, 31; J. M. Robins, "News in the '90s: Stretched to the Limit," *Channels*, September 1989, 42–54, cited in Shoemaker and Reese, *Mediating the Message*, 147.

57. Bill Headline, interview by author, July 28, 1995. Also see Martin Mayer, *Making News* (Boston: Harvard Business School Press, 1993), 206–24.

58. Mary Matalin and James Carville, *All's Fair: Love, War, and Running for President* (New York: Random House and Simon & Schuster, 1994), 189.

59. Howard Kurtz, interview by author, July 18, 1995; Epstein, *News from Nowhere*, 34.

60. Kimball, *Downsizing the News*, 53–58. The morale at the Washington bureau of CNN evident in my visit in the summer of 1995 presented a stark contrast to the atmosphere at the one network bureau I visited. Despite the fact that CNN watched costs just like any other news organization, the bureau chief was also confident that "even in dire [budgetary] circumstances the word would be 'do what you have to do'" (Bill Headline, interview by author, July 28, 1996). The energy and youth of the CNN Washington bureau were palpable. As a former NBC News correspondent confirmed, CNN "has become a very big news organization, with resources far outstripping any one of the three networks" (John Dancy, interviews by author, September 9, 12, and 18, 1996).

61. Auletta, *Three Blind Mice*.

62. Quoted in Ken Auletta, "How General Electric Tamed NBC News," *Washington Journalism Review*, November 1991, 36–41, cited in Shoemaker and Reese, *Mediating the Message*, 150.

63. Alan Murray, interviews by author, July 14 and 28, 1995.

64. R. W. Apple, interview by author, July 7, 1995; Richard Harwood, interview by author, July 18, 1995; Howard Kurtz, interview by author, July 18, 1995. Short-run concerns may drive policy, however, and in the near term, "improved quality, better service, and lower pricing all negatively affect a newspaper's bottom line" (Squires, *Read All About It!* 89).

65. For background, see Rodney Smolla, *Suing the Press* (New York: Oxford University Press, 1986); Lois G. Forer, *A Chilling Effect: The Mounting Threat of Libel and Invasion of Privacy Actions to the First Amendment* (New York: Norton, 1987); Donald M. Gillmor, *Power, Publicity, and the Abuse of Libel Law* (New York: Oxford University Press, 1992); Wat W. Hopkins, *Actual Malice: Twenty-five Years after Times v. Sullivan* (New York: Praeger Press, 1989). Also see Gaye Tuchman, "Objectivity as a Strategic Ritual: An Examination of Newsmen's Notions of Objectivity," *American Journal of Sociology* 77 (1972): 660–79.

66. Lee Ranie, interview by author, July 21, 1995.

67. Alger, *The Media and Politics*, 158.

68. Bagdikian, *The Media Monopoly*, 11.

69. Larry Makinson, *Follow the Money Handbook* (Washington, D.C.: Center for Responsive Politics, 1990), 6, 5–16. Exceptions were "labor," "miscellaneous industries," and "ideological/single issue" contributors. In each case, single-issue groups, individual trade associations, or federated unions gave more money than did individual media and publishing companies. The printed news companies participate as trade associations, even if they typically do not contribute as separate companies. Also

see Ken Auletta, "Annals of Communication: Pay Per Views," *New Yorker,* June 5, 1995, 52–56; Larry Makinson and Joshua Goldstein, *Open Secrets: The Encyclopedia of Congressional Money and Politics* (Washington, D.C.: Center for Responsive Politics and CQ Press, 1994).

70. Interestingly, the presence of strong media company interests does not necessarily mean unanimity within any one news organization. The *Wall Street Journal's* Washington bureau chief reported that even as lobbyists for Dow Jones were "pushing to maintain certain regulations and restrictions in order to protect the newspaper classified from competition from other media," the *Journal's* editorial position was "very pro deregulation" (Alan Murray, interviews by author, July 14 and 28, 1995; Mike Mills, interview by author, August 15, 1995).

71. Bagdikian, *The Media Monopoly,* 92. Jack Fuller, the publisher of the *Chicago Tribune,* notes that "many media firms (including the Tribune Co.) regularly employ full-time professionals in Washington to keep their positions in Congress. Their trade organizations engage in this as well, and delegations of publishers and broadcast executives often can be found in the offices of key legislators" (*News Values* [Chicago: University of Chicago Press, 1996], 80).

72. Bagdikian, *The Media Monopoly,* 91, 99–100. Other newspaper chain owners also benefited from this action, of course.

73. James Snider and Benjamin Page, "Does Media Ownership Affect Media Stands? The Case of the Telecommunications Act of 1996" (paper presented at the annual meeting of the Midwest Political Science Association, Chicago, April 1997), and "The Political Power of TV Broadcasters: Covert Bias & Anticipated Reactions" (paper presented at the annual meeting of the American Political Science Association, Washington, D.C., August 1997).

74. Snider and Page, "The Political Power of TV Broadcasters," 24–25.

75. Dennis Wharton, "Dole Demands Infopike Toll," *Daily Variety,* January 8, 1996, 5, cited in Snider and Page, "The Political Power of TV Broadcasters," 26–27.

76. Roya Akhavan and Gary Wolf, "American Mass Media and the Myth of Libertarianism: Toward an 'Elite Power Group' Theory," *Critical Studies in Mass Communication* 8 (1991): 139–51.

77. Carlin Romano, "The Grisly Truth about Bare Facts," in *Reading the News,* ed. Michael Schudson and Robert Karl Manoff (New York: Pantheon, 1986), 55–57; also see Tom Goldstein, *The News at Any Cost: How Journalists Compromise Their Ethics to Shape the News* (New York: Simon & Schuster, 1985), 103, 118–22, 192–93.

78. Todd Lappin, "The McCain Mutiny," *Wired,* June 1997, 123, cited in Snider and Page, "The Political Power of TV Broadcasters," 31; Bagdikian, *The Media Monopoly,* 11. Also see David H. Weaver and G. Cleveland Wilhoit, *The American Journalist in the 1990s* (Mahwah, N.J.: Erlbaum, 1996); Kenneth Dautrich and Jennifer Necci Dineen, "Media Bias: What Journalists and the Public Say about It," *Public Perspective* 7, no. 6 (1996): 7–14; Elisabeth Noelle-Neumann, "The Effect of Media on Media Effects Research," *Journal of Communication* 33, no. 3 (1993): 157–65.

79. Gans, *Deciding What's News,* 216–17; Warren Breed, "Social Control in the Newsroom: A Functional Analysis," *Social Forces* 33 (1955): 329–31.

80. Squires, *Read All About It!* 78. Also see Underwood, *When MBAs Rule the Newsroom;* McManus, *Market-Driven Journalism;* Bagdikian, *The Media Monopoly.* Further indicative of the collapse of the wall of separation is the fact that the editor at the *Philadelphia Inquirer,* one of the nation's leading newspapers, was also "placed in

charge of circulation and promotion, and made president of Philadelphia Newspapers Inc." (Shoemaker and Reese, *Mediating the Message,* 162).

81. Diamond, *Behind the Times,* 223-26. Kovach is now curator of the Nieman Foundation at Harvard University.

82. Underwood, *When MBAs Rule the Newsroom,* 48; John Robinson and Mark Levy, *The Main Source: Learning from Television News* (Beverly Hills, Calif.: Sage, 1986), 217.

83. Quoted in Auletta, *Three Blind Mice,* 466; Shoemaker and Reese, *Mediating the Message,* 146; McManus, *Market-Driven Journalism.*

84. "American Press Institute: 1988 Seminars," *Bulletin of the American Press Institute,* cited in Underwood, *When MBAs Rule the Newsroom,* 85. Also see Alison Carper, "Paint-by-Numbers Journalism: How Reader Surveys and Focus Groups Subvert a Democratic Press" (Discussion Paper D-19, the Joan Shorenstein Center on the Press, Politics and Public Policy, John F. Kennedy School of Government, Harvard University, Cambridge, Mass., April 1995).

85. The *New York Times* now uses color (as of October 1997), and the *Washington Post* is scheduled to do so as well. The exception may be the *Wall Street Journal,* which is a second paper to its readers and offers short news briefs but also contains more pointed features and news articles.

86. Walter Cronkite quoted in "The First Annual Theodore H. White Lecture with Walter Cronkite" (Joan Shorenstein Barone Center on the Press, Politics and Public Policy, John F. Kennedy School of Government, Harvard University, Cambridge, Mass., 1990, bound transcript of conference), 54.

87. Underwood, *When MBAs Rule the Newsroom,* 96-97, 99. On the growth of the Gannett model of journalism, see Underwood, *When MBAs Rule the Newsroom;* Squires, *Read All About It!;* Bagdikian, *The Media Monopoly.* Also see Underwood for a grim portrayal of *USA Today's* top-down control of news production. Underwood further observes that *USA Today* has become a more serious and substantial newspaper over time.

88. John Dancy, interviews by author, September 9, 12, and 18, 1996. Robinson and Levy report that these back-of-the-book network features happen to be the best comprehended stories of the network broadcast—probably because they are longer and done in advance and therefore are more polished and better honed to grab the attention of individual viewers (*The Main Source,* 188-91).

89. See Auletta, *Three Blind Mice;* Underwood, *When MBAs Rule the Newsroom.*

90. Abel quoted in Richard Parker, "Journalism and Economics: The Tangled Webs of Profession, Narrative, and Responsibility in a Modern Economy" (Discussion Paper D-25, the Joan Shorenstein Center on Press, Politics and Public Policy, John F. Kennedy School of Government, Harvard University, Cambridge, Mass., May 1997), 11. ABC News's Ted Koppel confesses, "Financial stories really bore me. It's a function of my own ignorance" (quoted in Parker, "Journalism and Economics," 3). On the low prestige of reporting economics, also see Stephen Hess, *The Washington Reporters* (Washington, D.C.: Brookings, 1981).

91. Parker, "Journalism and Economics," 11.

92. Ibid., 11-13. On the treatment of organized labor by news organizations, see Parenti, *Inventing Reality,* 83-94.

93. Mike Mills, interview by author, August 15, 1995.

94. Parker, "Journalism and Economics," 16-17.

95. Marvin Kalb quoted in Alger, *The Media and Politics,* 135.

96. Kimball, *Downsizing the News*, 6.

97. Shoemaker and Reese, *Mediating the Message*, 160; Bagdikian, *The Media Monopoly*, 94.

98. Michael Eisner, quoted in Utley, "The Shrinking of Foreign News," 8.

99. Bob Costas and NBC quoted in Utley, "The Shrinking of Foreign News," 8.

100. Utley, "The Shrinking of Foreign News," 8.

101. Peter Dreier quoted in Underwood, *When MBAs Rule the Newsroom*, 53; Bagdikian, *The Media Monopoly*, 25–26.

102. McManus, *Market-Driven Journalism*, 64–65, 69.

103. Ibid., 72.

104. William Blankenburg quoted in Baker, *Advertising and a Democratic Press*, 69.

105. Baker, *Advertising and a Democratic Press*, 66.

106. I follow the work of Jon Elster here. See Elster, *Ulysses and the Sirens: Studies in Rationality* (New York: Cambridge University Press, 1984).

107. Baker, *Advertising and a Democratic Press*, 78.

108. Harold Evans (currently an executive for Advance Publications, a former editor at Random House, and a former journalist) is quoted in Underwood, *When MBAs Rule the Newsroom*, 14. Also see Squires, *Read All About It!* 89–90; Goldstein, *The News at Any Cost*, 103. Only a handful of cities—New York, San Francisco, Boston, Denver, and Washington, D.C., among a few others—still have competing newspapers; there were *five hundred cities* with competing papers in 1930 (John Morton, interview by author, July 11, 1995).

109. Tim Russert, quoted in "The First Annual Theodore H. White Lecture with Walter Cronkite" (Joan Shorenstein Barone Center on the Press, Politics and Public Policy, John F. Kennedy School of Government, Harvard University, Cambridge, Mass., 1990, bound transcript of conference), 73.

110. Auletta, *Three Blind Mice*, 413, 478, 565; Bill Headline, interview by author, July 18, 1995; David Shribman, interviews by author, June 7 and July 18, 1995. Shribman is also the *Globe*'s assistant managing editor.

111. Oberdorfer, "A Journalist to His Profession," 147–48.

112. Kimball, *Downsizing the News*, 9.

113. Squires, *Read All About It!* 90. Also see Goldstein, *The News at Any Cost.*

FIVE Organizational News, Ordered News

1. The anthropologist Victor Turner uses "multivocality" to mean polysemy. After a brief description of the Ndembu culture, Turner says, "This brings me to another important property of many ritual symbols, their polysemy or *multivocality*. By these terms I mean that a single symbol may stand for many things. This property of individual symbols is true of ritual as a whole. For a few symbols have to represent a whole culture and its material environment" (*The Forest of Symbols* [Ithaca, N.Y.: Cornell University Press, 1966], 50). I am indebted to Chris Ansell for this reference.

2. Edward Jay Epstein, "The Selection of Reality," in *What's News*, ed. Elie Abel (San Francisco: Institute for Contemporary Studies, 1981), 122; Martin Mayer, *Making News* (Boston: Harvard Business School Press, 1993), 67. As David Altheide observes, there is a "vast difference between social phenomena and the physical world . . . Unlike physical things, human events cannot be divorced from the interpretive processes that create them . . . With social phenomena, we must realize that the meanings and

context of an act need to be clarified before we say what it is and what the facts are" (*Creating Reality: How TV News Distorts Events* [Beverly Hills, Calif.: Sage, 1974], 178).

3. Leon V. Sigal, *Reporters and Officials: The Organization and Politics of Newsmaking* (Lexington, Mass.: D.C. Heath, 1973), 1; Tom Wicker, *On Press* (New York: Viking, 1975), 177.

4. News stories may also be run without bylines, meaning that the reporter objected to the alteration of a story to the extent of pulling his or her name off it. Alternatively, a story without a byline may have been written by a stringer or taken from a news or wire service.

5. Herbert Gans, *Deciding What's News* (New York: Vintage, 1980), 97–98; Lee Ranie, interview by author, August 5, 1995. Paul Weaver describes the "editocracy" of news organizations (*News and the Culture of Lying* [New York: Free Press, 1994]).

6. A comment made by Walter Cronkite exemplifies the notion that news professionals are free to report what they want: "you really don't have any master to whom you must answer in television, in journalism. We are not beholden to any man or any cause or any purpose. We are as free as the birds in that regard" (quoted in "The First Annual Theodore H. White Lecture with Walter Cronkite" [Joan Shorenstein Barone Center on the Press, Politics and Public Policy, John F. Kennedy School of Government, Harvard University, Cambridge, Mass., 1990, bound transcript], 35). Yet not only does Cronkite ignore the subtle learning and socialization that he no doubt went through— learning what his bosses and the news ratings were calling for—but Cronkite himself was in a singularly distinct position as a journalist, one that few can ever match.

7. John Dancy, interviews by author, September 9, 12, 18, 1996. Dancy said the hardest part of his job was the script approval process: "You'd write a script, then call the nightly news . . . And then you'd have a conference about the story, the writing, the structure, the facts, the visual. Scripts tended to go through this mixmaster before they got on the air."

8. Alan Murray, interviews by author, July 14 and 28.

9. John Fialka, interview by author, June 29, 1995. Also see Chris Argyris, *Behind the Front Page: Organizational Self-Renewal in a Metropolitan Newspaper* (San Francisco: Jossey-Bass, 1974).

10. The same was true of other metropolitan newspapers, such as the *Boston Globe, Austin American-Statesman,* and *Dallas Morning News* (interviews with David Shribman, Rich Oppel, and Carl Leubsdorf, respectively). Shribman reports that the *Globe* printed "one hundred percent" of what the staff wrote, "not ninety-nine, one-hundred."

Warren Breed lists six reasons why few reporters have to be fired and most go along with editors' and publishers' policies: (1) the reporters are the employees of the publishers who own the paper and ultimately control its content, though that control may be exercised indirectly, (2) reporters feel obligated to their bosses, (3) reporters want to move upward in the organization, (4) there is no organized alliance to oppose the publishers, editors, and "safe" staffers, (5) reporters work in a generally comfortable and pleasant environment, and they like their occupation, and (6) getting new news is more important than ethics or objectivity ("Social Control in the Newsroom: A Functional Analysis," *Social Forces* 33 [1955]: 329–31).

11. David H. Weaver and G. Cleveland Wilhoit, *The American Journalist in the 1990s* (Mahwah, N.J.: Erlbaum, 1996), 150; Gans, *Deciding What's News;* Weaver, *News and the Culture of Lying,* 148.

12. Doyle McManus, interview by author, July 23, 1995. The Washington bureau of the *Los Angeles Times* had about forty-five persons with eight to twelve editors (about a 5:1 ratio); there were also the national editor, the deputy national editor, the managing editor and the editor-in-chief located in Los Angeles.

13. Bill Headline, interview by author, July 28, 1996.

14. Alan Murray, interviews by author, July 14 and 28, 1995; Gans, *Deciding What's News*, 78. The *Wall Street Journal* is somewhat of an exception, because there are no regular conferences held between the New York office and the Washington bureau. Rather, there is an 11:00 a.m. meeting in New York, and the Washington bureau is in touch with New York several times a day.

15. Cited in Edward J. Epstein, *News from Nowhere* (New York: Vintage Books, 1974), 4–5; also see William A. Henry III, "News as Entertainment," in *What's News*, ed. Elie Abel (San Francisco: Institute for Contemporary Studies, 1981), 133–58. Media theorist Bethami Dobkin presents journalists' storytelling in much the same way in her commentary on the Persian Gulf War. Narratives are divided into three phases: the presence of an initial puzzle, problem, or issue (the enigma); the building of tension and the development of possible resolutions to the problem (the suspension of the enigma); and the conclusion or satisfactory settling of the problem (the resolution of the enigma) ("Constructing News Narratives: ABC and CNN Cover the Gulf War," in *The Media and the Persian Gulf War*, ed. Robert Denton [Westport, Conn.: Praeger, 1993], 110).

16. Roper Center and Gannett Newseum survey of January 1997, reported in "News Junkies, News Critics," www.newseum.org/survey/index/html. Identifying which media sources they trusted, 53 percent of those surveyed said they trust "all" or "most" of what their local television anchors say, 45 percent said they trust all or most of what network television anchors say, and 31 percent said they believe all or most of what newspaper reporters write ($n = 1,500$).

17. John H. McManus, *Market-Driven Journalism: Let the Citizen Beware?* (Thousand Oaks, Calif.: Sage, 1994), 155; also see Altheide, *Creating Reality*. Although there are clearly differences in reportorial style between the video media and the printed press, the fact that stories have to be written in "inverted pyramid" form does not mean they are no longer narratives. On the contrary, even the dryly written news article written in an inverted pyramid form has its beginning, middle, end, protagonists, antagonists, and other features of drama. So even though a report in the printed press is not the equivalent of a mini-movie script, there is considerable overlap. The newsmagazines are editorial interpretations of politics and government, rather than summaries of the news, and newspapers are increasingly "magazinified" insofar as they assume that readers know the breaking news and want the news to be digested or analyzed in their paper. Again, this is analogous to the video media.

18. See David L. Paletz and Robert M. Entman, *Media Power Politics* (New York: Free Press, 1981). The pressure for television news to be presented as attractively as possible extends to the looks of the correspondents and news anchors. Douglas Gomery reports that the word in the halls of NBC was "Stop the ratings slide with peroxide." Jon Katz, the former executive producer of CBS Morning News, remarks, "The people who make the decisions in network news are all white middle-aged men, and in their desperate attempt to keep audiences from shrinking, they've turned to the Hollywood star system of the 1930s, to the era of dazzling blondes such as Jean Harlow" (quoted in Gomery, "News Workers and Newsmakers," in *The Future of News: Television–News–*

papers–Wire Services–Newsmagazines, ed. Philip Cook, Douglas Gomery, and Lawrence Lichty [Washington, D.C.: Woodrow Wilson Center Press; Baltimore: Johns Hopkins University Press, 1992], 125).

19. Epstein, *News from Nowhere,* 262–63.

20. John Dancy, interviews by author, September 3, 6, and 12, 1996.

21. Sigal, *Reporters and Officials.*

22. Doyle McManus, interview by author, July 25, 1995.

23. Mayer, *Making News;* Walter Cronkite quoted in "The First Annual Theodore H. White Lecture with Walter Cronkite" (Joan Shorenstein Barone Center on the Press, Politics and Public Policy, John F. Kennedy School of Government, Harvard University, Cambridge, Mass., 1990, bound transcript), 23; Altheide, *Creating Reality,* 103–12, 179.

24. Leo Rosten, *The Washington Correspondents* (New York: Arno Press, 1974 [1937]), 234–35; Epstein, "The Selection of Reality," 124. The computerization of news reporting facilitates centralized editing, moreover, since editors and even executives are able to obtain access to reporter's stories, previous drafts, and research notes. Weaver notes that news executives "deploy the epithets *professional* and *unprofessional* as justifications for preempting discussion and as tools of managerial control" (*News and the Culture of Lying,* 123).

25. Argyris, *Behind the Front Page;* Weaver, *News and the Culture of Lying,* 137–40; Edwin Diamond, *Behind the Times: Inside the* New New York Times (New York: Villard Books, 1994), 98–104.

26. John Dancy, interviews by author, September 3, 6, and 12, 1996; Gans, *Deciding What's News,* 97.

27. Weaver, *News and the Culture of Lying,* 113–15; Weaver points out that those who hire and fire editors make their own "occasional, unpredictable, arbitrary, and often whimsical" demands on the editors, with the result that editors highly value loyalty in their reporters, since they may have to make sudden requests of them. There is also a technical agenda of how to write, do layouts, follow special preferences, and the like. Similarly, Warren Breed comments that the policy of newspapers "contravenes" the "ethical norms of journalism" ("Social Control in the Newsroom," 327).

28. Also see Mark Hertsgaard, *On Bended Knee: The Press and the Reagan Presidency* (New York: Farrar, Straus & Giroux, 1988); Wicker, *On Press;* David Wise, *The Politics of Lying* (New York: Vintage, 1973). In another example, the University of California president was able to get a CBS chair to modify a documentary about "Berkeley Rebels."

29. Doug Underwood, *When MBAs Rule the Newsroom* (New York: Columbia University Press, 1993), 28. On the general point, also see Ben Bagdikian, *The Media Monopoly,* 4th ed. (Boston: Beacon Press, 1992); Reuven Frank, *Out of Thin Air* (New York: Simon & Schuster, 1991); James Squires, *Read All About It!* (New York: Times Books, 1993).

30. Epstein, *News from Nowhere,* 222.

31. Eric Elbot, "The Giants in Our Midst," *Media Ethics Update* 4, no. 2 (1992): 6, quoted in Pamela Shoemaker and Stephen Reese, *Mediating the Message: Theories of Influences on Mass Media Content,* 2d ed. (White Plains, N.Y.: Longman, 1996), 171; also see Epstein, *News from Nowhere,* 46.

32. Breed, "Social Control in the Newsroom," 328, 326–35. Also see Rosten, *The Washington Correspondents,* 132–37, 219–36.

33. Benjamin I. Page, *Who Deliberates? Mass Media in Modern Democracy* (Chicago: University of Chicago Press, 1996), 112–15.

34. Sigal, *Reporters and Officials;* Gaye Tuchman, *Making News: A Study in the Construction of Reality* (New York: Free Press, 1978).

35. For examples of hierarchical relationships in media firms, see the organizational charts in Shoemaker and Reese, *Mediating the Message,* 162, 164.

36. Underwood, *When MBAs Rule the Newsroom;* Squires, *Read All About It!;* Diamond, *Behind the Times;* McManus, *Market-Driven Journalism.*

37. Quoted in Bernard Roshco, *Newsmaking* (Chicago: University of Chicago Press, 1975), 110.

38. Grossman quoted in Ken Auletta, *Three Blind Mice* (New York: Random House, 1991), 404; David Broder, *Behind the Front Page* (New York: Simon & Schuster, 1987), 18. Also see F. B. Marbut, *News from the Capital: The Story of Washington Reporting* (Carbondale, Ill.: Southern Illinois University Press, 1971), 243–54.

39. John Zaller, "Strategic Politicians, Public Opinion, and the Gulf Crisis," in *Taken by Storm,* ed. W. Lance Bennett and David L. Paletz (Chicago: University of Chicago Press, 1994), 250–74; Hertsgaard, *On Bended Knee,* 44–45; Russell Neuman, Marion Just, and Ann Crigler, *Common Knowledge: News and the Construction of Political Meaning* (Chicago: University of Chicago Press, 1992).

40. Howard Kurtz, *Media Circus: The Trouble with American Newspapers* (New York: Times Books, 1993), 246–48; William Greider, interview by author, September 6, 1995; Rosten, *The Washington Correspondents,* 14. Also see W. Lance Bennett, *News: The Politics of Illusion,* 3d ed. (White Plains, N.Y.: Longman, 1996), 120–23. Broder observes that "the ethics issues and straddling the line or crossing the line" have "become so much worse since the time" that he wrote *Behind the Front Page* (interview by author, June 23, 1995).

41. David Halberstam, *The Powers That Be* (New York: Knopf, 1979), 578–79; Greider, cited in Hertsgaard, *On Bended Knee,* 44–45. Also see Jeff Cohen and Norman Solomon, *Adventures in Medialand* (Monroe, Maine: Common Courage Press, 1993), 8–10.

42. Associated Press, "Dining With Presidents: Albright to Zuckerman," *New York Times,* National Edition, October 20, 1997, A13.

43. Fred Dutton, interview by author, July 18, 1996.

44. Quoted in Thomas B. Rosenstiel, "Talk-Show Journalism," in *The Future of News: Television–Newspapers–Wire Services–Newsmagazines,* ed. Philip Cook, Douglas Gomery, and Lawrence Lichty (Washington, D.C.: Woodrow Wilson Center Press; Baltimore: Johns Hopkins University Press, 1992), 80.

45. Frank J. Murray, "Sam: A Press Corps 'Ayatollah' and How He Got That Way," *Washington Times,* November 7, 1988, quoted in S. Robert Lichter and Richard E. Noyes, *Good Intentions Make Bad News,* 2d ed. (Lanham, Md.: Rowman & Littlefield, 1996), 3.

46. Percentages taken from Weaver and Wilhoit, *The American Journalist in the 1990s.* One percent of American journalists are Asian American, and 0.6 percent are Native American. Also see Gans, *Deciding What's News,* 130–31; Hertsgaard, *On Bended Knee,* 82. Tom Wicker notes that "67 percent" of black journalists, "said their superiors were not 'committed to retaining and promoting black journalists.' But 94 percent of newsroom managers said their organizations had a 'serious commitment' to

that goal" (*Tragic Failure: Racial Integration in America* [New York: Morrow, 1995], 164–65).

47. Weaver and Wilhoit, *The American Journalist in the 1990s.*

48. Broder, *Behind the Front Page,* 329; Walter Cronkite quoted in "The First Annual Theodore H. White Lecture with Walter Cronkite" (Joan Shorenstein Barone Center on the Press, Politics and Public Policy, John F. Kennedy School of Government, Harvard University, Cambridge, Mass., 1990, bound transcript), 16–17. Also see William Glaberson, "The Media Business: Press," *New York Times,* January 31, 1994.

49. James Fallows, *Breaking the News* (New York: Pantheon, 1996); Broder, *Behind the Front Page,* 329; Hertsgaard, *On Bended Knee,* 80–81. Cokie Roberts was reported to be receiving speaking fees from the American Hospital Association at the same time she was reporting on the Clintons' health care package (Michael Blowen, "The Press: When the Watchdogs Become Lap Dogs," *Boston Globe,* October 22, 1996).

50. Stephen Hess, *News and Newsmaking* (Washington, D.C.: Brookings, 1996), 10–11, 16–17. Also see Broder, *Behind the Front Page,* 360–61; Penn Kimball, *Downsizing the News: Network Cutbacks in the Nation's Capital* (Washington, D.C.: Woodrow Wilson Center Press, 1994), 33–34; Tom Goldstein, *The News at Any Cost: How Journalists Compromise Their Ethics to Shape the News* (New York: Simon & Schuster, 1985), 73; Michael Parenti, *Inventing Reality: The Politics of the News Media,* 2d ed. (New York: St. Martin's Press, 1993), 62–63. Journalists are "insiders" to the extent that they have privileged access to information, share in confidential information that may not ever be publicized, and have social ties with top governmental actors; they are clearly not insiders to the extent that they do not participate directly in government or policy making.

51. Michael Kelly, "David Gergen, Master of the Game," *New York Times Magazine,* October 31, 1993, 64.

52. Mort Rosenblum, *Who Stole the News?* (New York: Wiley, 1993), 221.

53. Timothy Crouse, *The Boys on the Bus* (New York: Random House, 1973); Sigal, *Reporters and Officials;* Wicker, *On Press;* Gans, *Deciding What's News;* Stephen Hess, *The Washington Reporters* (Washington, D.C.: Brookings, 1981); Michael Robinson and Margaret Sheehan, *Over the Wire and on TV: CBS and UPI in Campaign '80* (New York: Russell Sage Foundation, 1983); F. Christopher Arterton, *Media Politics: The News Strategies of Presidential Campaigns* (Lexington, Mass.: Lexington Books, 1984); Hertsgaard, *On Bended Knee;* McManus, *Market-Driven Journalism;* Page, *Who Deliberates?* Jan Hook, a veteran congressional correspondent for the *Los Angeles Times,* remarks that the informal basis of cue-taking is journalists' cooperation, consistent with Sigal's point about the "consensibility" of the news: that it is a sociological product of news beats and newsrooms (interview by author, July 28, 1995). More generally, see Elisabeth Noelle-Neumann, "Kumulation, Konsonunz, und Öffenlichkeitseffekt: Ein neuer Ansatz zur Analyse der Wirkung der Massenmedien," *Publizistik* 18 (1973): 26–55.

54. Gans, *Deciding What's News,* 180.

55. The newspapers subscribe to the *New York Times* wire, which posts three "advisories" during the day (3:00–4:00 in the afternoon, around 6:00, and around 9:00–10:30 p.m., central time) as to the front-page stories for the next day's newspaper. On one occasion, a major U.S. newspaper pulled a front-page story on Bosnia when the *New York Times* ran a story on the same topic on its front page, presumably because the *Times's* story differed in some of its important details from this paper's story. This

newspaper's story was right, however, and the *Times* story had it wrong.

56. Jon Wolman, interview by author, July 27, 1995.

57. Jack Germond quoted in Don Campbell, *Inside the Beltway: A Guide to Washington Reporting* (Ames: Iowa State University Press, 1991), 12.

58. Rosenblum, *Who Stole the News?* 217.

59. Kelly, "David Gergen," 64; David Shribman, interviews by author, June 7 and July 18, 1995; R. W. Apple, interview by author, July 7, 1995; Alan Murray, interviews by author, July 14 and 28, 1995.

60. Page, *Who Deliberates?* 118; Kurtz, *Media Circus*, 7; Kenneth T. Walsh, *Feeding the Beast: The White House Versus the Press* (New York: Random House, 1996), 261–63; Roper Center, "News Junkies, News Critics." As the media scholars and social critics Harry Boyte and Nan Karl observe, "an enormous gap exists between what politicians say and what most people experience in their everyday lives" ("Renewing the Community," *Minneapolis Star Tribune,* September 25, 1995).

61. Bartholomew Sparrow and Salma Ghanem, "The Transparency of the News Media: Coverage of the Press by the Press" (paper presented at the annual meeting of the Midwest Political Science Association, Chicago, April 1996).

62. In fact, the norm of balanced reporting meshes with the idea of a pluralist political community: the fact that the United States is composed of many different groups that legitimately contend for voice, influence, and resources.

63. See Page, *Who Deliberates?*; Sigal, *Reporters and Officials;* Rich Oppel, interviews by author, May 3 and June 8, 1996.

64. See Gaye Tuchman, "Objectivity as Strategic Ritual: An Examination of Newsmen's Notions of Objectivity," *American Journal of Sociology* 77 (1973): 660–79.

65. Tuchman, *Making News;* Robert A. Hackett, "Decline of a Paradigm? Bias and Objectivity in New Media Studies," *Critical Studies in Mass Communication* 1 (1984): 229–59. There is the exception of the *Wall Street Journal's* features and editorials, which may not be consistent with the inside and back-page news stories.

66. Tuchman, "Objectivity as Strategic Ritual."

67. See ibid.; E. Barbara Phillips, "Approaches to Objectivity: Journalistic Versus Social Science Perspectives," in *Strategies for Communication Research,* ed. Paul M. Hirsh, Peter V. Miller, and F. Gerald Kline (Beverly Hills, Calif.: Sage, 1979), 68–69.

68. See Tuchman, "Objectivity as Strategic Ritual," 660; Steven B. Clayman, "From Talk to Text: Newspaper Accounts of Reporter-Source Interactions," *Media, Culture, and Society* 12 (1990): 79–103.

69. Oliver Gramling, *AP: The Story of News* (New York: Farrar & Rinehart, 1940), 20, cited in Roshco, *Newsmaking;* Steffens quoted in Tuchman, *Making News,* 159. Also see Frank Luther Mott, *The News in America* (Cambridge, Mass.: Harvard University Press, 1952), 72–73, 78–79; Denis McQuail, *Media Performance: Mass Communication and the Public Interest* (Newbury Park, Calif.: Sage, 1992), 186–87; David L. Shaw, "News Bias and the Telegraph," *Journalism Quarterly* 38 (1961): 3–12.

70. Gerald J. Baldasty, *The Commercialization of News in the Nineteenth Century* (Madison: University of Wisconsin Press, 1992), 7, 140–41.

71. Weaver, *News and the Culture of Lying,* 23. It was an editorial for the *Springfield Republican* written by Samuel Bowles in 1855 that distinguished between "news of fact and news of opinion."

72. Michael Schudson, *Discovering the News* (New York: Basic Books, 1978), 122–29.

73. Ibid., 156; Tuchman, *Making News,* 160.

74. Roshco, *Newsmaking,* 45–46. Even in New York, however, the *Times* shared the spotlight with the *Herald Tribune.*

75. See Tuchman, *Making News.*

76. Robert Entman, *Democracy without Citizens* (New York: Oxford University Press, 1989), 55; Erving Goffman, *Frame Analysis: An Essay on the Organization of Experience* (Boston: Boston University Press, 1974); Tuchman, *Making News;* Todd Gitlin, *The Whole World Is Watching* (Berkeley: University of California Press, 1980); Shanto Iyengar, *Who's Responsible?* (Chicago: University of Chicago Press, 1991); William A. Gamson, *Talking Politics* (Cambridge: Cambridge University Press, 1992). Thomas Patterson uses the word "schema" in *Out of Order* (New York: Knopf, 1993) to describe what appears to be the same phenomenon.

77. See Gans, *Deciding What's News,* 42–57; Benjamin I. Page and Robert Shapiro, *The Rational Public: Fifty Years of Trends in Americans' Policy Preferences* (Chicago: University of Chicago Press, 1992), 366–80; Neuman et al., *Common Knowledge,* 62–74; Roderick P. Hart, *Seducing America: How Television Charms the Modern Voter* (New York: Oxford University Press, 1994).

78. Page and Shapiro, *The Rational Public,* 380–90; Gans, *Deciding What's News,* 50–52 (I consider Gans's "news values" to be analogous to news "frames," since frames also prioritize and contrast social values for audiences); Neuman et al., *Common Knowledge,* 66–72. The use of news frames that select, define, and judge the news may still be consistent with the norm of impartial reporting, given that journalists themselves may be unaware or only partly aware of the frames into which they or their sources put the news (Entman, *Democracy without Citizens,* 57).

79. Entman, "Framing: Toward Clarification of a Fractured Paradigm," *Journal of Communication* 43, no. 4 (1994): 51–58. As William A. Gamson writes, "The various frames offered in media discourse provide maps indicating useful points of entry, and signposts at various crossroads highlight the significant landmarks and warn of the perils of other paths" (*Talking Politics,* 179).

80. Hart, *Seducing America,* 10. Also see Joshua Meyrowitz, *No Sense of Place: The Impact of Electronic Media on Social Behavior* (New York: Oxford University Press, 1986). A number of media studies are premised on the idea that television news is the only news that really matters (e.g., Robert J. Donovan and Ray Scherer, *Unsilent Revolution: Television News and American Public Life,* Woodrow Wilson Center Series [New York: Cambridge University Press, 1992]; Kathleen Hall Jamieson, *Dirty Politics: Deception, Distraction, and Democracy* [New York: Oxford University Press, 1992]; Matthew Kerbel, *Edited for Television* [Boulder, Colo.: Westview Press, 1994]).

81. Samuel P. Huntington, *American Politics: The Promise of Disharmony* (Cambridge, Mass.: Belknap Press, 1981).

82. David Croteau and William Hoynes, *By Invitation Only* (Monroe, Maine: Common Courage, 1994); also see Stephen D. Reese and Lucig H. Danielian, "The Structure of News Sources on Television: A Network Analysis of 'CBS News,' 'Nightline,' 'MacNeil/Lehrer,' and 'This Week with David Brinkley,'" *Journal of Communication* 44, no. 2 (1994): 84–107.

83. Sigal, *Reporters and Officials;* Tuchman, *Making News;* Gitlin, *The Whole World Is Watching;* Mark Fishman, *Manufacturing the News* (Austin: University of Texas Press, 1980); Epstein, *News from Nowhere;* Leon V. Sigal, "Sources Make the News," in *Reading the News,* ed. Michael Schudson and Karl Manoff (New York: Pantheon, 1986).

84. The chance that a reporter interviews someone as the proverbial "man (or

woman) on the street" or that someone is able to go on the air in a national call-in format is, of course, minuscule.

85. "Transparency" is my term for this phenomenon. See Epstein, "The Selection of Reality"; Hackett, "Decline of a Paradigm"; Joseph Turow, "Hidden Conflicts and Journalist Norms: The Case of Self-Coverage," *Journal of Communication* 44, no. 2 (1994): 29–46. Also see Trudy Lieberman, "Plagiarize, Plagiarize, Plagiarize . . . Only Be Sure To Call It Research," *Columbia Journalism Review*, July/August 1995, 21–25.

86. Epstein "The Selection of Reality."

87. Ibid., 132.

88. Henry, "News as Entertainment," 134.

89. Weaver, *News and the Culture of Lying*, 84–85.

90. Mary Matalin and James Carville, *All's Fair: Love, War, and Running for President* (New York: Random House and Simon & Schuster, 1994), 187.

91. Richard Horchler, quoted in Roshco, *Newsmaking*, 86. Also see Rosten, *The Washington Correspondents*.

92. W. Lance Bennett, Lynne A. Gressett, and William Haltom, "Repairing the News: A Case Study of the News Paradigm," *Journal of Communication* 35, no. 2 (1985): 50–68.

93. Daniel J. Boorstin, "From Newsgathering to News-making: A Flood of Pseudo-events," in *The Process and Effects of Mass Communication*, ed. W. Schramm and D. F. Roberts (Urbana: University of Illinois Press, 1971). Also see the classic study by Kurt Lang and Gladys Engel Lang on the 1951 MacArthur Day parade in Chicago ("MacArthur Day in Chicago," in *Politics and Television*, ed. Gladys Engel Lang and Kurt Lang [Chicago: Quadrangle, 1968]).

94. Snider and Page, "Does Media Ownership Affect Media Stands?" Even the extent to which the news is not "transparent"—the fact that journalists are taking up more and more time on television programs, offering more and more of their own opinion and analysis in the news proper, and becoming more and more visible as celebrities (Fallows, *Breaking the News;* Patterson, *Out of Order;* Patterson cited in "The Annual Theodore H. White Lecture with Cokie Roberts" [Joan Shorenstein Center on the Press, Politics and Public Policy, John F. Kennedy School of Government, Harvard University, Cambridge, Mass., 1994, bound transcript], 57)—is true only with respect to news anchors and other talking heads: the audience is still sheltered from the organizational and financial dimensions of news production. Indeed, the fact that the print or broadcast reporter has a byline that brings attention to that particular person obscures the camera crew, headline editor, producer, and layout editor, who may be every bit as crucial in the presentation of the news.

95. Schudson, *Discovering the News.*

96. Gans, *Deciding What's News;* Hess, *The Washington Reporters;* Larry Sabato, *Feeding Frenzy* (New York: Free Press, 1991); Sigal, *Reporters and Officials;* Kimball, *Downsizing the News.*

97. McQuail, *Media Performance*, 172–73. See R. A. Pride and B. Richards, "Denigration of Authority? TV News Coverage of the Student Movement," *Journal of Politics* 36 (1973): 637–60; R. A. Pride and G. L. Wamsley, "Symbol Analysis of Network Coverage of the Laos Incursion," *Journalism Quarterly* 49 (1974): 635–40; J. S. Fowler and M. E. Steele, "Degree of Conformity in Lead Stories in Early Network TV Newscasts," *Journalism Quarterly* 63 (1986): 19–23; J. S. Fowler and S. W. Showalte, "Evening Network News Selection: Confirmation of News Judgment," *Journalism Quarterly* 51

(1973): 212–15; C. R. Hofstetter, *Bias in the News: Network Television Coverage of the 1972 Election Campaign* (Columbus: Ohio State University Press, 1976); J. B. Lemert, "Content Duplication by the Networks in Competing Evening Newscasts," *Journalism Quarterly* 51 (1974): 238–44. Also see Croteau and Hoynes, *By Invitation Only*.

98. Neuman et al., *Common Knowledge*.

99. Grant McConnell, *Private Power and American Democracy* (New York: Vintage, 1966), 215. McConnell adds that such charges would "leave the agency politically helpless and unlikely to survive," a situation that does not apply so well to the news media, given their First Amendment protections (justifying a modicum of "irresponsibility" or "arbitrariness") and their independent and healthy financial base (unlike almost all federal agencies that depend on congressional appropriations).

100. See Tuchman, *Making News;* Gitlin, *The Whole World Is Watching;* Shoemaker and Reese, *Mediating the Message*.

101. See Karen Orren and Stephen Skowronek, "Beyond the Iconography of Order: Notes for a New Institutionalism," in *The Dynamics of American Politics: Approaches and Interpretations,* ed. Lawrence C. Dodd and Calvin Tillson (Boulder, Colo.: Westview Press, 1994), 311–30; Roger Friedland and Robert Alford, "Bringing Society Back In," in *The New Institutionalism in Organizational Analysis,* ed. Walter W. Powell and Paul J. DiMaggio (Chicago: University of Chicago Press, 1991), 232–63.

102. Doris Graber, *The Mass Media and American Politics,* 5th ed. (Washington, D.C.: CQ Press, 1997); Marion R. Just, Ann N. Crigler, Dean E. Alger, et al., *Crosstalk: Citizens, Candidates, and the Media in a Presidential Campaign* (Chicago: University of Chicago Press, 1996); Neuman et al., *Common Knowledge;* Page, *Who Deliberates?;* Thomas Patterson, *The Mass Media Election* (New York: Praeger, 1976); idem, *Out of Order*.

103. Richard Harwood, interview by author, July 18, 1995; Norm Kempster, interview by author, July 25, 1995. As Michael Nelson points out, however, the iron triangle works best *outside* the media spotlight, whereas the notion of the media as a fourth corner suggests publicity (personal communication, January 1998).

104. S. Robert Lichter, Stanley Rothman, and Linda S. Lichter, *The Media Elite* (Bethesda, Md.: Adler & Adler, 1986), 4–5; Weaver and Wilhoit, *The American Journalist in the 1990s,* 15–19; Lichter and Noyes, *Good Intentions Make Bad News;* Kenneth Dautrich and Jennifer Necci Dineen, "Media Bias: What Journalists and the Public Say About It," *The Public Perspective,* October/November 1996, 7–14; Michael Schudson, *The Power of the News* (Cambridge, Mass.: Harvard University Press, 1994), 124–41; S. Robert Lichter, "Consistently Liberal: But Does It Matter?" *Media Critic,* fall 1996, 34. Seven percent voted for George Bush, and 2 percent voted for Ross Perot.

105. Richard Harwood, interview by author, July 18, 1995; Rich Oppel, interviews by author, May 3 and June 9, 1996; also see Lichter, "Consistently Liberal," 30, 31, 39.

106. Roper Center, "News Junkies, News Critics."

107. Roshco, *Newsmaking;* Altheide, *Creating Reality;* Hackett, "Decline of a Paradigm?"; Weaver, *News and the Culture of Lying;* Hackett, "Decline of a Paradigm?"; Maxwell McCombs, Edna Einseidel, and David Weaver, *Contemporary Public Opinion: Issues and the News* (Hillsdale, N.J.: Erlbaum, 1991); Bennett, *News: The Politics of Illusion;* Patterson, *Out of Order*.

108. Epstein, "The Selection of Reality," 131.

109. Altheide, *Creating Reality,* 177. Although Epstein and Altheide write about the 1970s, the politics of the late 1960s and early 1970s were certainly as intense and divisive as those of the present.

110. R. Kent Weaver and Bert A. Rockman, eds., *Do Institutions Matter? Government Capabilities in the United States and Abroad* (Washington, D.C.: Brookings, 1993), 445–46.

111. Ibid., 459–60, 465–81, 446–53. The authors recognize that their cases are not compiled so as to allow for a comparison of third-tier variables (e.g., the news media) across countries.

SIX The Watchdogs That Didn't Bark

1. They also covered anticommunist stories well, as in the case of the murder of the Polish priest in 1984. See Edward S. Herman and Noam Chomsky's *Manufacturing Consent: The Political Economy of the Mass Media* (New York: Pantheon, 1988) for a comparison of U.S. news coverage of that story with coverage of the rape and murder of four nuns in El Salvador.

2. Reston, *The Artillery of the Press* (New York: Harper & Row, 1966). Also see Paul Weaver, *News and the Culture of Lying* (New York: Free Press, 1994). Authoritative sources also include the most prominent societal actors. The news media thus allowed Texaco to respond fully to the racism and anti-Semitism revealed in Texaco corporate documents in the fall of 1996, for instance.

3. This is but part of the story, of course, since there is an obvious partisan dimension of Republicans in Congress attacking the Democratic presidential administration.

4. W. Lance Bennett, "Towards a Theory of Press-State Relations in the United States," *Journal of Communication* 40, no. 2 (1990): 103–25; Mark Fishman, *Manufacturing the News* (Austin: University of Texas Press, 1980), 125. Also see Daniel Hallin, *The "Uncensored War": The Media and Vietnam* (New York: Oxford University Press, 1986); John Zaller, "Strategic Politicians, Public Opinion, and the Gulf Crisis," in *Taken by Storm: The Media, Public Opinion, and U.S. Foreign Policy in the Gulf War*, ed. W. Lance Bennett and David L. Paletz (Chicago: University of Chicago Press, 1994), 250–74; Edward Jay Epstein, *Between Fact and Fiction* (New York: Vintage Books, 1975).

5. Leon V. Sigal, "Sources Make the News," in *Reading the News*, ed. Michael Schudson and Karl Manoff (New York: Pantheon, 1986), 33.

6. See Bernard Roshco, "When Policy Fails: How the Buck Was Passed When Kuwait Was Invaded" (Discussion Paper D-15, the Joan Shorenstein Barone Center on the Press, Politics and Public Policy, John F. Kennedy School of Government, Harvard University, Cambridge, Mass., December 1992); Michael R. Gordon and Gen. Bernard E. Trainor, *The General's War* (Boston: Little, Brown), 22, 24, 28; Jim Naureckas, "Creating the New Hitler: The Gulf War," *The FAIR Reader: An EXTRA! Review of Press and Politics in the 1990s*, ed. Jim Naureckas and Janine Jackson (Boulder, Colo.: Westview Press, 1996), 27. Roshco argues that the State Department and Bush administration soft-pedaled their diplomacy with Iraq because they never imagined that Hussein and Iraq would take *all* of Kuwait and then seek to hold onto it. Also see Robert Denton, ed., *The Media and the Persian Gulf War* (Westport, Conn.: Praeger, 1993); H. Mowlana, G. Gerbner, and H. I. Schiller, *Triumph of the Image* (Boulder, Colo.: Westview Press, 1992); Benjamin I. Page, *Who Deliberates? Mass Media in Modern Democracy* (Chicago: University of Chicago Press, 1996); Jean Edward Smith, *George Bush's War* (New York: Henry Holt, 1992); Calvin F. Exoo, *The Politics of the Mass Media* (Minneapolis/St. Paul, Minn.: West, 1994), 3–17.

7. Jarol B. Manheim, "Strategic Public Diplomacy," in *Taken by Storm*, ed. W. Lance

Bennett and David Paletz (Chicago: University of Chicago Press, 1994), 140; John R. MacArthur, *Second Front: Censorship and Propaganda in the Gulf War* (New York: Hill & Wang, 1992), 46–77; Martin Yant, *Desert Mirage: The True Story of the Gulf War* (Buffalo: Prometheus Books, 1991), 54–61; Naureckas, "Creating the New Hitler," 19–51. The incubator baby story was repeated uncritically and unquestioningly throughout the news media.

8. MacArthur, *Second Front,* 163, 172–78; Yant, *Desert Mirage,* 91–92; Lawrence Freedman and Effraim Karsh, *The Gulf Conflict 1990–1991: Diplomacy and War in the New World Order* (Princeton, N.J.: Princeton University Press, 1993), 390; Jason DeParle, "Keeping the News in Step," in *The Media and the Gulf War: The Press and Democracy in Wartime,* ed. Hedrick Smith (Washington, D.C.: Foreign Policy Institute of the School of Advanced International Studies, Johns Hopkins University, 1992), 387; John J. Fialka, *Hotel Warriors: Covering the Gulf War* (Washington, D.C.: Woodrow Wilson Center Press, 1991), 59; MacArthur, *Second Front,* 163; Philip Taylor, *War and the Media: Propaganda and Persuasion in the Gulf War* (Manchester: Manchester University Press, 1992), 181–83, 259–63, 277–78; Naureckas, "Creating the New Hitler," 26–27.

9. Fialka, *Hotel Warriors,* 33–35, 58–59; Yant, *Desert Mirage,* 31–34, 208–9; DeParle, "Keeping the News in Step," in *The Media and the Gulf War,* ed. Hedrick Smith, 386–87; MacArthur, *Second Front,* 163, 202.

10. MacArthur, *Second Front,* 162, 172; Taylor, *War and the Media,* 220; Yant, *Desert Mirage,* 212; Dean E. Alger, *The Media and Politics,* 2d ed. (Belmont, Calif.: Wadsworth, 1996), 159–60.

11. Washington Bureau Chiefs, "Covering the Persian Gulf War," unpublished report, May 30, 1991, cited in Barrie Dunsmore, "The Next War: Live?" (Discussion Paper D-22, the Joan Shorenstein Center on the Press, Politics and Public Policy, John F. Kennedy School of Government, Harvard University, Cambridge, Mass., March 1996), 5; Washington Bureau Chiefs, letter to Defense Secretary Richard Cheney, April 29, 1991, cited in Dunsmore, "The Next War: Live?"

12. MacArthur, *Second Front,* 192; Naureckas, "Creating the New Hitler," 28–34.

13. See Benno Schmidt, "The First Amendment and the Press," in *What's News: The Media in America,* ed. Elie Abel (San Francisco: Institute for Contemporary Studies, 1981); Harold Hongju Koh, *The National Security Constitution: Sharing Power after the Iran-Contra Affair* (New Haven, Conn.: Yale University Press, 1990).

14. Mark Cook and Jeff Cohen write of the extent to which the same jingoist and uncritical reporting was evident in the news coverage of the Panama invasion ("Rallying 'Round the Flag: The Panama Invasion," in *The FAIR Reader: An EXTRA! Review of Press and Politics in the 1990s,* ed. Jim Naureckas and Janine Jackson [Boulder, Colo.: Westview Press, 1996], 11–19).

15. See Alexander Dallin, *Black Box: KAL 007 and the Superpowers* (Berkeley: University of California Press, 1985), 4–11; Allan Rachlin, *News as Hegemonic Reality: American Political Culture and the Framing of News Accounts* (Westport, Conn.: Praeger, 1988), 38–49.

16. David Pearson, *KAL 007: The Cover Up* (New York: Summit Books, 1987), 224. The bill gave the Reagan administration almost everything it wanted, including funding for nerve gas and the MX missile system (224–26). Soviet aircraft were also not allowed to land at Kennedy Airport on Long Island for a short while.

17. See Don Oberdorfer, *The Turn: From the Cold War to a New Era* (New York: Touch-

stone, 1992), 49–74. Also see Richard A. Brody, *Assessing the President: The Media, Elite Opinion, and Public Support* (Stanford, Calif.: Stanford University Press, 1991), 58, 73–74. Brody tracks the "rally" support for President Reagan as a result of the crash of KAL 007. Reagan's public opinion approval rose by about 23 percent for two days in a row shortly after the incident. Still, 56 percent of Americans did not think that the Reagan administration was being tough enough (Rachlin, *News as Hegemonic Reality*, 73).

18. For the "accepted" accounts of the downing of KAL 007, see Seymour Hersh, *The Target Is Destroyed: What Really Happened to Flight 007 and What America Knew about It* (New York: Random House, 1986), and Murray Sayle, "Closing the File on Flight 007," *New Yorker*, December 13, 1993, 90–101. For a dispassionate account of the tragedy shortly afterwards, see Dallin, *Black Box*. Also see the brief treatments of the KAL downing in George Shultz, *Turmoil and Triumph* (New York: Charles Scribner's Sons, 1993), 361–70, 463–64, and Oberdorfer, *The Turn*. For accounts that question these perspectives, see David Pearson, "KAL 007: What the U.S. Knew and When We Knew It," *The Nation*, August 18–25, 1984, 105–24; R. W. Johnson, *Shootdown: Flight 007 and the American Connection* (New York: Viking, 1986); Pearson, *KAL 007*.

19. See Michel Brun, *Incident at Sakhalin: The True Mission of Flight 007* (New York: Four Walls Eight Windows Press, 1996); John Keppel, "Korean Airlines Flight 007: Remarks at the Kennedy School of Government" (paper presented at the John F. Kennedy School of Government, Harvard University, Cambridge, Mass., April 1992).

20. Johnson, *Shootdown*, 321; Pearson, *KAL 007*, 142. See Pearson (*KAL 007*) on the Navy's lack of cooperation in releasing ship records. Also see John Keppel on the release of radar records by the ICAO, the United States, and Japan (*The MacNeil/Lehrer NewsHour*, August 31, 1984, Transcript #2330, Educational Broadcasting Corporation and GWETA, Arlington, Va.).

21. Brun, *Incident at Sakhalin*, 119–39.

22. Brun, *Incident at Sakhalin;* Alexander Shalnev, *Nightline*, May 22, 1991, American Broadcasting Companies, Inc., New York.

23. Brun, *Incident at Sakhalin*, 42–43.

24. Also see Dallin, *Black Box*, 25.

25. Johnson, *Shootdown*, 295–96; Pearson, *KAL 007*, 353.

26. On this and the following points, see Keppel, "Korean Air Lines Flight 007," and Brun, *Incident at Sakhalin*. Also see Patrice Le Beer, "Le Mystere du Vol 007," *Le Monde*, September 1, 1993, 4.

27. When an Air India 747 (Flight 182) crashed in the Indian Ocean on June 23, 1985, the black boxes were readily found in a four-mile stretch of seafloor at a depth of 6,700 feet—more than twice the depth of the deepest part of the KAL 007 search area in the Sea of Japan. One hundred bodies and much of the luggage were recovered from the Air India flight within two weeks (Pearson, *KAL 007*, 265).

28. This and the following points borrow from the letter of John Keppel to Sam Smith of *The Progressive Review*, May 28, 1996, and the letter of John Keppel to The Honorable Janet Reno, March 23, 1993 (copies of both letters are in my possession).

29. Keppel, "Cover-Up, Airliner Disasters, and the National Interest," unpublished manuscript, November 30, 1992.

30. Pearson, "KAL 007," 116–17; Pearson, *KAL 007*, 288–89, 299–301; Shalnev, "Nightline," May 22, 1991; Johnson, *Shootdown*, 242. The International Civil Aviation Organization (ICAO) conducted a study of the downing of KAL 007 but was not

instructed to rule on the intentionality of the flight (Pearson, *KAL 007*, 272). Nothing, then, can be inferred from the ICAO's report with respect to why the airliner ended up deep in Soviet airspace. Nor does the ICAO have independent investigatory authority; under the conditions of its charter, it has no power of subpoena and "cannot extrapolate beyond the limits of the information in its possession." It is completely dependent on the information that member governments voluntarily hand over (Pearson, *KAL 007*, 190-91). The ICAO report's "biases and limitations went unreported," however (272).

31. Keppel, "Annotated List of Events in KE 007 Flight," unpublished manuscript, August 8, 1992, 7; Johnson, *Shootdown*, 242. Hersh speculates that "ETP" means "equal time point."

32. Pearson, "KAL 007," 106; Pearson, *KAL 007*, 49; Oberdorfer, *The Turn*, 55; Rachlin, *News as Hegemony*, 41-43. The downing of KAL 902 in April 1978 happened at another sensitive moment: when Secretary of State Cyrus Vance of the Carter administration was in Moscow discussing arms control issues with Soviet Foreign Minister Andrei Gromyko.

33. Pearson, *KAL 007*, 291-92; Johnson, *Shootdown*, 149, 295.

34. Pearson, *KAL 007*, 97; Dallin, *Black Box*, 49.

35. Johnson, *Shootdown*, 97. Judge Clark was the decision maker at the NSC in the summer of 1983, when decisions were piling up and the Reagans were spending much of their time at the Santa Barbara ranch. The Biltmore Hotel in Santa Barbara, twenty miles from the Reagan ranch, was in effect "the temporary capital of the US," as the British political scientist R. W. Johnson describes the situation (*Shootdown*, 211-24). Bob Woodward writes that Clark stepped down because of political in-fighting (*Veil: The Secret Wars of the CIA 1981-1987* [New York: Pocket Books, 1987], 317-19).

36. David Shribman, "U.S. Experts Say Soviet Didn't See Jet Was Civilian," *New York Times*, October 7, 1983, A1; Tom Wicker, "A Damning Silence," *New York Times*, September 7, 1984, A27; Stephen S. Rosenfeld, "Flight 007: What We Know Now," *Washington Post*, October 21, 1983, A19; "Second Opinion; What Did the Soviets Know?" *Time*, October 17, 1983, 25; William Pfaff, *International Herald Tribune*, October 13, 1983, cited in Rosenfeld, "Flight 007."

37. Pearson, *KAL 007*, 296; Editorial, *Washington Post*, December 9, 1983, A22; Editorial, *Washington Post*, January 5, 1984, A22; Burt is quoted in Dallin, *Black Box*, 115, note 43. Also see Dallin, *Black Box*, 103.

38. See Pearson, *KAL 007*, 296-301.

39. See John W. R. Leppingwell, "Opening the KAL-007 Black Box: New Documents and Old Questions," *RFE/RI Research Report* 1, no. 44 (1992): 20-26.

40. Mark Hertsgaard, *On Bended Knee: The Press and the Reagan Presidency* (New York: Farrar, Straus & Giroux, 1988).

41. Hersh, *The Target Is Destroyed*, 168; Johnson, *Shootdown*, 242.

42. Jacques Ellul, quoted in Pearson, *KAL 007*, 260.

43. Pearson, *KAL 007*, 284-90, 297-301; Johnson, *Shootdown*, 148-49; Dallin, *Black Box*, 103.

44. Johnson, *Shootdown*, 69-76, 257-60; Pearson, *KAL 007*, 346-47; James Bamford, *The Puzzle Palace* (New York: Penguin Books, 1983), 161. The Krasnoyarsk radar was discovered by American spy satellites just weeks before the KAL 007 incident; its construction was in violation of the ABM Treaty.

45. Several key questions remain. What *did* cause the crash of KAL 007? Why have

the Soviets/Russians cooperated with the U.S. government's single-intruder thesis, from 1983 through the end of the cold war? Why have the principals in the matter on either side not been heard? With respect to the second question, Brun (*Incident at Sakhalin*) suggests that the Soviets cooperated out of fear of the United States and that the Russians have cooperated for reasons of economic dependence. He further points out that the Russians and Japanese have not, in fact, cooperated entirely: they each have released material that, upon close examination, is clearly inconsistent with the scenario that KAL 007 accidentally strayed off course and was then shot down by a single Soviet pilot. Regarding the third question (one that comes up often), it should be pointed out that dissenting or questioning individuals can be heard only if news organizations decide to go with the story.

46. Michel Brun and John Keppel, "KE 007 and the Danger of War," unpublished manuscript, June 1, 1992. Brun and Keppel review Soviet records to argue that the Soviets were extremely anxious about American and NATO intentions.

47. See Hersh, *The Target Is Destroyed*, 74; Brun, *Incident at Sakhalin*. If the U.S. government did *not* know that the Soviets had MiG 31s on hand, this fact would be embarrassing for U.S. military intelligence agencies to acknowledge.

48. This account follows Keppel's letter to The Honorable Janet Reno, March 23, 1993. Also see Pearson, *KAL 007*, 284–327, and Keppel's letter to Smith, May 28, 1996. Senator Patrick Leahy (D-Vt.), who sits on the Senate Intelligence Committee, at one point argued against Pearson's *Nation* article. He did so by using information furnished by intelligence officers, who briefed him just before his meeting with the press (Pearson, *KAL 007*, 291).

49. See David Wise, *The Politics of Lying* (New York: Vintage, 1973); William A. Gamson, *What's News? A Game Simulation of TV News* (New York: Basic Books, 1978); Hallin, *The Uncensored War;* Martha Joynt Kumar, *Wired for Sound and Pictures: The President and White House Communications Policies* (Baltimore: Johns Hopkins University Press, forthcoming); Hertsgaard, *On Bended Knee;* Robert Parry, *Fooling America: How Washington Insiders Twist the Truth and Manufacture the Conventional Wisdom* (New York: Morrow, 1992); Ted Galen Carpenter, *The Captive Press* (Washington, D.C.: Cato Institute, 1996), 228–47; Nik Gowing, "Real-time Television Coverage of Armed Conflicts and Diplomatic Crises: Does It Pressure or Distort Foreign Policy Decision?" (paper presented at the Joan Shorenstein Barone Center on the Press, Politics and Public Policy, John F. Kennedy School of Government, Harvard University, June 1994).

50. One is the news coverage of the defense budget, and of the black budget in particular, in the post–cold war era (e.g., Phil Patton, "Exposing the Black Budget," *Wired* [November 1995], 94–102). A second is news of foreign arms sales by American companies (see Sam Gejdenson and Toby Roth, "Arsenals Abroad," *New York Times,* July 13, 1997; Jeff Cole and Sarah Lubman, "Weapons Merchants Are Going Great Guns in Post–Cold War Era," *Wall Street Journal,* January 28, 1994, 1). The coverage of the "October Surprise" is another case. The phrase refers to the negotiations in the fall of 1980 between William Casey, and others working on behalf of Ronald Reagan, and Iranian officials in regard to ensuring that the Americans then held hostage by Iran would not be released in October 1980, prior to the general election between the incumbent, President Jimmy Carter, and the Republican nominee Ronald Reagan (this would have been the "October Surprise"). See Gary Sick, *October Surprise* (New York: Times Books, 1991); Barbara Honegger, *October Surprise* (New York: Tudor Publishing, 1989); Robert Parry, *Trick or Treason: The October Surprise Mystery* (New York: Sheridan

Square Press, 1993); Robert Parry, *The October Surprise X-Files: The Hidden Origins of the Reagan-Bush Era* (Arlington, Va.: The Media Consortium, 1996), and *October Surprise: Finally Time for the Truth* (Arlington, Va.: The Media Consortium, 1997).

51. In Bob Woodward's acclaimed no. 1 bestseller, *Veil: The Secret Wars of the CIA 1981–1987*, the official story of KAL 007 is taken as a given. Despite having remarkable access to CIA Director William Casey and the historical record of the CIA (332, 338, 345), Woodward did not inquire into the cause of the airline disaster. He also omits mention of the CIA's use of the money from the Savings and Loans disaster of the 1980s (see note 62, below). Nor does Woodward write of Casey's involvement in the October Surprise arms deal with Iran (see Sick, *October Surprise;* Honegger, *October Surprise*). On Woodward himself, see Len Colodny and Robert Gettlin, *Silent Coup: The Removal of a President* (New York: St. Martin's Press, 1991); Jim Hougan, *Secret Agenda: Watergate, Deep Throat and the CIA* (New York: Random House, 1984); and Len Colodny and Robert Gettlin, "Protecting the Myth: *The Washington Post* and the Second Watergate Cover-up," postscript to the paperback edition, *Silent Coup* (New York: St. Martin's Paperbacks, 1992). On the news media's coverage of domestic security with respect to federal agents' assault on the Waco, Texas, compound of the Branch Davidians, see Dick J. Reavis, *The Ashes of Waco: An Investigation* (New York: Simon & Schuster, 1995); David B. Kopel and Paul H. Blackmon, *No More Wacos: What's Wrong in Law Enforcement and How To Fix It* (Armonk, N.Y.: Prometheus Books, 1997). Also see the movie *Waco: The Rules of Engagement* (Dan Gifford, executive producer, 1997).

52. Sissela Bok, *Lying* (New York: Vintage, 1989), 172–73.

53. At $500 billion, the S&L disaster will cost every American $2,000. Martin Mayer (*The Greatest Ever Bank Robbery* [New York: Collier Books, 1992], 1–2) as well as Kitty Calavita, Henry N. Pontell, and Robert H. Tillman (*Big Money Crime* [Berkeley: University of California Press, 1997], 1) give the half-trillion-dollar price tag, Kathleen Day (*S&L Hell: The People and Politics behind the $1 Trillion Savings and Loan Scandal* [New York: Norton, 1993]) uses the $1 trillion tag, and James Ring Adams (*The Big Fix: Inside the S&L Scandal* [New York: Wiley, 1991], 36, 283, 306) uses the $1.5 trillion figure.

The Teapot Dome scandal involved oil reserves at Teapot Dome, Wyoming, and Elk Hills, California. In 1922, President Harding's secretary of the treasury, Albert Fall, leased the Teapot Dome and Elk Hills oil fields to Harry Sinclair and Edward Doheny, respectively, without competitive bidding. It turned out that both Sinclair and Doheny had "loaned" Fall sizable amounts of money, interest free. Fall was indicted for conspiracy and fined $100,000. Credit Mobilier was a construction company set up under a Pennsylvania charter by Congressmen Oakes Ames and Thomas Durant, both directors of the Union Pacific Railroad Company, and by other Union Pacific directors. The Union Pacific directors secured contracts through the Credit Mobilier company and made profits estimated at $7 million to $23 million, thereby depleting Union Pacific's congressional grants and leaving the railroad company in debt. Ames proceeded to sell Credit Mobilier shares to other members of Congress to forestall investigation.

54. L. William Seidman, *Full Faith and Credit* (New York: Times Books, 1993); James Sterngold, "For Some, It's Still a Wonderful Life," *New York Times*, National Edition, December 8, 1996, E3.

55. Howard Kurtz, *Media Circus: The Trouble with American Newspapers* (New York: Times Books, 1993), 61–68; Day, *S&L Hell;* Calavita et al., *Big Money Crime*, 17. Some

of the most notorious thrifts were Empire Savings and Loans of Mesquite, Texas; Centrust Savings Bank of Miami; the Butchers' United American Bank of Knoxville, Tennessee; Keating's Lincoln Savings and Loan of California; Mario Renda's First United Fund of Garden City, New York; Don Dixon's Vernon Savings and Loan of California; Mike Wise's (and Neil Bush's) Silverado Savings and Loan of Denver; Beverly Hills Savings and Loan; Sunbelt (known as "Gunbelt") Savings; Charles Knapp's Financial Corporation of America and its State Savings and Loan (California); and Lamar Savings and Loan of Austin, Texas.

56. Johnson quoted in "The Theodore H. White Lecture with Senator Warren B. Rudman" (Joan Shorenstein Barone Center on the Press, Politics and Public Policy, John F. Kennedy School of Government, Harvard University, Cambridge, Mass., 1992, bound transcript), 35.

57. Mayer, *The Greatest Ever Bank Robbery,* 3.

58. Ibid., 53, 58–59, 72–78, 115, 123, 132, 140–41, 162–63, 166, 170, 200, 222, 289, 293–96; Adams, *The Big Fix,* 20, 169; Calavita et al., *Big Money Crime,* 72–77; Day, *S&L Hell,* 126, 332, 350, 383–84; Seidman, *Full Faith and Credit,* 192, 226, 233–34. Many of the law firms subsequently had to pay millions of dollars in penalties for their actions on behalf of the S&Ls. Mayer tells of one occasion when a *Wall Street Journal* reporter named Charlie McCoy wanted to write about First Gibralter Savings of Texas: Texas lawyer and Democratic National Committee chair Robert Strauss, a friend of the S&L's owner, J. Livingston Kosberg, "chewed McCoy out on the telephone for a quarter of an hour, informing him that he was close to Warren Phillips, CEO of Dow Jones, and thus McCoy's employer, and Strauss would have his ass if there was stuff in the story of which Strauss disapproved" (*The Greatest Ever Bank Robbery,* 14).

59. Mayer, *The Greatest Ever Bank Robbery,* 140–41 and Appendix C; Day, *S&L Hell,* 210. Adams notes that, as the Federal Reserve chairman, Alan Greenspan presided over a further weakening of the federal regulation of the thrifts (*The Big Fix,* 64–65).

60. Calavita et al., *Big Money Crime,* 169.

61. Ibid., 42.

62. Adams, *The Big Fix,* 226; Mayer, *The Greatest Ever Bank Robbery,* 16, 53; Calavita et al., *Big Money Crime,* 170. One way for the S&Ls to show profits was to conduct fictitious land sales. Another way was to buy back from friends office buildings funded through the S&L, with the friends investing their profit in S&L stock and thus raising the nominal amount of S&L equity (Calavita et al., *Big Money Crime,* 12, 15).

Adams and the investigative journalists Stephen Pizzo, Mary Fricker, and Paul Muolo note the presence of the U.S. Central Intelligence Agency at a number of points in their investigation of the Bank Board and the financial improprieties of the thrifts (Adams, *The Big Fix,* 80, 85, 150–51; Pizzo, Fricker and Muolo, *Inside Job: The Looting of America's Savings and Loans* [New York: McGraw-Hill, 1989], 303–5).

63. Joseph Grundfest quoted in Adams, *The Big Fix,* 304.

64. Mayer, *The Greatest Ever Bank Robbery,* 97–98, 63.

65. Adams, *The Big Fix,* 17–18, 243–48, 251, 253–54. The "disgrace" of the Keating Five—Senators Cranston, DeConcini, McCain, Riegle, and Glenn—was their reaction to Gray's revelation of their support for (and their financial contributions from) Keating: all of the men attempted to deny or conceal their ties with Keating once the story broke (Mayer, *The Greatest Ever Bank Robbery,* 202; Seidman, *Full Faith and Credit,* 232–34).

66. Adams, *The Big Fix,* 47–48, 229–31, 259–60. Adams points out that the House

Ethics Committee was also negligent for not taking action against House Speaker Jim Wright for attempting to fire a Bank Board member (48–50).

67. Adams, *The Big Fix*, 305. See Adams as well as Mayer (*The Greatest Ever Bank Robbery*) for the names of the many members of the House and Senate who received money from the thrifts.

68. Cited in Adams, *The Big Fix*, 308.

69. Ned Eichner, *The Thrift Debacle* (Berkeley: University of California Press, 1989), 130–32, 134; Mayer, *The Greatest Ever Bank Robbery*, 61, 57–89. Pratt went to Merrill Lynch after leaving the Bank Board. Fernand St. Germain, congressional representative from Rhode Island, went on to lose his reelection bid of 1988 and then went to work as a lobbyist for the S&Ls.

70. Mayer, *The Greatest Ever Bank Robbery*, 58; also see Calavita et al., *Big Money Crime*, 94–97. Gray was chair of the Federal Home Loan Bank Board from May 1983 to 1985.

71. Mayer, *The Greatest Ever Bank Robbery*, 202, 259, 269, 271–79; Seidman, *Full Faith and Credit*.

72. Eichner, *The Thrift Debacle*, 135–36; Mayer, *The Greatest Ever Bank Robbery*, 97; Seidman, *Full Faith and Credit*, 181.

73. See Day, *S&L Hell*, 135–37; Kurtz, *Media Circus*, 57–58, 65; Seidman, *Full Faith and Credit*, 79, 183.

74. See Day, *S&L Hell*, 217–19, 316–17; Mayer, *The Greatest Ever Bank Robbery*, 237; Kurtz, *Media Circus*, 57, 65–66; Seidman, *Full Faith and Credit*, 111.

75. Adams, *The Big Fix*, 59; Mayer, *The Greatest Ever Bank Robbery*, 261; Kurtz, *Media Circus*, 58. Both Texas Senator (and Dukakis Vice President) Lloyd Bentsen and House Speaker Jim Wright told the Dukakis campaign to lay off the thrift issue (William Greider, *Who Will Tell the People: The Betrayal of American Democracy* [New York: Touchstone Books, 1992], 75; Seidman, *Full Faith and Credit*, 189–90).

76. Kurtz, *Media Circus*, 58–61.

77. Ibid., 47–48.

78. Adams, *The Big Fix*, 35, 41, 60. This conclusion came despite revelations of Wright's receipt of a free Cadillac (which Wright did not mention) and a book deal serving as a conduit for the contribution of campaign funds (34–35).

79. Kurtz, *Media Circus*, 53–54, 61.

80. Adams, *The Big Fix*, 283–84 (Adams, a writer for the *Wall Street Journal*, indentifies the *Journal*'s editorial page as Milken's "unpaid defender" [285]); Sterngold, "For Some, It's Still a Wonderful Life"; Eichler, *The Thrift Debacle*, 139. Sterngold claims that "few people seemed to care" when Charles Keating was released, that the United States has "moved on," and that records show that the "chicanery of some savings and loan owners . . . accounted for a modest portion of the losses—perhaps 5 percent." None of these claims is substantiated by a single reference to a government document or identifiable source. Eichler notes that the bailout figure is low for at least four reasons that overstate the assets of the S&Ls.

81. See Stephen Hess, *The Washington Reporters* (Washington, D.C.: Brookings, 1981).

82. Kurtz, *Media Circus*, 49; Stephen Hess, in "The Theodore H. White Lecture with Senator Warren B. Rudman" (Joan Shorenstein Barone Center on the Press, Politics and Public Policy, John F. Kennedy School of Government, Harvard University, Cambridge, Mass., 1992, bound transcript), 39; Seidman, *Full Faith and Credit*, 193.

83. Adams, *The Big Fix,* 284; Calavita et al., *Big Money Crime,* 17–18. Many of the books on the S&Ls also personalize the problem by focusing on the outrageous actions and fraud perpetrated by some of the most egregious thrift owners (e.g., Day, *S&L Hell,* and Pizzo et al., *Inside Job*).

84. Kurtz, *Media Circus.*

85. Mayer, *The Greatest Ever Bank Robbery,* 28.

86. As one Washington, D.C., man asked Danny Wall in a House Banking Committee hearing on the hundreds of millions of dollars being made by Ron Perelman, "Why is it only white folks who get that kind of deal?" (quoted in Mayer, *The Greatest Ever Bank Robbery,* 259). Howard Kurtz observes that a recent parallel to the S&L scandal is the story of the Orange County (California) financial disaster (interview by author, July 25, 1995).

87. James Kinsella, *Covering the Plague: AIDS and the American Media* (New Brunswick, N.J.: Rutgers University Press, 1989); Timothy E. Cook and David C. Colby, "The Mass-Mediated Epidemic: The Politics of AIDS on the Nightly Network News," in *AIDS: The Making of a Chronic Disease,* ed. Elizabeth Fee and Daniel M. Fox (Berkeley: University of California Press); Timothy E. Cook, "Notes for the Next Epidemic, Part One: Lessons from the News Coverage of AIDS" (Discussion Paper D-12, the Joan Shorenstein Barone Center on the Press, Politics and Public Policy, John F. Kennedy School of Government, Harvard University, Cambridge, Mass., October 1991); Randy Shilts, *And The Band Played On: Politics, People, and the AIDS Epidemic* (New York: Penguin, 1987).

88. Cook, "Notes for the Next Epidemic."

89. Randy Shilts, *And The Band Played On,* 294, 183–84, 617.

90. David C. Colby and Timothy E. Cook, "Epidemics and Agendas: The Politics of Nightly News Coverage of AIDS," *Journal of Health Politics, Policy and Law* 16 (1991): 245.

91. Shilts, *And The Band Played On,* 110.

92. Ibid., 601. Also see Sandra Panem, *The AIDS Bureaucracy* (Cambridge, Mass.: Harvard University Press, 1988), 120–24; Cook, "Notes for the Next Epidemic," 2–5.

93. Shilts, *And The Band Played On,* 384. On the *New York Times's* and Associated Press's handling of the AIDS story, see Kinsella, *Covering the Plague,* 48–58, 68–86.

94. Shilts, *And The Band Played On,* 126, 172, 183; Russell Neuman, Marion Just, and Ann Crigler, *Common Knowledge* (Chicago: University of Chicago Press, 1992), 118. There are comparative cases: Legionnaire's disease in the mid-1970s; the toxic waste discovered in 1978 in Love Canal, New York; and the Tylenol poisoning of 1982 (Shilts, *And The Band Played On,* 143–44, 268; Mayer, *Making News*).

95. Shilts, *And The Band Played On,* 535–36. On the lack of funding from the Reagan administration, also see Kinsella, *Covering the Plague,* 3; Charles Perrow and Mauro F. Guillén, *The AIDS Disaster: The Failure of Organizations in New York and the Nation* (New Haven, Conn.: Yale University Press, 1980), 50–52. Curiously, these authors do not address the failure of news organizations.

96. Shilts, *And The Band Played On,* 617; also see Cook and Colby, "The Mass-Mediated Epidemic."

97. Shilts, *And The Band Played On,* 617–18.

98. Colby and Cook, "Epidemics and Agendas," 244; Shilts, *And The Band Played On,* 267, 320, 350–51, 577–79; Opinion Roundup, "AIDS: A Multi-Country Assessment," *Public Opinion* 10, no. 2 (1988): 36–39, cited in Neuman et al., *Common Knowl-*

edge, 48. Also see Shilts on the general tardiness of the news media's focus on AIDS (*And The Band Played On*, 600–601).

99. David R. Boldt, "Aiding AIDS: The Story of a Media Virus," *Media Critic*, fall 1996, 48–57; Amanda Bennett and Anita Sharpe, "AIDS Fight Is Skewed By Federal Campaign Exaggerating Risks," *Wall Street Journal*, May 1, 1996, 1; Michael Fumento, *The Myth of Heterosexual AIDS: How a Tragedy Has Been Distorted by the Media and Partisan Politics* (New York: Basic Books, 1990). Also see the work of John Crewdson of the *Chicago Tribune*.

100. Colby and Cook, "Epidemics and Agendas," 246; Shilts, *And The Band Played On*, 617.

101. Naessens studied physics, biology, and chemistry at the Union Scientifique Francaise in Lille during World War II, but he did not get the degree equivalent from the postwar de Gaulle government—a fact that led to accusations that he did not have a college degree.

102. Naessens quoted in Raymond Keith Brown, *AIDS, Cancer and the Medical Establishment* (New York: Robert Speller, 1986), 104.

103. Bechamp's best known book was *Le Sang* (1908), translated as *The Blood*.

104. Cited in "Seeing Is Believing: Gaston Naessens and the New Biology: Part I," *Bio/Tech News* (Portland, Ore.), special issue, 1993, 3. Naessens uses similar phrasing: "Conventionalists say that cancer is a local affliction that becomes generalized. I say 'Cancer is a general systemic illness that becomes localized'" (quoted in Christopher Bird, *The Persecution and Trial of Gaston Naessens* [Tiberon, Calif.: H. R. Kramer, 1991], 178). Also see Christopher Bird, "What Has Become of the Rife Microscope?" *New Age*, March 1976, 41–47.

105. Dr. Yale quoted in "Seeing Is Believing," 4; Louisa Williams, "From Bechamp's Microzyma to Naessens' Somatid," *The American Raum and Zeit: The New Dimension in Scientific Research* 3, no. 1 (1991): 52–53. Also see Christopher Bird, "What Has Become of the Rife Microscope?" 41–47. The research by Rife and others using his equipment was opposed by many of his contemporaries, who, without the special optical equipment, could not duplicate their findings.

106. Lini S. Kadaba, "A Brave, Lonely Fight," *Chicago Tribune*, September 9, 1994, Evening Update Edition, 7; Karen Hayes, "Norwell Youth Now Free of Cancer, Tests Show," *Boston Globe*, April 6, 1995, A32; Robin Estrin, "Boy Who Ran Away from Chemotherapy Cancer-Free," *Portsmouth (N.H.) Herald*, November 23, 1995, 8; Jim Memmott, "Woman Fights Cancer by Using Alternative Drug," *Rochester Democrat and Chronicle*, December 10, 1995, 1B; Paul Buker, "Exploring the Options," *The Oregonian*, October 25, 1996, Sect. A; Anita Messina, "Introducing the Controversial 714-X," *The Citizen* (Auburn, New York), October 31, 1996, C1; Steve Wieberg, "Boise State Coach Watches Team from Afar," *USA Today*, October 17, 1996, 1C. Other stories predate 1994.

107. Raymond Keith Brown, "AIDS: A Perspective," *American Clinical Products Review*, November 1987, 44–47; P. A. MacOmber, "Cancer and Cell Wall Deficient Bacteria," *Medical Hypotheses* 32 (1990): 1–9; *Health Consciousness* 11, no. 6 (1990): 12–26; Williams, "From Bechamp's Microzyma to Naessens' Somatid," 52–56; Leslie Kenton, "What the Microscope Can Reveal," *International Journal of Alternative and Complementary Medicine*, January 1992, 11–12; "Blood Feud," *Saturday Night*, December 1992, 51ff; Judith Hooper, "Unconventional Cancer Treatments," *Omni*, February 1993, 59ff; Stephanie Hiller, "A New Answer to Cancer," *Yoga Journal*, September/October

1993, 40ff; "Seeing Is Believing," 1–8; "Somatids, 714-X and Curing Cancer: Gaston Naessens and the New Biology, Part II," *Bio/Tech News* (Portland, Ore.), special issue, 1993, 1–12; Steven Elswick, "The Amazing Wonders of Gaston Naessens," *Nexus 2*, no. 18 (1994): 43–45; Roxanne Davies, "Choosing Complementary Cancer Treatments," *Health Action*, July 1995, reprint; *The Cancer Chronicles* (special double issue) 5, nos. 5/6 (1995): 1–16.

108. See Brown, *AIDS, Cancer and the Medical Establishment*; Bird, *Gaston Naessens*; Richard Walters, *Options: The Alternative Cancer Therapy Book* (Garden City Park, Wash.: Avery, 1992); Leon Chaitow and James Strohecker, *You Don't Have To Die* (Puyallup, Wash.: Future Medical Publishing, 1994); Ross Pelton with Lee Overholzer, *Alternative in Cancer Therapy: The Complete Guide to Non-traditional Treatments* (New York: Fireside, 1994); Ralph W. Moss, *Cancer Therapy: The Independent Consumer's Guide to Non-Toxic Treatment and Prevention* (New York: Equinox Press, 1993).

109. See Bird, *Gaston Naessens*.

110. Stephen Budiansky, "Cures or Quackery?" *U.S. News*, July 17, 1995, 48–51.

111. Denis McQuail, *Media Performance: Mass Communication and the Public Interest* (Newbury Park, Calif.: Sage, 1992), 174–75. The *FAIR Reader* gives other examples of such neglect: foreign nationals in the case of the Panamanians killed in the U.S. invasion of 1989 and the American workers made worse off as a result of NAFTA (12, 132).

112. Page, *Who Deliberates?*; Bennett and Paletz, eds., *Taken by Storm*.

113. Quoted in *The MacNeil/Lehrer NewsHour*, August 31, 1984, Transcript #2330 (Educational Broadcasting Corporation and GWETA, Arlington, Va.). Eagleburger added, "What all of these arguments come down to, including Mr. Keppel's, is that senior U.S. government officials, including either implicitly or explicitly the President of the United States, engaged in a conspiracy which put at risk the lives of 269 innocent people . . . Neither the President nor the senior officials of the U.S. government play with people's lives this way."

114. Barbara Allen, Paula O'Laughlin, Amy Jasperson, and John L. Sullivan, "The Media and the Gulf War: Framing, Priming, and the Spiral of Silence," *Polity* 27 (1994): 277, 272–73.

115. Allen et al., "The Media and the Gulf War," 278–79. Also see Carol Cohn, "The Language of the Gulf War," *Center Review: Publication of the Center for Psychological Studies in the Nuclear Age* (Harvard Medical School) 5 (1991).

116. See, especially, Pearson, *KAL 007*; Johnson, *Shootdown*; Rachlin, *News as Hegemonic Reality*, 35–92.

117. Tom Brokaw on the NBC Nightly News, June 17, 1982, quoted in Cook and Colby, "The Mass-Mediated Epidemic," 93; also see Cook and Colby for an account of the news media's framing of the AIDS story (84–122). In smaller and alternative publications, the Naessens case has been portrayed as one of the individual entrepreneur—the underdog—tackling big government and the medical-industrial complex.

118. Quoted in Kurtz, *Media Circus*, 43. Also see Everette Dennis et al., *The Media at War: The Press and the Persian Gulf Conflict* (New York: Gannett Foundation Media Center, 1991); Smith, ed., *The Media and the Gulf War*; MacArthur, *Second Front*; Fialka, *Hotel Warriors*; Kurtz, *Media Circus*.

119. Cited in McQuail, *Media Performance*, 38–39. I take these as representative of the news media. Also see McManus on the discrepancy between the behavior of news

organizations and the professed ethics of journalists (*Market-Driven Journalism: Let the Citizen Beware?* [Thousand Oaks, Calif.: Sage, 1994], 168–69).

120. See Mayer, *Making the News*.

121. There are several other examples of stories gone unreported by the U.S. news media. One is that bribes were paid to the Brazilian government by Raytheon Corporation for a $1.4 billion Amazon radar surveillance system (Reuters, "'Pink File' Scandal Hits Brazil Government," December 8, 1995; idem, "Brazil Scandal Seen Hampering Reform Drive," December 14, 1995; idem, "Brazil President Backs Down from Amazon Contracts," December 16, 1995). A second is that clean-up of radioactive waste from decades of cold war nuclear weapons production is going to cost from $230 billion to $350 billion (Associated Press, "Cleanup of Radioactive Waste to Cost at Least $230 Billion," *Austin American-Statesman*, April 14, 1995). Another is Larry Agran's 1992 Democratic candidacy for the presidency (S. Robert Lichter and Richard E. Noyes, *Good Intentions Make Bad News*, 2d ed. [Lanham, Md.: Rowman & Littlefield, 1996], 167–68); on Agran, also see Janny Scott, "Finally '92 Candidate Is Getting Say, in Court," *New York Times*, August 28, 1996, B1. Pamela Shoemaker and Stephen D. Reese point out unreported stories of nuclear mishaps, preparation for biological warfare, the fact that the space shuttle carries plutonium, and Third World toxic waste dumping (*Mediating the Message: Theories of Influences on Mass Media Content* [White Plains, N.Y.: Longman, 1994], 95). Also see Herman and Chomsky, *Manufacturing Consent*; Hertsgaard, *On Bended Knee*.

Some of these stories are included in the Project Censored yearbook list, which explains 25 stories that did not receive significant attention by the major media. The list is compiled by twelve seminar researchers and then winnowed down by a panel of nineteen writers and journalists. In 1990 and 1991, the top "censored" stories were the lead-up and conduct of the Gulf War, and in other years Project Censored has focused on media concentration and disinformation campaigns by the executive branch (Carl Jensen and Project Censored, *Censored: The News That Didn't Make the News—and Why, The 1994 Project Censored Yearbook* [New York: Four Walls Eight Windows Press, 1994], 183–89).

122. Diane Vaughan, *The Challenger Launch Decision: Risky Technology, Culture, and Deviance at NASA* (Chicago: University of Chicago Press, 1996), 394. Neuman et al. refer to the middle and late 1980s as a period of "politics as usual" because there was no war, no energy or hostage crisis, and no popular uprisings (as there were in the 1960s and early 1970s) (*Common Knowledge*, 41).

123. For example, Ken Auletta, *Three Blind Mice: How the Three Networks Lost Their Way* (New York: Random House, 1991); Ben Bagdikian, *The Media Monopoly*, 4th ed. (Boston: Beacon Press, 1992); Doug Underwood, *When MBAs Rule the Newsroom* (New York: Columbia University Press, 1993); James Squires, *Read All About It!* (New York: Times Books, 1993); Neuman et al., *Common Knowledge*; Marion R. Just, Ann N. Crigler, Dean E. Alger, et al., *Crosstalk: Citizens, Candidates, and the Media in a Presidential Campaign* (Chicago: University of Chicago Press, 1996); Diane C. Mutz, "Contextualizing Personal Experience: The Role of Mass Media," *Journal of Politics* 56 (1994): 689–714.

124. These mistakes are especially striking in view of the fact that the cases meet three out of four of Herbert Gans's substantive criteria for importance: the stories "impact the nation and the national interest," they "impact on large numbers of people,"

and they have "significance for the past and future." The cases do not match Gans's criterion of "rank[ing] in governmental and other hierarchies." The fact that these news stories did not rank in the U.S. government—despite the fact that they meet the other three of Gans's criteria—points to the importance of the media as an index of governmental positions (*Deciding What's News* [New York: Vintage, 1980], 147–52). Jack Fuller notes that "loyalty to country" should be a central and enduring value of journalists (*News Values: Ideas for an Information Age* [Chicago: University of Chicago Press, 1996], 89–91), but he does not address how one defines such loyalty.

125. Thomas Patterson, *Out of Order* (New York: Knopf, 1993). Also see William A. Gamson, *Talking Politics* (Cambridge: Cambridge University Press, 1992), 179–80; Joel Kotkin and David Friedman, "Clueless: Why the Elite Media Don't Understand America," *The American Enterprise*, March/April 1998, 28–32.

126. Tom Wicker, interview by author, December 6, 1996. Also see Gaye Tuchman, *Making News: A Study in the Construction of Reality* (New York: Free Press, 1978); Todd Gitlin, *The Whole World Is Watching* (Berkeley: University of California Press, 1980); Fishman, *Manufacturing the News.*

127. Gitlin, *The Whole World Is Watching*, 254–55, 269–70, 274; Tuchman, *Making News*; also see Gans, *Deciding What's News.*

128. James G. March and Johan P. Olsen, *Rediscovering Institutions: The Organizational Basis of Politics* (New York: Free Press, 1989), 47.

129. Rick Marin and T. Trent Gegax, "Conspiracy Mania Feeds Our Growing National Paranoia," *Newsweek*, December 30, 1996/January 6, 1997, 64–71, 72. Also see Liz Spayd, "Welcome to the State of Paranoia: Why Americans Wallow in Waco and Whitewater," *Washington Post*, July 23, 1995, C1; Tina Rosenberg, "Crazy for Conspiracies," *New York Times*, December 31, 1996, A13; Philip Weiss, "Clinton Crazy," *New York Times Magazine*, February 23, 1997, 34.

130. Tuchman, *Making News*, 87.

131. E. E. Schattschneider, *The Semisovereign People* (Hinsdale, Ill.: Dryden Press, 1975 [1960]), 106–7.

132. Michael Kelly, "David Gergen, Master of The Game," *New York Times Magazine*, October 31, 1993, 64, 65. Matthew Kerbel uses slightly different words to describe the same phenomenon: "Through publicity, the media made the press manipulation of the war room legitimate. Being a hired gun became cool" (*Remote and Controlled* [Boulder, Colo.: Westview Press, 1995], 83). Also see Kevin Phillips, *Arrogant Capital* (Boston: Back Bay Books, 1995).

SEVEN Reforming Political Communication

1. The Gallup Poll, 1993, quoted in Matthew R. Kerbel, *Remote and Controlled* (Boulder, Colo.: Westview Press, 1995), 14.

2. Reginald Stuart, "A Year of Sizzle Boosts Audiences, Arms Our Critics," *The Quill* 82, no. 9 (1994): 56; *The People, the Press, and Their Leaders* (Times-Mirror Center for the People and the Media, 1995).

3. Jon Katz, "The Capital Gang Bang: The Failure of the Washington Press Corps," *Rolling Stone*, August 19, 1993, 37ff.

4. See Kerbel, *Remote and Controlled;* Paul Weaver, *News and the Culture of Lying* (New York: Free Press, 1994). In response to the statement "I don't think public officials care much about what people like me think," 64 percent of those surveyed in 1990 by the National Election Studies agreed, and 23 percent disagreed; in 1960, 15 percent agreed

and 73 percent disagreed. In response to the question "Would you say that the government is pretty much run by a few big interests looking out for themselves or that it is run for the benefit of all people?", 76 percent of those polled in 1992 said "few big interests," and 20 percent said "benefit of all"; in 1964, 29 percent answered "few big interests," and 64 percent responded "benefit of all" (cited in Weaver, *News and the Culture of Lying*, 19).

5. See Benjamin I. Page, *Who Deliberates? Mass Media in Modern Democracy* (Chicago: University of Chicago Press, 1996); Thomas Patterson, *Out of Order* (New York: Knopf, 1993); Russell Neuman, Marion Just, and Ann Crigler, *Common Knowledge: News and the Construction of Political Meaning* (Chicago: University of Chicago Press, 1992).

6. Stinchcombe, *Theoretical Methods in Social History* (New York: Academic Press, 1978), 40, cited in Elisabeth Clemens, *The People's Lobby* (Chicago: University of Chicago Press), 323.

7. I do not mention or recommend several reforms. I agree with Kerbel, for one, that electronic "town meetings" and talk radio are poor substitutes for genuine reforms. They represent the promise and appearance of participation and engagement, but they are necessarily highly restricted in the number and range of views that get expressed and are not good at holding politicians accountable (*Remote and Controlled*, 131–33).

8. Edwin Baker notes that the effect of this taxation and subsidy plan would likely be increased cover prices for low-circulation, advertising-rich publications and lowered cover prices for high-circulation publications that receive proportionately less in advertising revenues. But the exact effects on cover prices, circulation, and investment by media companies in news coverage would depend on the specific market and management strategies (*Advertising and a Democratic Press* [Princeton, N.J.: Princeton University Press, 1994], 83–91). This reform is consistent with Weaver's recommendation that news organizations reorient themselves away from advertisers and toward readers (*News and the Culture of Lying*, 209–10).

9. Weaver, *News and the Culture of Lying*, 211.

10. Ibid.; Dean E. Alger, *The Media and Politics*, 2d ed. (Belmont, Calif.: Wadsworth, 1996), 104–5, 112–15.

11. Benno Schmidt, "The First Amendment and the Press," in *What's News: The Media in America*, ed. Elie Abel (San Francisco: Institute for Contemporary Studies, 1981), 60, 80; also see "The National Entertainment State," editorial, *The Nation*, June 3, 1996, 23–27. Schmidt equivocates at the end of the article, claiming that big media are better able to counteract big government. Since there is reason to believe that more overlap than antagonism exists between news organizations and the government, I emphasize Schmidt's first point and read him as supportive of a diverse marketplace of ideas.

12. Learned Hand quoted in Schmidt, "The First Amendment and the Press," 60.

13. Research on the effects of newspaper monopolies in what had been formerly two-newspaper markets is inconclusive. The general effects of monopolization on local content, diversity of information, and editorial independence have been small or unclear (Denis McQuail, *Media Performance: Mass Communication and the Public Interest* [Newbury Park, Calif.: Sage, 1992], 115–17).

14. Commission on the Freedom of the Press, *Government and Mass Communications*, vol. 2 (Chicago: University of Chicago Press, 1947), 537, 585–86. Also see McQuail, *Media Performance*, 37.

15. For purposes of calculating this aggregate audience reach, UHF stations were attributed with only 50 percent of the audience of VHF stations (because UHF signals deteriorate more rapidly than VHF signals). This rule went into effect after the 12—12—12 rule of media ownership (12 FM, 12 AM, and 12 TV stations) passed in 1984. Also see Neil Hickey, "Revolution in Cyberia," *Columbia Journalism Review*, July/August 1995, 40–47.

16. Commission on Freedom of the Press, *Government and Mass Communications*, 537–94. For a discussion of newspaper monopolies, see Bagdikian, *The Media Monopoly*; Robert Entman, *Democracy without Citizens* (New York: Oxford University Press, 1989), 95–96.

17. See, for instance, John Ellis, "Nine Sundays: A Proposal for Better Campaign Coverage" (Joan Shorenstein Barone Center on the Press, Politics and Public Policy, John F. Kennedy School of Government, Harvard University, Cambridge, Mass., n.d.). Also see Fred Wertheimer, "TV Ad Wars: How To Reduce the Costs of Television Advertising in Our Political Campaigns" (paper presented at the Joan Shorenstein Center on the Press, Politics and Public Policy, John F. Kennedy School of Government, Harvard University, Cambridge, Mass., December 1996). Former NBC News president Larry Grossman also attacks the ill-effects of money on contemporary politics (*The Electronic Republic* [New York: Viking, 1995], 182–86). I do not discuss the desirable reform of PBS and the Corporation for Public Broadcasting. See Entman, *Democracy without Citizens*, 135–36; Kerbel, *Remote and Controlled*, 133–34; Laurence Jarvik, *PBS: Behind the Screen* (Rocklin, Calif.: Prima, 1995); Grossman, *The Electronic Republic*, 210–17; David Croteau and William Hoynes, *By Invitation Only* (Monroe, Maine: Common Courage, 1994), 107–69; Jeff Cohen and Norman Solomon, *Adventures in Medialand* (Monroe, Maine: Common Courage, 1993), 231–33.

18. George Will and others caricature the public finance of campaigns as politicians on welfare. They neglect the fact that the public pays for the present system of campaign finance in the currency of bad policy and policy inaction, given the ability of special interests, whether a particular industry, union, or age group, to veto legislation with broad public appeal. (Nor would the public financing of electoral campaigns cost more than a few dollars per person a year.)

19. Kerbel remarks, "Proactive change is more likely to come about from reformers tinkering with the rules of the game, a shift that could be more meaningful if it involves party rather than media reform. This may seem an odd claim, given the argument that party reform got us into the present situation. But if the media have become the default vehicle for performing functions that were better handled by parties, perhaps playing with the rules a bit more is not such a bad thing" (*Remote and Controlled*, 140–41).

20. See Fuller, *News Values*. Also see Norman H. Nie, Jane Junn, and Kenneth Stehlik-Barry, *Education and Democratic Citizenship in America* (Chicago: University of Chicago Press, 1996).

21. For other journalistic reforms, including the expansion and reinforcement of the role of media ombudsmen, see Larry Sabato, *Feeding Frenzy* (New York: Free Press, 1991), 226–44. Also see the reforms listed by John Robinson and Mark Levy, *The Main Source: Learning from Television News* (Beverly Hills, Calif.: Sage, 1986), 223–27.

22. Patterson, *Out of Order*; Kerbel, *Remote and Controlled*. These reforms are consistent with S. Robert Lichter and Richard E. Noyes's suggestions that journalists "lose the attitude" (*Good Intentions Make Bad News*, 2d ed. [Lanham, Md.: Rowman & Lit-

tlefield, 1996], 272–74) and "cover the campaign" (274–76). For reforms in the coverage of politicians' personal lives, see Sabato, *Feeding Frenzy*, 213–25.

23. Patterson, *Out of Order*, 43; Fuller, *News Values*, 192.

24. Tim Weiner, "CIA Chief Disciplines Official for Disclosure," *New York Times*, December 6, 1996, A20.

25. Kenneth T. Walsh, *Feeding the Beast: The White House Versus the Press* (New York: Random House, 1996), 270–71; Tom Rosenstiel quoted at 270.

26. Philip Shenon, "Schwarzkopf Says He Doubts Chemical Arms Caused Health Troubles of Gulf Veterans," *New York Times*, December 6, 1996, A36. Just below the story on Schwarzkopf was a story on the destruction of an Iraqi ammunition depot that had stored nerve gas and other chemical weapons; the reporter had his or her byline stripped ("Pentagon Describes Contents of Bunker," *New York Times*, December 6, 1996, A36).

27. Philip Shenon, "Pentagon Says It Knew of Chemical Arms Risks," *New York Times*, February 26, 1997, A11; idem, "Gulf War Panel Will Investigate Warning Lapse," *New York Times*, February 27, 1997, A1.

28. Weaver, *News and the Culture of Lying*, 197–203; John Dancy, interviews by author, September 9, 12, and 18, 1996. There is already evidence that some shows do exactly this. Between stories about O. J. Simpson in January 1997, for instance, ABC's *Prime Time* ran programs on Newt Gingrich's ethics problems and on rape and genocide in Rwanda.

29. Weaver, *News and the Culture of Lying*, 207–9.

30. Jason Vest, "Will Microsoft Squash the Alternative Press?" *U.S. News*, July 28, 1997, 45.

31. James Fallows, *Breaking the News: How the Media Undermine American Democracy* (New York: Pantheon, 1996); Chris Conte, "Civic Journalism: Can Press Reform Revitalize Democracy," *CQ Researcher* 6 (1996): 817–40; Jay Rosen, *Getting the Connections Right* (New York: Twentieth Century Fund Press, 1996); "Civic Journalism . . . What's Happening?" *Civic Catalyst* (Pew Center for Civic Journalism), June 1995, 4ff; Jay Rosen, "Public Journalism: A Case for Public Scholarship," in *Standing with the Public: The Humanities and Democratic Practice*, ed. James F. Veninga and Noëlle McAfee (New York: Kettering Foundation Press, 1997), 126. Civic journalism is further consistent with Weaver's proposed reform that journalists define themselves as "citizens, not professionals" (*News and the Culture of Lying*, 205–7). Also see Walsh, *Feeding the Beast*, 303–5.

32. The Harwood Group, cited in Fuller, *News Values*, 194; Fuller, *News Values*, 194; Ed Fouhy, interview by author, September 7, 1995; John Mashek, interview by author, July 18, 1995.

33. Although the experiment in civic journalism in the fall of 1996 in North Carolina received a great deal of criticism (e.g., William E. Jackson Jr., "The Press Cops Out," *New York Times*, October 7, 1996; Curtis Willkie, "'Public Journalism' Plays Out in N.C.," *Boston Globe*, October 30, 1996, A1; Michael Kelly, "'Media Culpa,'" *New Yorker*, November 4, 1996, 45–49; Lawrence Jarvik, "Pitfalls of 'Public Journalism,'" *Washington Post*, November 16, 1996; Brian McQuarrie, "Press Critic Decries 'Civic Journalism,'" *Boston Globe*, November 15, 1996), the full story has not yet been told. Even if the North Carolina experiment in the news coverage of the Helms-Gantt senate race did err, one can hardly condemn a whole set of ideas (civic journalism) on the basis of one example (the North Carolina senatorial election campaign). Furthermore,

a sole focus on North Carolina neglects the dozens of other communities where local newspapers are to varying degrees implementing civic journalism.

34. Commission on the Freedom of the Press, *A Free and Responsible Press: A General Report on Mass Communication: Newspapers, Radio, Motion Pictures, Magazines, and Books* (Chicago: University of Chicago Press, 1947), 18, emphasis added. The commission was composed of a number of academics as well as the chair of the Federal Reserve Bank of New York. See Richard N. Rosenfeld, *American Aurora, A Democratic Republican Returns* (New York: St. Martin's, 1997).

35. See Conte, "Civic Journalism"; Neuman et al., *Common Knowledge;* Roderick P. Hart, *Seducing America: How Television Charms the Modern Voter* (New York: Oxford University Press, 1994); also see "Civic Journalism . . . What's Happening," *Civic Catalyst.*

36. James Fallows, who advocates civic journalism in the last chapter of *Breaking the News,* had the chance to put his ideas into practice at *U.S. News.* See, for example, James Fallows, "Walking the Walk," interview by Alicia C. Shepard, *American Journalism Review,* November 1996, 40. *U.S. News* still very much engages in service journalism, however (see the discussion of market journalism in Chapter 4). Also see William John Fox, "Junk News" (Discussion Paper D-26, the Joan Shorenstein Center on the Press, Politics and Public Policy, John F. Kennedy School of Government, Harvard University, Cambridge, Mass., August 1997).

37. Edwin Diamond and Robert A. Silverman, *White House to Your House* (Cambridge, Mass.: MIT Press, 1994), 103; Weaver, *News and the Culture of Lying,* 24–25. Then there is President Nixon's lie in March 1969 about the bombing of Cambodia. Although the United States dropped 110,000 tons of bombs over the course of fourteen months, Nixon said, "It never happened" (Ben Bradlee, "The Annual Theodore H. White Lecture with Ben Bradlee" [Joan Shorenstein Center on the Press, Politics and Public Policy, John F. Kennedy School of Government, Harvard University, Cambridge, Mass., 1991, bound transcript]).

38. See Doris Graber, *Processing the News: How People Tame the Information Tide* (White Plains, N.Y.: Longman, 1984), 203; Patterson, *Out of Order,* 187.

39. Weaver, *News and the Culture of Lying,* 31.

40. Bradlee, "The Theodore H. White Lecture with Ben Bradlee." Robert Donovan and Ray Scherer make the interesting suggestion that journalists could adopt the style of sports reporting to cover politics. Sports reporting is colorful and rarely objective; it identifies with a team (i.e., with a mission and a community) and then comments boldly about how well the coach or players are doing to realize the promise of that team (*Unsilent Revolution: Television News and American Public Life,* Woodrow Wilson Center Series [New York: Cambridge University Press, 1992], 283–91).

41. Howell Raines, "The Fallows Fallacy," *New York Times,* February 24, 1996, A14. Columnist and reporter Maureen Dowd criticizes civic journalism, too: "We don't need Mr. Fallows's version of 'public journalism,'" since Fallows romanticizes the past ("Raffish and Rowdy," *New York Times,* March 31, 1996, E15).

42. Rich Oppel, interviews by author, May 3 and June 8, 1996; Buzz Merritt quoted in Fouhy, "Setting the Record Straight," *Civic Catalyst,* October 1996, 3.

43. David Broder gave the keynote address at the James K. Batten Symposium on Civic Journalism, Washington, D.C., September 13, 1995; Fuller, *News Values,* 193–94.

44. Jon Roe, "When Citizens Asked the Questions, Viewers Tuned In," *Civic Catalyst,* January 1997, 9; Tom Bier, "Ratings: A Runaway Winner," *Civic Catalyst,* October 1995, 11.

45. On the use of the word "terrorism," see David Paletz, J. Z. Ayanian, and P. A. Fozzard, "The I.R.A., the Red Brigades, and the F.A.L.N. in the New York Times," *Journal of Communication* 32, no. 2 (1982): 162–71; McQuail, *Media Performance,* 247.

46. See Weaver, *News and the Culture of Lying,* 201.

47. See David L. Altheide, *Creating Reality: How TV News Distorts Events* (Beverly Hills, Calif.: Sage, 1974), 28; John H. McManus, *Market-Driven Journalism: Let the Citizen Beware?* (Thousand Oaks, Calif.: Sage, 1994), 208–10.

48. See, for instance, Page, *Who Deliberates?* 126–27; Weaver, *News and the Culture of Lying,* 215–16.

49. Although total book sales have increased on a per capita basis, sales of new books that relate to politics (history, law, sociology, economics, and general works) have declined slightly in number from 1980 through 1991.

50. Hart, *Seducing America.*

51. CommerceNet and Nielsen Media Research cited in the *Washington Post,* March 13, 1997.

52. On the survival of newspapers, see Fuller, *News Values,* 223–31; Richard Harwood, "Commentary," in *The Future of News: Television–Newspapers–Wire Services–Newsmagazines,* ed. Philip Cook, Douglas Gomery, and Lawrence Lichty (Washington, D.C.: Woodrow Wilson Center Press; Baltimore: Johns Hopkins University Press, 1992), 104–9; John Morton, interview by author, July 11, 1995.

53. The omission of the middle-man is called "disintermediation" in business language. I use the word "de-mediate" to specify the excision of the news *media* from the mediation of political information.

54. See David Bank, "How Net Is Becoming More Like Television," *Wall Street Journal,* December 13, 1996, A1. For an example of the weak commercial impact of the Internet at present, see Thomas Weber, "Simplest E-Mail Queries Confound Companies," *Wall Street Journal,* October 21, 1996, B1. Thirty-two percent of persons say they use the Internet for e-mail, 24 percent for research, 22 percent for news and information, 19 percent for entertainment, 13 percent for education, and 8 percent for chat lines and chat rooms (Odyssey Ventures, Inc., cited in Thomas Weber, "Who Uses the Internet?" *Wall Street Journal,* December 9, 1996, R6ff).

55. See, for instance, the discussion by Thomas W. Benson, "Desktop Demos: New Communication Technologies and the Future of the Rhetorical Presidency," in *Beyond the Rhetorical Presidency,* ed. Martin J. Medhurst (College Station: Texas A&M Press), 70–72.

56. Much of the following material comes from the honors thesis of Sharad Sushil Khandelwal, "Illusions of Technology: An Examination of How Advanced Technology Affects Political Dissent," University of Texas at Austin, May 1995. Former NBC News president Lawrence Grossman believes that the technologies of freedom will put too much power in the hands of individual citizens. Unlike Orwell's Big Brother image of the government monitoring citizens, Grossman believes the future will evidence information flow in all directions, from the top down as well as from the bottom up (*The Electronic Republic,* 12–13).

57. Peter F. Eder, "Privacy on Parade," *The Futurist,* July-August 1994, 38; Barbara Starr, "Woolsey: Why the CIA Is Still in Need of Human Touch," *Jane's Defense Weekly,* August 1994, 4.

58. Khandelwal, "Illusions of Technology," 52.

59. Erik Ness, "Big Brother @ Cyberspace," *The Progressive,* December 1994, 22;

Karen Nussbaum and Virginia doRivage, "Computer Monitoring," *Business and Society Review,* winter 1986, 16.

60. Also see John Thompson on how the media decouple space and time in human relations (Thompson, *The Media and Modernity: A Social Theory of the Media* [Stanford, Calif.: Stanford University Press, 1995]).

61. Joshua Meyrowitz, *No Sense of Place: The Impact of Electronic Media on Social Behavior* (New York: Oxford University Press, 1986).

62. E. E. Schattschneider, *The Semisovereign People: A Realist's View of Democracy in America* (Hinsdale, Ill.: Dryden Press, 1975 [1960]), 34–35; David B. Truman, *The Governmental Process: Political Interests and Public Opinion,* 2d ed. (New York: Knopf, 1971 [1951]).

63. Mancur Olson, *The Logic of Collective Action* (Cambridge, Mass.: Harvard University Press, 1965). Olson directly confronts established theories of group action and prominently mentions the work of David Truman. At one point, Olson writes, "Large or latent groups will *not* organize for coordinated action merely because, as a group, they have reason for doing so" (65).

64. Weber, "Who Uses the Internet?"; Amy Harmon, "Blacks Found to Trail Whites in Cyberspace," *New York Times,* April 17, 1998, A1.

65. Walter Lippmann, *Public Opinion* (New York: Free Press, 1922), 229; Graham quoted in Bernard Roshco, *Newsmaking* (Chicago: University of Chicago Press, 1975), 122. Also see Patterson, *Out of Order,* 28, 206; idem, *The Mass Media Election* (New York: Praeger, 1980), 173–74; Sabato, *Feeding Frenzy,* 245–46; Bernard Roshco, "When Policy Fails: How the Buck Was Passed When Kuwait Was Invaded" (Discussion Paper D-15, the Joan Shorenstein Barone Center for the Press, Politics and Public Policy, John F. Kennedy School of Government, Harvard University, Cambridge, Mass., December 1992), 29–30.

INDEX

ABC, 79, 100, 106, 184, 206n.4; affiliates, 86; cost-cutting and, 85–86; market journalism and, 83; news production, 113. *See also* Capital Cities/ABC; Walt Disney Company

ABC News, xiii, 18, 21, 50, 86, 116, 184, 194; as authoritative, 132; libel and, 89; morale, 87; *Prime Time*, 189, 263n.28; soft news and, 97, 189

Abel, Elie, 97

Adams, James, 156, 160

Advertising, 30, 52, 231n.14; dependence of news organizations on, 76–80, 93, 122, 172, 182; negative, 30; news subsidy, 102–3; political, 29–30, 31, 52, 77

Agran, Larry, 259n.121

AIDS, xv, 24, 140–41, 162–65, 170; institutional media and, 170–75

Ailes, Roger, 34

Albright, Madeleine, 63, 125

Alternative press, 182, 190, 197

Altheide, David, 16, 111, 135, 196, 238n.2

"American Creed," 125

American Press Institute, 96

Anonymous sources, 68. *See also* Leaks

Ansolabehere, Stephen, 30, 31

Apple, R. W. (Johnny), 32, 88

Argyris, Chris, 111

Ariel Sharon v. Time, 89

Arledge, Roone, 79

Arnett, Peter, 143

Arterton, F. Christopher, 32, 37

Asner, Ed, 77

Associated Press (AP), 22; as authoritative, 86, 119, 132; Naessens and, 168; objectivity and, 122

Library of Congress Cataloging-in-Publication Data

Sparrow, Bartholomew H., 1959–
    Uncertain guardians : the news media as a political institution / Bartholomew H.
Sparrow.
        p.   cm. — (Interpreting American politics)
    Includes bibliographical references and index.
    ISBN 0-8018-6035-0 (alk. paper). — ISBN 0-8018-6036-9 (pbk. : alk. paper)
    1. Journalism—Political aspects—United States.   2. Mass media—Political
aspects—United States.   3. Press and politics—United States.   4. Press—United
States—Influence.   I. Title.   II. Series.
PN4888.P6S68   1999
070.4'49324'0973—dc21   98-44281
                                                                                    CIP